224

# PRINCIPLES OF STATISTICS

# THE

# CENTURY

# PSYCHOLOGY

# SERIES

---

*Editors*
Kenneth MacCorquodale
Gardner Lindzey
Kenneth E. Clark

# PRINCIPLES
# OF STATISTICS

## TRADITIONAL AND BAYESIAN

## Victor E. McGee

*Dartmouth College*

New York

APPLETON-CENTURY-CROFTS
Educational Division
MEREDITH CORPORATION

*To MARIE, BETH, and BILL*

# Preface

This text is directed at the social science student who is hoping to read the literature critically and with understanding, or wants to conduct research in the general social science area, or both. Since it is common practice for reviewers of prospective journal publications to examine the statistical handling of data, it is therefore true that the large majority of published papers contain one or more references to statistical analyses. From the reader's point of view, an accurate understanding of an experimental report is critically dependent upon an understanding of the statistical analysis conducted by the author of the paper. A major goal of this text is that a serious student, having completed the course contained in these chapters, will be able to read the literature critically—not only to recognize the kind of analysis described in an article but also to be able to decide whether the investigator was justified in performing that analysis. If this level of sophistication can be reached, then this same student will know how to handle data obtained from his own experiments.

This text is aimed at practitioners rather than theoreticians. Since many students complain about all the mathematics and all the theory in a statistics course, a distinction is made between two roles: the role of the experimenter and the role of the statistician. From time to time, the text is written in the form of a dialogue between these two "players," and the theme of the first nine chapters (The Traditional Approach) is embodied in a split-page diagram which is found repeatedly in the text. On the left-hand side of the page, an experimental situation is described in terms of *what is known* and *what is not known*—this defines the experimenter's point of view. On the right-hand side of the page, a statistical model is described in terms of *what is assumed* and *what is concluded on the basis of these assumptions*—this defines the statistician's point of view. When an experimenter and a statistician get together, their dialogue centers around the problem of fluctuation. The experimenter knows some things for sure, but he is aware that if the experiment is replicated, the results will be different. The statistician addresses himself to the question: Under what circumstances (assumptions) can I make precise statements about fluctuation? The experimenter and the statistician have to agree on the assumptions—or the dialogue ends.

This text is selective in terms of what material is covered. In order to pursue the study of statistical principles relentlessly, it has been necessary to pass over certain aspects of more standard statistics courses. For example, the various graphical ways of presenting data have been omitted on the grounds that no statistical principles are involved. Where summary numbers in common usage (for example, medians, percentiles, stanines) cannot be presented within the framework of a well-defined statistical model, they have been relegated to brief mention. The increasingly large variety of nonparametric statistics has also been excluded on two grounds: they will be easily understood if the parametric models of this text (Chapters 1 through 9) are understood, and there are a number of well-written texts directed exclusively at nonparametric test procedures.

This text offers an introduction to the Bayesian approach (Chapters 10 and 11) in the hopes that experimenters will become more experimental, that hypotheses will not only be rejected but also vindicated from time to time, and that the dialogue between experimenter and statistician will place the heavier load of responsibility on the experimenter. Nowadays it is common for colleges and universities to have two courses—one called "Statistics" and the other called "Experimental Design." Typically, the latter course defines a number of factorial designs which are recommended for use by the experimenter. The reason they are recommended is that there exists a very well used traditional model (the $F$-model of Chapters 6 and 7) which can handle data from such designs. Regardless of the merits of this procedure, it seems worth while for experimenters in general to pay increasingly more attention to *what* they are interested in studying rather than in *how* they ought to perform the experiment. The Bayesian approach offers a flexibility which is refreshing, a compatibility with common sense which seems uncommon, and an opportunity for an experimenter to define hypotheses of interest *to him* rather than hypotheses of interest to a statistical model.

In an effort to achieve the goals set up for this text, the following criteria were adopted:

1. The style should be informal and direct.

2. Visual illustrations should become a part of the experimenter's statistical imagery. Hence, the "theme" diagram is repeatedly presented as reinforcement, and the student is urged to draw rough diagrams of distributions whenever possible.

3. The presentation of descriptive statistics and statistical models should be sensitive to both the need for an intuitive grasp as well as the need for efficient computation.

4. The mathematics behind statistical models should be presented—on the understanding that this belongs properly to the role of the statistician rather than to the role of the experimenter. Chapter 4 illustrates this point. The student is to read Chapter 4 through the eyes of an interested experimenter. It is designed to serve as a reference chapter and should be used whenever he wants to be sure what the assumptions behind a statistical model are.

5. Where possible, formal arguments should be paralleled with concrete computations. In some chapters this is handled in a double-column format—theory on the left and a worked example following step by step on the right.

6. The exercises should form an integral part of the course. It is extremely important for the student to attempt as many of the exercises as possible. An author is hard-put to present in a book what he feels he can present as an instructor. To bridge the gap between talking and writing, the exercises are invaluable.

7. Applied statistics should be examined in the context in which it is applied, namely, in the literature. The student is urged to make constant reference to the journals in his field of interest. Many of the exercises in this text come from the literature, and references are given so that the student can see applied statistics in action.

8. Where possible, the organization of chapters and sections of chapters should follow the same plan so that the learning process is facilitated.

It has been rather a long time since this text was first conceived, and the years since then have been beneficial. Some of the impractical dreams had to be abandoned, and some new thoughts made their appearance. Throughout this time, the students I have taught have been a constant source of encouragement and a valuable source of criticism, and this text has benefited from their scrutiny. My colleague Jack Baird took the trouble to read the complete manuscript, and his comments were greatly appreciated. Many others have read portions of the text, and to them I am grateful. A special debt of thanks belongs to members of the Engineering Department of the University of Wisconsin–Milwaukee for "mothering" me during two months of intensive writing on the book and to the community of deans at Indiana University of Pennsylvania for similar succor. Concerning Chapters 10 and 11, I owe a tremendous debt to Myron Tribus, Dean of the Thayer School of Engineering at Dartmouth College, as indicated in the introduction to Part Two of this text. Much of the material in these two chapters is merely a restructuring and rewording of material contained in his own book (referenced later). In the role of instructor, colleague, and collaborator, he has enthusiastically supported my attempts to make this Bayesian approach relevant in a social science context.

In the words of a college president, I address my reader: "Your business here is learning, and I'm hoping to be with you all the way!"

VICTOR E. MCGEE

# Contents

*one*

---

# *THE TRADITIONAL APPROACH*

# INTRODUCTION TO PART ONE

ORIENTATION. As mentioned in the Preface, this text is aimed at social science students who need to read the literature critically and to perform analyses on their own experimental data. The literature makes constant reference to traditional statistical models, and so the principles underlying these models must be thoroughly understood. Since the basis of all statistical models is the concept of sampling fluctuation, there is a heavy emphasis on this throughout the text. Whenever an experimenter performs an experiment and obtains data, these data will be designated statistical data, where the implication is that a replication of the experiment will show the evidence of sampling fluctuation. Data are often summarized in terms of a mean (the mean score on a given test is 73, etc.), and from sample to sample the value of this mean fluctuates. This is sampling fluctuation. Two experimenters perform the same experiment. One says that there is no significant difference between his experimental subjects and his controls. The other says that there is. This is the result of sampling fluctuation. If an opinion poll suggests that candidate X will win over candidate Y, and Y wins the actual election, this is evidence of sampling fluctuation (among other things). *To understand traditional statistical models, you must have a thorough grasp of the concept of sampling fluctuation.*

PREPARATION. Although you may find an integral sign once in a while, this text does not require calculus. If you assume the role of the experimenter (and this is what the author assumes), then the required preparation includes addition, subtraction, multiplication, division, raising quantities to various powers, taking square roots, and the ability to substitute given values for variables in equations. The last is perhaps most important. From time to time equations will have to be used to compute various statistics (summary numbers, such as the mean, variance, correlation). They will usually be algebraic equations, in that several symbols will be used, and your job will be to distinguish what is known and what is not known. The values of the knowns are entered in the equation in order to find out the value of the unknown. This is formally designated as specializing. For example, if $y = 2a + 3b$, then we are talking about a general functional relationship between $y$ and values of $a$ and $b$. If we specialize when $a = 1$ and $b = 2$, we find $y = 8$.

If you attempt to assume the role of the statistician from time to time (and this is what the author hopes), then essentially the same preparation will carry you most of the way. However, there are references to special functions, together with ways and means of handling them, and to formidable-looking equations. These should not upset you. They are presented merely because the role of the statistician is being expounded. You are not expected to be a statistician. *This text aims to prepare you to be able to converse intelligently with a statistician.*

ORGANIZATION.    Chapter 1 is an overview. It is aimed at giving you an intuitive feeling for the all-important concept of sampling fluctuation. Along the way it develops the theme diagram, and in Section 1-4 some examples of dialogues between experimenter and statistician are given. At the appropriate place later on in the text you will be urged to reread Section 1-4. Chapter 2 discusses commonly used summary numbers (statistics). In this chapter the notion of sampling fluctuation is held in abeyance, but you should know that every one of the statistics (summary numbers) discussed fluctuates from sample to sample. Chapter 3 introduces the basic equipment of statistical models—the normal distribution family and simple independent random sampling (SIRS).

Chapter 4 deserves a special place. Note first that it is part of the statistician's role to know everything in this chapter. From the experimenter's point of view this should be considered a reference chapter. It contains the assumptions underlying the commonly used traditional statistical models, and whenever you forget the foundations of these models, you should refer to the appropriate section of Chapter 4. Your instructor may choose to read this chapter piecemeal—Sections 4-1 to 4-3 in sequence; Section 4-5 with Chapter 5, which is the study of the $t$-model and $t$-testing; Section 4-6 with Chapters 6 and 7, which are the chapters dealing with the $F$-model and analysis of variance; Section 4-4, and possibly also Section 4-8, with Chapter 8, which is the study of the chi-square goodness-of-fit model and contingency table data; and Section 4-7 with various exercises and other parts of the text.

Chapter 9 introduces the statistical study of the correlation coefficient and simple linear regression. Since the principles of sampling fluctuation are more difficult in connection with this material, Section 9-2 might well be omitted in a first course.

A NOTE TO THE INSTRUCTOR.    The author has been privileged to teach statistics with the aid of a fine time-sharing computer system that is readily available to both faculty and students. The main advantage of this system is the speed with which we can simulate sampling procedures and obtain many, many (large or small) samples for the purposes of studying sampling fluctuation. In the absence of this facility the first two appendices may be used to good advantage. Appendix A contains the more familiar random numbers, which we call values sampled by SIRS from a rectangular distribution on the interval (0,1). Appendix B contains the less familiar random normal deviates, which we call values sampled by SIRS from ND(0,1). Several of the exercises are organized around the use of these appendices.

Concerning the exercises that make reference to specific articles in the literature, it was suggested (too late) that Bobbs-Merrill reprints should have been selected so that students could purchase a few useful illustrations from this series. This is a good idea and can be handled in this way if so desired.

A NOTE TO THE STUDENT. You are urged to consider the following study aids while you proceed through this text. (*i*) Use lots of paper while you read. Jot down equations; draw rough sketches of distributions; make quick calculations to see whether the reported calculations are in the "ballpark"; keep track of the symbols used. (*ii*) Make use of the theme diagram as often as possible and particularly when you are reading the literature. (*iii*) Do as many of the exercises as possible, and do them diligently. Answers are not as important as the principles involved. (*iv*)Talk to a fellow student in the course. Unless you are specifically instructed to proceed on your own, it is valuable to join forces with another person in the course for the purpose of doing an exercise diligently and critically. Some of the exercises are specially designed for this kind of discussion. They have no correct or incorrect numerical answer; they are for meditation.

Remember the famous dictum of Piaget: "Activity precedes thought." As you develop intuitive imagery for the concepts of statistics, let it be kinesthetic (write often), let it be visual (read the text often), let it be auditory (discuss matters with your instructor and with fellow students). Finally let your study be distributed study (rather than massed toward the end of the term). The study of statistical principles cannot be crammed. There is no royal road to becoming an expert. Consistent grappling with the concepts and the practice of statistics is the only proven way.

REFERENCES. It is good practice to browse in a library even when the course is statistics! In this text we make repeated reference to two authoritative books:

Cramer, Harald. *Mathematical methods of statistics.* Princeton University Press, Princeton, N.J., 1946.
Kendall, M. G., and Stuart, A. *The advanced theory of statistics.* Vol. 1. Hafner Publishing Company, New York, 1958.

# Populations, Samples, and Summary Numbers

## 1-1  INTRODUCTION

### 1-11  Sets of Numbers

Here is a set of numbers.

```
4 2 1 3 2 3 2 5 3 2 2 4 3 4 3 6 5 3 3 5
3 3 3 6 6 3 3 1 1 4 5 4 5 3 3 4 3 2 3 3
2 2 2 3 2 1 3 3 6 2 3 4 3 6 3 4 4 3 1 6
4 1 3 3 3 3 2 5 4 2 4 1 3 5 2 3 3 3 4 4
2 1 3 3 4 2 4 3 3 1 4 4 4 1 2 2 1 4 2 3
6 3 3 4 5 2 2 4 4 4 3 5 3 3 3 1 4 3 6 4
3 5 6 3 1 3 4 3 1 6 3 1 2 2 2 3 4 3 3 3
4 2 3 4 1 2 6 6 1 3 3 3 2 1 4 2 3 4 2 4
4 2 2 2 3 2 3 1 1 2 3 4 3 4 2 3 3 3 3 1
6 2 2 6 4 3 2 4 2 3 4 3 1 2 2 5 4 4 3 4
4 4 5 3 1 3 2 6 3 1 2 5 2 3 6 3 3 3 1 3
5 3 4 2 2 3 2 2 4 2 2 3 4 3 3 3 2 3 4 4
3 3 3 5 3 4 3 3 2 3 3 3 2 3 2 2 4 6 3 2
4 2 2 1 4 2 4 5 3 2 6 4 4 6 1 3 5 3 4 3
1 2 4 6 2 2 2 6 2 5 2 2 2 2 3 2 3 5 4 2
1 4 2 1 3 2 5 4 2 2 3 3 3 4 1 4 1 2 3 3
4 2 4 3 1 4 4 4 1 4 2 2 4 5 2 3 4 3 5 3
3 3 2 3 6 4 3 5 3 2 6 4 3 6 6 3 3 2 2 6
3 5 2 2 3 3 2 2 3 3 2 5 3 4 2 3 5 3 4 3
3 2 6 4 2 2 1 5 2 3 4 3 4 1 3 1 4 3 5 2
```

How do we describe them?

We begin by rearranging the set. There are just six distinct values—1, 2, 3, 4, 5, and 6—and they occur with varying frequency. For instance, the distinct value 1 occurs 37 times, and the distinct value 3 occurs 134 times. Checking each distinct value in this manner, we arrive at an equivalent way of writing the set:

| Distinct value | Frequency of occurrence |
| --- | --- |
| 1 | 37 |
| 2 | 95 |
| 3 | 134 |
| 4 | 79 |
| 5 | 28 |
| 6 | 27 |

This is a compact way of describing a set of numbers, and is known as a *frequency distribution.*

There are various ways of representing frequency distributions pictorially. One is the *histogram*, which, for the set of numbers on page 7, would appear as in Figure 1-1.

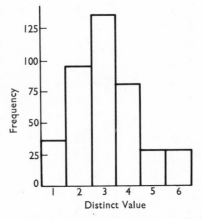

FIGURE I-I.   Histogram of "parent" set

Thus, when we think of a *set* of numbers we may imagine (*i*) a wild array of numbers showing no semblance of organization, (*ii*) a set of distinct numbers together with their frequency of occurrence (the frequency distribution), or (*iii*) a diagrammatic representation of the distribution (such as a histogram).

## 1-12   Subsets

Consider a large bowl containing 400 marbles. On each marble is painted a number, and the 400 numbers in the bowl are the same as those on page 7.

In the bowl there are now two sets—a set of marbles and a set of numbers—and there is a one-to-one correspondence between the marbles and the numbers. Suppose that we wish to select just 40 marbles (numbers) from the bowl. To do so requires the use of some selection procedure called a *sampling plan*, and the 40 marbles (numbers) chosen according to some sampling plan constitute a *subset*, or sample.

Here is one possible sampling plan. Mix the marbles in the bowl thoroughly, and, without looking, pull out 40 marbles (numbers). This procedure generates a subset of marbles (numbers), and the sampling plan is known as *random sampling without replacement*.

Here is another possible sampling plan. Mix the marbles in the bowl thoroughly, and, without looking, pull out one marble. Record the number on this marble, and replace it in the bowl. Mix again, and, without looking, pull out one marble. Record the number on this marble, and replace it in the bowl. Repeat until 40 numbers have been recorded. These 40 numbers constitute a subset of numbers, and the sampling plan is known as *random sampling with replacement*.

By way of illustration the following subset of 40 numbers was obtained using random sampling with replacement:

```
4  3  2  1  2  2  2  3  4  2  3  5  3  3  3  4  4  2  2  4
3  4  3  3  3  3  2  3  4  6  4  6  2  4  1  2  3  2  4  1
```

Describing this subset in terms of its frequency distribution, we have:

| Distinct value | Frequency of occurrence |
|:---:|:---:|
| 1 | 3 |
| 2 | 11 |
| 3 | 13 |
| 4 | 10 |
| 5 | 1 |
| 6 | 2 |

Using the same sampling plan a second time, we may obtain another subset as follows:

```
2  2  4  3  4  5  4  4  6  5  5  4  2  3  3  1  5  3  5  5
3  1  2  2  3  6  3  5  3  3  1  3  4  4  4  3  3  4  4  1
```

The frequency distribution of this subset is as follows:

| Distinct value | Frequency of occurrence |
|:---:|:---:|
| 1 | 4 |
| 2 | 5 |
| 3 | 12 |
| 4 | 10 |
| 5 | 7 |
| 6 | 2 |

We may apply the sampling plan as many times as we wish to obtain as many subsets (samples) as we wish, but the two subsets obtained above are enough to demonstrate the following important fact. Using the same sampling plan on a given *parent* set, we obtain many different subsets. This variability is known as *sampling fluctuation*. To illustrate this point, consider the following table showing the frequency distribution for subsets 1 and 2 above:

|  Subset 1  |  Subset 2  |
| --- | --- |
| 1 /// | 1 //// |
| 2 ///////////// | 2 ///// |
| 3 ////////////// | 3 //////////////// |
| 4 ////////// | 4 /////////// |
| 5 / | 5 /////// |
| 6 // | 6 // |

Recapitulating, note that when we think about *subsets* of numbers, we imagine (*i*) a set of numbers, because a subset is a set in its own right and therefore may be regarded as a wild array of numbers, as a frequency distribution, or as a histogram; (*ii*) a larger "parent" set of numbers from which the subset has been selected; (*iii*) a sampling plan that indicates how the subset and the parent set are related; and (*iv*) the sampling fluctuation from subset to subset obtained under the same sampling plan.

## 1-13  Summary Numbers

Any set of numbers—and this includes subsets—can be summarized in many different ways. Consider subset 1 in Section 1-12. There are 40 numbers in this subset. How can we summarize them in terms of just one number? All we have to do is define some numerical operation that produces just one number. For example, we calculate the mean of the numbers in subset 1 by summing the 40 numbers and dividing by 40 to produce

$$\text{Mean of subset 1} = 3.025$$

Thus the mean is a *summary number*. It is computed according to a well-defined numerical operation—sum the 40 numbers and divide by 40—that reduces the 40 numbers to just one number. Any well-defined numerical operation that reduces the 40 numbers of subset 1 to just one number produces a summary number. Thus it should be clear that for a given set of numbers there are many permissible summary numbers.

Here is another numerical operation that may be applied to the numbers in subset 1:

Numerical operation:    (1) Square the numbers in subset 1.
                        (2) Sum these squares.
                        (3) Divide the sum by 40.

1. Here are the squares of the numbers in subset 1:

16  9  4  1  4  4  4  9  16  4  9  25  9  9  9  16  16  4  4  16
9  16  9  9  9  9  4  9  16  36  16  36  4  16  1  4  9  4  16  1

2. Here is the sum of these squares:

Sum of squares $= 421$    Sum of square = sum of each $n$ squared

3. Here is the sum divided by 40:

$$\text{Mean square} = \frac{421}{40} = 10.525 = \frac{\text{Sum of Squares}}{n}$$

The mean square is another summary number for subset 1.

When we think about *summary numbers*, we are considering some well-defined numerical operations that have been applied to the numbers in a set. Each distinct numerical operation will produce one summary number.

## 1-14  A Diagram

A convenient summary of what has been said above may be presented in the form of a diagram that will have important uses throughout much of the text. We shall give a brief description of the diagram (Figure 1-2) here:

1. PARENT SET.  This is the set of numbers with which we begin. It will, in the future, be called the *population*.

2. SAMPLING PLAN.  If we intend to select a subset of numbers from the population, we must describe the sampling plan by which we make the selection.

3. SUBSETS.  Applying the sampling plan, we may obtain from the population many subsets, which from now on will be called *samples*. Note that the same sampling plan will produce a variety of samples. This is known as sampling fluctuation.

4. NUMERICAL OPERATIONS.  In order to summarize the numbers in any given sample, we have to define the numerical operations that produce the summary numbers.

5. SUMMARY NUMBERS.  For each numerical operation we determine a summary number for each sample. If we define two numerical operations, there will be two summary numbers for each sample.

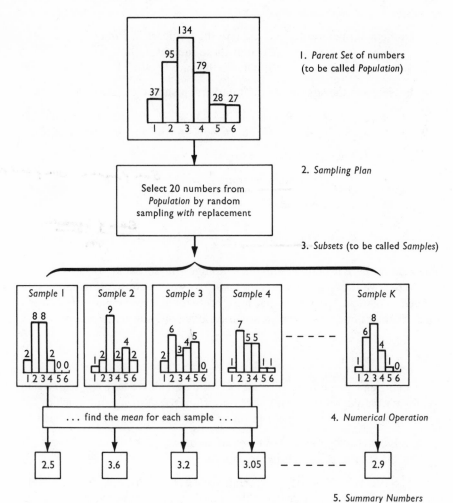

FIGURE 1-2.   A diagram to summarize Section 1-1

## EXERCISES

1. The 400 numbers on page 7 were produced by a computer, and the order of presentation may be thought of as random. Thus each row, containing 20 numbers, may be thought of as a sample from the parent set.
   (a) What kind of sampling plan are we considering if we think of row 1 as a sample?
   (b) Compute the means for the first five and the last five rows.
   (c) Draw histograms for the first five rows (samples) in order to see the kind of sampling fluctuation involved. For the same five samples examine the summary numbers (means) as another illustration of sampling fluctuation.
2. Consider the following very small population (parent set): [0,1,2,3,5,5,9].

(a) Choose a sample containing four numbers, using random sampling without replacement, and compute the mean. Repeat 20 times.

(b) Choose a sample containing four numbers, using random sampling with replacement, and compute the mean. Repeat 20 times.

(c) Compare the 20 means from (a) with those from (b). Does the sampling plan make a difference?

(d) Compute the mean of the means from (a) and from (b). How do they compare?

3. If you select a reasonably small sample from a reasonably large population, is there likely to be much difference between sampling with replacement and sampling without replacement?

## 1-2   THE EXPERIMENTER'S VIEWPOINT

### 1-21   A Problem

What is the mean height of male students entering American colleges and universities in the academic year 1968–69?

### 1-22   The Population

In this section we aim to be realistic, viewing the above problem through the eyes of a practical experimenter. We ask first about the population in this problem.

The population consists of two sets: (i) the population is a set of male students; (ii) the population is a set of measures, say, height in inches. There is a one-to-one correspondence between these two sets, since each height is that of one male student. However, the experimenter does consider these two sets in a definite order. Clearly, if he is to determine the height of every male student, he must first have the students to measure. So let us consider the population first as a set of male students.

It is not practical to list the names of every member of the population. Instead, either explicitly or implicitly, the experimenter defines a set of rules for membership in the population, and an accurate statement of the problem includes some of the explicit rules for membership. For example, the problem stated above includes the following explicit rules for membership:

Rule 1. A member must be of the male sex.

Rule 2. A member must be an entering freshman in 1968.

Rule 3. A member must be entering an American college or university.

Some rules for membership are not made explicitly but are just as certainly intended. For example, we can conceive of a person satisfying the above three rules and yet having no legs. Clearly such a student would be disqualified for population membership. In any given problem the experimenter has to decide which rules should be made explicit and which can be assumed implicitly.

The terminology that has become widely used to describe these rules for membership includes the term *independent variable*. An equivalent way of saying that we have defined the rules for membership is to say that we have defined the independent variables that are relevant to the problem. It is useful to consider each rule for membership as having to do with one independent variable. Thus Rule 1 above deals with the independent variable "sex." This variable has only two values—male and female—and the rule tells us which of these values is allowed in the problem.

Having considered the population as a set of people, defined by a set of rules for membership, let us now consider it as a set of measures (of height). Whereas the rules for membership define the independent variables relevant to the problem, the measure of height is known as the *dependent variable*. The measure of height depends on who is being measured, and the "who" is defined in terms of the rules for membership (the independent variables).

Now if you were the experimenter faced with answering the question in Section 1-21, what would you do? In all probability you would do the following: (*i*) You would not try to deal with the whole population of male students. (*ii*) You would select a sample from this population. (*iii*) You would measure the height of the members of the sample. (*iv*) You would make some statement concerning the original problem.

This is a reasonable approach and is the kind we are concerned with in this text. Given this approach, what can we conclude about the experimenter's viewpoint concerning the population for the original problem?

From the practical point of view of the experimenter the concept "population" is usually intangible (in that he will not be working with the population at all); involves a set of *objects*—in this case, people—that are identified in terms of rules for membership; and involves a set of *measures* that to all intents and purposes is unknown.

### 1-23  A Sampling Plan

The experimenter wishes to choose a sample of members from the population of members. Just how he goes about this will be called his *sampling plan*. However, it must at once be acknowledged that, if the whole population is not available to the experimenter, there is no way for him to know precisely what his sampling plan really is. Another way of saying this is that the experimenter rarely knows the relationship between his sample and the population. The best he can do is to state accurately how he obtained his sample. In the literature you will find sample members identified as "subjects" and you will read descriptions of sampling plans such as "100 subjects were chosen at *random* from the freshman class," "a *representative* sample of 300 English themes was chosen," or even such honest reports as "50 subjects were used in this experiment on the basis of *availability*." A popular criticism of certain unpopular studies (such as those dealing with the sexual behavior of the American female, for example) is that "the experimenter used a *biased* sample."

Let us consider each of these sampling plans in the case of the problem above.

1. RANDOM SAMPLING.   If all the members of the population were marbles and if their heights were painted on each particular marble, then we could put all the marbles in a large bowl and apply random sampling without replacement, as defined in Section 1-12. Since the whole population of members is not available, we cannot do this. The practical equivalent of such a procedure is as follows. Assuming that there is no special reason why only tall students (or, for that matter, only short students) would gravitate to New York City's colleges and universities, an experimenter might write to every New York City college and university, asking that someone select every tenth entering freshman (from an alphabetical list) in each institution and measure their height. If there were no knowledge to the contrary, this would be an acceptable random sample.

2. REPRESENTATIVE SAMPLING.   The problem at hand is not the best one to use in a discussion about representative sampling. A better illustration could be given in the area of opinion polling. If you planned to measure the popularity of the President, you would do well to interview a representative sample of voters. However, in the problem about the height of male students entering colleges and universities an experimenter might attempt to obtain a representative sample as follows. He would determine that there are so many large state universities, so many private colleges, so many colleges or universities concentrating on basketball (attracting the tall freshmen), and so on. Based on this survey, he might randomly select 50 colleges and universities that he judged to be representative of the national situation. Within the chosen institutions he might then select 10 percent of the freshmen by an acceptable random procedure. The final sample would be called a representative sample.

3. AN AVAILABLE SAMPLE.   Much research is based on available samples. Indeed psychological research on human subjects has been characterized as the study of college sophomores, and it is customary for students in introductory psychology courses to be rewarded for participating in psychological experiments. In many instances there is nothing seriously inadequate about this procedure. For the problem at hand an experimenter at the University of Michigan might well choose as his sample the entering male students at his institution. The university is large, the sample is available, and not many of the entering freshmen are likely to have been admitted by the basketball coach. Such an available sample would qualify as the practical equivalent of both a random sample and a representative sample.

4. BIASED SAMPLING.    Wherever something is known about a sample to make its randomness suspect, the sample is called a biased sample. Among experimenters the term "biased" carries with it something in the nature of illegality, but from the statistician's point of view such connotations are not permitted. Biased samples are perfectly legal. They may simply be biased for a particular reason, and the experimenter would do well to concentrate on the relationship between his sample and the population to which he wishes to generalize. If he cannot be reasonably sure that his sample is a random sample from the population of interest, then he must call it a biased sample; in this way he has stated the relationship between the sample and the population. Inferences based on biased samples can certainly be made, but they will not be the same as those based on random samples. For example, if a political-opinion pollster predicts the results of a presidential election after polling the opinions of Democrats only, then his predictions will not be the same as those based on representative opinion polling.

The choice of a sampling plan is an intimate part of any experimental work, and the experimenter should try to make an accurate statement concerning his plan, so that generalization from the sample data to the unknown population data becomes more appropriate.

### 1-24    A Sample

From the experimenter's point of view the population of members is usually unknown (except insofar as rules for membership can specify them), the population of measures is consequently unknown, and the sampling plan cannot be known precisely. But the one thing he does know for sure is the sample of members and the sample of measures obtained on them.

In an experimental inquiry the experimenter proceeds inductively from what he does know to what he would like to know. It is convenient at this stage to consider the population measures to be what he would like to know. More accurately it is only certain characteristics of the population that he would like to know. In reading the experimental literature you are advised to develop the habit of asking three questions: (*i*) what does the experimenter know for sure, (*ii*) what assumptions does he make, and (*iii*) are his inferences consistent with what he knows and what he assumes? The second and third questions will be handled later, but the first one can be answered here. The sample measures constitute the experimenter's certain knowledge. (We are tacitly assuming that the experimenter does not blunder when he obtains measures on his sample members.)

### 1-25    Statistics (Summary Numbers)

By definition a *statistic* is a summary number. If we define a numerical operation to be applied to the sample measures so as to produce a single number, then this number is a statistic. As indicated in Section 1-13, it is possible to generate a great variety of different summary numbers for a given set of numbers. In the same way, for a given set of sample measures it is possible to generate a great variety of different statistics (summary numbers). However, in spite of the potentially unlimited variety of possibilities there are only a few types of statistics that are really useful. Among the useful statistics are two that are more important than all the rest:

1. The *mean*, a familiar summary number
2. The *variance* (or its square root, called the *standard deviation*), which is a summary number indicating the variability or "spread-out-ness" or dispersion of the set of measures.

There will not be many more statistics of concern to us in this text.

To emphasize the importance of summarizing data in the form of a statistic, we digress a moment to the following problem. You approach an official of the College Boards and ask him how the high school seniors scored on the SAT-M this year. Now what kind of answer would you expect? Remember that there may have been something like 750,000 students taking the SAT-M this year and each of them has a score on the test. Here is one way he might answer you: "The 750,000 scores were 456, 712, 365, 501, ... ," continuing through all the scores. This would take a few weeks off your life and his, and it would certainly not be very helpful. It is evident that this vast set of scores must be summarized in some manner. Suppose that he answered you as follows: "Well, in the last few years the mean has been 500, but this year it was 515." This is a much more reasonable answer and would be quite acceptable. The College Board official has summarized the 750,000 numbers using just one number, the mean. Surely this is a very useful statistic.

Returning to the original problem, the experimenter has defined rules for membership in the population, has chosen a sample of members according to some specified sampling plan, and has measured the height in inches of each member of the sample. Suppose that there are 1,000 members in his sample and therefore 1,000 heights. The next step would be to summarize these 1,000 heights in the form of useful statistics. The mean height is obviously an important statistic to compute, since the original question was concerned with it. The experimenter finds that

Mean height of sample members = 67.5 in.

This is his first statistic.

It will become something of a habit to compute at least two statistics for every set of sample data you work with: the mean and the standard deviation (remember, if you square the standard deviation, you have the variance). We already know how to compute the mean, and Chapter 2 shows how to compute the standard deviation. It suffices at present to state that the experimenter finds that

Standard deviation of sample measures = 1.95 in.

This is his second statistic.

The experimenter does not know the set of population measures, but he does know the set of sample measures. He summarizes the sample measures in the form of statistics. Since statistics are calculated according to well-defined numerical operations, the experimenter makes no assumptions when computing them. No inferences are made when a set of measures is summarized in the form of a single number—a statistic. It is a purely mechanical operation.

## 1-26   Inference

We cannot say too much about statistical inference at this early stage in the text, but we do ask what answer the experimenter will give to the original question in Section 1-21. The mean height for the 1,000 sample members is 67.5 in. Does the experimenter say that the mean height of male students entering American colleges and universities in the academic year 1968–69 is 67.5 in.? This statement goes beyond the facts. It would be better to state that the mean height of the population is likely to be close to the mean height of the sample. But how likely?

As soon as we go beyond the facts, we have to employ the concept of probability, which we shall introduce more formally later. The reason why the experimenter cannot be confident that the population mean is the same as the sample mean is that for any specified sampling plan there is sampling fluctuation. If he had chosen a different sample of 1,000 members, according to the same sampling plan, his new sample mean would, in general, be different from the first one. The value of a statistic is affected by sampling fluctuation. Thus the experimenter must reason as follows:

1. I have one sample of measures, and my one sample mean is 67.5 in.

2. There are many other possible samples that could have been selected, and each one could have been summarized in the form of a mean.

3. In general the value of this statistic, the mean, would vary from sample to sample.

4. If I generalize from the sample to the population, then I must acknowledge this sampling fluctuation.

For the moment we shall leave the discussion at this point.

## 1-27   The Experimenter's Diagram

A convenient summary of the experimenter's viewpoint is presented in Figure 1-3. We describe it briefly as follows:

1. POPULATION.   An incomplete rectangle designates the population, since it is unknown except in terms of some specified rules for membership.

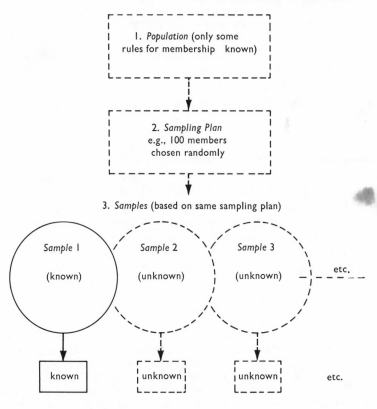

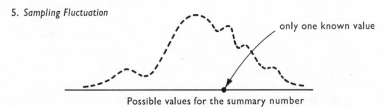

FIGURE 1-3. The experimenter's diagram—solid lines indicate what is known; dashed lines indicate what is not known.

2. SAMPLING PLAN.  An incomplete rectangle designates the sampling plan, since it is also unknown. The experimenter nevertheless does make some attempt to describe what kind of plan was attempted.

3. SAMPLES.  Only one sample is known and it is designated by means of a solid circle. All other possible samples are indicated by incomplete circles, since they are unknown. They are retained in the diagram to remind the experimenter that other samples are possible.

4. STATISTICS.   Each statistic is indicated by means of a small square below the sample circle. For the known sample the statistic is designated by means of a solid square. For all other possible (but unknown) samples the statistics are shown by means of incomplete squares. Note that the diagram shows only one statistic below each sample circle. It is possible, of course, to have many squares appended to each sample circle, one square for each new type of statistic.

5. SAMPLING FLUCTUATION.   To illustrate what is known and what is not known, the diagram includes a distribution that shows the sampling fluctuation of the values of a specific statistic. Suppose that you had 500 samples instead of just one. Then it would be possible to calculate 500 means. These 500 means would be a set of 500 numbers, and we could represent them in the form of a histogram, for example. In Figure 1-3 we represent the distribution of the sample means as a dotted line because we really do not know what it is. All we know is one mean, and it is indicated as a solid point on the distribution.

## EXERCISES

1. An experimenter is interested in knowing something about the frequency of usage of the five vowels—*a, e, i, o, u*—in the written English language. He defines rules for membership (in this case the rules would specify which written materials would be acceptable members of the population) and proceeds to sample as follows: He chooses a book that satisfies the rules for membership (assume the obvious: this book qualifies!), turns to any page, and examines the first 50 vowels on the page.
   (*a*) What kind of sampling plan is this?
   (*b*) Organize the 50 vowels in the form of a frequency distribution, and draw a histogram. Does it matter in which order you consider the five vowels?
   (*c*) Let $a = 1$, $e = 2$, $i = 3$, $o = 4$, and $u = 5$, and summarize the sample in the form of a mean. (Note that we cannot talk about a mean until we have arbitrarily assigned numbers to the vowels.)
   (*d*) Repeat steps *a* to *c* several times in order to expose sampling fluctuation. (Note that sampling fluctuation can be demonstrated by presenting a series of histograms—the different shapes indicate fluctuation—or by presenting a series of sample means or any other summary number.)
2. Consider the statement "Young ladies smoke more heavily than young men." Plan an experiment to investigate this assertion, defining (*a*) explicit rules for membership, (*b*) the sampling plan, (*c*) the dependent measure, that is, what would be measured, (*d*) the summary numbers (statistics) you might use, and (*e*) the sampling fluctuation. Suppose that you completed the experiment and were asked if young ladies smoke more heavily than young men. How would you answer the question?
3. Draw a diagram for Exercise 2, and make it specific to that exercise.
4. Consult a recent issue of the *Journal of Experimental Psychology* or any journal of your choice, select any article in that issue, and describe the experiment in the form of a diagram similar to Figure 1-3, that is, from the experimenter's point of view. In the appropriate sections of the diagram, spell out (*a*) the rules for

membership, explicit and implicit, (*b*) the sampling plan, (*c*) the sampling data actually used, (*d*) the summary numbers actually used, (*e*) the kind of sampling fluctuation to be expected, and (*f*) the conclusion reached by the experimenter.

## 1-3  THE STATISTICIAN'S VIEWPOINT

### 1-31  Statistical Model

The statistician is concerned with making imprecise notions precise. Therefore, instead of dealing with a real-world problem, which is always infinitely complex and inherently imprecise, he deals with a *model*—a mathematically based model, which is defined precisely. Instead of dealing with an unknown population, he must make the population known. Instead of dealing with an unknown sampling plan, he must make the sampling plan known. Instead of dealing with an unknown sampling fluctuation, he must make the sampling fluctuation known. Keeping the story simple, we characterize a statistical model as follows:

1. Define a population.
2. Define a sampling plan.
3. Generate every possible sample under this sampling plan.
4. Summarize every one of these samples by means of one or more statistics.
5. Define the sampling fluctuation of each statistic.

These five steps constitute a statistical model.

An equivalent characterization is as follows:

1. *If* the population is defined precisely, and
2. *If* the sampling plan is defined precisely,

*then* it will be theoretically possible:

3. To generate every possible sample under this sampling plan,
4. To summarize every possible sample in terms of a specific statistic,
5. And thereby determine the sampling fluctuation of this statistic.

These characterizations of a statistical model are naive, because a statistician does not, in fact, generate every possible sample. If the population is defined to be infinite, then according to any sampling plan there will be an infinite number of samples, so that he cannot generate every possible one. Thus, from the statistician's point of view the problem is as follows:

Under what conditions can I proceed mathematically from a defined population and a defined sampling plan to a defined sampling fluctuation of a given statistic?

In other words, what kinds of population and what kinds of sampling plan can the statistician work with if he wishes to obtain knowledge of the sampling fluctuation of a given statistic?

### 1-32   Choosing a Population

A parent set of numbers, that is, a population, can be represented as a wild array of numbers, a frequency distribution, or some kind of picture that shows the shape of the frequency distribution. In a statistical model the shape of the population distribution is often represented in the form of an equation.

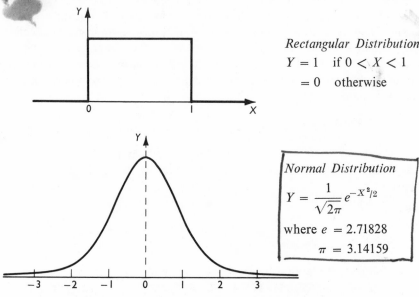

*Rectangular Distribution*

$$Y = 1 \quad \text{if } 0 < X < 1$$
$$= 0 \quad \text{otherwise}$$

*Normal Distribution*

$$Y = \frac{1}{\sqrt{2\pi}} e^{-X^2/2}$$

where $e = 2.71828$

$\pi = 3.14159$

FIGURE 1-4.   Two populations of interest to the statistician

Consider Figure 1-4. In the case of the *rectangular distribution*, note that all values of $x$ between 0 and 1 are equally represented in the population. We say that all these values are equally likely to occur if we sampled randomly from a rectangular population distribution. Values of $x$ that are less than zero and values of $x$ that are greater than unity do not occur at all in the population.

In passing, note that, if we could program a computer to sample randomly from a population distribution such as this rectangular distribution, then we should have a *random-number generator*. Numbers between 0 and 1 would be produced randomly by the computer. Many computers do have something equivalent to this built into them.

The second illustration in Figure 1-4 shows the *normal distribution*. The equation in this case is a little more exotic, but the principle is the same. For any given value of $x$ we compute the corresponding value of $y$. For this kind of population distribution the values of $x$ do not occur with constant probability in any interval. Values of $x$ close to zero occur more often than those farther away from zero. The normal distribution is symmetrical, and in fact the tails of the distribution go on to infinity in both directions.

Note two things about these population distributions. ($i$) They are *continuous* as opposed to *discrete*. Every conceivable $x$-value is involved in the domain of the distribution—not just the integers, not just the rational numbers. In the real world all measurements are discrete. A thermometer can measure only one or two decimal places, a surveyor's theodolite can measure angles to only one decimal place of a second of arc, a psychologist can measure level of anxiety only on a crude discrete scale. The statistician can also define populations that concern themselves with discrete values of $x$, but he has the option of using continuous distributions as well. The experimenter does not have this option. ($ii$) The area under these two population distributions is unity. This is easy to see in the case of the rectangular distribution but will have to be taken on faith in the case of the normal distribution (at least until Chapter 3). Such distributions are called *frequency functions* (close relatives of frequency distributions), and for the time being we shall say that, when the statistician defines his population, he does so by specifying a frequency function.

In Part One we are concerned primarily with only one frequency function, the normal distribution. The most common statistical models in use today are all based on this population distribution. The statistician, therefore, chooses as his population the normal distribution.

### 1-33   Choosing a Sampling Plan

The statistician has chosen a population distribution, the normal distribution, and it involves infinitely many values of $x$. Under these conditions there is no difference between sampling with replacement and sampling without replacement. (Are you convinced that this is so?) We therefore consider defining a *simple independent random sampling plan*, which we denote as an SIRS plan:

> Simple independent random sampling (*SIRS*) ensures that all permissible samples have an equal chance of being drawn and that all samples are independent of one another.

The word "independent" here means something precise. It is defined in Section 3-14, but a sense of what is meant can be gained by considering two events $A$ and $B$. If $A$ and $B$ are independent of each other, then knowing $A$ does not give us any information about $B$, and vice versa.

The most common statistical models in use today are based on a normal population distribution and a simple independent random-sampling plan. The statistician, therefore, chooses as his sampling plan the SIRS plan.

### 1-34  Generating Many Samples

We have already noted that the statistician does not in fact generate every permissible sample under a given sampling plan. However, for pedagogical reasons, it is useful to proceed as if he did. Thus for a normal population and SIRS plan we might imagine the statistician generating many samples of size $N$, that is, $N$ numbers in each sample. We say that he generates all permissible samples of size $N$.

### 1-35  Summarizing Each Sample

To keep the discussion clear, let us consider only one statistic, the mean. Every permissible sample may be summarized in terms of its mean; that is, we obtain a value for this statistic for every sample. Since we are thinking about the complete set of possible samples, we obtain the complete set of values for this statistic under the given population (a normal distribution) and the given sampling plan (a SIRS plan).

### 1-36  The Sampling Distribution of a Statistic

Until now we have been talking about the sampling fluctuation of the values of a statistic. From now on we shall use the correct technical term, the *sampling distribution of a statistic*. The complete set of values for the statistic defines its sampling distribution. Note again that the complete set of values for a statistic can be regarded as a wild array of numbers, as a frequency distribution or frequency function, or as a picture showing the shape of the distribution of numbers.

Recapitulating, the statistician's viewpoint concerning a statistical model involves:

1. Specifying the population—a normal distribution
2. Specifying the sampling plan—a SIRS plan
3. Determining the sampling distribution of a statistic

In the statistical models that we deal with, the sampling distributions are often specified as equations. Some of these equations appear to be very complicated and may well involve mathematical concepts that are unfamiliar. However, an experimenter is not expected to be able to derive these equations; his role is merely to understand what a sampling distribution is.

### 1-37  Statistics and Parameters

If a population set of numbers is being summarized, then such a summary number is called a *parameter*. If a sample set of numbers is being summarized, then such a summary number is called a *statistic*.

Since an experimenter does not deal with populations, the term "parameter" is usually reserved for the statistician. There is something fixed about a parameter; there is something variable about a statistic. Since there is only one population for a given model, there is only one value for a given parameter. However, under a specific sampling plan there are many permissible samples and hence many permissible values for a given statistic.

### 1-38   The Statistician's Diagram

A convenient summary of the statistician's viewpoint is presented in Figure 1-5. We describe it briefly as follows:

1. POPULATION.   A solid rectangle designates the population, since it must be known in the statistical model. The normal distribution is most commonly used in statistical models, and it has to be specified in terms of two parameters, a mean and a standard deviation.

2. SAMPLING PLAN.   A solid rectangle designates the sampling plan, since it is a known sampling plan—an SIRS plan.

3. MANY POSSIBLE SAMPLES.   Solid circles designate the many possible samples, all of which may conceivably be known.

4. STATISTICS.   Solid squares below each sample indicate that, in principle, all values of the statistic are known.

5. SAMPLING DISTRIBUTION.   If all the values of a statistic are known, then its sampling distribution can be defined. The figure illustrates the case of the sampling distribution of a mean based on samples of size 100.

### EXERCISES

1. Appendix A contains five-digit numbers that were produced by a random-number generator on a computer. If you imagine that each five-digit number is a decimal fraction (for example, the number 59981 is read 0.59981), then the numbers in this appendix can be interpreted as values sampled by SIRS from a rectangular distribution between 0 and 1.
   (a) Consider the first column of Appendix A, and draw up a histogram for the 40 numbers on the intervals: <0.1, 0.1 to 0.2, 0.2 to 0.3, . . . , 0.8 to 0.9, 0.9 to 1.0. You should decide whether 0.10000 belongs in the first or second interval, etc.
   (b) By adding up the 40 numbers in column 1, compute the *true* mean.
   (c) Compute what is known as the *grouped* mean as follows: Find the frequency of the numbers in the first interval, and consider each of them to be the number 0.05000, that is, the midpoint of the interval; find the frequency of the numbers in the second interval, and consider each of them to be 0.15000; etc. Find the mean of these new numbers. (Note that we lose some information when we group data in this manner. The numbers 0.51111 and 0.53333 both

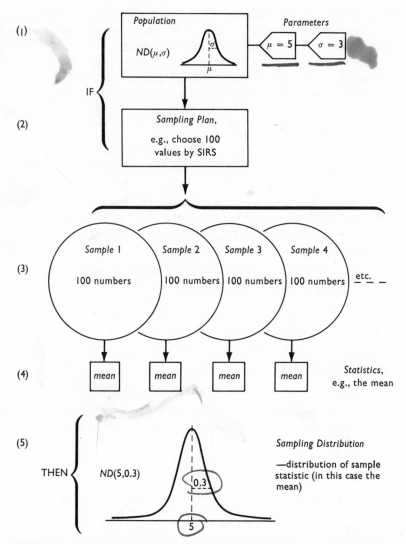

FIGURE 1-5.  The statistician's diagram—a description of the statistical model

belong to the interval 0.5 to 0.6, and their true mean is 0.52222. When we
compute their grouped mean, both take on the new value 0.55000, the
interval midpoint, and so the grouped mean is 0.55000.)

2. Rectangular distributions can be discrete as well as continuous. The simplest
   discrete rectangular distribution has only two values, each of which is as likely as
   the other. Consider tossing a fair coin. It has two possible outcomes, head and
   tail, and since the coin is fair, these outcomes are equally likely. Appendix A
   can be used to simulate a coin-tossing experiment. For example, we might
   consider reading the separate digits across row 1 of the table. If the digit is
   0, 1, 2, 3, or 4, then call it head; if it is 5, 6, 7, 8, or 9, then call it tail.

(a) Treating each row of the table as an experiment involving 50 tosses of a fair coin, compute the number of heads in 50 tosses. Do this for the first 10 rows.

(b) How many heads would you expect in 10 repetitions of 50 tosses? How many occurred according to the tabled values?

(c) If you want to consider a biased coin instead of a fair one, all you have to do is let the digits 0, 1, and 2 stand for head and the rest of the numbers stand for tail. This will bias the coin in favor of giving tails 70 percent of the time, in the long run. Repeat parts (a) and (b) of this exercise using the biased coin.

3. Appendix B contains a table of numbers that may be regarded as values selected by SIRS from a normal distribution with a mean equal to zero and a standard deviation equal to unity. (Do not worry at this point about these parameters. Just look at Figure 1-4 to get a feeling for this very important population.) We take up the serious study of normal distributions in Chapter 3, but by way of preliminary exposure do the following exercises:

(a) Theory suggests that about 68 percent of the values selected from a ND(0,1) should be between $-1.0$ and $+1.0$. Check this, using the 400 numbers in Appendix B.

(b) Theory suggests that about 5 times in 100 we are likely to get normal-deviates (the nickname for values on the horizontal axis of the standard normal distribution) that are bigger than 1.95 or smaller than $-1.95$. Another way of saying this is that the absolute (positive) value of the normal-deviate is larger than 1.95 about 5 times in 100. Check this.

(c) Find the means of the first five rows in Appendix B, one row at a time.

(d) Find the means of the first five columns in Appendix B, one column at a time.

(e) Theory suggests that the mean of a sample should be close to the mean of the population (zero in this case). If the sample size is small, as in (c), then the fluctuation of sample means will be greater than if the sample size is larger, as in (d). Check this by examining the five means of (c) and the five means of (d). Does this make sense to you? (To intuit this important concept, think of your bowling average based on separate sets of 3 games; based on separate sets of 30 games.)

## 1-4 COOPERATION BETWEEN EXPERIMENTER AND STATISTICIAN

### 1-41 Introduction

This chapter is an overview. The stage has now been set for a consideration of what goes on in a statistical analysis. From the experimenter's point of view sample data are available and summary statistics can be computed. In the face of this limited knowledge he would like to make inferences about the unknown population or about the relationship between his sample data (known) and the population data (unknown). From the statistician's point of view, *if* he knows the population and *if* he knows the sampling plan, *then*, under certain circumstances, he can make statements about the sampling distribution of a statistic (summary number). When the experimenter and the statistician get together, one or more of the following problems is handled:

1. ESTIMATING A POPULATION PARAMETER.    A statistical model requires that the population be specified completely. Sometimes this requires specifying one or more parameters (two, in the case of the normal population), and the experimenter and statistician cooperate by estimating the parameter value or values from the sample data.

2. DETERMINING A CONFIDENCE INTERVAL FOR A PARAMETER.    We have just talked about a *point* estimate of a parameter, that is, giving the parameter one value. We now consider an *interval* estimate of a parameter. The experimenter wants to be able to say that he is 90 percent confident that the parameter value lies between this value and that value. The experimenter and the statistician cooperate by making use of sample data and a statistical model to arrive at such a confidence region for a parameter.

3. TESTING A HYPOTHESIS.    The statistician sets up a statistical model, and some of the values of the parameters are hypothesized, as opposed to being estimated. Given these hypothesized values of the parameters and the complete statistical model, the experimenter can test to see whether his sample data can reasonably be considered a SIRS sample from the hypothesized population.

The actors on this stage are (*i*) sample data (known), (*ii*) statistics based on these sample data (known), (*iii*) population parameters in the statistical model (estimated or hypothesized), (*iv*) sampling plan in the statistical model (almost invariably SIRS), and (*v*) sampling distribution based on the statistical model (known under the assumptions of the statistical model). These items are amplified in Chapters 2 to 9. In the meantime we shall discuss an artificial problem in the form of a dialogue between an experimenter $E$ and a statistician $S$. As far as possible, technical details are omitted in an attempt to make the discussion maximally intelligible. Leaving the question of point estimation aside, we shall consider two approaches to the problem, one aimed at finding confidence intervals and the other aimed at a test of significance.

The problem is as follows. $E$ measures the height of 100 male students entering American colleges and universities in the academic year 1968–1969 and summarizes these 100 measures in the form of two statistics:

$$\text{Mean} = 70 \text{ in.}$$
$$\text{Standard deviation} = 10 \text{ in.}$$

Now $E$ ponders two questions. (*i*) If the 100 sample members constitute a random sample from the population of members, how can I use my sample data to make some intelligent inferences about the unknown population measures? (*ii*) If some competent authority, such as a spokesman for the President's Council on Physical Fitness, tells me that the population mean is, in fact, 65 in, how can I determine whether my sample mean of 70 in. is significantly different from this? Let us consider each of these questions in turn.

## 1-42 Confidence Intervals

*E* has computed a sample mean of 70 in. He believes that his sample was a random sample from the population, and he wishes to make a statement about the population mean. His hunch is that the population mean is likely to be about 70 in. give or take a few inches. This region in which he believes the population mean will lie is known as a *confidence region*. *E* is concerned about how much confidence he can place in such a confidence region.

Consider the following dialogue between *E* and *S*:

*E*  I don't know the set of population measures, but I did make an effort to define rules for membership pretty carefully, and I have some confidence that the sample I chose is, in fact, a random sample.

*S*  Well, I like to work with a normally distributed population. Is that all right with you?

*E*  Sure. A lot of measures like heights and weights and IQs seem to be distributed in a sort of bell shape, much like the normal distribution.

*S*  To be precise, I need to know the mean and the standard deviation for my normal population. These two parameters must be specified.

*E*  Since I have absolutely no idea about the population of heights, the best I can do is let you use my sample mean (70 in.) and my sample standard deviation (10 in.) as estimates of your population parameters.

*S*  Fine, and I will accept your word that the sampling plan is essentially a simple random sampling plan. And you were working with a sample containing 100 members?

*E*  That's correct. I used only one sample and therefore obtained only one mean, and I know that the value of a statistic varies from sample to sample. Can you tell me what sort of sampling fluctuation occurs under these circumstances?

*S*  Yes, as a matter of fact I can prove the following: if the population is a normal distribution with mean = 70 and standard deviation = 10 and if the sampling plan is a SIRS plan, then the sampling distribution of the mean turns out to be another normal distribution, this time with a mean = 70 and a standard deviation = 1.

*E*  Really? That standard deviation for the sampling distribution is rather small, isn't it?

*S*  Yes, it is, and if your sample had contained 10,000 members the standard deviation of the sampling distribution would have been just 0.1. It makes sense, though, because the larger the size of the sample, the smaller the fluctuation in the value of a statistic.

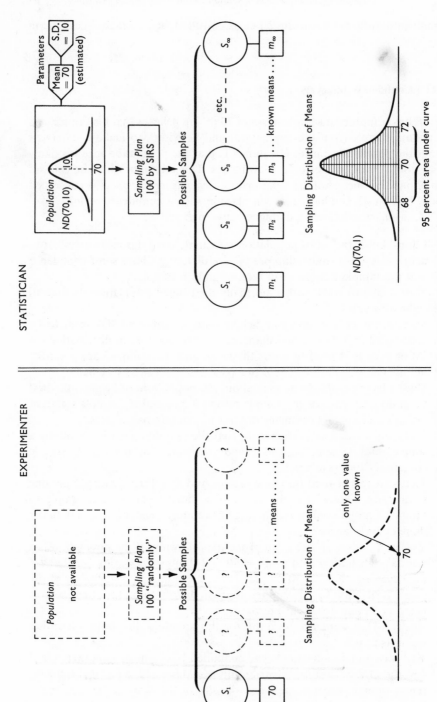

FIGURE 1-6. Diagram summarizing the determination of confidence intervals

*E*   All right. Now I want to define a confidence region that hopefully includes the true value of the population mean.

*S*   The sampling distribution of the mean is a normal distribution, as I told you, and I can also tell you that 95 percent of this distribution is contained between the values 68 and 72. In other words I can say with 95 percent confidence that the sample means will lie between 68 and 72, that is, if our statistical model is accepted.

*E*   Then I will say, with 95 percent confidence, that the true population mean lies between 68 and 72 in.

Figure 1-6 summarizes this discussion.


## 1-43   Test of Significance

*E* has computed a sample mean of 70 in. and a sample standard deviation of 10 in. His sample of 100 members was chosen on the basis of availability, and he suspects that it might well be something other than a random sample from the underlying population. He believes that the population mean is actually 65 in., and knowing about sampling fluctuation, he would like to determine whether his sample could be called a random sample or whether it is more likely to be a biased sample.

Consider the following dialogue:

*E*   A spokesman for the President's Council on Physical Fitness told me that the population mean height is 65 in., and in my sample of 100 members I calculated a sample mean of 70 in. Could this difference be accounted for by sampling fluctuation alone, or is it conceivable that I don't really have a random sample from the population?

*S*   We'll try to answer that by creating a statistical model. Assume that the population is a normal distribution and that the sampling plan is a SIRS plan. This will be the model. Now what parameters should I use for my population?

*E*   Well, you will have to let the mean be 65 in., because that is the true population mean. Since I have no information about the population standard deviation, I guess we'll have to estimate it by using the sample standard deviation.

*S*   All right, the population is normally distributed with mean 65 and standard deviation 10. Let us consider what would happen if we used a SIRS plan to obtain all permissible samples of size 100. I can prove for you that the sampling distribution of the sample means would be another normal distribution, with mean 65 and standard deviation 1.

*E*   Now where does my one obtained sample mean (70 in.) fit in?

*S*   According to our statistical model we must find out what the chances are of obtaining a sample mean as large as 70 or larger. If you look at Figure 1-7, you will notice that the area under the sampling distribution to the

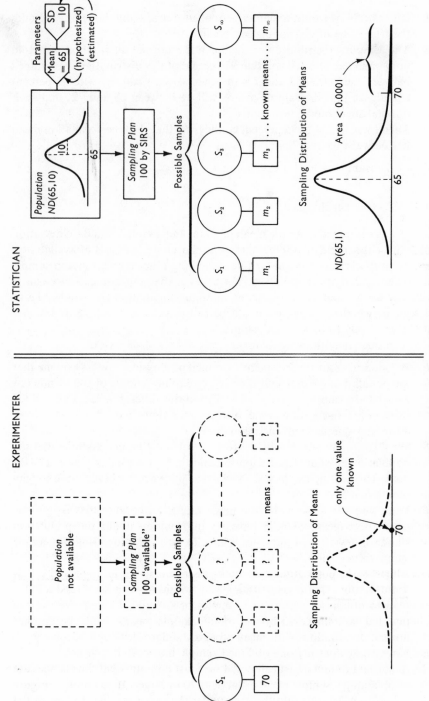

FIGURE I-7. Diagram summarizing the test of a hypothesis

right of 70 is extremely small. In fact it is less than 0.0001. According to the model, then, we will say that the chances of obtaining a sample mean as large as 70 are less than 1 in 10,000. I would say this was pretty slim evidence in support of the hunch that your sample is a random sample from the population.

E   I agree. As a matter of fact a lot of social scientists will reject the model if the chances are less than 5 in 100. So in this case I will argue that my sample is most unlikely to be a random sample from the population as stated in the model and that my sample mean is significantly different from the stated population mean—in fact, it is significant beyond the 0.0001 level.

Figure 1-7 summarizes this discussion.


## 1-44   Conclusion

The framework for Part 1 has been developed in this chapter. We must now amplify several points. First, the experimenter must become thoroughly acquainted with the most important summary numbers (statistics), namely, the mean and the standard deviation (or variance). He must be able to compute them quickly and efficiently, and he must be able to use them freely. Chapter 2 discusses this material and, in addition, a few other statistics that one meets in the literature. One of the important uses of the mean and standard deviation is in the definition of a standard score. This is also discussed in Chapter 2.

Second, the experimenter must become thoroughly acquainted with the normal distribution and the process of sampling from it. These matters are discussed in Chapter 3.

Third, although the experimenter may not have a strong mathematical background, he will do well to observe the statistician in action as he proceeds from a population and a sampling plan to a well-defined sampling distribution. With the use of diagrams, such as Figure 1-5, these processes are discussed in Chapter 4. The reader is urged to examine this chapter no matter how ill at ease he may feel in the presence of ominous-looking equations. The diagrams will help to structure his reading.

Fourth, the experimenter must learn to cooperate with the statistician so that he can use the important sampling distributions that are provided in Chapter 4. The three most common are the $t$-distribution, which is discussed in Chapter 5; the $F$-distribution, which is discussed in Chapters 6 and 7; and the $\chi^2$ (chi-square) distribution, which is discussed in Chapter 8.

Finally, Chapter 9 deals with problems of regression analysis. This material does not fit easily into the framework but is of sufficient importance in the literature to warrant a place in the text.

## EXERCISES

1. Consider the following unusual experiment. You want to know the mean height of twenty-year-old American girls, and you decide to use a sample size of just one, that is, one sample member and one measurement of height.
   (a) What rules for membership would this one sample member have to satisfy?
   (b) How could you justify that your sampling plan was random?
   (c) What kind of sampling fluctuation would you be aware of?
   (d) If you had to estimate (a point estimate) the population parameter (mean height of the population of twenty-year-old American girls), what would this estimate be?
   (e) If you could be sure that the sampling plan was a SIRS plan, what could you say about the population distribution and the sampling distribution of the mean of a sample of size one?
2. If in Exercise 1 your interest had been in the body temperature of each population member and the sample size was still one, would the situation be any different? Consider what you know about the distribution of height and body temperature. (The point of Exercises 1 and 2 is that the experimenter always has more or less knowledge about the distribution of measures for a population. Such *a priori* knowledge helps him decide whether inferences based on sample data are plausible or not. Consider what would happen, for instance, if the one sample member had a body temperature of 104°.)
3. To get an intuitive feeling for confidence intervals, consider the following exercises:
   (a) Looking at someone, estimate his body weight. Now ask yourself how sure you are of this estimate. How much would you bet in exchange for a dollar that the true weight is exactly what you estimated? If you needed to be correct within only 5 pounds (more or less), how much would you bet in exchange for a dollar? Clearly, as the interval increased, you would feel more sure of winning a dollar rather than losing, whatever you bet. The more you are prepared to bet, the greater your confidence.
   (b) Next time you talk to someone over the telephone, preferably someone you have not met before, estimate his body weight. Repeat (a) in this case. Would the confidence regions have to be bigger or smaller under these circumstances for a given bet?
4. To get an intuitive feeling for tests of significance, consider the following exercises:
   (a) When you buy light bulbs for ordinary household use, you typically accept them as a SIRS sample from all such bulbs, that is, the population of bulbs. How many bad bulbs would it take to make you fairly sure that your purchase was not a SIRS sample?
   (b) All cars need to be serviced from time to time. You can think of this as a sample of troubles from the population of troubles that cars typically suffer from. How many troubles would you need to convince you that your car's troubles seemed like something other than a random sample of troubles; that is, when would you reject the hypothesis that this is a SIRS sample of troubles?

# Useful Summary Numbers (Descriptive Statistics)

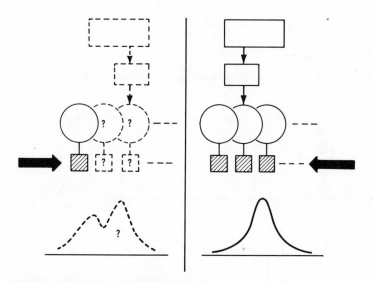

## 2-1 SOME WARM-UP EXERCISES

### 2-11 Distributions to Work With

Summary numbers describe particular characteristics of distributions. That is why they are often called *descriptive statistics*. Since distributions come in a wide variety of shapes, we wish to work with summary numbers that are sensitive to these shapes. Figure 2-1 presents a set of eight different distributions that are used for illustrative purposes in this chapter.

These eight distributions are designed to be treated as four pairs. For example, distributions *A* and *B* have identical shape, but the numbers in *B* are greater than those in *A*. The technical jargon is that *A* and *B* differ only with respect to *central tendency*. Distributions *C* and *D* differ from each other in

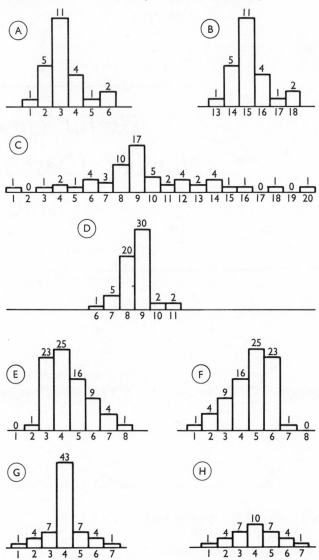

FIGURE 2-1.  Eight distributions for use in this chapter—numbers on top of the histogram columns indicate frequency of occurrence of the value listed below the columns

that C is more widely *dispersed* than D. The distinct values in distribution C have a greater *range* than those in distribution D. Distributions E and F illustrate *skewness*. E slopes more gradually to the right than to the left and is known as a right-skewed distribution. F slopes more gradually to the left than to the right and is known as a left-skewed distribution. Finally, distributions G and H are designed to illustrate what is known as "peakedness" or _kurtosis_. $G$ is a rather flat distribution compared with $H$, since $H$ has a more pronounced peak on the distinct value 4.

We shall now examine sets of statistics that are sensitive to the above shape characteristics.

## 2-12   Moments about Zero

A summary number may be obtained by defining a numerical operation that reduces a set of numbers to one number. Consider the following _family of numerical operations:_

1. Raise all the numbers in the set to some power.
2. Add all these new numbers.
3. Divide by $N$ (the number of elements in the set).

We call this a family of numerical operations because we can raise the numbers in the set to the first power, the second power, the third power, the fourth, the fifth, the sixth, and so on. In each case we obtain one summary number. Thus we say that this family of numerical operations produces a family of statistics, and they are known as the _moments about zero_. There is a first moment about zero, a second moment about zero, a third, a fourth, and so on.

Consider distribution $A$. There are 24 numbers in this set: one 1, five 2s, eleven 3s, four 4s, one 5, and two 6s. If we raise these 24 numbers to the second power, there will still be 24 numbers: one 1, five $2^2$s, eleven $3^2$s, four $4^2$s, one $5^2$, and two $6^2$s. If we raise them to the third power, there will be one 1, five 8s, eleven 27s, four 64s, one 125, and two 216s. And so we could go on. For illustrative purposes let us compute the first three moments about zero for distribution $A$.

THE FIRST MOMENT ABOUT ZERO $(m_1')$.   Raising the 24 numbers to the first power is to leave them as they are. Thus all we have to do is to add the 24 numbers and divide by 24, and this is, in fact, what we do to compute the mean of a set of numbers. So the first moment about zero is the mean. Consider the two ways of doing this calculation shown in Table 2-1.

THE SECOND MOMENT ABOUT ZERO $(m_2')$.   Raise the numbers to the second power, that is, square them; add them; and divide by 24. This produces the second moment about zero, $m_2'$, as shown in Table 2-2.   An alternative procedure is shown in Table 2-3.

THE THIRD MOMENT ABOUT ZERO $(m_3')$.   Raise the numbers to the third power, add them, and divide by 24. This produces the third moment about zero, $m_3'$. Check that the answer is $m_3' = 47.96$.

Now it is time to introduce some useful symbols. Consider the 24 numbers in distribution $A$ again. Instead of writing them on 24 marbles, let

Table 2-1

(a)          (b)

| Distribution A | Distinct value (x) | Frequency (f) | Product (fx) |
|---|---|---|---|
| 1 | 1 | 1 | 1 |
| 2  2  2  2  2 | 2 | 5 | 10 |
| 3  3  3  3  3  3  3  3  3  3  3 | 3 | 11 | 33 |
| 4  4  4  4 | 4 | 4 | 16 |
| 5 | 5 | 1 | 5 |
| 6  6 | 6 | 2 | 12 |
| Sum of first powers = 77 | | Total = 24 | Total = 77 |

$$\text{Mean of first powers} = \frac{77}{24} = 3.21$$

$$\text{that is,} \quad m_1' = 3.21$$

us identify a variable $X$ that can take on 24 values. We identify these 24 values for $X$ by means of subscripts as follows: $X_1$, $X_2$, $X_3$, $X_4$, . . . , $X_{24}$. The 24 numbers in distribution $A$ are now attached to these symbols in any order you wish, just as long as all 24 numbers are accounted for. Here is one way we may make the correspondence:

$$X_1 = 1 \quad X_2 = 2 \quad X_3 = 2 \quad X_4 = 2 \quad X_5 = 2 \quad X_6 = 2$$
$$X_7 = 3 \quad X_8 = 3 \quad X_9 = 3 \quad X_{10} = 3 \quad X_{11} = 3 \quad X_{12} = 3$$
$$X_{13} = 3 \quad X_{14} = 3 \quad X_{15} = 3 \quad X_{16} = 3 \quad X_{17} = 3 \quad X_{18} = 4$$
$$X_{19} = 4 \quad X_{20} = 4 \quad X_{21} = 4 \quad X_{22} = 5 \quad X_{23} = 6 \quad X_{24} = 6$$

If you wish to talk about any one of these values in general but none in particular, then you may talk about the $i$th value, where $i$ can be any one of the values 1 to 24. We designate the $i$th value $X_i$ (read "$X$ sub $i$"). When $i = 17$, we are talking about the value 3 ($X_{17} = 3$), for example.

Another symbol that is very useful is the Greek capital sigma, $\Sigma$, which stands for "the sum of." As you become more familiar with it, you will no doubt begin to call it "sum" or "sigma"; and if we have to add many

Table 2-2

| Distribution A | | |
|---|---|---|
| 1 | Square the numbers → | 1 |
| 2  2  2  2  2 | | 4  4  4  4  4 |
| 3  3  3  3  3  3  3  3  3  3  3 | | 9  9  9  9  9  9  9  9  9  9  9 |
| 4  4  4  4 | | 16  16  16  16 |
| 5 | | 25 |
| 6  6 | | 36  36 |

Add them      281
Divide by 24      11.71

$$\text{that is,} \quad m_2' = 11.71$$

Table 2-3

| Distinct value (x) | Squared ($x^2$) | Frequency (f) | Product ($fx^2$) |
|---|---|---|---|
| 1 | 1 | 1 | 1 |
| 2 | 4 | 5 | 20 |
| 3 | 9 | 11 | 99 |
| 4 | 16 | 4 | 64 |
| 5 | 25 | 1 | 25 |
| 6 | 36 | 2 | 72 |
| | | Total = $\overline{24}$ | Total = $\overline{281}$ |

that is, $m_2' = 11.71$

$X$-values, we shall say "sigma $X$." To illustrate its usefulness, consider adding the values $X_1$, $X_2$, $X_3$, and $X_4$:

$$X_1 + X_2 + X_3 + X_4 = 1 + 2 + 2 + 2 = 7$$

Another way of writing this is as follows:

$$\sum_{i=1}^{4} X_i = 7$$

In words the symbols on the left of this equation are meant to convey the idea that values of the type $X_i$ are to be added together for all values of $i$ from 1 to 4. More briefly we say, sigma $X$ sub $i$ for $i$ going from 1 to 4.

Using this notation, we now rewrite the first three moments about zero for distribution $A$:

$$m_1' = \frac{\sum_{i=1}^{24} X_i}{24}$$

$$m_2' = \frac{\sum_{i=1}^{24} X_i^{2}}{24}$$

$$m_3' = \frac{\sum_{i=1}^{24} X_i^{3}}{24}$$

Where there can be no doubt as to the range of the subscript $i$, we do not bother to elaborate the sigma symbol. Thus, in general, we write:

$$m_1' = \frac{\sum X}{N} \quad \text{mean}$$

$$m_2' = \frac{\sum X^2}{N} \tag{2-1}$$

$$m_3' = \frac{\sum X^3}{N}$$

where $N$ is the number of observations being considered.

A family of moments about zero has been defined. Is such a set of statistics (summary numbers) useful? Yes, they are for the following reasons:

1. They are easy to understand.

2. They are all "means"—$m_1'$ is the mean of the first powers, $m_2'$ is the mean of the second powers, and so on—and the first moment about zero is *the* mean, that is, the commonly accepted version of "mean."

3. They are all computed directly from the raw data as opposed to some transformation of the raw data. This becomes very important when we start looking for the most efficient formula for computing a given statistic.

4. If you ever plan to try to follow the work of mathematical statisticians, you will surely come across these moments about zero.

## 2-13  Moments about the Mean

Consider distribution $H$ in Figure 2-1. Imagine that the 34 numbers in this distribution are, in fact, 34 scores obtained by 34 students in a spelling test. What is the mean score on this test? The first moment about zero is the mean:

$$m_1' = \frac{\sum_{i=1}^{34} X_i}{34} = 4$$

The mean is important enough to deserve a special symbol, and we call it $\bar{X}$ (read "X-bar"). Thus, for distribution $H$, $\bar{X} = 4$. Now one of the most common transformations applied to raw data is to subtract the mean from the raw data. If we do this to the 34 scores, we obtain 34 *deviations from the mean*. In symbols the $i$th deviation from the mean is

$$(X_i - \bar{X})$$

We write it within parentheses because it is, in fact, just one number, in spite of the fact that the symbols make it look like two things. Since deviations from the mean are so common in statistical calculations, it is convenient to designate them with lower-case symbols, as follows:

$$x_i = (X_i - \bar{X})$$

In distribution $H$ there are seven 3s. These are raw data. If we subtract the mean ($= 4$) from each of these 3s, we obtain $-1$ (minus one) seven times; that is, there will be seven deviations from the mean equal to minus one. The 10 scores of 4 become 10 deviations from the mean of zero; the 4 scores of 6 become 4 deviations from the mean of 2; and so on.

*Moments about the mean* are defined exactly like moments about zero except that we work with deviations from the mean instead of the raw data. Whereas moments about zero are designated $m_1'$, $m_2'$, $m_3'$, and so on, moments about the mean are designated without the prime: $m_1$, $m_2$, $m_3$, and so on. Consider the $H$ distribution again:

Raw data: $\qquad\qquad\qquad\quad$ $X_i$ for $i = 1$ to 34

Deviations from the mean: $\quad$ $x_i$ for $i = 1$ to 34

Using the deviations from the mean, we define the moments about the mean as follows:

$$m_1 = \frac{\sum x_i}{34} \qquad \text{first moment about the mean}$$

$$m_2 = \frac{\sum x_i^2}{34} \qquad \text{second moment about the mean}$$

$$m_3 = \frac{\sum x_i^3}{34} \qquad \text{third moment about the mean}$$

$$m_4 = \frac{\sum x_i^4}{34} \qquad \text{fourth moment about the mean}$$

etc.

Thus these moments are also "means." The first moment about the mean is the mean of the first powers of the deviations from the mean, the second moment about the mean is the mean of the second powers of the deviations from the mean, and so on. An equivalent designation of these moments about the mean is the following:

$$m_1 = \frac{\sum (X_i - \bar{X})}{34}$$

$$m_2 = \frac{\sum (X_i - \bar{X})^2}{34}$$

$$m_3 = \frac{\sum (X_i - \bar{X})^3}{34}$$

$$m_4 = \frac{\sum (X_i - \bar{X})^4}{34}$$

etc.

$$(2\text{-}2)$$

By way of illustration we compute the first three moments about the mean for distribution $H$. First assign the 34 numbers by one-to-one correspondence with the 34 symbols $X_1$ to $X_{34}$, as follows:

$$X_1 = 1 \quad X_2 = 2 \quad X_3 = 2 \quad X_4 = 2 \quad X_5 = 2 \quad X_6 = 3$$
$$X_7 = 3 \quad X_8 = 3 \quad X_9 = 3 \quad X_{10} = 3 \quad X_{11} = 3 \quad X_{12} = 3$$
$$X_{13} = 4 \quad X_{14} = 4 \quad X_{15} = 4 \quad X_{16} = 4 \quad X_{17} = 4 \quad X_{18} = 4$$
$$X_{19} = 4 \quad X_{20} = 4 \quad X_{21} = 4 \quad X_{22} = 4 \quad X_{23} = 5 \quad X_{24} = 5$$
$$X_{25} = 5 \quad X_{26} = 5 \quad X_{27} = 5 \quad X_{28} = 5 \quad X_{29} = 5 \quad X_{30} = 6$$
$$X_{31} = 6 \quad X_{32} = 6 \quad X_{33} = 6 \quad X_{34} = 7$$

Now subtract the mean ($\bar{X} = 4$) from each of these raw scores:

$$x_1 = -3 \quad x_2 = -2 \quad x_3 = -2 \quad x_4 = -2 \quad x_5 = -2 \quad x_6 = -1$$
$$x_7 = -1 \quad x_8 = -1 \quad x_9 = -1 \quad x_{10} = -1 \quad x_{11} = -1 \quad x_{12} = -1$$
$$x_{13} = 0 \quad x_{14} = 0 \quad x_{15} = 0 \quad x_{16} = 0 \quad x_{17} = 0 \quad x_{18} = 0$$
$$x_{19} = 0 \quad x_{20} = 0 \quad x_{21} = 0 \quad x_{22} = 0 \quad x_{23} = 1 \quad x_{24} = 1$$
$$x_{25} = 1 \quad x_{26} = 1 \quad x_{27} = 1 \quad x_{28} = 1 \quad x_{29} = 1 \quad x_{30} = 2$$
$$x_{31} = 2 \quad x_{32} = 2 \quad x_{33} = 2 \quad x_{34} = 3$$

THE FIRST MOMENT ABOUT THE MEAN ($m_1$). Raise the deviations from the mean to the first power—that is, leave them as they are—add them, and divide by 34:

```
-3
-2  -2  -2  -2
-1  -1  -1  -1  -1  -1  -1
 0   0   0   0   0   0   0  0  0  0
 1   1   1   1   1   1   1
 2   2   2   2
 3
```

Sum of first powers of deviations = 0

Mean of first powers of deviations = 0

that is,    $m_1 = 0$

(In passing, note that the first moment about the mean is always zero, no matter what distribution we are working with.)

THE SECOND MOMENT ABOUT THE MEAN ($m_2$). Raise the deviations to the second power—that is, square them—add them, and divide by 34:

```
9
4  4  4  4
1  1  1  1  1  1  1
0  0  0  0  0  0  0  0  0  0
1  1  1  1  1  1  1
4  4  4  4
9
```

Sum of second powers of deviations = 64

Mean of second powers of deviations = $\dfrac{64}{34} = 1.88$

that is,    $m_2 = 1.88$

THE THIRD MOMENT ABOUT THE MEAN ($m_3$).   Raise the deviations to the third power, add them, and divide by 34:

$$
\begin{array}{lllllllll}
-27 \\
-8 & -8 & -8 & -8 \\
-1 & -1 & -1 & -1 & -1 & -1 & -1 \\
0 & 0 & 0 & 0 & 0 & 0 & 0 & 0 & 0 & 0 \\
1 & 1 & 1 & 1 & 1 & 1 & 1 \\
8 & 8 & 8 & 8 \\
27
\end{array}
$$

Sum of third powers of deviations = 0

Mean of third powers of deviations = 0

that is,     $m_3 = 0$

(In passing, note that for all symmetrical distributions the third moment about the mean is zero.)

A family of moments about the mean has been defined. Is such a set of summary numbers (statistics) useful? They are for the following reasons:

1. They are easy to understand.

2. They are all means—$m_1$ is the mean of the first powers of the deviations, $m_2$ is the mean of the second powers, and so on—and the second moment about the mean is a very important one. It is called *variance*. (Note in passing that, if you take the square root of $m_2$, you have the *standard deviation*.)

3. The first moment about the mean is always zero. (One way to interpret this is to say that, if you wish to transform a set of numbers into another set of numbers that has a mean of zero, you subtract the mean from the raw data. Subtracting the mean yields deviations from the mean, and the mean of these deviations is zero.)

4. Mathematical statisticians use these sets of moments to define distributions. Thus you might come across something called a moment-generating function, which generates all the moments of a distribution.

## 2-14   Alternative Symbolism

Consider $N$ scores designated $X_1$ to $X_N$. Then the formulas for moments about zero and moments about the mean are given in Equations (2-1) and (2-2) respectively. An alternative way of designating these scores would be to designate the distinct scores $Y_1$ to $Y_n$, where $n$ is the number of distinct scores, and for each distinct score identify the frequency of occurrence by the symbols $f_1$ to $f_n$. Thus we could write the frequency distribution as follows:

| Distinct score | Frequency of occurrence |
|:---:|:---:|
| $Y_1$ | $f_1$ |
| $Y_2$ | $f_2$ |
| $Y_3$ | $f_3$ |
| . | . |
| . | . |
| . | . |
| $Y_n$ | $f_n$ |

Using this symbolism, the formulas for moments about zero would be

$$m_1' = \frac{\sum_{i=1}^{n} f_i Y_i}{N} \quad \text{mean}$$

$$m_2' = \frac{\sum_{i=1}^{n} f_i Y_i^2}{N} \qquad (2\text{-}1')$$

$$m_3' = \frac{\sum_{i=1}^{n} f_i Y_i^3}{N}$$

etc.

and the formulas for moments about the mean would be

$$m_1 = \frac{\sum_{i=1}^{n} f_i (Y_i - m_1')}{N}$$

$$m_2 = \frac{\sum_{i=1}^{n} f_i (Y_i - m_1')^2}{N} \qquad \text{variance} \qquad (2\text{-}2')$$

$$m_3 = \frac{\sum_{i=1}^{n} f_i (Y_i - m_1')^3}{N}$$

etc.

where $m_1' =$ the mean of the $N$ scores. We say that $f_i$ is the frequency of occurrence of the $i$th distinct value $Y_i$.

## EXERCISES

1  Compute $m_1'$ for distributions $C$ and $D$.
2. Compute the first four moments about zero for distribution $H$.
3. Compute $m_1$ for distribution $A$.
4. Compute $m_2$ for distribution $G$, and compare with $m_2$ for distribution $H$. Can you explain the difference?
5. Use Equations (2-1′) and (2-2′) to compute the first three moments about zero and the first three moments about the mean for distribution $H$.
6. Consider the distinct value $Y_i$. If we subtract the mean of a set of numbers from it, we obtain a deviation from the mean, $(Y_i - m_1')$. Designate this deviation score as $y_i = (Y_i - m_1')$ and rewrite Equations (2-2′) in terms of $y_i$.
7. Consider Equations (2-1) and (2-2). It is of considerable value to express moments about the mean in terms of moments about zero because moments about zero deal with the raw scores, whereas moments about the mean deal with transformed scores (the deviation scores are transformed scores), and it is more efficient to perform computations on raw scores. See if you can prove the following relationships:

(a) $m_1 = 0$ (always)

(b) $m_2 = m_2' - (m_1')^2$

(c) $m_3 = m_3' - 3(m_2')(m_1') + 2(m_1')^3$

(d) $m_4 = m_4' - 4(m_3')(m_1') + 6(m_2')(m_1')^2 - 3(m_1')^4$

8. Even if you cannot prove the relationships in Exercise 7, verify that they are true, using distribution $H$. Exercise 2 asks for the first four moments about zero for distribution $H$. Compute the first four moments about the mean, using Equations (2-2) or (2-2′). Then use the relations (a), (b), (c), and (d) from Exercise 7 to verify their correctness.

## 2-2  THE VITAL STATISTICS

### 2-21  Mean

Having introduced the moments, we now use them to define the most common descriptive statistics. There are only four that concern us here:

1. Mean, which is defined in terms of $m_1'$
2. Variance, which is defined in terms of $m_2$
3. Skewness, which is defined in terms of $m_3$
4. Kurtosis, which is defined in terms of $m_4$

The last one is interesting but not often used in the literature.

The mean is a statistic that indicates the central tendency of a distribution of numbers. In Figure 2-1 distributions $A$ and $B$ have identical shape but different central tendencies. This is described in terms of the two means:

Mean of distribution $A$:      $\bar{A} = 3.21$
Mean of distribution $B$:      $\bar{B} = 15.21$

In general, for any distribution of $N$ numbers, $X_1$ to $X_N$,

*The mean is defined as*

$$\bar{X} = \frac{\sum X_i}{N} \qquad (2\text{-}3)$$

*This is also $m_1'$.*

## 2-22   Variance and Standard Deviation

The variance is a statistic that indicates the dispersion or variability of the numbers in a distribution. It is defined as the second moment about the mean or, equivalently, as the mean of the squared deviations from the mean. Given a set of numbers, we define the numerical operation that produces the variance as follows:

1. Find the mean of the numbers.
2. Subtract the mean from each number in the set.
3. Square these deviations from the mean.
4. Find the mean of these squared deviations.

In Figure 2-1 distributions $C$ and $D$ illustrate a wide dispersion and a narrow dispersion respectively. Applying the numerical operation above to these two distributions of numbers, we obtain

Variance for distribution $C$: $\qquad s_C^2 = 11.346$
Variance for distribution $D$: $\qquad s_D^2 = \phantom{1}0.781$

The symbol for variance is $s^2$, where $s$ stands for standard deviation. Thus variance is the standard deviation squared, or, stated the other way around, the standard deviation is the square root of the variance. We append a subscript to the $s^2$ to designate which distribution is being referred to. Note that distribution $C$ has a large variance and distribution $D$ has a small one.

The square root of the variance for distributions $C$ and $D$ gives the standard deviation for the two distributions:

Standard deviation for distribution $C$: $\quad s_C = 3.368$
Standard deviation for distribution $D$: $\quad s_D = 0.884$

In general, for any distribution of $N$ numbers, $X_1$ to $X_N$,

*The variance is defined as*

$$s_X^2 = \frac{\sum (X_i - \bar{X})^2}{N}$$

*This is also $m_2$.*

$$(2\text{-}4)$$

*The standard deviation is*

$$s_X = \sqrt{\frac{\sum (X_i - \bar{X})^2}{N}}$$

*This is also $\sqrt{m_2}$.*

## 2-23   Skewness

The skewness is a statistic that describes the asymmetry of the numbers in a distribution. It is defined in terms of the third moment about the mean and the standard deviation. If we divide the third moment about the mean by the standard deviation raised to the third power, then we have the skewness, which is designated $g_1$ (g sub one). Given a set of numbers, we define the numerical operation that produces the skewness as follows:

1. Find the mean of the numbers.
2. Find the standard deviation $s$ of the numbers.
3. Find the third moment about the mean $m_3$ of these numbers.
4. Divide $m_3$ by $s^3$.

In Figure 2-1 distributions $E$ and $F$ illustrate a right-skewed distribution and a left-skewed distribution respectively. Applying the numerical operation above to these two distributions, we obtain

Skewness for distribution $E$:     $g_1 = +0.714$
Skewness for distribution $F$:     $g_1 = -0.714$

Thus a right-skewed distribution, such as $E$, is also called a positive-skewed distribution, and a left-skewed distribution, such as $F$, is also called a negative-skewed distribution. In Section 2-13, $m_3$ was computed for distribution $H$ and turned out to be zero. Thus the skewness for distribution $H$ is zero. Obviously, since distribution $H$ is symmetrical, it is not skew.

In general, for any distribution of $N$ numbers, $X_1$ to $X_N$,

*The skewness is defined as*

$$g_1 = \frac{\sum (X - \bar{X})^3 / N}{[\sum (X - \bar{X})^2 / N]^{3/2}} \tag{2-5}$$

*This is also $m_3/s^3$.*

## 2-24   Kurtosis

The kurtosis is a statistic that indicates the peakedness of a distribution of numbers. It is defined in terms of the fourth moment about the mean, the standard deviation, and a constant. If we divide the fourth moment about the mean by the standard deviation raised to the fourth power, and then subtract a constant, 3, we have the kurtosis, which is designated $g_2$ (g sub two). Given a set of numbers, we define the numerical operation that produces the kurtosis as follows:

1. Find the mean of the numbers.
2. Find the standard deviation $s$ of the numbers.
3. Find the fourth moment about the mean $m_4$ of the numbers.
4. Divide $m_4$ by $s^4$, and then subtract 3.

In Figure 2-1 distributions $G$ and $H$ illustrate a rather peaked distribution and a rather flat distribution respectively. Applying the numerical operation above to these two distributions, we obtain

Kurtosis for distribution $G$:     $g_2 = 1.973$
Kurtosis for distribution $H$:     $g_2 = -0.476$

Thus a rather peaked distribution has positive kurtosis, and a rather flat distribution has negative kurtosis. Somewhere between there must be some kind of distribution that is neither peaked nor flat. As a matter of convention the normal distribution is considered to be neither peaked nor flat. Thus we wish to ensure that the kurtosis of a normal distribution is zero. If we compute $m_4/s^4$ for a normal distribution, we find it to be 3. Hence the formula for kurtosis involves a $-3$.

In general, for any distribution of $N$ numbers, $X_1$ to $X_N$,

*The kurtosis is defined as*

$$g_2 = \frac{\sum (X_i - \bar{X})^4 / N}{[\sum (X_i - \bar{X})^2 / N]^2} - 3 \qquad (2\text{-}6)$$

*This is also* $(m_4/s^4) - 3$.

## 2-25  Efficient Computation

The experimenter should develop an intuitive feeling for the statistics he uses, but when he is faced with the task of actually computing such statistics, he should know how to do so with maximum efficiency.

Consider the computation of the variance of a set of numbers. The formula given in Equation (2-4) is

$$s^2 = \frac{\sum (X - \bar{X})^2}{N}$$

In Exercise 7 of Section 2-1 it was pointed out that another formula for variance is

$$s^2 = m_2' - (m_1')^2 = \frac{\sum X^2}{N} - \left(\frac{\sum X}{N}\right)^2 \qquad (2\text{-}7)$$

Now these two formulas are, in fact, identical, but Equation (2-7) is the more efficient computational formula. There is no better way of convincing yourself that this is so than by taking a set of numbers, say, distribution $A$, and computing the variance by both formulas.

In general the formula that deals directly with the raw data is more efficient than one that deals with transformed data, and if you wish to compute the four vital statistics, the following efficient procedure is recommended:

1. Compute the four quantities

$$\text{Sum of } X: \qquad \sum X$$
$$\text{Sum of } X^2: \qquad \sum X^2$$
$$\text{Sum of } X^3: \qquad \sum X^3$$
$$\text{Sum of } X^4: \qquad \sum X^4$$

2. Using these sums, compute the first four moments about zero:

$$m_1' = \frac{\sum X}{N} \qquad m_3' = \frac{\sum X^3}{N}$$
$$m_2' = \frac{\sum X^2}{N} \qquad m_4' = \frac{\sum X^4}{N}$$

3. Using these moments about zero, compute

$$m_2 = m_2' - (m_1')^2$$
$$m_3 = m_3' - 3(m_2')(m_1') + 2(m_1')^3 \qquad\qquad (2\text{-}8)$$
$$m_4 = m_4' - 4(m_3')(m_1') + 6(m_2')(m_1')^2 - 3(m_1')^4$$

4. Now refer to Equations (2-3) to (2-6) to obtain

$$\text{Mean} = m_1'$$
$$\text{Variance} = m_2 = s^2$$
$$\text{Skewness} = \frac{m_3}{s^3}$$
$$\text{Kurtosis} = \frac{m_4}{s^4} - 3$$

Of course, if you wish to compute only the mean and the variance, you have only to compute the two basic quantities $\sum X$ and $\sum X^2$.

## EXERCISES

1. Compute the first three vital statistics for distributions $C$ and $D$, using the efficient procedures outlined in Section 2-25.
2. Compute the skewness of distributions $E$ and $F$ to verify the results given in the text.

3. Compute the kurtosis of distributions $G$ and $H$ to verify the results given in the text.
4. Consider distribution $H$. Obtain the mean and standard deviation for this distribution.
   (a) Now multiply all the scores in $H$ by 2, and recompute the mean and standard deviation.
   (b) Multiply the original scores in $H$ by 3, and recompute the mean and standard deviation.
   (c) At this point can you write down the mean and standard deviation for the set of scores obtained by multiplying the original $H$ scores by 7; by 10; by $-2$?
5. Consider distribution $H$ again.
   (a) Suppose that you multiplied by 2 and added 5 to every original score in $H$. What would be the new mean and standard deviation?
   (b) Suppose that you multiplied by $-3$ and added 100 to every original score in $H$. What would be the new mean and standard deviation?
   (c) Suppose that you multiplied by any real number $a$ and added any real number $b$. What would be the new mean and standard deviation?

## 2-3 THE STANDARD SCORE

### 2-31 An Example

Twenty-five students were administered the Cureton Multi-Aptitude Test, with the following results for Mechanical Comprehension:

$$
\begin{array}{lllll}
X_1 = 6 & X_6 = 10 & X_{11} = 9 & X_{16} = 10 & X_{21} = 11 \\
X_2 = 11 & X_7 = 5 & X_{12} = 6 & X_{17} = 8 & X_{22} = 3 \\
X_3 = 11 & X_8 = 10 & X_{13} = 11 & X_{18} = 7 & X_{23} = 12 \\
X_4 = 12 & X_9 = 9 & X_{14} = 12 & X_{19} = 6 & X_{24} = 4 \\
X_5 = 10 & X_{10} = 8 & X_{15} = 12 & X_{20} = 4 & X_{25} = 7
\end{array}
$$

The experimenter's statistical reflex, on seeing a set of measures, is to calculate the mean and the standard deviation. Thus

$$
\bar{X} = \frac{\sum_{i=1}^{25} X_i}{N} = \frac{214}{25} = 8.56
$$

and

$$
s_X = \sqrt{\frac{\sum (X_i - \bar{X})^2}{N}} = \sqrt{\frac{\sum X_i^2}{N} - \bar{X}^2}
$$

$$
= \sqrt{\frac{2{,}022}{25} - 8.56^2} = 2.758
$$

The problem we now wish to consider is how to transform the 25 raw scores into 25 standard scores. First, what do we mean by standard scores? To gain an intuitive feeling for this concept, consider the following problem. Suppose

that you are told that subject 23 got a raw score of 12 on Mechanical Comprehension, and suppose that you know nothing else. Then ask yourself whether
this is a good or a bad score. You cannot answer this until you know how
other people score on the test. Suppose someone tells you that for a given
reference group (25 students) the mean raw score is 8.56. Now you know at
least that subject 23 scored 3.44 raw score points above the mean. You know
his deviation from the mean score, which tells you something more than the
raw score alone. But you still cannot know whether this 3.44 is exceptional
or not. Does a deviation score of $+3.44$ points mean that subject 23 is
exceptionally good at mechanical comprehension, or is it quite common for
students to score $+3.44$ points above the mean? You can answer this only
if you know the original dispersion of scores in the reference group. Suppose
now you are told that the standard deviation for the reference group is 2.758
units. This adds more information. We can compute that subject 23 scored

$$\frac{3.44}{2.758} = 1.247 \qquad \frac{Score}{Std\ dev}$$

standard deviations above the mean. Since every 2.758 raw-score units equals
one standard-deviation unit, we can express each subject's score in standard-
deviation units above or below the mean. This is the unit that has been
accepted as the standard-score scale.

To recapitulate, in order to have a standard-score scale we must have:

1. A reference group
2. The mean of the reference group, so that each subject's score can be
transformed into a deviation from the mean
3. The standard deviation of the reference group, so that deviations
from the mean can be expressed in standard-deviation units.

The effect of such a transformation of raw scores is twofold: (a) the standard
scores have a mean of zero (the mean of deviation scores is always zero;
compare $m_1$, the first moment about the mean); and (b) the standard scores
have a standard deviation of unity (the unit on the standard-score scale is one
standard deviation, so that the standard deviation is one unit).

## 2-32 The z-Score (Standard-score) Transformation

Given a set of numbers $X_1$ to $X_N$, In the example the raw scores are $X_1$
with mean $\bar{X}$ and standard deviation to $X_{25}$.
$s_X$, we transform raw scores into
standard scores, also known as
z-scores, by means of the following
formula:

For subject 23 we have

$$z_i = \frac{(X_i - \bar{X})}{s_X} \qquad\qquad z_{23} = \frac{(12 - 8.56)}{2.758} = 1.247 \qquad (2\text{-}9)$$

Stated verbally, we subtract the mean and divide by the standard deviation.

Never forget that a reference group is involved. We may also state this transformation in the following way. Change the *origin* of the score scale by subtracting the mean $\bar{X}$—that is, put the origin of the transformed scale at the (raw) mean; and change the *scale* of the score scale by dividing by the standard deviation $s_X$—that is, make the unit of the transformed scale equal to one (raw) standard deviation.

Verify that the standard scores for the 25 subjects above are

$$
\begin{array}{llll}
z_1 = -0.928 & z_7 = -1.291 & z_{13} = \quad 0.885 & z_{19} = -0.928 \\
z_2 = \quad 0.885 & z_8 = \quad 0.522 & z_{14} = \quad 1.247 & z_{20} = -1.653 \\
z_3 = \quad 0.885 & z_9 = \quad 0.160 & z_{15} = \quad 1.247 & z_{21} = \quad 0.885 \\
z_4 = \quad 1.247 & z_{10} = -0.203 & z_{16} = \quad 0.522 & z_{22} = -2.016 \\
z_5 = \quad 0.522 & z_{11} = \quad 0.160 & z_{17} = -0.203 & z_{23} = \quad 1.247 \\
z_6 = \quad 0.522 & z_{12} = -0.928 & z_{18} = -0.566 & z_{24} = -0.566
\end{array}
$$

*A raw score is converted to standard-score form by subtracting the mean and dividing by the standard deviation of some reference group.*

## 2-33   Other Transformations

The $z$-score transformation is known as a *linear* transformation, because the graph of raw scores against $z$-scores is a straight-line graph. Although the standard-score transformation is most important in statistics, there are other linear transformations that have become important in the world of the experimenter. For example, the College Board scores are often reported on a scale that has a mean of 500 and a standard deviation of 100. This could be called the College Board scale. Students in introductory psychology courses are often introduced to the $T$-score scale, which has a mean of 50 and a standard deviation of 10. Given any set of numbers, it is possible to transform them into a $z$-scale, a College Board scale, the $T$-scale, or any other kind of scale. We shall not spend too much time on these transformations, since they do not constitute principles of statistics. They are purely numerical operations on numbers. But it is useful to know the following procedure.

If you have a set of numbers whose mean is $\bar{X}$ and whose standard deviation is $s_X$ and you wish to transform the numbers into new numbers that have a mean of $\bar{Y}$ and a standard deviation of $s_Y$, then you may do so as follows:

Convert to a $z$-scale (standard scale) by (1) subtracting the mean $\bar{X}$ and (2) dividing by the standard deviation $s_X$.

Convert the $z$-scale into the desired scale by (3) multiplying by the desired standard deviation $s_Y$ and (4) adding the desired mean $\bar{Y}$.

If the new numbers are called $Y_i$ for $i = 1$ to $N$, then we may write a single equation to describe these four operations:

$$Y_i = \frac{(X_i - \bar{X})}{s_X} s_Y + \bar{Y} \qquad (2\text{-}10)$$

### EXERCISES

1. Convert the 34 raw scores of distribution $H$ into standard scores.
2. In Table 2-4 the scores of 25 subjects on seven subtests of the Cureton Multi-Aptitude Test Battery are presented. Consider subtests $C$ and $E$.
   (a) Compute the mean and standard deviation for these two subtests.
   (b) Now consider subject 2. He scored 11 on test $C$ and 10 on test $E$. The question we want to ask is whether this subject did better, relative to the other 24 subjects, on test $C$ than on test $E$? The way to answer this question is to convert the two scores into standard scores. Do so and come to some conclusion about the question posed.
   (c) Now consider subjects 15 and 22. If you add the two raw scores for subject 15, you get 15; and if you add the two raw scores for subject 22 you get 13. Suppose that you converted their scores to standard scores before adding. Which subject would come out ahead?
3. For subtest $G$ in Table 2-4 convert all the raw scores into $z$-scores, and verify that the mean of the $z$-scores is zero and the standard deviation is unity.
4. For the first five subjects in Table 2-4 convert their scores on subtest $G$ into (a) the College Board scale, (b) the $T$-score scale, and (c) a scale with mean $= 5$ and standard deviation $= 2$.

## 2-4  A STATISTIC THAT INDICATES RELATIONSHIP

### 2-41  Data to Work With

When an experimenter selects a sample of members, he often wishes to measure more than one dependent variable per member. For example, in Section 2-31 the experimenter worked with just one score for each of his 25 subjects, but the administration of the Cureton Multi-Aptitude Test yields several scores for each subject. Table 2-4 presents the data obtained on seven subtests of the Cureton Multi-Aptitude Test when administered to a class of 25 students. These data will serve our purpose both for illustrating the text and for the exercises that follow. In what follows immediately we consider only the tests designated $C$ and $G$ in the table.

The experimenter has a sample consisting of 25 students. Two dependent

Table 2-4   Data from the Administration of the Cureton Multi-Aptitude Test Battery to 25 Subjects

Tests: (A) Number Series
      (B) Figure Classification
      (C) Mechanical Comprehension
      (D) Word Recognition
      (E) Scrambled Letters
      (F) Checking
      (G) Paper Form Board

| Subject | A | B | C | D | E | F | G |
|---------|---|---|---|---|---|---|---|
| 1 | 9 | 13 | 6 | 12 | 9 | 23 | 4 |
| 2 | 9 | 12 | 11 | 15 | 10 | 26 | 5 |
| 3 | 6 | 12 | 11 | 11 | 5 | 28 | 6 |
| 4 | 7 | 13 | 12 | 11 | 6 | 22 | 4 |
| 5 | 5 | 12 | 10 | 11 | 2 | 17 | 5 |
| 6 | 9 | 12 | 10 | 14 | 6 | 17 | 4 |
| 7 | 10 | 10 | 5 | 9 | 7 | 21 | 3 |
| 8 | 8 | 11 | 10 | 9 | 5 | 21 | 6 |
| 9 | 9 | 12 | 9 | 10 | 5 | 25 | 6 |
| 10 | 10 | 12 | 8 | 10 | 5 | 24 | 2 |
| 11 | 8 | 13 | 9 | 15 | 7 | 25 | 5 |
| 12 | 10 | 10 | 6 | 13 | 6 | 21 | 3 |
| 13 | 8 | 12 | 11 | 10 | 9 | 18 | 4 |
| 14 | 10 | 14 | 12 | 11 | 10 | 24 | 6 |
| 15 | 8 | 10 | 12 | 10 | 3 | 10 | 8 |
| 16 | 9 | 14 | 10 | 11 | 8 | 19 | 5 |
| 17 | 6 | 9 | 8 | 11 | 7 | 22 | 5 |
| 18 | 8 | 10 | 7 | 7 | 3 | 19 | 6 |
| 19 | 8 | 11 | 6 | 11 | 5 | 14 | 4 |
| 20 | 9 | 10 | 4 | 11 | 5 | 21 | 1 |
| 21 | 9 | 12 | 11 | 14 | 9 | 17 | 6 |
| 22 | 10 | 14 | 3 | 9 | 10 | 28 | 5 |
| 23 | 8 | 12 | 12 | 8 | 6 | 18 | 6 |
| 24 | 10 | 11 | 4 | 13 | 10 | 22 | 2 |
| 25 | 10 | 10 | 7 | 10 | 6 | 22 | 3 |

measures of interest are mechanical ability, as defined by the score on test C (Mechanical Comprehension), and spatial ability, as defined by the score on test G (Paper Form Board). Thus each sample member has two scores, and we are looking for a statistic (summary number) that will indicate the relationship or "co-relation" between the two sets of scores on the same subjects. Are the two scores for a given subject related in any way? If he scores high on test $C$, will he score high or low on test $G$?

## 2-42   How to Represent Bivariate Data

In Chapter 1 we stated that a set of numbers could be thought of as a wild array of numbers, a frequency distribution, or a histogram (or some other picture of the distribution). How shall we think about bivariate data? For each of the $N$ members in a set we have two numbers, which constitute bivariate data. Now we may wish to treat the two dependent measures quite separately, and so we simply have two sets of numbers; but it is important to remember that the two measures per subject (or sample member) are inexorably paired with each other. The terminology that emphasizes this point is as follows. We say that for each member of the set we have an *ordered two-tuple* of measures. The word "ordered" is used to indicate that the two dependent measures are written in the same order for all members of the set, and the word "two-tuple" indicates that there are two dependent measures. If we measure three dependent measures per subject, we have ordered three-tuples, and the data in Table 2-4 are arranged in ordered seven-tuples.

We are now in a position to be consistent with what we said in Chapter 1. A univariate distribution of numbers can be thought of as a wild array of numbers, a frequency distribution, or a histogram. A bivariate distribution of ordered two-tuples can be thought of as a wild array of ordered two-tuples, a bivariate frequency distribution, or a picture of the distribution (this time in three dimensions).

In the case of tests $C$ and $G$ in Table 2-4 here is an array of ordered two-tuples:

|       |        |        |        |        |        |        |
|-------|--------|--------|--------|--------|--------|--------|
| (6,4) | (11,5) | (11,6) | (12,4) | (10,5) | (10,4) | (5,3) |
| (10,6)| (9,6)  | (8,2)  | (9,5)  | (6,3)  | (11,4) | (12,6)|
| (12,8)| (10,5) | (8,5)  | (7,6)  | (6,4)  | (4,1)  | (11,6)|
| (3,5) | (12,6) | (4,2)  | (7,3)  |        |        |       |

Note that by convention we write the score on test $C$ first.

To describe these ordered two-tuples as a bivariate frequency distribution, we have to determine their distinct values, and then find the frequency of occurrence of each. We do this in the form of a *scatterplot* as shown at the top of page 56. The 10 distinct values obtained on test $C$ are written horizontally, and the 8 distinct values obtained on test $G$ are written vertically. This makes a grid of 80 cells, each representing a possible two-tuple. The top right-hand cell indicates the ordered two-tuple (12,8), and since this occurred once, we enter a 1 there. The ordered two-tuple (6,4) occurred twice in the set of bivariate data, and therefore we enter a 2 in the corresponding cell. The completed diagram is the bivariate analog of the frequency distribution.

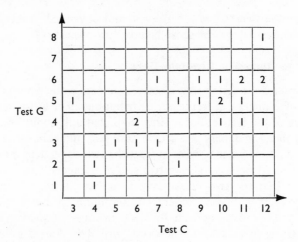

Test C

Note that, if we sum the frequencies in each row, we obtain what is known as the *marginal distribution* of $G$:

| $G$ | $f$ |
| --- | --- |
| 8 | 1 |
| 7 | 0 |
| 6 | 7 |
| 5 | 6 |
| 4 | 5 |
| 3 | 3 |
| 2 | 2 |
| 1 | 1 |

This is nothing more or less than the frequency distribution for test $G$, but when we are considering a bivariate distribution, it is known as a marginal distribution, that is, a distribution in the margin.

Similarly we could sum the frequencies in each column to obtain the marginal distribution of $C$:

| $C$ | $f$ |
| --- | --- |
| 12 | 4 |
| 11 | 4 |
| 10 | 4 |
| 9 | 2 |
| 8 | 2 |
| 7 | 2 |
| 6 | 3 |
| 5 | 1 |
| 4 | 2 |
| 3 | 1 |

Again this is nothing more nor less than the frequency distribution for test $C$.

If you wish to make a pictorial representation of a bivariate frequency distribution, you will need a third dimension. For example, you could build up a solid histogram on the basis of the scatterplot shown above. In each cell in the scatterplot you could simply place as many blocks as the frequency of occurrence required. If you try to picture a trivariate distribution, you are on your own.

### 2-43   The Correlation Coefficient

In the scatterplot shown above there appears to be a positive relationship between the scores on test $C$ and test $G$. By this we mean that larger scores on test $C$ tend to go with larger scores on test $G$ and smaller scores on test $C$ tend to go with smaller scores on test $G$. We now define a statistic that gives a numerical measure of such a relationship. It is known as the *correlation coefficient* and is designated $r$. Subscripts are appended to $r$ to indicate the two dependent measures. Thus we wish to find the value of $r_{CG}$ (or $r_{GC}$). Here is the numerical operation:

1. Transform the raw scores on test $C$ to standard-score form; that is, obtain the set of $z$-scores for test $C$.
2. Transform the raw scores on test $G$ to standard-score form; that is, obtain the set of $z$-scores for test $G$.
3. For each subject multiply the two $z$-scores together; that is, obtain the $z$-score product for each subject.
4. Add all 25 $z$-score products.
5. Divide the sum by 25; this will be $r_{CG}$.

The formula that expresses this numerical operation is

$$r_{CG} = \frac{\sum (z_C z_G)}{25}$$

Never forget that this formula refers to ordered two-tuples, so that the product $z_C z_G$ is the product for one sample member.

Table 2-5 shows the details of the calculation of $r_{CG}$ according to the formula above.

The last column mean, being the average of $z$-score products, is the correlation coefficient between tests $C$ and $G$:

$$r_{CG} = r_{GC} = \frac{\sum z_C z_G}{25} = 0.6361$$

In general, given two dependent measures $X$ and $Y$ on each of $N$ sample members,

The correlation coefficient is defined as

$$r_{XY} = \frac{\sum (z_X z_Y)}{N} \tag{2-11}$$

where
$$z_X = \frac{(X - \bar{X})}{s_X} \qquad z_Y = \frac{(Y - \bar{Y})}{s_Y}$$

Table 2-5  Computation of the Correlation Coefficient between Scores on Tests $C$ and $G$ ($C$ = Mechanical Comprehension; $G$ = Paper Form Board)

| Subject | $C$ | $G$ | $z_C$ | $z_G$ | $z_C z_G$ |
|---------|-----|-----|--------|--------|-----------|
| 1 | 6 | 4 | −0.928 | −0.355 | 0.3297 |
| 2 | 11 | 5 | 0.885 | 0.279 | 0.2467 |
| 3 | 11 | 6 | 0.885 | 0.913 | 0.8079 |
| 4 | 12 | 4 | 1.247 | −0.355 | −0.4430 |
| 5 | 10 | 5 | 0.522 | 0.279 | 0.1457 |
| 6 | 10 | 4 | 0.522 | −0.355 | −0.1854 |
| 7 | 5 | 3 | −1.291 | −0.989 | 1.2770 |
| 8 | 10 | 6 | 0.522 | 0.913 | 0.4768 |
| 9 | 9 | 6 | 0.160 | 0.913 | 0.1457 |
| 10 | 8 | 2 | −0.203 | −1.624 | 0.3297 |
| 11 | 9 | 5 | 0.160 | 0.279 | 0.0445 |
| 12 | 6 | 3 | −0.928 | −0.989 | 0.9183 |
| 13 | 11 | 4 | 0.885 | −0.355 | −0.3142 |
| 14 | 12 | 6 | 1.247 | 0.913 | 1.1391 |
| 15 | 12 | 8 | 1.247 | 2.182 | 2.7211 |
| 16 | 10 | 5 | 0.522 | 0.279 | 0.1457 |
| 17 | 8 | 5 | −0.203 | 0.279 | −0.0567 |
| 18 | 7 | 6 | −0.566 | 0.013 | −0.5166 |
| 19 | 6 | 4 | −0.928 | −0.355 | 0.3297 |
| 20 | 4 | 1 | −1.653 | −2.258 | 3.7328 |
| 21 | 11 | 6 | 0.855 | 0.913 | 0.8079 |
| 22 | 3 | 5 | −2.016 | 0.279 | −0.5625 |
| 23 | 12 | 6 | 1.247 | 0.913 | 1.1391 |
| 24 | 4 | 2 | −1.653 | −1.624 | 2.6843 |
| 25 | 7 | 3 | −0.566 | −0.989 | 0.5596 |
| Sum | 214 | 114 | 0.000 | 0.000 | 15.9029 |
| Mean | 8.56 | 4.56 | 0.000 | 0.000 | 0.6361 |
| Standard deviation | 2.76 | 1.58 | 1.000 | 1.000 | |

## 2-44   Additional Comments on the Correlation Coefficient

The correlation coefficient is used so often in the literature that it deserves additional comment. It is a summary number, that is, a statistic, that indicates the measure of the linear relationship between two sets of measures on the same subjects. It is a little difficult at this stage to say why it is linear as opposed to nonlinear. In Chapter 9 it will become more evident that $r_{XY}$ is a measure of linear association between $X$ and $Y$.

The maximum value that $r$ can attain is $+1$ and represents what is known as perfect positive relationship. The minimum value that $r$ can attain is $-1$ and represents what is known as perfect negative relationship. When $r = 0$, we say that there is no linear relationship between the two variables under consideration, or you may say that they are linearly independent. When $r$ has a value somewhere between 0 and $+1$, we talk about imperfect positive relationship; and when $r$ lies between 0 and $-1$, we talk about imperfect negative relationship. These cases are summarized in Figure 2-2.

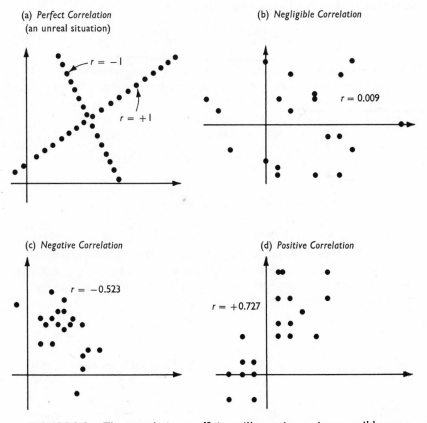

FIGURE 2-2.   The correlation coefficient: illustrating various possible cases

Sometimes you will find that $r$ is called the *Pearson product-moment correlation coefficient*. Since we have already introduced moments about zero and moments about the mean, it is easy to introduce product moments. Consider a set of $N$ ordered two-tuples $(X_1, Y_1)$ to $(X_N, Y_N)$. If we convert all the $X$ values to deviations from the mean, calling them $x_1$ to $x_N$, and all the $Y$ values to deviations from the mean, calling them $y_1$ to $y_N$, then we can define a family of product moments as follows:

$$m_{11} = \frac{\sum (x_i^1 y_i^1)}{N} \qquad \text{first product moment}$$

$$m_{22} = \frac{\sum (x_i^2 y_i^2)}{N} \qquad \text{second product moment}$$

$$m_{33} = \frac{\sum (x_i^3 y_i^3)}{N} \qquad \text{third product moment}$$

etc.

We are interested only in the first product moment (about the mean), and we can write it in this equivalent form:

$$m_{11} = \frac{\sum (X_i - \bar{X})(Y_i - \bar{Y})}{N} = C_{XY} \qquad (2\text{-}12)$$

This first product moment about the mean is used frequently in the study of mental-test theory and elsewhere, and it has its own special name—*covariance*, which is designated $C_{XY}$. The covariance, that is, the first product moment, is a statistic (summary number) that indicates how two variables co-vary.

We digress for a moment to examine Equation (2-11):

$$r_{XY} = \frac{\sum z_X z_Y}{N} = \frac{\sum (X_i - \bar{X})(Y_i - \bar{Y})/(s_X s_Y)}{N}$$

$$= \frac{\sum (X_i - \bar{X})(Y_i - \bar{Y})/N}{s_X s_Y} = \frac{C_{XY}}{s_X s_Y}$$

In other words, Equation (2-11) clearly involves the use of the first product moment $C_{XY}$. Hence the name product-moment correlation coefficient.

There is one further digression that the interested reader will find valuable. If we rewrite the equations for the variance of $X$ and $Y$, we can see how similar they are to the covariance equation:

Variance of $X$:
$$s_X^2 = \frac{\sum (X_i - \bar{X})(X_i - \bar{X})}{N} = C_{XX}$$

Variance of $Y$:
$$s_Y^2 = \frac{\sum (Y_i - \bar{Y})(Y_i - \bar{Y})}{N} = C_{YY}$$

Covariance of $X$ and $Y$:
$$\frac{\sum (X_i - \bar{X})(Y_i - \bar{Y})}{N} = C_{XY}$$

Indeed, it is often useful to think of the variance of $X$ as the covariance of $X$ and $X$, and we designate this $C_{XX}$. Similarly the variance of $Y$ can be designated $C_{YY}$. Using this notation, we find that the standard deviations for $X$ and $Y$ are

$$s_X = \sqrt{C_{XX}}$$

and
$$s_Y = \sqrt{C_{YY}}$$

Thus the equation for $r_{XY}$ can be rewritten in the easily remembered form

$$r_{XY} = \frac{C_{XY}}{\sqrt{C_{XX}C_{YY}}} \tag{2-13}$$

### 2-45   An Efficient Computational Equation

Equations (2-11) and (2-13) are helpful for developing an intuitive feeling for the correlation coefficient, but they are not efficient as computational equations. If you were communicating with a high-speed computer and were trying to compute $r_{XY}$ using Equation (2-11), your flow diagram would look something like this:

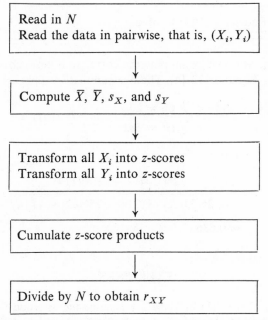

A much more efficient equation for computing $r_{XY}$ is the following:

$$r_{XY} = \frac{N \sum (XY) - (\sum X)(\sum Y)}{\sqrt{N \sum (X^2) - (\sum X)^2} \sqrt{N \sum (Y^2) - (\sum Y)^2}} \tag{2-14}$$

This equation can be derived without too much difficulty from Equation (2-13). Now although it may look formidable, note that we need to compute only five quantities to be able to use Equation (2-14): $\sum X$, $\sum Y$, $\sum X^2$, $\sum Y^2$, and $\sum (XY)$.

Thus, in contrast to the flow chart given above, the following flow chart shows how $r_{XY}$ may be computed most efficiently:

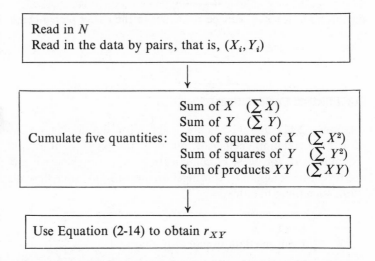

By way of illustration we recompute the correlation between scores on tests $C$ and $G$, using Equation (2-14). The five cumulative sums are

$$\sum C = 214 \quad \sum C^2 = 2{,}022$$
$$\sum G = 114 \quad \sum G^2 = 582 \quad \sum (CG) = 1{,}045$$

Substituting, we obtain

$$r_{CG} = \frac{25(1{,}045) - (214)(114)}{\sqrt{25(2{,}022) - (214)^2}\sqrt{25(582) - (114)^2}}$$

$$= 0.636$$

## EXERCISES

1. On the basis of the data in Table 2-4 examine the assertion that mechanical ability, as measured by test $C$, is more closely related to spatial ability, as measured by test $G$, than to mathematical ability, as measured by test $A$. Compute $r_{CA}$ and compare with $r_{CG}$.
2. Is $r_{CA} = r_{AC}$?
3. Compute the correlation coefficient between tests $D$ and $E$.

4. See if you can prove that the efficient formula for computing covariance is

$$C_{XY} = \frac{N \sum XY - (\sum X)(\sum Y)}{N^2}$$

If this is so, then write the equivalent efficient formulas for computing

$$s_X^2 = C_{XX} \quad \text{and} \quad s_Y^2 = C_{YY}$$

Putting these together in the form of Equation (2-13), show how we arrive at the efficient formula for computing $r_{XY}$ (Equation 2-14).

5. Use the efficient formulas in Exercise 4 to compute the covariance $C_{CG}$ (for tests $C$ and $G$), the covariance $C_{CC}$ (variance of test $C$), the covariance $C_{GG}$ (variance for test $G$), and then put them together in the form of Equation (2-13) to compute $r_{CG}$.

## 2-5  SOME ODDS AND ENDS

### 2-51  Grouping Data into Intervals

So as not to confuse the discussion, we have thus far kept to distributions involving whole numbers. Very often, however, the sample measures are not whole numbers, so that grouping the data into convenient intervals becomes necessary. For example, consider the following 20 measures:

5.0  8.9  4.6  4.1  4.9  6.3  3.7  3.5  2.7  2.3

4.1  4.8  5.7  4.4  5.1  6.2  4.7  5.4  5.4  6.0

To make a reasonable histogram out of these numbers, we have to choose intervals, find the frequency of occurrence within the intervals, and plot the frequencies. Table 2-6 is one such choice for intervals:

Table 2-6

| Interval | Frequency | Midpoint of interval |
|---|---|---|
| $8.5 \leqslant X < 9.5$ | 1 | 9.0 |
| $7.5 \leqslant X < 8.5$ | 0 | 8.0 |
| $6.5 \leqslant X < 7.5$ | 0 | 7.0 |
| $5.5 \leqslant X < 6.5$ | 4 | 6.0 |
| $4.5 \leqslant X < 5.5$ | 8 | 5.0 |
| $3.5 \leqslant X < 4.5$ | 5 | 4.0 |
| $2.5 \leqslant X < 3.5$ | 1 | 3.0 |
| $1.5 \leqslant X < 2.5$ | 1 | 2.0 |

Note that the $X$-value dividing two intervals is arbitrarily put into the higher interval. With this frequency distribution we could draw a histogram, and typically we would say that there was one value of 9, four 6s, eight 5s, five 4s, one 3, and one 2. In other words, once the grouping is accomplished, all values within an interval are considered to take on the value of the midpoint of the interval.

COMMENT. Before the age of computers it was customary to take time out to consider how to compute means, standard deviations, and other statistics for grouped data. Since grouping involves a loss of information, in that all values falling in an interval are considered to take on the value of the midpoint of the interval, the values of the statistics so computed needed to be corrected for such things as size of the interval, location of the interval, and so on. Clearly if the interval is large enough, all the values will fall in it. Then all values take on the value of the midpoint of the interval, and there is no dispersion. Nowadays we seldom need to go through the ritual of grouping, computing statistics on grouped data, and then correcting for grouping.

## 2-52  Ranking Data and Percentiles

In educational testing—both standardized testing, like the College Boards, and classroom testing—it is a matter of some importance to order the scores and to determine percentile ranks for them. We shall not spend too much time on such matters here, because they do not fit easily into the framework of elementary statistical principles. In practice, percentile ranks are not often recognized as statistics, which they are, and if we wanted to learn about the sampling fluctuation of percentile ranks we could not do so in an elementary text.

Consider the 20 scores given in Section 2-51. Perform the following operations on the data: (*i*) Order them from largest to smallest; (*ii*) assign frequencies of occurrence to each distinct value; (*iii*) determine the frequency

Table 2-7

| (*i*) | (*ii*) | (*iii*) | (*iv*) |
|-------|--------|---------|--------|
| 8.9 | 1 | 19 | 95% |
| 6.3 | 1 | 18 | 90 |
| 6.2 | 1 | 17 | 85 |
| 6.0 | 1 | 16 | 80 |
| 5.7 | 1 | 15 | 75 |
| 5.4 | 2 | 13 | 65 |
| 5.1 | 1 | 12 | 60 |
| 5.0 | 1 | 11 | 55 |
| 4.9 | 1 | 10 | 50 |
| 4.8 | 1 | 9 | 45 |
| 4.7 | 1 | 8 | 40 |
| 4.6 | 1 | 7 | 35 |
| 4.4 | 1 | 6 | 30 |
| 4.1 | 2 | 4 | 20 |
| 3.7 | 1 | 3 | 15 |
| 3.5 | 1 | 2 | 10 |
| 2.7 | 1 | 1 | 5 |
| 2.3 | 1 | 0 | 0 |

of occurrence below each distinct score; and (*iv*) convert this frequency to a percentage frequency. The results are shown in Table 2-7.

The last column is the column of percentile ranks. The jargon is as follows. A student who scores 8.9 points is at the 95th percentile; or the 95th percentile is a score of 8.9 points; or the percentile rank of a score of 8.9 points is 95.

## 2-53 The Median

When distributions are skew to the right or left, it can sometimes happen that the mean gives a rather unrealistic picture of the central tendency of the distribution. For instance, suppose that five subjects score the following:

1 1 1 2 9

The mean of these scores is 2.8. If we leave out the fifth subject, the mean is 1.25. In other words, an extreme point can make the mean less than helpful in some instances. In the real world of educational tests and measurements it often happens that test scores distribute themselves in a skew fashion, and when instructors issue final grades for course work, it often happens that there are extreme scores at one or other or both ends of the score scale. Under these circumstances the median is used to indicate the central tendency of the distribution. The median is a statistic (summary number) that is defined as a point on the score scale above and below which 50 percent of the cases lie. As such it is closely related to the 50th percentile, that is, the score below which 50 percent of the cases lie. However, the definition is not quite satisfactory as we now show. Consider the example given in Section 2-52. The 50th percentile is the score 4.9. But only 9 cases fall above this score. Hence it does not satisfy the definition of median given above. As a matter of fact any value between 4.8 and 4.9 satisfies the definition, but which one value is the median? By convention in this case we take the midpoint between 4.8 and 4.9, and the median is 4.85. Consider the following scores:

1 1 1 1 1 2 2 2 3 3 3 3 3

There are 13 scores. The central tendency is very clearly the value 2. However, there are only 5 scores above 2 and only 5 scores below 2, and this is not 50 percent above and below. However, by convention the definition is stretched a little to allow us to call 2 the median in this case.

On a continuous distribution, one of interest to the statistician, the median is defined as that point on the abscissa which divides the area under the curve into two equal parts. This is not an ambiguous definition. In this case the median is a parameter.

For every symmetrical distribution the median coincides with the mean. Thus, for the normal distribution the mean, median, and mode all coincide, where by "mode" we refer to the point on the abscissa with the greatest ordinate value. For discrete distributions we identify the mode as the most frequently occurring value. If a distribution has two distinct modes, we call it a bimodal distribution.

In this text we do not consider the median in the framework of a statistical model; hence we mention it only briefly.

## EXERCISES

1. (a) Using the data in Section 2-51, compute the mean and the standard deviation of the grouped data. (Remember that all values in an interval assume the value of the midpoint of the interval.)

   (b) A correction known as Sheppard's correction may be applied to the moments of a distribution when they are computed from grouped data. For example, the variance $m_2$ is corrected as follows:

$$m_2 \text{ (corrected)} = m_2 \text{ (grouped)} - \tfrac{1}{12}h^2$$

   where $h$ is the width of the interval. Determine whether this correction helps in the case of the data in Section 2-51.

   (c) Try another grouping for the data in Section 2-51. For example, simply drop all decimal points and recompute the mean, standard deviation, and corrected standard deviation for this new grouping.

2. Consider the following data:

$$5.4 \quad 3.4 \quad 4.1 \quad 5.5 \quad 5.0 \quad 8.7 \quad 6.6 \quad 7.0 \quad 4.9 \quad 6.1$$
$$8.1 \quad 5.2 \quad 5.3 \quad 4.3 \quad 5.3 \quad 4.5 \quad 3.2 \quad 2.4 \quad 6.1 \quad 7.1$$

   (a) Compute the mean and the standard deviation.

   (b) Order the data from largest to smallest value. Compute percentile ranks for each of the distinct scores.

   (c) Group the data according to the same plan, as in Section 2-51, and recompute the percentile ranks, this time for the midpoint values.

   (d) Consider the score 6.6. What is its percentile rank as computed from (b) and from (c)? Repeat for the score 5.4.

3. A common procedure for preparing data for the computation of the median is as follows: (i) group the data into intervals (this includes the case of not grouping, that is, letting each data point define its own interval) that are ordered from largest values on the top to smallest values on the bottom; (ii) determine the frequencies of occurrence within each interval; (iii) cumulate the frequencies from the bottom; and (iv) find the interval in which the median falls (that is, if there are $N$ data points, find the interval in which the cumulative frequency reaches or passes $N/2$). Then the following formula is applied:

$$\text{Median} = X_L + \left[ \frac{(N/2) - f_b}{f_i} \right] i$$

where $X_L$ = lower limit of interval containing median

$\quad\quad f_b$ = cumulative frequency below this interval

$\quad\quad f_i$ = frequency (not cumulative frequency) within this interval

$\quad\quad i$ = interval width

Apply this formula to compute the median for the following data sets:

(a) The data in Exercise 2 above, ungrouped.

(b) The data in Exercise 2 above, grouped as in Exercise 2c.

(c) The data set [1,2]. Show that this set of $N = 2$ numbers should not be handled by means of the formula.

(d) The data set [1,2,2]. Note that the definition of median given in the text does not fit the value computed for this data set.

# Useful Statistical Models (Population and Sampling Plan)

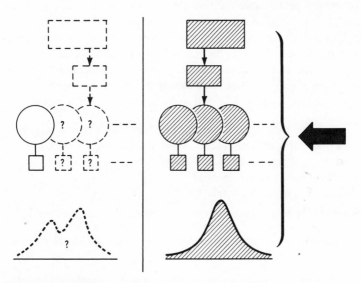

## 3-1 PRELIMINARIES

### 3-11 The Statistician's Viewpoint

If a social scientist wants to publish a paper in an academic journal, he is required to write up his experiment in such a way as to make it possible for another experimenter to *replicate* it; that is, he must define the conditions of his experiment with sufficient clarity that it is, in principle, possible for someone else to repeat it. Whether or not someone else does, in fact, repeat the experiment is of no consequence to the present discussion. From the statistician's point of view any experiment that can, in principle, be replicated produces what are known as *statistical data*. In terms of the basic diagram we might say that the solid circle indicating what the experimenter *does know* is a set of statistical data. The broken-line circles, indicating what the experimenter *might have known* had he used another sample, show what might have been obtained if the experiment had been replicated: "The chief object of statistical theory is to investigate the possibility of drawing valid inferences from statistical data, and to work out methods by which such inferences may be obtained." [1]

### 3-12   Some Definitions

1. VARIABLE.   What do we mean when we talk about a variable $X$? The symbol $X$ is the name of the variable. It signifies a set of *permissible values*. For example, the statement "$X$ is a variable designating the even numbers between 9 and 21" means that $X$ (the name) can take on any one of the following permissible values: 10, 12, 14, 16, 18, 20. Consider the statement "$E$ is a variable designating the eye color of human beings." This variable $E$ can take on any one of the following permissible values: blue, green, brown, mixed. In other words, the permissible values of a variable need not always be numerical values. It is always possible, however, to assign numbers to permissible values. For example, we might agree to make the following identities: blue = 1, green = 2, brown = 3, and mixed = 4.

The *experimenter* deals with variables that have numerical values (height, trials, test score, etc.) and variables that have nonnumerical values (hair color, personality traits, political party, etc.).

The *statistician* deals only with variables that have numerical values.

*A variable is a name for any one of a set of permissible values.*

2. FUNCTION.   A function is a rule. Consider an elementary function such as

$$Y = 2X$$

The right-hand side of this equation gives the rule whereby values of the variable $X$ are converted into values of the variable $Y$. For any value of $X$, the rule is to double it to obtain a value of $Y$. In general, if we have a set of

---

[1] Harald Cramer. *Mathematical methods of statistics*. Princeton, N.J.: Princeton University Press, 1946, p. 138. The reader is urged to read Chapter 13 (pp. 137–151) in this reference. It is a short chapter, written by an authority in the field of statistics, and involves no sophisticated mathematics. As a general principle, it makes good sense to make excursions into the literature of the mathematical statistician from time to time. For example, if you want to know what the statistician means by a "random variable" or a "function," then you should browse in a mathematics library, find a good mathematical statistics text, and use the subject index to locate what you want to know.

permissible values for a variable $X$, then we can define any rule we please to assign new values based on these old values. We designate the general rule $f(X)$, which we read "function of $X$," and we write $Y = f(X)$.

> *A function is a rule that assigns to every permissible value of a set some definite value.*

If the rule specifies that the definite values be numbers, then we speak about a numerically valued function.

3. RANDOM VARIABLE. This is a difficult term to define. Perhaps the easiest way to grasp its meaning is to consider it a special variable. It is "special" in the sense that it involves not only a set of permissible values but also a function defined on them. The function indicates the frequency of occurrence, or the probability, of each of the permissible values. Thus we may contrast the notion of a variable $X$ and the notion of a random variable $X$ as follows:

1. The *variable* $X$ is a name for any one of the following permissible values: 1, 2, 3, 4, 5, 6, 7, 8, or 9. We make no statement about their frequency of occurrence.

2. The *random variable* $X$ is a name for any one of the following permissible values: 1, 2, 3, 4, 5, 6, 7, 8, or 9, where the probabilities of their occurrence are $p_1$, $p_2$, $p_3$, $p_4$, $p_5$, $p_6$, $p_7$, $p_8$, and $p_9$.

Referring to an authoritative text again, consider the following quotation: "The idea of a variable [whose permissible values] can appear with varying degrees of probability has been elevated into a distinct concept, that of a random variable." [2]

In terms of definitions 1 and 2, we might say that a random variable is both a variable and a function.

> *A random variable is (i) a name for any one of a set of permissible values and (ii) a rule that assigns to each of these permissible values a probability of occurrence.*

This definition can be abbreviated as follows: a random variable is a function defined on a set of permissible values, and we shall talk about the *distribution* of a random variable, meaning the shape of the function.

WARNING. One of the confusing aspects of the concept "random variable" is the word "random." In our colloquial use of the word "random,"

[2] M. G. Kendall and A. Stuart. *The advanced theory of statistics.* Vol. 1. New York: Hafner, 1958, p. 187.

we think of something unpredictable. Do not forget that a random variable is a function and that a function is a rule that assigns some definite value as the probability of occurrence of each of the permissible values. A random variable implies some definite function shape. Uncertainty arises only when we sample from such a distribution.

## 3-13   Fundamentals of Probability

Until now we have made use of the word "probability" on the assumption that everybody has some intuitive feel for the concept. We shall now make it precise.

Consider a conventional die. Throw the die 10 times, and observe the frequency of occurrence of 6. Suppose that 6 occurs twice. The frequency of occurrence of the distinct value 6 is 2, and the *relative frequency* of occurrence of 6 is $\frac{2}{10}$, or 0.2. Throw the die 100 times, and note the frequency of occurrence of a 6—say, 18. Then the relative frequency of occurrence of a 6 is $\frac{18}{100}$, or 0.18. If the die is not loaded, you will find that the *long-run relative frequency* stabilizes around a value close to $\frac{1}{6}$, or 0.16; that is, in the long run the relative frequency of 6 tends to become more and more stable, and the stable value is around $\frac{1}{6}$.

If we call the throw of a die an experiment, then the following (modified) definition given by Cramer may be used as a definition of probability:

Whenever we say—that the probability of an event $E$ with respect to a particular experiment is equal to $P$, the concrete meaning of this assertion will simply be the following: In a long series of repetitions of the experiment, it is practically certain that the relative-frequency of $E$ will be approximately equal to $P$. This statement will be referred to as the relative-frequency interpretation of the probability $P$.[3]

The event $E$ in the example above would be the occurrence of 6.

Now let us note certain properties of relative frequencies. The maximum value of a relative frequency is unity. If we toss a coin 100 times and obtain 100 heads, then the relative frequency of occurrence of heads is $\frac{100}{100}$, that is, 1. The minimum value of a relative frequency is zero. If we toss a coin 100 times and observe no heads whatsoever, then the relative frequency of "head" is $\frac{0}{100}$, that is, 0. Since the probability $P$ is defined as a long-run relative frequency, we note that the maximum value of $P$ is unity and the minimum value of $P$ is zero. In fact, a probability measure can assume any value from 0 to 1 inclusive, and we express this symbolically as

$$0 \leq P \leq 1$$

Next consider what we mean by a set of *mutually exclusive and exhaustive events*. In the case of the die, there are six mutually exclusive and exhaustive outcomes. One throw of the die will give a 1 or a 2 or a 3 or a 4 or a 5 or a 6.

---

[3] Cramer, *op. cit.*, pp. 148–149.

No two of these events can occur together, so that they are mutually exclusive; and at least one of them must occur on any one throw, so that the six possibilities exhaust the set of outcomes.

In general, if we have a mutually exclusive and exhaustive set of $N$ events, $E_1$ through $E_N$, and if we assign a probability measure to each event,

$$p(E_1), p(E_2), p(E_3), \ldots, p(E_N)$$

then the sum of these probabilities will be unity; that is,

$$p(E_1) + p(E_2) + p(E_3) + \cdots + p(E_N) = 1$$

$$\text{or} \quad \sum_{i=1}^{N} p(E_i) = 1$$

This is a property of relative frequencies when we are dealing with mutually exclusive and exhaustive events.

The simplest illustration of this fact is the following. Toss a coin 100 times, and observe that the number of heads is, say, 40. Then the relative frequency of occurrence of the event "heads" is $\frac{40}{100}$, and the relative frequency of occurrence of the event "tails" is $\frac{60}{100}$. The two events, "heads" and "tails," constitute a mutually exclusive and exhaustive set of events, and we note that the sum of the relative frequencies is unity:

$$\frac{40}{100} + \frac{60}{100} = 1$$

A final property of the relative-frequency interpretation of probability in the case of mutually exclusive and exhaustive events is the following: Consider two mutually exclusive events $E_1$ and $E_2$. If the probabilities assigned to them are $p(E_1)$ and $p(E_2)$, respectively, then the probability "either $E_1$ or $E_2$ occurs" is simply the sum of these two probabilities. We express this symbolically as

$$p(E_1 + E_2) = p(E_1) + p(E_2)$$

The expression $(E_1 + E_2)$ may be read as "$E_1$ or $E_2$ or both," but in the case of mutually exclusive events "or both" does not apply. Note that this *law of addition* for mutually exclusive events can be extended very easily. If we have $N$ mutually exclusive and exhaustive events, $E_1$ through $E_N$, then

$$p(E_1 + E_2 + \cdots + E_N) = p(E_1) + p(E_2) + \cdots + p(E_N)$$

$$= 1$$

This statement expresses the fact that the probability of at least one of the $N$ possible events occurring is unity. Obviously one event has to occur.

SUMMARY. The relative-frequency interpretation of probability for the case of $N$ mutually exclusive and exhaustive events, $E_1$ through $E_N$, includes the following properties:

1. RANGE OF THE PROBABILITY MEASURE. The probability measure $p(E_i)$ for the $i$th event is restricted to the range.

$$0 \leq p(E_i) \leq 1 \tag{3-1}$$

2. SUM OF ALL PROBABILITY MEASURES. The sum of the $N$ probability measures, $p(E_1)$ through $p(E_N)$, is unity:

$$\sum_{i=1}^{N} p(E_i) = 1 \tag{3-2}$$

3. THE ADDITION LAW. The probability of either $E_1$ or $E_2$ is the sum of the separate probabilities of $E_1$ and $E_2$:

$$p(E_i + E_j) = p(E_i) + p(E_j) \qquad \text{for } i \neq j \tag{3-3}$$

## 3-14  Joint Events and Conditional Probability

The major purpose of this section is to give a precise definition of *independence*. The reader is warned that the experimenter's use of the terms "dependent variable" (referring to a sample measure) and "independent variable" (referring to a rule for membership) is quite distinct from the statistician's concept of statistical dependence and statistical independence. We are here concerned with the statistician's viewpoint.

To set the stage, consider the following situation. Suppose that you are working in the admissions office of a university and are asked to answer the following questions:

1. What is the probability of an entering freshman's scoring above 700 on both the verbal and the math sections of the Scholastic Aptitude Test (SAT)?

2. If you know that a certain applicant scored above 700 on the SAT-Verbal section, what is the probability that he also scored above 700 on the SAT-Math section?

Question 1 refers to a *joint* probability—that of two events occurring at the same time. Question 2 refers to a *conditional* probability—that of one event conditional on the occurrence of another.

Let us define two symbols $A$ and $B$ as follows:

$A$ = "Student scores more than 700 on SAT-Verbal."
$B$ = "Student scores more than 700 on SAT-Math."

Then we designate questions 1 and 2 as follows:

Question 1 asks, "What is $p(AB)$?" *joint A and B*
Question 2 asks, "What is $p(B \mid A)$?" *conditional B given A*

We read these symbolic expressions as follows: (i) $p(AB)$ means "the probability of the joint occurrence of $A$ and $B$," and (ii) $p(B \mid A)$ means "the probability of $B$ given that $A$ is true."

In general, for any experiment in which more than one event can occur on any single trial, we need to define joint probabilities, such as $p(AB)$, and conditional probabilities, such as $p(B \mid A)$.

Consider an experiment in which two events may occur on any given trial. One of the events is a member of a mutually exclusive and exhaustive set of events:

$$A_1, A_2, A_3, \ldots, A_m$$

The other event is a member of a mutually exclusive and exhaustive set of events:

$$B_1, B_2, B_3, \ldots, B_n$$

For the $A$-set there exist a set of probabilities

$$p(A_1), p(A_2), \ldots, P(A_m)$$

that satisfy Equations (3-1) to (3-3). Similarly, for the $B$-set there exist a set of probabilities

$$p(B_1), p(B_2), \ldots, p(B_n)$$

that satisfy Equations (3-1) to (3-3).

Consider the event $A_i$ and the event $B_j$. We wish to define a joint probability $p(A_iB_j)$ and a conditional probability $p(B_j \mid A_i)$.

Consider the two questions mentioned above. The mutually exclusive and exhaustive events on SAT-V are

$$A_1 = \text{SAT-V score} > 700$$
$$A_2 = \text{SAT-V score} \leq 700$$

The mutually exclusive and exhaustive events on SAT-M are

$$B_1 = \text{SAT-M score} > 700$$
$$B_2 = \text{SAT-M score} \leq 700$$

Let

$$p(A_1) = 0.20$$
$$p(A_2) = 0.80$$

Let

$$p(B_1) = 0.10$$
$$p(B_2) = 0.90$$

Consider the event $A_1$ and the event $B_1$.
Examine $p(A_1B_1)$ and $p(B_1 \mid A_1)$.

It is not difficult to give a relative-frequency interpretation to the joint probability. Repeat the experiment, say, 1,000 times, and observe the relative frequency of occurrence of the ordered two-tuple $(A_i, B_j)$. In the long run this relative frequency approaches a stable value that is, by definition, the probability of the joint occurrence of $A_i$ and $B_j$.

The conditional probability is defined as follows:

$$p(B_j \mid A_i) = \frac{p(A_iB_j)}{p(A_i)}$$

Similarly

$$p(A_i \mid B_j) = \frac{p(A_iB_j)}{p(B_j)}$$

Suppose $p(A_1B_1) = 0.05$ (probability of getting more than 700 on both SAT-V and SAT-M is 0.05).

$$p(B_1 \mid A_1) = \frac{p(A_1B_1)}{p(A_1)}$$
$$= \frac{0.05}{0.20} = 0.25$$

$$p(A_1 \mid B_1) = \frac{p(A_1B_1)}{p(B_1)}$$
$$= \frac{0.05}{0.10} = 0.50$$

The conditional probability formula can be rearranged to give

$$p(A_iB_j) = p(A_i)p(B_j \mid A_i) = p(B_j)p(A_i \mid B_j)$$

which is known as the *multiplication law* of probability. Using more general symbols, we define

*The multiplication law:*
$$p(AB) = p(A)p(B \mid A) = p(B)p(A \mid B) \qquad (3\text{-}4)$$

We are now in a position to define independence.

If $p(A_iB_j) = p(A_i)p(B_j)$, then $A_i$ and $B_j$ are said to be independent of each other. Conversely we may say that if $A_i$ and $B_j$ are independent events, then

$$p(A_iB_j) = p(A_i)p(B_j)$$

Referring to the multiplication law, note that this definition of independence implies

$$p(A_i \mid B_j) = p(A_i)$$
$$p(B_j \mid A_i) = p(B_j)$$

when $A_i$ and $B_j$ are independent.

$p(A_1B_1) = 0.05$, $p(A_1) = 0.20$, and $p(B_1) = 0.10$. Therefore, $p(A_1B_1) \neq p(A_1)p(B_1)$, so that $A_1$ and $B_1$ are not independent events.

$p(A_1 \mid B_1) = 0.50$ and $p(A_1) = 0.20$, so that knowing $B_1$ has a considerable effect on the probability of $A_1$ being true. Similarly $p(B_1 \mid A_1) = 0.25$ and $p(B_1) = 0.10$, so that knowing $A_1$ has a considerable effect on the probability of $B_1$ being true. $A_1$ and $B_1$ are clearly dependent.

Summarizing these results and using more general symbols, we have

If $A$ and $B$ are independent events, then $p(AB) = p(A)p(B)$.    (3-5)
If $p(AB) = p(A)p(B)$, then $A$ and $B$ are independent events.

COMMENT ON THE ADDITION LAW FOR THE GENERAL CASE.   The addition law (3-3) is specific to the case of a set of mutually exclusive and exhaustive events. When events are not mutually exclusive and exhaustive, we need a more general form of the addition law:

The general law of addition:

$$p(A + B) = p(A) + p(B) - p(AB) \qquad (3\text{-}6)$$

Note that this more general law includes Equation (3-3) as a special case. When $A$ and $B$ are exclusive $p(AB)$ is zero and Equation (3-6) is identical to Equation (3-3).

## 3-15   Bayes' Theorem

We shall make just one more digression before picking up the thread of Chapters 1 and 2. There is an important theorem, due to Bayes, which follows easily from the multiplication law. Since $p(AB) = p(A)p(B \mid A)$ and $p(AB) = p(B)p(A \mid B)$, it follows that

$$p(A)p(B \mid A) = p(B)p(A \mid B)$$

Rearranging this equation, we obtain Bayes' theorem:

$$p(B \mid A) = p(B) \frac{p(A \mid B)}{p(A)}$$

This theorem is the cornerstone of Part Two of this text and will be considered at length in Chapters 10 and 11. For now we shall simply rephrase it in a form that is more easily remembered. Suppose that you are an experimenter entertaining two mutually exclusive and exhaustive hypotheses $H_1$ and $H_2$. Before you do any experiment, you reach the conclusion that the probability of $H_1$ being true is 0.5 (that is, there is a 50:50 chance of $H_1$ being true). Now you do an experiment and collect some data $D$. How do the data $D$ affect the chances of $H_1$ being true? Using Bayes' theorem, we write

$$\underset{\substack{\text{posterior} \\ \text{probability}}}{p(H_1 \mid D)} = \underset{\substack{\text{prior} \\ \text{probability}}}{p(H_1)} \underset{\substack{\text{likelihood} \\ \text{ratio}}}{\frac{p(D \mid H_1)}{p(D)}}$$

In other words, we say that prior to running an experiment, we have a *prior probability* of $H_1$ being true. This is $p(H_1)$. After running an experiment and obtaining data $D$, we want to know the *posterior probability* of $H_1$ being true. This is $p(H_1 \mid D)$. Bayes' theorem gives us a rule whereby we can convert the prior probability into a posterior probability. This rule involves multiplying the prior probability by the *likelihood ratio*, $p(D \mid H_1)/p(D)$. Verbalizing this likelihood ratio, we say that it is the ratio of the probability of getting the data, $D$, given that $H_1$ is true, to the probability of getting the data anyway. The expression "getting the data anyway" will be handled in Part Two, but we shall anticipate the useful *extension rule* by noting that

$$p(D) = p(DH_1) + p(DH_2)$$

Remember that $H_1$ and $H_2$ are mutually exclusive and exhaustive hypotheses (or events if you like), so that

$$p(H_1 + H_2) = 1$$

Hence we can say that the probability of getting the data $D$ anyway means the probability of getting the data under $H_1$ or under $H_2$, and there are no other ways of getting the data. Using the addition law, we have

$$p(D) = p(DH_1 + DH_2) = p(DH_1) + p(DH_2)$$

We now use the multiplication law twice on the right-hand side of the equation to obtain

$$p(D) = p(H_1)p(D \mid H_1) + p(H_2)p(D \mid H_2)$$

In general, if there are $N$ mutually exclusive and exhaustive hypotheses, we may write Bayes' theorem as follows:

$$p(H_i \mid D) = p(H_i) \frac{p(D \mid H_i)}{\sum\limits_{i=1}^{N} p(H_i)p(D \mid H_i)} \tag{3-7}$$

AN EXAMPLE.   A $2\frac{1}{2}$-year-old boy develops a nasty-looking rash all over his body and says to his mother, "I eat pill." He cannot be more explicit than that, and the mother notes to her consternation that five bottles of pills are emptied out on the floor of the bathroom. Each bottle contained the same number of pills, but one of them contained a toxic medication that should never be given to small children. Referring to *Baby and Child Care* by Dr. Spock, she notes that 80 percent of the children who swallow the toxic pill come out in a serious rash, whereas the chances of getting a rash from the pills in the other four bottles are only 10 in 100 (10 percent). The mother entertains two hypotheses:

$$H_1 = \text{"My boy ate a toxic pill."}$$
$$H_2 = \text{"My boy ate a nontoxic pill."}$$

Not knowing anything to the contrary, she establishes the prior probabilities of these two hypotheses:

$$p(H_1) = \tfrac{1}{5}$$
$$p(H_2) = \tfrac{4}{5}$$

since only one of the five bottles contained toxic pills. Her information from Dr. Spock's book leads her to the following conditional probabilities:

$$p(S \mid H_1) = 0.80$$

$$p(S \mid H_2) = 0.10$$

where $S$ stands for the symptoms, that is, the rash on the body. Knowing that she must exercise plausible reasoning in the determination of a posterior probability, she makes use of Bayes' theorem:

$$p(H_1 \mid S) = p(H_1) \frac{p(S \mid H_1)}{p(H_1)p(S \mid H_1) + p(H_2)p(S \mid H_2)}$$

$$= (0.2) \frac{(0.80)}{(0.2)(0.80) + (0.8)(0.10)} = 0.667$$

Given the symptoms and the other relevant information, the mother concludes that the chances of her boy having eaten a toxic pill are 2 out of 3.

## EXERCISES

1. In the expression "Hearing acuity is a function of age," what do we mean by the word "function"?
2. (a) A spelling test composed of 100 items (scored 1 if correct and 0 if incorrect) is administered to fifth-graders. If we call the score on this test a random variable, what do we mean?
   (b) A sample of 50 subjects yields 50 measurements on critical fusion frequency (CFF), the frequency at which a flickering light appears to be steady. The mean CFF is computed. Is this mean CFF a random variable?
   (c) Discuss the statement "Every statistic is a random variable." Where does the sampling distribution of a statistic fit into this discussion?
3. A chemistry professor keeps a record of the way in which lab students read the last digit when measuring the volume of liquids in a burette. In $N = 1,590$ cases he finds the following frequency distribution:

| Digit | 0 | 1 | 2 | 3 | 4 | 5 | 6 | 7 | 8 | 9 |
|---|---|---|---|---|---|---|---|---|---|---|
| Frequency | 375 | 132 | 129 | 118 | 123 | 252 | 117 | 118 | 143 | 83 |

   (a) Express these frequencies as relative frequencies.
   (b) Check the rules expressed in Equations (3-1) to (3-3).
   (c) What is the probability that students round the last digit to 0 or 5? (As an exercise in good statistical thinking, you might be critical of the wording of this question. Consider sampling fluctuation and the definition of probability, for example.)
   (d) Do the digits 0 to 9 constitute a mutually exclusive and exhaustive set of outcomes? [4]

   [4] The data for this exercise comes from H. A. Laitenen. *Chemical analysis*. New York: McGraw-Hill, 1960, p. 554.

4. In which of the cases in Table 3-1 are the events $A$ and $B$ independent? Fill in the empty cells wherever possible.

Table 3-1

|     | $p(A)$ | $p(B)$ | $p(AB)$ | $p(A \mid B)$ | $p(B \mid A)$ |
|-----|--------|--------|---------|---------------|---------------|
| (a) | 0.50   | 0.50   | 0.25    | ?             | ?             |
| (b) | 0.30   | ?      | 0.21    | 0.50          | ?             |
| (c) | 0.30   | 0.70   | ?       | 0.30          | ?             |
| (d) | 0.30   | 0.70   | ?       | ?             | 0.30          |
| (e) | ?      | ?      | 0.40    | 0.80          | 0.50          |
| (f) | ?      | ?      | 0.33    | 0.55          | 0.66          |
| (g) | 0.10   | ?      | 0.05    | 0.05          | ?             |
| (h) | ?      | 0.80   | 0.70    | ?             | 0.60          |
| (i) | 0.40   | ?      | 0.20    | ?             | 0.50          |

5. For each of the cases in Exercise 4 try to compute $p(A + B)$.
6. Suppose that you are taking two courses this semester. One is a math course, and you are convinced that your chances of passing it are 6 in 10. The other is a tough Russian course, and you doubt your ability to pass it. If you feel that you are going to pass at least one course with a probability of 0.75 and you estimate that your chances of passing both courses are just 1 in 10, what is the probability of your passing Russian?
7. If events $A$ and $B$ are mutually exclusive, can they be independent?


## 3-2 THE NORMAL DISTRIBUTION

### 3-21 Introduction

In Section 1-36, it was stated that the statistician's viewpoint concerning a statistical model involved (*i*) the specification of a population distribution, usually an equation (and usually the normal distribution equation); (*ii*) the specification of a sampling plan, usually a SIRS plan; and (*iii*) the determination of the sampling distribution of a statistic. In this chapter we deal with the normally distributed population in Section 3-2; the process of sampling from a normal distribution using an SIRS plan in Section 3-3; and the determination of one particular sampling distribution (that of the mean) in Section 3-4. In Chapter 4 a number of other important sampling distributions are discussed. Chapters 5 to 8 then return to the realm of the experimenter as he makes use of the statistician's models.

The *normal distribution* is a theoretical population, and the summary numbers for a population are called *parameters*. Hence the normal distribution is characterized by means of parameters. As a matter of fact, we need to specify two parameters for a normal distribution—the shape of the distribution is completely known once we specify a *mean* (the first parameter) and a *standard deviation* (the second parameter). For this reason it is often called a *two-parameter distribution*. (A statistical model based on a normal distribution is called a *parametric model*, and if we go on to define a test of significance based on this kind of model, we say that we have defined a *parametric test*.)

Greek letters are used to designate population parameters. Roman letters are used to designate sample statistics. Thus we refer to the normal distribution as

$$ND(\mu,\sigma)$$

where $\mu$ is the mean and $\sigma$ is the standard deviation. If we specify $\mu$ and $\sigma$, then $ND(\mu,\sigma)$ is completely specified.

$ND(\mu,\sigma)$ is the distribution that statisticians have found most amenable to the task of producing sampling distributions. It is not a distribution that could ever be observed in the real world. It is an equation. It happens to represent a shape that approximates many real-world distributions, that is, outcomes of experiments, and it has long been known as the *normal law of error*. It was in 1733 that the great mathematician De Moivre first con-conceived of the *normal equation*, and then later, in connection with their work on errors of observation, Gauss and Laplace rediscovered it. Consequently it is sometimes referred to as the Gaussian distribution, sometimes as the Gauss-Laplace distribution, sometimes simply as the law of error.

### 3-22   The General Normal Distribution: ND($\mu,\sigma$)

The general equation for a normal distribution with mean $\mu$ and standard deviation $\sigma$ is

$$Y = \frac{1}{\sqrt{2\pi}\,\sigma}\, e^{-(X-\mu)^2/2\sigma^2} \qquad ND(\mu,\sigma) \qquad (3\text{-}8)$$

where $\pi$ (= 3.1415926) and $e$ (= 2.718281828) are constants, $\mu$ and $\sigma$ are specified parameters, and $X$ is the random variable. We say that $X$ is a normally distributed random variable, meaning (*i*) it is a name for any one of a set of permissible values and (*ii*) Equation (3-8) specifies the function defined on these permissible values. Note that all values of $X$ from $-\infty$ to $+\infty$ are permissible.

In order to make it clear that Equation (3-8) expresses $Y$ as a function of $X$, consider what the equation looks like when we replace $\pi$ and $e$ by their numerical values and when we specify the two parameters. ND(5,3) is

$$Y = \frac{1}{\sqrt{(2)(3.14159)(3)}}(2.71828)^{-(X-5)^2/2(3^2)}$$

Choose a value of $X$, and with a little effort you can find the corresponding value for $Y$. Clearly this sort of computation should be done by a computer rather than by hand. A very simple computer program may be written according to the following flow diagram:

Read in the values chosen for $\mu$ and $\sigma$: for example,

$$\mu = 2.5$$
$$\sigma = 1.3$$

Decide which range of $X$ values is to be considered: for example,

$$X = -4 \text{ to } +9 \text{ in steps of } 0.5$$

For each of these $X$ values compute the corresponding $Y$ value, using Equation (3-8). Print out the $(X, Y)$ pairs.

Such a program was used to produce the various normal distributions shown in Figure 3-1. Notice how the shape of a normal distribution depends on the values chosen for the two parameters $\mu$ and $\sigma$.

Note the following facts about the normal distribution:

1. It is a continuous distribution. All values of $X$ from minus infinity to plus infinity are permissible.

2. The first parameter $\mu$ indicates the central tendency of the distribution.

3. The second parameter $\sigma$ indicates the dispersion or spread of the distribution.

4. The distribution is symmetrical. Hence the skewness parameter $\gamma_1$ is zero.

5. By definition this is the distribution that is neither peaked nor flat; that is, it has zero kurtosis. The kurtosis parameter $\gamma_2$ is zero. (Note that this is true for all normal distributions, regardless of whether they look flat or peaked. The kurtosis involves a ratio of the fourth moment about the mean to the fourth power of the standard deviation. This ratio is constant for all normal distributions.)

6. The area under the normal curve is unity. When we deal with a discrete number of permissible values for $X$ and assign probability measures to each, the sum of the probabilities must be unity (see Section 3-13). When we deal with a continuous set of permissible values and assign probability measures on this set, then the integral over the set (that is, the area under the curve)

(a) The effect of varying $\mu$ and keeping $\sigma$ constant

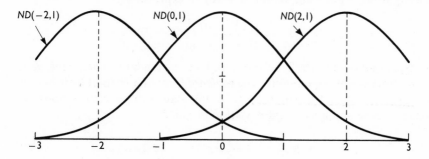

(b) The effect of varying $\sigma$ and keeping $\mu$ constant

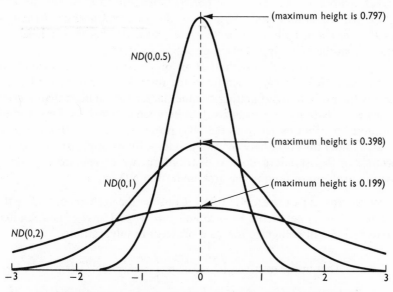

FIGURE 3-1.   The family of normal distributions: ND($\mu,\sigma$)

must be unity. We shall have more to say about this shortly. In the meantime note that this property expresses the fact that the normal distribution is a *probability distribution*. The function shown in Equation (3-8) is a special function—it is a probability function.

## 3-23   The Standard Normal Distribution: ND(0,1)

In Section 2-3 it was shown that a given set of raw scores could be converted into standard scores (or z-scores) by subtracting the mean and dividing by the standard deviation. If you look at Equation (3-8), you will notice that the exponential factor involves an expression

$$-\frac{1}{2}\left[\frac{(X-\mu)}{\sigma}\right]^{2}$$

The expression within the brackets is, in fact, a standard score. This gives rise to a very simple equation for the *standard* form of a normal distribution. The standard normal distribution (like any standardized distribution) has a mean of zero and a standard deviation of unity:

$$Y = \frac{1}{\sqrt{2\pi}}e^{-z^2/2} \qquad \text{ND}(0,1) \qquad (3\text{-}9)$$

Here we use the symbol $z$ in place of $X$ to emphasize the fact that this is the equation for the standard normal distribution. (Of course it makes no difference what symbol we use, but a few conventions help to keep our thinking straight.) We sometimes talk about $z$ as the *standard normal deviate* or simply the *normal deviate*. (It is a "deviate" measure, because it measures deviation from the mean in standard-deviation units.)

The standard normal distribution is of considerable importance in statistics, and so it has been tabled for ready reference. What we really need to know is the probability of getting $z$-values larger (or smaller) than a given value or the probability of getting $z$-values between two given values, and on a continuous distribution (such as the ND) probability can be thought of as area—area under the curve between two $z$-values, for example. In view of the importance of this standard normal distribution, we digress for a while to discuss the problem of finding the area under the ND curve.

FINDING THE AREA UNDER ND(0,1).   Consider the problem of finding the area under ND(0,1) between $z = -\infty$ and $z = +\infty$. Those of you familiar with integration will recognize this as a problem in integration:

$$\text{Area under curve} = \int_{-\infty}^{+\infty} Y\,dz = \int_{-\infty}^{+\infty}\frac{1}{\sqrt{2\pi}}e^{-z^2/2}\,dz$$

Those of you who are not familiar with integration can understand the problem as follows: First, since infinity is not a very practical quantity to deal with, consider finding the area under the curve between $-5$ and $+5$. There is very little area outside this range of $z$-values. Next, chop up ND(0,1) into very thin slices, find the areas of these small slices (approximately), and then add them to get an approximation to the area between $-5$ and $+5$. Figure 3-2 illustrates the procedure. An exaggerated slice $ABCD$ is shown. Now, how shall we approximate the area of this slice, knowing that the curve $AD$ is not a straight line? Briefly, note that we can do one of two things: (*a*) we can think of $ABCD$ as a trapezoid (all sides straight lines and $AB$ parallel to $DC$), and then the approximate area is $(AB + DC) * BC/2$,

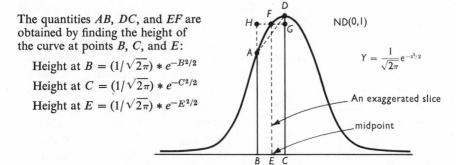

The quantities $AB$, $DC$, and $EF$ are obtained by finding the height of the curve at points $B$, $C$, and $E$:

Height at $B = (1/\sqrt{2\pi}) * e^{-B^2/2}$

Height at $C = (1/\sqrt{2\pi}) * e^{-C^2/2}$

Height at $E = (1/\sqrt{2\pi}) * e^{-E^2/2}$

ND(0,1)

$Y = \dfrac{1}{\sqrt{2\pi}} e^{-z^2/2}$

— An exaggerated slice

midpoint

1. Trapezoid Rule: Area of trapezoid $ABCD = \left[\dfrac{AB + DC}{2}\right] BC$

2. Midpoint Rule: Area of rectangle $BCGH = EF * BC$

3. Simpson's Rule: Approximate area under curve = (trapezoid area)/3
   $+\ 2(\text{midpoint area})/3 = (BC/6) * (AB + 4 * EF + DC)$

FIGURE 3-2. A practical way to approximate the area under ND(0,1) between $z = B$ and $z = C$

where $*$ means multiplied by; (*b*) we can use the so-called midpoint rule, where we find the height of the curve at the midpoint $E$ (between $C$ and $B$) and compute the area of the rectangle $BCGH$. This rectangle area approximates the area under the curve slightly better than the trapezoid area. The thinner the slices, the better the overall approximation to the desired area.

It may be of interest to some readers to know that a combination of the midpoint rule and the trapezoid rule is better than either one alone. If we take one-third of the trapezoid area plus two-thirds of the midpoint area, we obtain *Simpson's rule* for approximating the area under a curve. The formula for this approximation is

$$\text{Area} = \frac{1}{3}\left[\frac{(AB + DC)}{2}\right] * BC + \frac{2}{3}(EF * BC)$$

$$= \frac{BC}{6} * (AB + 4 * EF + DC)$$

It is very easy to use this formula in a computer program to approximate areas under the normal distribution or any other distribution of interest. By way of illustration, consider the outputs from such a computer program in Table 3-2. Comparing these values with those listed in the tables (Appendix C) for ND(0,1), we see clearly that the approximations obtained by Simpson's rule are very stable even for small numbers of slices.

In fact, the tabled values for the standard normal distribution were obtained by a different procedure (as explained in Appendix C), but for the

Table 3-2

| From $z =$ | To $z =$ | No. slices | Approximate area according to | | |
|:---:|:---:|:---:|:---:|:---:|:---:|
| | | | Trapezoid | Midpoint | Simpson |
| $-5$ | $+5$ | 100 | 0.9999 | 0.9999 | 0.9999 |
| $-5$ | $+5$ | 10 | 0.9999 | 0.9999 | 0.9999 |
| 0 | 1 | 100 | 0.3413 | 0.3413 | 0.3413 |
| 0 | 1 | 10 | 0.3411 | 0.3414 | 0.3413 |
| 1.96 | 7 | 100 | 0.0250 | 0.0249 | 0.0249 |
| 1.96 | 7 | 10 | 0.0274 | 0.0237 | 0.0250 |

student who likes to get his hands on the computer, Simpson's rule can be a useful tool. For all readers it is suggested that freehand drawings of the normal distribution (or other distributions to be introduced in the next chapter), together with shaded areas under the curve, can help to keep the thinking clear when it comes to making probability statements concerning normally distributed random variables.

### 3-24  Frequency Function and Distribution Function

Two terms that the statistician uses very often are *frequency function* and *distribution function*. For the case of the ND(0,1) the frequency function (F.F.) is Equation (3-9). For the case of the general normal distribution the frequency function is Equation (3-8). In other words, a frequency function is a close relative of what we called a frequency distribution in Chapter 1.

The distribution function is a *cumulative* frequency function. In other words, if we define a new function for the ND(0,1), so that for each value of $z$ we obtain the area under the curve to the left of this $z$-value, then this new function is the distribution function for a ND(0,1). In symbols the statistician designates these two functions as follows:

Frequency function for ND(0,1):    $f(z) = \dfrac{1}{\sqrt{2\pi}} e^{-z^2/2}$

Distribution function for ND(0,1):    $F(z) = \displaystyle\int_{-\infty}^{z} \dfrac{1}{\sqrt{2\pi}} e^{-X^2/2} \, dX$

A lowercase $f(z)$ is used to designate the frequency function and an uppercase $F(z)$ is used for the distribution function. To show the distinction between *discrete* and *continuous* distributions in the matter of frequency functions and distribution functions, Figure 3-3 should be consulted.

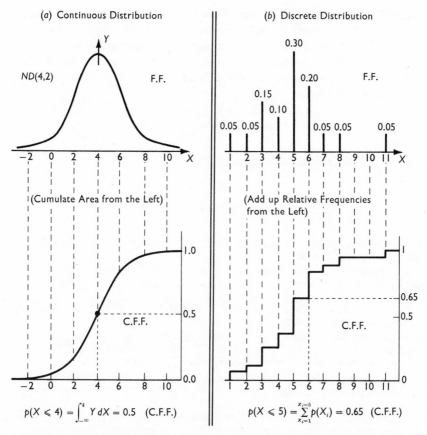

FIGURE 3-3. The relationship between the frequency function (F.F.) and the cumulative frequency function (C.F.F.) of discrete and continuous distributions

DISCRETE DISTRIBUTIONS.  The frequency function for a discrete distribution is a rule that assigns to each of the distinct values of $X$ a probability measure. In this case we may talk about the probability of occurrence of any particular value $X_i$. The distribution function for a discrete distribution is a rule which assigns to each of the distinct values of $X$ a measure that indicates the probability of obtaining a value of $X$ less than or equal to the given value. Thus we may write

$$F(X_4) = p(X \leq X_4) = \sum_{i=1}^{4} p(X_i)$$

CONTINUOUS DISTRIBUTIONS.  The frequency function for a continuous distribution is a rule that assigns to each of the permissible values of $X$ a probability density. We are not permitted to talk about the probability of any particular value (unless we say that the probability is zero—an infinite number of permissible values cannot have finite probabilities of occurrence if the sum of the probabilities is to be unity). Instead we may talk about the probability of obtaining an $X$-value within some interval on the $X$-scale. The distribution function for a continuous distribution is a rule that assigns to a given value $X_i$ the probability of obtaining a value of $X$ less than or equal to $X_i$. Thus we may write

$$F(X_i) = p(X \leq X_i) = \int_{-\infty}^{X_i} f(X)\, dX$$

where $f(X)$ is the frequency function of $X$.

### EXERCISES

1. This exercise is designed to make you thoroughly comfortable with the equation for the normal distribution.
   (a) Compute $Ax^B$, where $A = 2$, $B = 3$, and $x = 0, 1, 2, 3, 4$.
   (b) Compute $Ax^{-B}$, where $A = 2$, $B = 3$, and $x = 0, 1, 2, 3, 4$. (Is there any problem when $x = 0$?)
   (c) Compute $Ax^{-B}$, where $A = 0.4$, $x = 3$, and $B = 0, 1, 2, 3$. (Is there any problem when $B = 0$?)
   (d) Compute $Ax^{-B}$, where $A = 0.4$, $x = 3$, and $B = -1, -2, -3$.
   (e) Compute $Ax^{-B^2}$, where $A = 0.4$, $x = 3$, and $B = -1, 0, +1$. (This is very close to the standard normal distribution. To make it more accurate, $A$ would have to be $1/\sqrt{2\pi}$ and $x$ would have to be $e = 2.71828$. Then we should have the function

$$Y = \frac{1}{\sqrt{2\pi}} e^{-B^z}$$

   which is the standard normal distribution.)
   *Note:* It would help materially if you did this exercise with a piece of graph paper handy. As you compute the values asked for, plot them on the graph paper. Then, using the standard normal distribution tables (Appendix C), take the time to plot ND(0,1), so that your proprioceptors get the feel of a normal distribution.
2. Using the tables for ND(0,1) and the equation for the general normal distribution, ND($\mu,\sigma$), see if you can generate some of the values for (a) ND(0,2), (b) ND(3,1), (c) ND(3,2), (d) ND(50,10).
3. The normal distributions have two tails going out to infinity in both directions. Using the tabled values for ND(0,1), find the normal deviate values $+K$ and $-K$ such that the area in the two tails sums to (a) 0.10, (b) 0.05, (c) 0.01. (*Note:* Draw rough graphs as you perform each part of the exercise.)
4. Repeat Exercise 3 for ND(5,3).
5. Repeat Exercise 3 where the interest is now in just one tail. In other words, what is the value of $K$ if the area in one tail is (a) 0.10, (b) 0.05, and (c) 0.01? What would these one-tail critical values be for ND(5,3)? What would these one-tail values be for ND($\mu,\sigma$)? (*Note:* This is an important exercise. In later chapters we shall have occasion to use this information repeatedly.)

## 3-3 SAMPLING FROM A NORMAL DISTRIBUTION

Since the normal distribution is a theoretical population distribution forming the backbone of many statistical models, we should learn how to sample from such a distribution. The statistician is going to be saying that, *if* the population is normally distributed and *if* we sample $N$ values using a SIRS plan, *then* the sampling distribution of some statistic is such-and-such. Clearly we must know what is meant by simple independent random sampling (SIRS) from a normal distribution.

There is no way in which we can conceive of an infinite bowl containing an infinite number of numbered marbles, or of thoroughly mixing such a set of marbles, or of pulling out $N$ of them without looking. Instead we must make use of the following information: The tables for ND(0,1) show that the area to the right of $z = 1$ is 0.1587 and that the area to the right of $z = 0$ is 0.5000. Thus the area between $z = 0$ and $z = 1$ is the difference between these two areas, that is, 0.3413. We interpret this information as follows: If we sample by a SIRS plan from a ND(0,1), then we shall expect (in the long run) that 34.13 percent of the sampled values lie between $z = 0$ and $z = 1$. Similarly we should expect in the long run that 68.26 percent of the sampled values lie between $z = -1$ and $z = +1$; that 95 percent of the sampled values lie between $z = -1.96$ and $z = +1.96$; that 99 percent of the sampled values lie between $z = -2.58$ and $z = +2.58$; and so on. Extreme values, outside the range $-3 < z < +3$, would be expected very rarely. For example, we should expect to get a sampled value of $z = 3.1$ or larger only about once every 1,000 values.

Thus, although it may be difficult to conceive of the actual manner in which values are sampled from a normal distribution, it is possible to know what kind of results to expect. If we sample 100 values from ND(0,1) by a SIRS plan, then we shall expect about 68 percent of the values to lie between $z = -1$ and $z = +1$, but we shall not be surprised if the actual percentage is only 60 percent, since we know about sampling fluctuation.

Here is one way to sample independently and randomly (that is, using a SIRS plan) from a normal distribution with mean $M$ and standard deviation $S$. We consider what is known as an *algorithm*. An algorithm is a ritual which may appear to be mysterious but which does, in fact, accomplish what we want it to. Leaving the details to the mathematical statistician, we present an algorithm that has been shown to accomplish SIRS from a ND($M$,$S$). We write it in the computer language BASIC, using just three instructions:

```
1   LET X = SQR (−2 * LOG (RND))
2   LET T = 2 * 3.1415926 * RND
3   LET A = X * SIN(T) * S + M
```

The value $A$ in line 3 may be assumed to have been sampled according to a SIRS plan from the ND($M$,$S$).

The three lines of the program are explained as follows:

*Line* 1. RND refers to a random number between 0 and 1. Given a computer system that includes a random-number generator, that is, can produce numbers between 0 and 1 at random, the first instruction calls for one such number, RND; computes the natural logarithm of this number, LOG(RND); multiplies by minus 2; takes the square root; and names this final quantity $X$.

*Line* 2. A second random number is called for here; it is multiplied by $2\pi$; and the answer is called $T$. ($\pi$ is taken to be 3.1415926.)

*Line* 3. The trigonometric sine function of $T$, SIN($T$), is multiplied by $X$ (from line 1) and also by the standard deviation $S$ of the normal distribution from which we are sampling; then the mean $M$ is added and the result is called $A$. This quantity is a value obtained by SIRS from ND($M$,$S$).

| X-Interval | Frequency | |
|---|---|---|
| ⩽20 | 11 | |
| 20–22 | 3 | |
| 22–24 | 5 | |
| 24–26 | 20 | |
| 26–28 | 27 | * |
| 28–30 | 46 | ** |
| 30–32 | 87 | **** |
| 32–34 | 122 | ***** |
| 34–36 | 193 | ********* |
| 36–38 | 242 | *********** |
| 38–40 | 319 | ************** |
| 40–42 | 444 | ********************* |
| 42–44 | 536 | ************************** |
| 44–46 | 622 | ******************************* |
| 46–48 | 663 | ********************************* |
| 48–50 | 819 | ***************************************** |
| 50–52 | 820 | ***************************************** |
| 52–54 | 794 | **************************************** |
| 54–56 | 750 | ************************************** |
| 56–58 | 718 | ************************************ |
| 58–60 | 617 | ******************************* |
| 60–62 | 508 | ************************* |
| 62–64 | 483 | ************************ |
| 64–66 | 349 | ***************** |
| 66–68 | 258 | ************ |
| 68–70 | 180 | ********* |
| 70–72 | 140 | ****** |
| 72–74 | 96 | **** |
| 74–76 | 57 | ** |
| 76–78 | 34 | * |
| 78–80 | 15 | |
| 80+ | 22 | * |

*Note:* The intervals mentioned above are of the following form:

$$68 < X \leqslant 70$$

FIGURE 3-4. Results obtained using the algorithm to sample 10,000 values from a normal distribution with mean 50 and standard deviation 10

Table 3-3

|  | Population, ND(50,10) | Sample, 10,000 values by SIRS |
|---|---|---|
| Mean | $\mu = 50$ | $\bar{X} = 50.1543$ |
| Standard deviation | $\sigma = 10$ | $s_X = 9.83816$ |
| Skewness | $\gamma_1 = 0$ | $g_1 = -0.01627$ |
| Kurtosis | $\gamma_2 = 0$ | $g_2 = -0.04510$ |

Repeat this process as many times as you wish in order to obtain as many sampled values as needed.

Note that this algorithm depends on the generation of a random number between 0 and 1. We mean by this that RND is a random variable. The set of permissible values for RND is all values between 0 and 1, and the function defined on these permissible values is the uniform function (rectangular distribution)—all values are equally likely (have equal probability density).

To illustrate the use of this algorithm, consider sampling 10,000 values from a ND(50,10). With this many sampled values we should expect the sample distribution to look very much like ND(50,10). Figure 3-4 shows the results. Comparing the population parameters with the obtained sample statistics, we have Table 3-3. Evidently the algorithm is reasonably efficient.

## EXERCISES

1. If we sample one value by SIRS from ND(0,1), what will be the sampling distribution of this value?
2. (a) Using the tabled values for ND(0,1), determine normal deviate values so as to split the area under the curve into 10 equal parts. (If you start at minus infinity, how far do you have to go before you have an area of 0.1? From this point how much farther do you have to move to the right to get another 0.1 area? $\cdots$ etc.) Draw a rough graph of this operation.
   (b) Now use Appendix B, which contains 10 columns of 40 numbers that may be assumed to have been sampled by SIRS from ND(0,1). With reference to your findings in Exercise 2a and taking one column of Appendix B as your sample, find out how many cases fall into the 10 intervals on the ND(0,1).
   (c) What would you expect to find in a sample of 10,000? How many cases would you expect to find in each of the 10 intervals on the normal deviate scale?
   (d) Repeat Exercise 2b using two or three different columns of Appendix B. This will give you evidence of sampling fluctuation.
3. How would you convert the values in Appendix B to suitable values for a ND(3,2)? For the general case, ND($\mu,\sigma$)?
4. Draw up the statistician's diagram for sampling 10 values (a row in Appendix B) by SIRS from ND(0,1). Choose three or four rows as three or four possible samples, and compute the means for these samples. (Follow the guidelines in Figure 1-5.)

## 3-4 THE SAMPLING DISTRIBUTION OF THE MEAN

### 3-41 The Additive Property of Normal Distributions

What does it mean to "add" two independent normally distributed random variables? Let $X$ and $Y$ be two random variables, where

$$X \text{ is ND}(2,1) \quad \text{and} \quad Y \text{ is ND}(3,2)$$

We want to know what it means to talk about the sum $(X + Y)$, and we want to know how this sum is distributed.

First, note that the sum $(X + Y)$ is another random variable and as such has a range of permissible values and a probability distribution defined over this range. Since the range of $X$ and $Y$ is minus infinity to plus infinity, so also is the range of $(X + Y)$. In order to find out about the distribution of $(X + Y)$, consider the following procedure:

1. Using the algorithm on p. 87, sample one value from $X$.
2. Using the algorithm on p. 87, sample one value from $Y$.
3. Add these two SIRS values together to get one value for $(X + Y)$.
4. Repeat steps 1 through 3 as many times as possible (which is of course impossible, since there are an infinite number of such repetitions).

The set of sums $(X + Y)$ so obtained will indicate the distribution of the random variable $(X + Y)$.

The statistician does not, in fact, use this brute-force method of studying the distribution of $(X + Y)$. Working mathematically, he comes up with the following conclusion:

> *The addition theorem for normally distributed random variables: If $X$ is ND$(\mu_1,\sigma_1)$ and $Y$ is ND$(\mu_2,\sigma_2)$ and $X$ and $Y$ are independent, then the sum $(X + Y)$ is a random variable that is*
>
> $$\text{ND}(\mu_1 + \mu_2, \sqrt{\sigma_1{}^2 + \sigma_2{}^2})$$

AN EXAMPLE.   Suppose $A$ and $B$ are independent random variables, where $A$ is ND$(-1.0, 0.6)$ and $B$ is ND$(+1.0, 0.8)$. What is the distribution of $(A + B)$?

Rewriting the theorem for this problem, we have the following: If $A$ and $B$ are independent random variables distributed as mentioned above, then the sum $(A + B)$ is a random variable which is ND$(-1.0 + 1.0,$ $\sqrt{0.6^2 + 0.8^2})$, that is, ND$(0,1)$.

This result may be tested empirically as follows: Use the algorithm to obtain SIRS values from the $A$-distribution and the $B$-distribution. If we are sampling from the $A$-distribution, then line 3 of the BASIC program will read

$$\text{LET } A = X * \text{SIN}(T) * (0.6) + (-1.0)$$

What would line 3 read if we were sampling from the $B$-distribution? If we paired an $A$-value with a $B$-value to get a sum $(A + B)$ and repeated this operation, say, 1,000 times, we could compute the mean of the 1,000 $(A + B)$-values and their standard deviation. In an actual test of this problem, the results were as follows:

Mean of 1,000 sampled values of $(A + B) = 0.00767$

Standard deviation of these values $= 1.0307$

Of course, this summary of the 1,000 obtained values of $(A + B)$ cannot prove that the distribution of $(A + B)$ is normal. It shows only that the obtained mean and standard deviation of 1,000 values of $(A + B)$ are close to what the theorem says they should be.

AN IMPORTANT EXTENSION.    It is very simple for the statistician to prove and quite straightforward for the experimenter to understand that the addition theorem for independent random variables can be extended as follows:

*The extended addition theorem: If $X_1$ through $X_n$ are n independent normally distributed random variables, where $X_1$ is $ND(\mu_1, \sigma_1)$, $X_2$ is $ND(\mu_2, \sigma_2), \ldots, X_n$ is $ND(\mu_n, \sigma_n)$, then the sum $(X_1 + X_2 + \cdots + X_n)$ is a random variable which is normally distributed with*

$$\text{Mean} = \mu_1 + \mu_2 + \mu_3 + \cdots + \mu_n$$

$$\text{Standard deviation} = \sqrt{\sigma_1^2 + \sigma_2^2 + \sigma_3^2 + \cdots + \sigma_n^2}$$

AN EXAMPLE.    Suppose that you sample by SIRS from $ND(5,2)$. Consider sampling five values, adding them together, and then repeating the process indefinitely. What would be the distribution of the sum of these five values? We interpret the problem in terms of the extended addition theorem above. If we had five independent random variables each of which was $ND(5,2)$, then the sum of these random variables would be a random variable that was normally distributed with

$$\text{Mean} = 5 + 5 + 5 + 5 + 5 = 25$$

and

$$\text{Standard deviation} = \sqrt{2^2 + 2^2 + 2^2 + 2^2 + 2^2} = \sqrt{20} = 4.472$$

Be sure that you understand this example before you move to the next section.

## 3-42   The Sampling Distribution of the Mean

We take a moment here to reestablish our footing. This chapter has involved several excursions into the domain of the statistician, and it has involved the presentation of the machinery with which he works when he produces a statistical model. Remember that a statistical model consists of three items:

1. The specification of a *population distribution*, and we are here concerned only with the normal distribution.

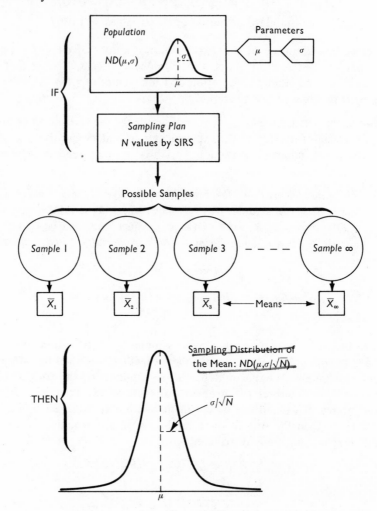

FIGURE 3-5.   Sampling distribution of the mean—based on a normally distributed population and an SIRS sampling plan

2. The specification of a *sampling plan*, and we are here concerned only with the SIRS plan.

3. The determination of the *sampling distribution of a statistic*, and in this section the statistic of interest is the mean.

We have considered the normally distributed population (Section 3-2) and how to sample from it by SIRS (Section 3-3). Now we turn to the third aspect, namely, the determination of the sampling distribution of a statistic—the mean. Figure 3-5 tells the story in diagrammatic form.

PROBLEM.   *If* the population is $ND(\mu,\sigma)$ and *if* the sampling plan is the SIRS plan, *then* what is the sampling distribution of the mean of $N$ sampled values? The answer is

> *The sampling distribution of the mean of N values sampled by SIRS from a $ND(\mu,\sigma)$ is another normal distribution, having a mean of $\mu$ and a standard deviation of $\sigma/\sqrt{N}$.*

*Heuristic Proof.*   We need three results:

1. If $X$ is a random variable with mean $\mu$, then random variable $kx$, where $k$ is a constant, has mean $k\mu$.

If $X$ is a random variable having mean $= 4$, then $(-2) * X$ is a random variable having mean $= -8$.

2. If $X$ is a random variable with standard deviation $\sigma$, then $kX$ is a random variable having standard deviation $|k|\,\sigma$, where $|k|$ is the positive value of $k$.

If $X$ is a random variable with standard deviation $= 2.5$, then $(-2) * X$ is a random variable with standard deviation $= 5.0$.

3. We also make use of the extended addition theorem for independent random variables.

Consider sampling $N$ values by SIRS from $ND(\mu,\sigma)$. Interpreting this as an example of the extended addition theorem, we know that the sum of these $N$ values is a random variable that is normally distributed with

$$\text{Mean} = \mu + \mu + \cdots + \mu = N\mu$$

$$\text{Standard deviation} = \sqrt{\sigma^2 + \sigma^2 + \cdots + \sigma^2} = \sqrt{N\sigma^2}$$

But this is the distribution of the sum $(X_1 + X_2 + \cdots + X_N)$; we want the distribution of the mean $(X_1 + X_2 + \cdots + X_N)/N$. The relationship between the mean and the sum is

$$\text{Mean} = k(\text{sum})$$

where $k = 1/N$.

Thus, using results (1) and (2) above, we can make the following statement: If the sampling distribution of the sum of $N$ values (sampled by SIRS from ND($\mu,\sigma$)) is the ND($N\mu,\sqrt{N}\sigma$), then the sampling distribution of the mean is the ND($\mu$, $\sigma/\sqrt{N}$).

AN EXAMPLE. What is the sampling distribution of the mean of 16 values sampled by SIRS from a population that is ND(5,2)? The sampling distribution of the mean is a normal distribution with mean $= 5$ and standard deviation $= 2/\sqrt{16} = 0.5$.

Consider what the sampling distribution of the mean would be if we changed the size of the sample:

| Sample size $N$ | Sampling distribution |
|:---:|:---:|
| 1 | ND(5,2) |
| 4 | ND(5,1) |
| 16 | ND(5,0.5) |
| 100 | ND(5,0.2) |
| 1,000 | ND(5,0.063) |

This trend—smaller and smaller standard deviation of the sampling distribution of the mean as $N$ increases—expresses the well-known fact that averages based on many data points are more stable than averages based on few data points. (Consider your own bowling average or a baseball player's batting average.) Remember, however, that we are making the assumption here that the population is a normally distributed population. We shall relax this restriction in the next chapter. (At this point the reader should reread Section 1-43.)

## EXERCISES

1. If we sample 10 values from a ND(0,1) by SIRS, what will be the sampling distribution of the mean? Is the mean a random variable? If so, identify the permissible values for the mean and the probability distribution on these permissible values.
2. Exercise 1 should be done prior to this one. In order to perform an empirical check on the answer to Exercise 1, do the following:
   (a) With the help of some fellow students find the means for each of the 40 rows in Appendix B.
   (b) How many of these means would you expect to fall within one standard deviation of the mean of the sampling distribution of the means? Check to see whether the empirical check bears this out.
   (c) How many of the 40 means would you expect to fall outside the range of $+2$ to $-2$ standard deviations (on the sampling distribution)? Does the empirical check come close to the expected value?
3. The addition theorem says that, if $X$ is ND(0,1) and $Y$ is independently ND(0,1), then the sum $(X + Y)$ has what kind of distribution?

4. To perform an empirical check on the conclusion to Exercise 3, do the following:

   (a) Regard column 1 of Appendix B as successive samplings by SIRS from $X$; regard column 2 of Appendix B as successive samplings from $Y$. To get 40 values of $(X + Y)$, simply add the corresponding values in columns 1 and 2.

   (b) Find the mean and the standard deviation for these 40 values of $(X + Y)$. How do these statistics compare with what the theorem states?

5. For each of the statistical models in Table 3-4 give the sampling distribution of the mean.

Table 3-4

|      | Population | Sampling plan |
|------|------------|---------------|
| (a) | ND(0,1) | 1 by SIRS |
| (b) | ND(9,9) | 81 by SIRS |
| (c) | ND(0,9) | 81 by SIRS |
| (d) | ND(2.3,7.2) | 113 by SIRS |

6. In each of the cases in Table 3-5, give the sampling distribution of the sum of the sampled values.

Table 3-5

|      | Population | Sampling plan |
|------|------------|---------------|
| (a) | ND(0,1) | 1 by SIRS |
| (b) | ND(9,9) | 81 by SIRS |
| (c) | ND(0,9) | 81 by SIRS |
| (d) | ND(2.3,7.2) | 113 by SIRS |

7. Determine the population distribution for each of the following cases. The sampling distribution of the mean is ND(0,1) when

   (a) 10 values were sampled by SIRS,

   (b) 81 values were sampled by SIRS,

   (c) 121 values were sampled by SIRS,

   (d) $N$ values were sampled by SIRS.

8. The SAT-V and SAT-M scores for the population of high school seniors are assumed normally distributed with mean 500 and standard deviation 100. What is the distribution of the sum of the SAT-V and SAT-M scores? (Assume independence of SAT-V and SAT-M scores.)

9. Continuing with Exercise 8, if the football coach is told that he cannot consider football prospects who score less than 700 on their combined score (SAT-V + SAT-M), what proportion of the population is being denied him? (Draw a graph to help solve this one.)

10. According to the assumptions in Exercise 8, what are the chances of a student's scoring more than 1,500 on his combined SAT-V and SAT-M tests?

# Useful Sampling Distributions

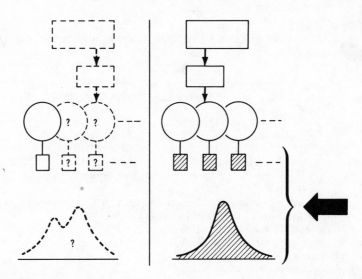

## 4-1 INTRODUCTION

The social science literature abounds with the use of three major statistical tests—the $t$-test, the $F$-test, and the chi-square ($\chi^2$) goodness-of-fit test. These three tests are based upon three sampling distributions—the $t$-distribution, the $F$-distribution, and the $\chi^2$-distribution. And these three sampling distributions are based upon three statistical models—Student's "model $t$," Fisher's $F$-model, and Pearson's $\chi^2$-model. "Student" is the pen name of an English statistician, W. S. Gossett, and R. A. Fisher and Karl Pearson are the names of two other famous statisticians. Whenever an experimenter makes use of one of these tests, he must examine the assumptions underlying it, so as to be able to decide whether or not it is appropriate to use the test. For example, if the experimenter uses a $t$-test on his data and the conditions of his experiment violate the assumptions underlying the $t$-model, then he is misapplying the $t$-test. In terms of the dialogue between the experimenter, $E$, and the statistician, $S$, no cooperation is possible until $E$ and $S$ have reached a mutual understanding of (*i*) the assumptions underlying the statistical model and (*ii*) the conditions underlying the experiment. The latter are best explained by $E$ and the former by $S$. And it is healthy for $E$ to recognize that sometimes no test is better than any test. Unfortunately there is an attitude prevalent among many social science researchers that unless data are analyzed according to some statistical model, they should not be reported. Such an attitude shows a lack of good (statistical) breeding, and the only way to combat it is to become thoroughly versed in the underlying assumptions of the commonly used statistical models.

This chapter is offered as a kind of reference source. It contains in concise form the basic statistical models and the equations for the basic sampling distributions. In principle the story is simple. Given a population and a sampling plan, the model tells us the shape of the sampling distribution of the statistic of interest. In detail the story is more sophisticated. The equations specifying the sampling distributions of the $t$-statistic, the $F$-statistic, and the $\chi^2$-statistic are not simple. The matter of proof that the sampling distributions are what they are said to be is also quite complicated, especially in the case of the $\chi^2$-statistic (which, by the way, is the easiest statistic to use in practice).

In order to present the material to the experimenter's maximum advantage, technical details have been omitted, and the serious student is directed to authoritative source materials for further information. Each model is treated in the same way, using five headings—the population, the sampling plan, the statistic of interest, the sampling distribution of this statistic, and the assumptions underlying the model. Then an example is given.

The reader is encouraged to go through this chapter in the following manner. Keep plenty of paper handy, and for each section draw a diagram of the statistical model. When it comes to the equations for the sampling distribution of the various statistics, try to sketch the shape of the distribution and get an idea of where its mean is likely to be and some indication of the standard deviation. The exercises at the end of each section are designed to establish some confidence in the use of these statistical models, and you should find yourself able to do most of the exercises.

There is one new term in this chapter, *standard error*, and you should note that a standard error is (*i*) a standard deviation and (*ii*) the standard deviation of a sampling distribution. In other words, when you are considering a particular statistic and its sampling distribution, it is conventional to call the standard deviation of the sampling distribution by another name, the standard error of the statistic.

## 4-2 THE SAMPLING DISTRIBUTION OF THE MEAN

### 4-21 The Model

POPULATION.   Let the population be $ND(\mu,\sigma)$.

SAMPLING PLAN.   Let the sampling plan be $n$ values chosen from $ND(\mu,\sigma)$ by SIRS.

STATISTIC.   The summary number of interest is the mean:

$$\bar{X} = \frac{\sum X_i}{n} \tag{4-1}$$

SAMPLING DISTRIBUTION.   If every permissible sample could be obtained according to the sampling plan above and from the population above and if each of these samples were summarized in terms of the mean $\bar{X}$, then the complete set of means would have the following distribution:

$$Y_{(n)} = f(\bar{X}) = \frac{1}{\sqrt{2\pi}\,(\sigma/\sqrt{n})}\, e^{-(\bar{X}-\mu)^2/(2\sigma^2/n)} \tag{4-2}$$

This is simply $ND(\mu,\sigma/\sqrt{n})$. Note that we attach a subscript to the symbol $Y$. There is one such sampling distribution for each distinct value of $n$, the sample size. In other words, Equation (4-2) describes a family of distributions. Note also that we write $f(\bar{X})$ to emphasize the fact that this sampling distribution is a function of the sample mean, $\bar{X}$.

ASSUMPTIONS.   The population is assumed normally distributed, and the sampling plan is assumed to be SIRS. Check Section 4-23, however, to see when these assumptions can be relaxed somewhat.

### 4-22 An Example

Consider the population of scores on the SAT-V. The experimenter and the statistician agree that the population may be considered $ND(500,100)$. The experimenter wishes to take samples of size 100 from 250 colleges around the country in order to see what the mean SAT-V score is at each of these colleges. What he is really aiming at is a classification of colleges into better than average, average, and worse than average. In preparation for this task, he must know something about the sampling distribution of the mean of samples of size 100. If the sampling plan is SIRS, then he can use the model in Section 4-21 to reach the following conclusion. The sample mean for

$n = 100$ cases is normally distributed with a mean of 500 and a standard error given by

$$\frac{100}{\sqrt{100}} = 10$$

This is ND(500,10), and the equation of this sampling distribution, according to Equation (4-2), is

$$Y_{(100)} = \frac{1}{\sqrt{2\pi}\,(100/\sqrt{100})}\, e^{-(\bar{X}-500)^2/(2*100^2/100)}$$

$$= \frac{1}{\sqrt{2\pi}\,(10)}\, e^{-(\bar{X}-500)^2/(200)}$$

## 4-23 Notes

It is important to note that even if the population is not normally distributed, we can still say something useful about the sampling distribution of the mean. Consider the following model:

POPULATION. Unknown except for two parameters. The mean is $\mu$, and the standard deviation is $\sigma$. (Think of a very skewed distribution.)

SAMPLING PLAN. Choose $n$ values by SIRS.

STATISTIC. Summarize the $n$ values in terms of the mean $\bar{X}$.

SAMPLING DISTRIBUTION. Although all the details of the shape of the sampling distribution of $\bar{X}$ cannot be known precisely, we can say that the mean of the sampling distribution is $\mu$ and the standard error is $\sigma/\sqrt{n}$. Furthermore, we can say that as the sample size gets larger and larger, this sampling distribution looks more and more like a normal distribution. This last fact is based upon a most important theorem known as the *central limit theorem*, and the interested reader is urged to look it up in an authoritative mathematical statistics text. No matter what shape the original population distribution, if the sampling plan is SIRS, then the mean of $n$ sampled values tends (and this means "tends as $n$ goes to infinity") to be normally distributed with mean $\mu$ and standard error $\sigma/\sqrt{n}$.

UNBIASEDNESS. The statistician is interested in certain formal properties of statistics. One of these properties is unbiasedness. If the *expected value* (and this is the mean) of a sample statistic (e.g., the mean, $\bar{X}$) for a SIRS sample of size $n$ is equal to the population parameter (e.g., the mean, $\mu$), then the statistic, $\bar{X}$, is called an *unbiased* statistic. In symbols this is written

$$E(\bar{X}) = \mu \qquad \text{for samples of size } n \qquad (4\text{-}3)$$

When we talk about expected value, we are talking about the mean of the sampling distribution. Note that this definition of unbiasedness is not concerned with approximations as *n* tends to infinity. If the statistician is interested in what happens to the statistic as the sample size increases indefinitely, then we say he is interested in *asymptotic* properties of sampling distributions.

To anticipate an important practical matter in the next section of this chapter (Section 4-3), consider the following:

CONSISTENCY.  A sample statistic is called a consistent statistic if its expected value approaches the population parameter as the sample size increases indefinitely. In symbols

$$E(\bar{X}) \to \mu \qquad \text{as the sample size } n \to \infty \qquad (4\text{-}4)$$

*The sample mean $\bar{X}$ is both an unbiased statistic and a consistent statistic.*

## EXERCISES

1. For each of the population distributions and sample sizes in Table 4-1 (*i*) sketch the population distribution, (*ii*) assume an SIRS plan, (*iii*) sketch the sampling distribution of the mean, and (*iv*) identify the mean and standard error of the sampling distribution:

Table 4-1

|     | Population | Sample size |
| --- | --- | --- |
| (*a*) | ND(0,1) | $n = 9$ |
| (*b*) | ND(0,1) | $n = 100$ |
| (*c*) | ND(100,10) | $n = 100$ |
| (*d*) | ND(−3.5,1.6) | $n = 37$ |

2. Assuming a SIRS plan, what are the population distributions that give rise to the sampling distributions of the mean in Table 4-2?

Table 4-2

|     | Sampling distribution | Sample size |
| --- | --- | --- |
| (*a*) | ND(0,1) | $n = 9$ |
| (*b*) | ND(17,1.2) | $n = 100$ |
| (*c*) | ND(−5.9,0.63) | $n = 41$ |

3. On a regular piece of graph paper draw, roughly, the sampling distributions of the mean when the population is ND(0,16), the sampling plan is SIRS, and the sample sizes are $n = 1, 4, 16, 256$. (Draw them all on one piece of graph paper so that you can see how with increasing *n* the sampling distribution concentrates more and more around the value 0.)

4. To illustrate the points made in Section 4-23, consider the following discrete population:

| Distinct values | 1 | 2 | 3 | 4 | 5 | 6 | 7 | 8 | 9 |
|---|---|---|---|---|---|---|---|---|---|
| Probability | 0.5 | 0.3 | 0.1 | 0.05 | 0.01 | 0.01 | 0.01 | 0 | 0.02 |

Draw a histogram for this population, and compute its mean and standard deviation; that is, compute these two vital parameters.

(a) According to Section 4-23, what would the mean and standard error be for the sampling distribution of the mean of 9 values sampled from this population by SIRS?

(b) A computer program was written to simulate sampling from this population (which is very skewed) with the results in Table 4-3.

Table 4-3

| Number of samples | Sample size | Mean* | Standard error* |
|---|---|---|---|
| 100 | 9 | 1.98 | 0.508 |
| 100 | 9 | 1.88 | 0.513 |
| 100 | 25 | 1.97 | 0.319 |
| 100 | 25 | 1.96 | 0.309 |
| 100 | 100 | 1.96 | 0.142 |
| 100 | 100 | 1.94 | 0.141 |

* These columns refer to the mean of 100 means and the standard error for 100 means.

Do these empirical checks agree reasonably with the statements in Section 4-23?

## 4-3  THE SAMPLING DISTRIBUTION OF THE VARIANCE

### 4-31  The Model

POPULATION.   Let the population be $ND(0,\sigma)$. (Since variance is independent of the origin, we might as well work with a mean of 0.)

SAMPLING PLAN.   Choose $n$ values from $ND(0,\sigma)$ by SIRS.

STATISTIC.   The summary number of interest is the variance:

$$s^2 = \frac{\sum (X_i - \bar{X})^2}{n} \tag{4-5}$$

SAMPLING DISTRIBUTION.   If every permissible sample could be obtained according to the sampling plan above and from the population above and if each sample were summarized in terms of $s^2$, then the complete set of values

$$s^2 = \frac{\Sigma (X_i - \bar{X})^2}{n}$$

of $s^2$ would have the following properties:

becomes
1 bias

$$\text{Mean of sampling distribution of } s^2 = \frac{(n-1)}{n}\sigma^2$$

$$\text{(4-6)}$$

$$\text{Standard error} = \sqrt{\frac{2(n-1)}{n^2}}\sigma^2$$

Note that the statistician does not say that the sampling distribution is a normal distribution. He cannot offer an equation in this case. He can offer only these two characteristics of the distribution.

ASSUMPTIONS. The population is assumed normally distributed, and the sampling plan is assumed to be SIRS. Note that as $n$ gets larger, the quantity $(n-1)/n$ gets closer to unity. For small values of $n$, the expected value of the sample variance is noticeably smaller than the population parameter.

### 4-32  An Example

Consider the SAT population once again, that is, ND(500,100). Suppose that we sample $n = 100$ values by SIRS and compute the sample variance, $s^2$. What is the sampling distribution of this variance?

We cannot give an equation for this sampling distribution, but we do know two of its characteristics. The mean of the sampling distribution of $s^2$ is

$$\frac{(n-1)}{n}\sigma^2 = \frac{(100-1)}{100}100^2 = 9{,}900$$

and the standard error of the sampling distribution of $s^2$ is

$$\sqrt{\frac{2(n-1)}{n^2}}\sigma^2 = \sqrt{\frac{2(100-1)}{100^2}}100^2 = 1{,}407$$

Remember that we are talking about variances here, not standard deviations. There are some mathematical niceties concerning the sampling distribution of the standard deviation that we shall ignore, and we shall note merely that the mean of the sampling distribution of $s$ would be approximately

$$\sqrt{\frac{(n-1)}{n}}\sigma = \sqrt{9{,}900} = 99.5$$

that is, a little less than the population value of 100.

## 4-33   Notes

Even if the population is not normally distributed, the statistician can show that the expected value of the sample variance, $s^2$, is as stated in Equation (4-6). In other words, we have the following model:

POPULATION.   Any distribution with a mean of zero and a standard deviation of $\sigma$.

SAMPLING PLAN.   Choose $n$ values by SIRS plan.

STATISTIC.   $s^2$ as defined in Equation (4-5).

Then the sampling distribution of the variance, $s^2$, will have an expected value (a mean) equal to

$$\frac{(n-1)}{n}\sigma^2$$

Now what would the statistician say about unbiasedness and consistency?

Is $s^2$ an unbiased statistic? No. In order for $s^2$ to be an unbiased statistic, we would have to have the following:

$$E(s^2) = \sigma^2 \qquad \text{for sample size } n$$

This is not the case. Instead we have

$$E(s^2) = \frac{(n-1)}{n}\sigma^2 \qquad \text{for sample size } n \qquad (4\text{-}7)$$

Instead of the sample variance $s^2$ having an expected value equal to the population variance $\sigma^2$, it turns out to be something less than the population parameter. For example, if our sample size is $n = 10$, then Equation (4-7) tells us that the sampling distribution of the variance, $s^2$, will have an expected value of $\frac{9}{10}\sigma^2$. Thus the statistician calls $s^2$ (as computed from Equation 4-5) a biased statistic.

Is $s^2$ a consistent statistic? Yes. By definition (see Equation 4-4), if the expected value of the sample statistic approaches the value of the population parameter as the sample size increases indefinitely, then that statistic is a consistent statistic. Note what happens to the fraction $(n-1)/n$ as the value of $n$ goes to infinity:

$$\lim \frac{(n-1)}{n} \qquad \text{as } n \to \infty = 1$$

Therefore, we can write

$$E(s^2) \to \sigma^2 \qquad \text{as sample size } n \to \infty \qquad (4\text{-}8)$$

Thus the statistician calls $s^2$ a consistent statistic.

## 4-34  Should You Use $n$ or $(n-1)$?

Since the standard deviation (or variance) is such an important statistic in practical experimentation and since the statistician calls $s^2$ a biased statistic, it is of considerable interest to the experimenter to try to "unbias" his biased statistic. The point is that when an experimenter and a statistician get together, their dialogue might be something like this:

$E$   I have $n$ data points, $X_1$ through $X_n$, and I computed the sample variance as follows:

$$s^2 = \frac{\sum (X_i - \bar{X})^2}{n}$$

$S$   Do you know what the population variance should be?

$E$   No, I don't know what $\sigma^2$ is, so let's use $s^2$ as an estimate of $\sigma^2$.

$S$   Well, you shouldn't do that. As a descriptive statistic $s^2$ is perfectly all right, but if you are trying to estimate the population parameter $\sigma^2$, then we know $s^2$ is a biased estimate. The sampling distribution of $s^2$ has an expected value, or a mean value, of $[(n-1)/n]\sigma^2$. In other words, the expected value of $s^2$ is always less than $\sigma^2$. It is biased because it underestimates $\sigma^2$.

$E$   What should I do to get an unbiased estimate of $\sigma^2$?

$S$   If you divide by $(n-1)$ instead of by $n$ when you compute the sample variance, you will have an unbiased statistic, which will serve as an unbiased estimate of the population variance, $\sigma^2$.

$E$   In other words, you are asking me to use the following formula for sample variance:

$$\hat{s}^2 = \frac{\sum (X_i - \bar{X})^2}{(n-1)} \tag{4-9}$$

$S$   Yes, and it's a good idea to use the symbol $\hat{s}^2$ for this statistic to make it quite clear that it is an unbiased estimate of a population parameter.

COMMENTARY.   The statistic $s^2$ as defined above (and in Equation 4-5) is a perfectly good statistic (that is, summary number), but if you are trying to estimate the population variance, then you should use $\hat{s}^2$ as defined in Equation (4-9). In other words, in answer to the question "Should you use $n$ or $(n-1)$ in the denominator when computing sample variance?" use $(n-1)$ if you want an unbiased estimate of the population parameter.

We now show, without comment, why $\hat{s}^2$ is unbiased:

$$\hat{s}^2 = \frac{\sum (X_i - \bar{X})^2}{(n-1)} = \frac{n}{n-1} s^2$$

Therefore,

$$E(\hat{s}^2) = E\left(\frac{n}{n-1} s^2\right) = \frac{n}{n-1} E(s^2)$$

$$= \frac{n}{n-1} \frac{n-1}{n} \sigma^2 = \sigma^2$$

Thus the expected value of $\hat{s}^2$ is shown to be $\sigma^2$, and this is the definition of unbiasedness.

*The sample variance, $s^2$, is a consistent statistic but biased. The sample variance, $\hat{s}^2$, is both a consistent and an unbiased statistic.*

## EXERCISES

1. Draw a diagram for the model that describes the sampling distribution of the variance $s^2$. What would be the difference between this diagram and the one for $\hat{s}^2$?
2. Using the data from Exercise 1 in Section 4-2, compute the mean and standard error for the sampling distribution of the sample variance $s^2$.
3. (a) If $X$ is a random variable having mean $M$, what will be the mean of the random variable $cX$, where $c =$ constant?
   (b) The sample variance $s^2$ is a random variable having a mean value of $[(n-1)/n]\sigma^2$. First express $\hat{s}^2$ in the form $cs^2$ (that is, find $c$) and then determine the mean value of the random variable $\hat{s}^2$.
   (c) If $X$ is a random variable having variance $V$, what will be the variance of the random variable $cX$?
   (d) What will be the variance of the random variable $\hat{s}^2$?
4. In conjunction with the results of Exercise 3 repeat Exercise 2 for the case of $\hat{s}^2$ rather than $s^2$.

## 4-4  THE $\chi^2$ (CHI-SQUARE) DISTRIBUTION

### 4-41  The $\chi^2$-Model

POPULATION.  Let the population be $ND(0,1)$.

SAMPLING PLAN.  Choose $n$ values by SIRS.

STATISTIC.  Let the $n$ sample values be designated $X_1$ through $X_n$. Then the summary number of interest is defined:

$$\chi^2 = X_1^2 + X_2^2 + X_3^2 + \cdots + X_n^2 = \sum_{i=1}^{n} X_i^2 \qquad (4\text{-}10)$$

SAMPLING DISTRIBUTION.  If every permissible sample size $n$ could be obtained using the sampling plan above and the population above and if

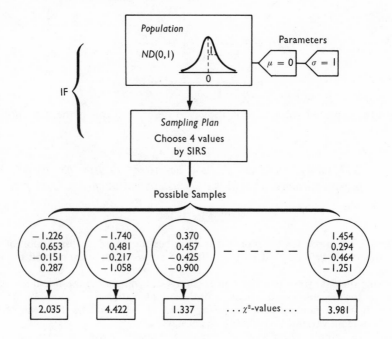

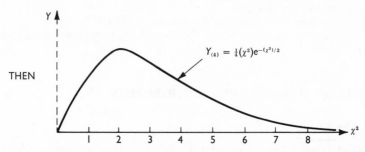

FIGURE 4-1.   The $\chi^2$-model: illustrated for the case of the chi-square distribution with four degrees of freedom

every such sample were summarized in terms of a $\chi^2$-value, then the complete set of $\chi^2$-values would have the following distribution (frequency function):

$$Y_{(n)} = f(\chi^2) = \frac{1}{2^{n/2}\Gamma(n/2)} (\chi^2)^{(n/2)-1} e^{-(\chi^2)/2} \qquad (4\text{-}11)$$

Note that, since chi-square is a sum of squares, $Y$ is defined only for $\chi^2 > 0$. Note also that we append a subscript to $Y$ to indicate the size of the sample. In other words Equation (4-11) describes a family of chi-square distributions, one for each distinct value of $n$. (See Figure 4-1.) The quantity $n$ is known as the *degrees of freedom* (df), and so we talk about a chi-square distribution with $n$ degrees of freedom.

ASSUMPTIONS.    (*i*) ND(0,1); (*ii*) SIRS sampling plan. In Chapter 8, however, we shall see how another summary number is approximately distributed as a chi-square variable, and the assumptions there are different.

THE GAMMA FUNCTION.    Equation (4-11) contains a factor $\Gamma(n/2)$, which is known as a gamma function. It is simply a rule by which the value $n/2$ is converted into another value, called "gamma of $n$ over 2." The formal definition of a gamma function is

$$\Gamma(p) = \int_0^\infty x^{p-1}e^{-x}\,dx \qquad \text{for } p > 0 \qquad (4\text{-}12)$$

but for our purposes we need only know what values it takes on in the following two cases: (*i*) when $n$ is divisible by 2 and (*ii*) when $n$ is not divisible by 2.

(*i*) *n* DIVISIBLE BY 2.    If $N = n/2$, then

$$\Gamma(N) = (N-1)(N-2)(N-3)\cdots 3 \times 2 \times 1 = (N-1)!$$

For example, if $n = 12$, then $N = n/2 = 6$ and $\Gamma(6) = 5! = 120$.

(*ii*) *n* NOT DIVISIBLE BY 2.    If $N = n/2$, then

$$\Gamma(N) = (N-1)(N-2)(N-3)\cdots (2.5)(1.5)(0.5)(\sqrt{\pi})$$

In particular, if $N = 0.5$, then

$$\Gamma(N) = \Gamma(0.5) = \sqrt{\pi}$$

For example, if $n = 9$, then $N = 4.5$ and

$$\Gamma(4.5) = (3.5)(2.5)(1.5)(0.5)(\sqrt{\pi})$$
$$= 11.6353$$

In general, the gamma function has the following property:

$$\Gamma(N) = (N-1)\Gamma(N-1)$$

## 4-42    An Example

Consider the standard normal population, ND(0,1). Suppose that we select six values from this distribution by SIRS, and we summarize these six numbers by obtaining their sum of squares. This sum of squares will be a chi-square value. What is the sampling distribution of this statistic?

In this case $n = 6$, and if we let $C$ stand for various chi-square values, we make use of Equation (4-11) to define the sampling distribution of $C$:

$$Y_{(6)} = f(C) = \frac{1}{2^{6/2}\Gamma(6/2)} C^{(6/2)-1}e^{-C/2}$$

$$= \frac{1}{(8)*(2!)} C^2 e^{-C/2}$$

$$= \tfrac{1}{16}C^2 e^{-C/2}$$

Anticipating a result in Section 4-43, we can state that the mean of this distribution is equal to 6 ($= n$) and the standard error is equal to 3.464 ($= \sqrt{2n}$).

Suppose that I select six values from the ND(0,1) by SIRS and you selected five values. Then the sampling distribution of the $\chi^2$-statistic for my six values will be

$$Y_{(6)} = \tfrac{1}{16}C^2 e^{-C/2}$$

and the sampling distribution of the $\chi^2$-statistic for your five values would be

$$Y_{(5)} = \frac{1}{7.52} C^{1.5}e^{-C/2}$$

If we cooperate to the point of putting our sampled values together before computing a $\chi^2$-value, we shall have 11 values from the ND(0,1), and the sampling distribution of the $\chi^2$-value, based on 11 sampled values, will be

$$Y_{(11)} = \frac{1}{2,369.0} C^{4.5}e^{-C/2}$$

This process can be repeated indefinitely. The mean of a chi-square distribution with 6 df is 6. The mean of a chi-square distribution with 5 df is 5. And the mean of the chi-square distribution with $(6 + 5) = 11$ df is 11.

### 4-43   Properties of the $\chi^2$-Distribution

We are dealing with a family of distributions, since for every distinct value of $n$ there is a distinct chi-square distribution. As $n$ increases, the chi-square distribution moves out along the abscissa, and the variance of the distribution increases. Two summary numbers tell the story. The chi-square distribution with $n$ degrees of freedom has

$$\text{Mean} = n$$
$$\text{Variance} = 2n$$

Thus we can draw up Table 4-4.

ADDITIVE PROPERTY. Another important property of chi-square distributions is that they are additive. Given a random variable $A$ that is distributed as a $\chi^2$-variable with $m$ df and an independent random variable $B$

Table 4-4

| Degrees of freedom (df) | Mean | Variance |
|:---:|:---:|:---:|
| $n = 1$ | 1 | 2 |
| $n = 2$ | 2 | 4 |
| $n = 5$ | 5 | 10 |
| $n = 10$ | 10 | 20 |
| etc. | | |

that has a $\chi^2$-distribution with $n$ df, then the random variable $(A + B)$ will also be a chi-square variable, this time having $(m + n)$ df.

AREA UNDER $\chi^2$-CURVE. The area under any chi-square curve is unity. In mathematical language we are saying that the integral of $Y_{(n)}$ in Equation (4-11) from 0 through $+\infty$ is unity. Thus the chi-square distributions are probability distributions. For example, if we consider a chi-square distribution with 10 degrees of freedom and we find the area under the curve beyond the value $\chi^2 = 18.306$, it will turn out to be 0.05. We interpret this by saying that under the $\chi^2$-model the probability of obtaining a chi-square value as large as 18.306 or larger is 0.05. We say that there is a 5 percent chance of obtaining a $\chi^2$-value as large as 18.306 or larger.

THE NORMAL DISTRIBUTION APPROXIMATION. As the degrees of freedom ($n$) increase, the chi-square distribution begins to look more and more like a normal distribution, except, of course, that it does not extend to minus infinity. In view of this property, tables for the chi-square distribution do not usually go beyond $n = 30$ (see Appendix D). For values of $n$ beyond 30, we make use of the following normal approximation:

1. Compute the value of $\chi^2$.
2. Compute the quantity $C = \sqrt{2\chi^2} - \sqrt{2n - 1}$.
3. Then $C$ is approximately distributed as a ND(0,1).

By way of example, consider the chi-square distribution with 30 degrees of freedom. Appendix D shows that the probability of obtaining a chi-square value as large as 40.255 or larger is 0.10; that is, the area under the curve to the right of 40.255 is 10 percent, or 0.10. Now, if we use the normal approximation to the chi-square distribution, we have the following results:

1. $\chi^2 = 40.255$
2. $C = \sqrt{(2)(40.255)} - \sqrt{(2)(30) - 1} = 1.29$
3. Looking up the ND(0,1) tables (Appendix C), we find that the area to the right of 1.29 is 0.0985, or 9.85 percent.

Evidently the normal approximation is reasonably good for $n = 30$, and it gets better as $n$ increases beyond 30.

## EXERCISES

1. By definition $0! = 1$. With this information compute the value of the gamma function for the values 1, 2, 3, 4, 5, 6, 7, 8, 9, 10.
2. By definition $\Gamma(0.5) = \sqrt{\pi}$. With this information compute the value of the gamma function for the values 1.5, 2.5, 3.5, 4.5, 5.5, 6.5, 7.5, 8.5, 9.5.
3. Using a piece of standard graph paper, try to make a plot of the chi-square distribution with 4 df. Indicate on the graph where the mean of the distribution is, and compute the standard error of the distribution.
4. If $n$ is the number of degrees of freedom, work out the equations for the sampling distribution of $\chi^2$ with (a) $n = 1$ df, (b) $n = 2$ df, (c) $n = 3$ df. Simply use Equation (4-11), and simplify to some convenient point.
5. *Stirling's approximation.* You may have noticed in computing the gamma values above that as $m$ gets large, $\Gamma(m)$ gets very large; and it is inconvenient to work with factorials when the numbers are large. Stirling has given us a very useful approximation for $N!$ as follows:

$$N! = \Gamma(N + 1) = \left(\frac{N}{e}\right)^N \sqrt{2\pi N}$$

How close is this approximation for $N = 5$, 10, 15?

## 4-5   THE $t$-DISTRIBUTION

### 4-51   The $t$-Model

POPULATION.   The statistician assumes a normally distributed population, $ND(0,\sigma)$.

SAMPLING PLAN.   Choose one value from this distribution and call it $X_0$. Then choose $n$ more values by SIRS and call them $X_1$ through $X_n$.

STATISTIC.   The summary number called $t$ was originally defined as follows:

$$t = \frac{X_0}{\sqrt{\sum_{i=1}^{n} X_i^2 / n}} \tag{4-13}$$

Why was it defined this way? Student first conceived of $t$ as the ratio of a value of the random variable $X$ to an independent estimate of its standard deviation. In Equation (4-13) the numerator is a value of the random variable $X$, and the denominator is an independent estimate of the standard deviation of $X$. In fact, the $t$-statistic is very much like a standard score. To obtain a standard score, we subtract the mean (which is zero in the case above) and divide by the standard deviation. Equation (4-13) is therefore a very close relative of a standard score.

SAMPLING DISTRIBUTION.   If every permissible sample of size $(n + 1)$ could be obtained from the $ND(0, \sigma)$ by SIRS and if every such sample were summarized in the form of a *t*-statistic, then the complete set of *t*-values would have the following distribution (frequency function):

$$Y_{(n)} = f(t) = \frac{1}{\sqrt{n\pi}} \frac{\Gamma([n + 1]/2)}{\Gamma(n/2)} \left(1 + \frac{t^2}{n}\right)^{-(n+1)/2} \tag{4-14}$$

Note that we append a subscript to $Y$ to indicate the degrees of freedom. Equation (4-14) is the sampling distribution of a *t* statistic with *n* df. Note also that the gamma function appears in both the numerator and the denominator. For example, if $n = 20$, we should have to evaluate $\Gamma(10.5)$ in the numerator and $\Gamma(10)$ in the denominator. Refer to Section 4-41 to find out how to evaluate these gamma values.

ASSUMPTIONS.   (*i*) Normally distributed population and (*ii*) SIRS sampling plan—to choose $(n + 1)$ values. Note that we said above that the mean of the population is zero. It is not necessary for this to be the case. If the mean is anything other than zero, we simply subtract it from all the *X*-values.

### 4-52   A Modified *t*-Model (The One Most Commonly Used)

POPULATION.   Let the population be normally distributed with mean $\mu$, which is usually hypothesized to be some particular value, and standard deviation $\sigma$, which is always estimated by $\hat{s}$ (that is, the unbiased sample standard deviation).

SAMPLING PLAN.   Choose *m* values by SIRS.

STATISTIC.   Let the *m* values for one sample be designated $X_1$ through $X_m$. Then the *t*-statistic is defined as

$$t = \frac{(\bar{X} - \mu)}{\hat{s}/\sqrt{m}} \tag{4-13'}$$

where

$$\hat{s} = \sqrt{\frac{\sum (X_i - \bar{X})^2}{m - 1}}$$

At this point you might refer to Section 2-3 (on standard scores) in order to recognize this formula for *t* as a close relative of the standard score. Consider the sampling distribution of a mean $\bar{X}$. Its expected value is $\mu$, and its standard error is $(\sigma/\sqrt{m})$. Thus the standard form for a mean $\bar{X}$ would be

$$\frac{(\bar{X} - \mu)}{\sigma/\sqrt{m}}$$

In Equation (4-13′) we obtain a sample mean $\bar{X}$, subtract the hypothesized mean $\mu$, and divide by $(\hat{s}/\sqrt{m})$, which is an estimate of the standard error of the mean. Thus we have something very close to a standard form.

In view of the fact that we estimate the standard error, we lose one degree of freedom, and we say that Equation (4-13′) defines a $t$-statistic with $(m - 1)$ df.

SAMPLING DISTRIBUTION.   The sampling distribution of this $t$-statistic—Equation (4-13′)—is a $t$-distribution with $(m - 1)$ df. Thus, we substitute

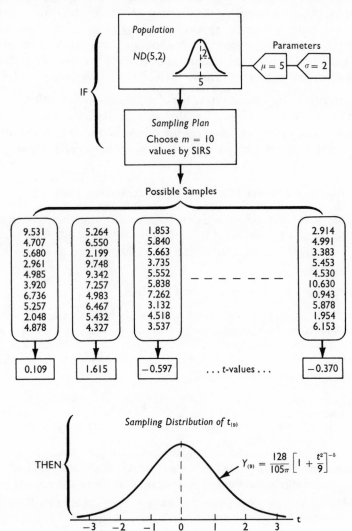

FIGURE 4-2.   The $t$-model: illustrated for the case of 10 values sampled from a population which is ND(5,2)

$(m - 1)$ for $n$ in Equation (4-14) to get the equation for the sampling distribution.

Figure 4-2 indicates the structure of the $t$-model.

ASSUMPTIONS.   In applications involving the use of the $t$-model, we assume a normally distributed population (of measures) and a SIRS sampling plan. We lose one degree of freedom for each parameter that has to be estimated from the sample data.

### 4-53   An Example

Consider a normally distributed population ND(5,2). Suppose that we sample 10 values from this population by SIRS and summarize them in the form of a $t$-value, according to Equation (4-13'). What is the sampling distribution of such $t$-values?

Substituting $(10 - 1)$ for $m$ in Equation (4-14'), we obtain

$$Y_{(10-1)} = \frac{1}{\sqrt{(10 - 1)\pi}} \frac{\Gamma(10/2)}{\Gamma([10 - 1]/2)} \left(1 + \frac{t^2}{10 - 1}\right)^{-10/2}$$

$$= \frac{128}{105\pi} \left(1 + \frac{t^2}{9}\right)^{-5}$$

This distribution is symmetrical about $t = 0$, and it looks very much like a normal distribution—in fact, like ND(0,1). The larger the degrees of freedom, the more closely the $t$-distribution resembles the ND(0,1).

### 4-54   Properties of the t-Distribution

We are dealing with a family of distributions, since for every distinct value of $m$ there is a distinct $t$-distribution. However, all $t$-distributions have a mean of zero, are symmetrical about this value, and for $m > 3$ the standard error of the distribution with $(m - 1)$ df is

$$\sqrt{\frac{(m - 1)}{(m - 3)}}$$

Thus we can draw up Table 4-5.

INDEPENDENCE FROM POPULATION VARIANCE.   A most important property of this sampling distribution is that it is independent of the population parameter, $\sigma^2$. From the experimenter's point of view, this means that if he wishes to summarize his sample data in the form of a $t$-value, he may do so as soon as he defines $\mu$, the population mean. As soon as he does so, the sampling distribution of $t$ can be known exactly. Thus, if the experimenter

Table 4-5

| Sample size $m$ | Degrees of freedom (df $= m - 1$) | t-distribution | |
|---|---|---|---|
| | | Mean | Standard error |
| 3 | 2 | 0 | Undefined |
| 4 | 3 | 0 | 1.732 |
| 5 | 4 | 0 | 1.414 |
| 10 | 9 | 0 | 1.134 |
| 20 | 19 | 0 | 1.057 |
| 30 | 29 | 0 | 1.036 |

decides to check a *null hypothesis*, that $\mu = 0$, his *t*-statistic will have the form

$$t = \frac{\text{sample mean } \overline{X} - 0}{\text{standard error of sample mean, } \overline{X}} \tag{4-15}$$

and if he assumes that (*i*) the population from which he sampled was normally distributed with a mean of zero and an unknown standard deviation and (*ii*) his sample data were obtained by SIRS from this population, then it is appropriate to make use of the sampling distribution of *t*. This procedure is known as testing the significance of the difference between a sample mean, $\overline{X}$, and some hypothetical population mean, $\mu$. When $\mu = 0$, we say that we are examining a null hypothesis.

THE NORMAL DISTRIBUTION APPROXIMATION.    As the degrees of freedom get larger and larger, the *t*-distribution begins to look more and more like the standard normal distribution, ND(0,1). Thus the tables for the *t*-distribution conclude with a set of values for $n = \infty$ degrees of freedom. These values are those obtained from ND(0,1). The reader is urged to check Appendix C (the ND(0,1) tables) with Appendix E (the *t*-distribution tables) to satisfy himself that this is the case.

THE *t*-DISTRIBUTION IS A PROBABILITY DISTRIBUTION.    The area under the *t*-curve is unity for all values of *n* (the degrees of freedom). In mathematical language we say that the integral of $Y_{(n)}$ with respect to *t*, evaluated from minus infinity to plus infinity, is unity. Thus the *t*-distributions are probability distributions. Looking at the tables (Appendix E), we can say that the area under the *t*-curve (with 10 df) to the right of 2.228 is 0.025, or 2.5 percent; that is, given the assumptions of the *t*-model, we should expect *t*-values as large as 2.228 or larger 2.5 percent of the time.

## EXERCISES

1. For $n = 4, 5, 6, 7, 8$, and 9, work out the equation of the sampling distribution of the $t$-statistic with $n$ df. Use Equation (4-14).
2. Using Appendix C (the normal tables), draw the standard normal distribution on a piece of ordinary graph paper. For a $t$-distribution with 4 df, plot some points on the same graph to get an idea of the relationship between ND(0,1) and $t_4$.
3. Using Appendix E (the $t$-tables), complete the following exercises:
   (a) How much area is there to the right of $t = 1$ for a $t$-distribution with 10 df? 15 df? 20 df? 100 df?
   (b) How much area is there to the right of $t = 2$ for a $t$-distribution with 10 df? 15 df? 20 df? 100 df?
   (c) What $t$-values correspond to an area of (a) 0.05 in the right tail of the distribution, (b) 0.05 in the left tail of the distribution, (c) 0.025 in the left tail of the distribution, when there are 17 df?
4. In Figure 4-2 the sample data are presented along with the summary number $t$. Check two of the samples to see if Equation (4-13') gives the same answer.

## 4-6  THE $F$-DISTRIBUTION

### 4-61  The $F$-Model

POPULATION.  Let the population be ND(0,$\sigma$).

SAMPLING PLAN.  Choose $(m + n)$ values by SIRS.

STATISTICS.  It is convenient to think of these $(m + n)$ values as making up two samples, one of size $m$ and the other of size $n$. Then the summary number of interest (to Fisher, in his work on analysis of variance—Chapters 6 and 7 in this text) is

$$F = \frac{\sum_{i=1}^{m} X_i^2 \big/ m}{\sum_{j=1}^{n} Y_j^2 \big/ n} \qquad (4-16)$$

where $X_i$ $(i = 1, \ldots, m)$ and $Y_j$ $(j = 1, \ldots, n)$ are the sampled values. Note that this summary number is the ratio of two *mean squares*. A mean square is a close relative of variance.

SAMPLING DISTRIBUTION.  If every permissible sample of size $(m + n)$ could be obtained using the sampling plan above and the population above, and if every such sample were summarized in terms of an $F$-statistic, then the complete set of $F$-values would have the following distribution (frequency function):

$$Y_{(m,n)} = f(F) = \frac{\Gamma[(m + n)/2]}{\Gamma[m/2]\Gamma[n/2]} m^{m/2} n^{n/2} \frac{F^{(m-2)/2}}{(mF + n)^{(m+n)/2}} \qquad (4-17)$$

Note that we append two subscripts to $Y$ to indicate degrees of freedom in the numerator ($m$) and degrees of freedom in the denominator ($n$), respectively. Again this is a family of sampling distributions, one for each ($m,n$) combination.

ASSUMPTIONS. Again the assumptions are a normally distributed population and a SIRS sampling plan. An additional assumption is known as the *equal-variance* assumption. The two samples, one of size $m$ and the other of size $n$, are assumed to come from the same population or from populations having the same variance.

### 4-62   The *F*-Model Used in Practice

POPULATION.   Let the population be $ND(\mu, \sigma)$, where $\mu$ is hypothesized and $\sigma$ is estimated in one or more ways from the sample data. (See Chapters 6 and 7 for more on this point.)

SAMPLING PLAN.   Choose ($m + n$) values by SIRS.

STATISTICS.   The summary number of interest is a ratio of two independent estimates of the population variance, for example,

$$F = \frac{\sum (X_i - \overline{X})^2/(m - 1)}{\sum (Y_j - \overline{Y})^2/(n - 1)} \qquad (4\text{-}16')$$

Note that the degrees of freedom in the numerator are ($m - 1$), not $m$. The variance estimate in the numerator is based on ($m - 1$) independent squares so that there are only ($m - 1$) df. Similarly, there are ($n - 1$) df for the denominator. In fact, the numerator and denominator in Equation ($4\text{-}16'$) are unbiased estimates of the parameter $\sigma^2$. See Section 4-33 for a discussion of unbiasedness.

SAMPLING DISTRIBUTION.   The sampling distribution of this *F*-statistic with ($m - 1, n - 1$) df is as in Equation (4-17), with $m$ and $n$ replaced by ($m - 1$) and ($n - 1$), respectively.

ASSUMPTIONS.   The assumptions of normality (normally distributed population) and a SIRS sampling plan are required for this model. Within reason, departures from strict normality and strict independence have been found to be not too harmful to the model. We also make the equal-variance assumption, which is sometimes known as *homoscedasticity*.

Figure 4-3 illustrates the *F*-model and shows the shape of the *F*-distribution with (4,8) df.

Equation (4-17) involves three gamma functions. For example, if we are dealing with an *F*-distribution with (5,10) df, we shall have to evaluate $\Gamma(7.5)$, $\Gamma(2.5)$, and $\Gamma(5.0)$. Refer to Section 4-41 to find out how to evaluate these gamma functions.

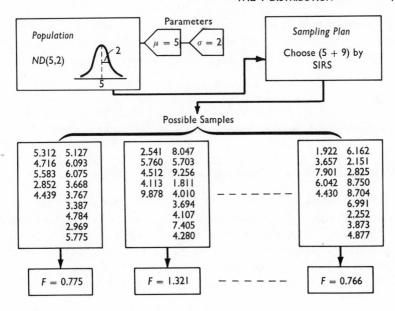

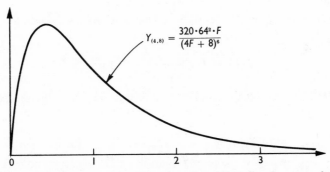

Sampling Distribution of $F_{(4,8)}$

$$Y_{(4,8)} = \frac{320 \cdot 64^2 \cdot F}{(4F + 8)^6}$$

FIGURE 4-3.   The F-model: illustrated for the case of (5 + 9) values sampled from a population which is ND(5,2)

## 4-63   An Example

Figure 4-3 illustrates the case of sampling (5 + 9) values by SIRS from ND(5,2). A computer program was written to simulate the sampling procedure, and a number of different samples resulted. For each of these samples, the 14 values were treated as two samples, the first being used to compute the numerator in Equation (4-16′) and the second the denominator. If the assumptions of the model are upheld, then the sampling distribution of the $F$-statistic should be

$$Y_{(4,8)} = \frac{\Gamma(6)}{\Gamma(2)\Gamma(4)} 4^2 8^4 \frac{F^{(4-2)/2}}{(4F + 8)^{(4+8)/2}}$$

$$= \frac{320 * 64 * 64 * F}{(4F + 8)^6}$$

A computed graph of this distribution is shown in Figure 4-3.

## 4-64  Properties of the $F$-Distribution

We are dealing with a family of distributions, since for different values of $m$ and $n$ we have different $F$-distributions. Consider now an $F$-distribution with $(p,q)$ df. The range of values for $F$ is zero through plus infinity. For values of $p$ (numerator degrees of freedom) less than 3, the distribution is J-shaped. For values of $p$ greater than or equal to 3, the distribution is positively skewed (that is, skewed to the right) and has a distinct maximum value (mode) when

$$F = \frac{(p - 2)}{p} \frac{q}{(q + 2)} \qquad (4\text{-}18)$$

EXPECTED VALUE (MEAN) OF $F$.   The mean of the sampling distribution of $F_{(p,q)}$ is

$$E(F) = \bar{F} = \frac{q}{(q - 2)} \qquad \text{for } q > 2 \qquad (4\text{-}19)$$

STANDARD ERROR OF $F$.   The standard deviation of the sampling distribution of $F$ is

$$\text{se of } F_{(p,q)} = \sqrt{\frac{2q^2(p + q - 2)}{p(q - 2)^2(q - 4)}} \qquad \text{for } q > 4 \qquad (4\text{-}20)$$

By way of illustration, consider the following special cases:

$p = 3, q = 5$.   The $F$-distribution with $(3,5)$ df has a mode at $F = \frac{5}{21}$, a mean value of $\bar{F} = \frac{5}{3}$, and a standard error $\text{se}_F = \frac{10}{3}$.

$p = 9$, $q = 20$.   The $F$-distribution with $(9,20)$ df has a mode at $F = \frac{70}{99}$, a mean value of $\bar{F} = \frac{10}{9}$, and a standard error $\text{se}_F = 0.68$.

AREA UNDER THE $F$-CURVE.   The area under every $F$-distribution is unity. In mathematical language we say that the integral of $Y_{(p,q)}$ in Equation (4-17) with respect to $F$, evaluated from zero through plus infinity, is unity. Thus the $F$-distributions are probability distributions. Looking at the $F$-tables (Appendix F), we can say that the area under an $F$-distribution with $(4,20)$ df to the right of $F = 2.87$ is 0.05, or 5 percent, that is, given the assumptions of the $F$-model, the probability of obtaining an $F$-value as large as 2.87 or larger is 0.05. Alternatively, we might say that if we repeatedly sampled $(5 + 21)$ values from a normally distributed population by SIRS and summarized every sample in terms of the $F$-statistic, then we should expect 5 percent of the samples to have $F$-values as large as 2.87 or larger.

RELATIONSHIP BETWEEN $t$ AND $F$. The $F$-distribution, like the $t$-distribution and the $\chi^2$-distribution, does tend to normality as the degrees of freedom, $p$ and $q$, become larger and larger. Of more practical importance, however, is the fact that whenever $p = 1$, then $F_{(1,q)} = t^2_{(q)}$. In other words, if we examine the statistic $t^2$ instead of the statistic $t$, we find that the sampling distribution of $t^2$ with $q$ df is exactly the same as the sampling distribution of $F$ with $(1,q)$ df. We shall make use of this fact in Chapter 5 (on the $t$-test).

## EXERCISES

1. Insert the following values for numerator and denominator degrees of freedom in Equation (4-17), and simplify the equation as far as possible:
   (a) $m = 1, n = 4$      (c) $m = 3, n = 20$
   (b) $m = 4, n = 8$      (d) $m = m - 1, n = n - 1$
2. For each of the distributions above, compute the mode, the mean, and the standard error wherever possible.
3. Table 4-6 gives the ordinate values for various $F$-distributions identified at the top of the columns. For each of these distributions compute the mode, mean,

Table 4-6

| Abscissa | Ordinate | | | |
|---|---|---|---|---|
| | $F_{(1,5)}$ | $F_{(4,4)}$ | $F_{(8,8)}$ | $F_{(16,16)}$ |
| 0.0 | $\infty$ | 0.000 | 0.000 | 0.000 |
| 0.2 | 0.754 | 0.578 | 0.260 | 0.035 |
| 0.4 | 0.476 | 0.624 | 0.607 | 0.387 |
| 0.6 | 0.348 | 0.549 | 0.704 | 0.781 |
| 0.8 | 0.271 | 0.457 | 0.650 | 0.889 |
| 1.0 | 0.219 | 0.375 | 0.546 | 0.785 |
| 1.2 | 0.181 | 0.307 | 0.440 | 0.612 |
| 1.4 | 0.152 | 0.253 | 0.348 | 0.447 |
| 1.6 | 0.130 | 0.210 | 0.274 | 0.316 |
| 1.8 | 0.112 | 0.175 | 0.216 | 0.220 |
| 2.0 | 0.097 | 0.148 | 0.170 | 0.153 |
| 2.2 | 0.085 | 0.125 | 0.135 | 0.106 |
| 2.4 | 0.075 | 0.107 | 0.108 | 0.074 |
| 2.6 | 0.067 | 0.092 | 0.087 | 0.051 |
| 2.8 | 0.059 | 0.080 | 0.070 | 0.036 |
| 3.0 | 0.053 | 0.070 | 0.057 | 0.026 |
| 4.0 | 0.032 | 0.038 | 0.022 | 0.005 |
| 5.0 | 0.021 | 0.023 | 0.010 | 0.001 |

and standard error, and on one piece of graph paper plot the four distributions on top of one another.

4. In Figure 4-3 check the value of the $F$-statistic in the first sample. What is the probability of getting an $F$-value as large as this or larger?


## 4-7  THE BINOMIAL DISTRIBUTION

In Sections 4-2 through 4-6 the statistician has in a sense displayed his wares. He has presented a number of statistical models all based on normally distributed populations and all requiring simple independent random sampling (SIRS). From the point of view of the experimenter, these models are very useful but not comprehensive enough, since some experiments deal with populations that are essentially qualitative in nature; that is, the attributes of interest to the experimenter may be qualitative. In this section (4-7) and the next (4-8) we present models that are not based on the normal distribution. First we consider the binomial model and then the multinomial model.


### 4-71  The Binomial Model

POPULATION. Imagine an infinite population of members. Each member is either an $H$ or a $T$; that is, there are only two kinds of members. The only population parameter of interest is the summary number $\pi$, where $\pi =$ proportion of $H$'s in the population. Given $\pi$, we know $(1 - \pi)$, which is the proportion of $T$'s in the population. (To intuit this kind of population, just think of a coin and every possible toss of this coin. The population of outcomes consists of an infinite number of $H$'s and $T$'s. If it is a fair coin, then the parameter $\pi = 0.5$.)

SAMPLING PLAN. Choose $n$ members from this population by SIRS.

STATISTIC. The summary number of interest is $n_H =$ number of $H$'s in the $n$ sample members (or $n_T = n - n_H =$ number of $T$'s in the $n$ sample members).

SAMPLING DISTRIBUTION. Every statistic is a random variable, and every random variable defines a set of permissible values and a probability function defined on them. In this binomial model the range of permissible values for $n_H$ (the statistic) is as follows:

$$n_H \text{ can be } 0, 1, 2, 3, 4, \ldots, (n - 1), n$$

There are no other values that $n_H$ can be. The probability function defined on these permissible values is as follows: Let $r$ $(= 0, 1, 2, 3, \ldots, n)$ be the general value of $n_H$. Then the probability that $n_H = r$ is

$$\binom{n}{r} \pi^r (1 - \pi)^{n-r}$$

where

$$\binom{n}{r} = \frac{n!}{r!(n-r)!}$$

By convention some special notation has been introduced for this important distribution. The notation $b(r;n,\pi)$ is used to indicate the binomial probability of $r$ successes (where success $= H$ in the case above) when $n$ values are sampled by SIRS from a binomial population with parameter $\pi$. Thus the sampling distribution for $n_H$ (number of successes) is as follows:

$$b(0;n,\pi) = \binom{n}{0} \pi^0 (1 - \pi)^{n-0} = (1 - \pi)^n$$

$$b(1;n.\pi) = \binom{n}{1} \pi^1 (1 - \pi)^{n-1} = \frac{n}{1} \pi (1 - \pi)^{n-1}$$

$$b(2;n,\pi) = \binom{n}{2} \pi^2 (1 - \pi)^{n-2} = \frac{n(n-1)}{1 \times 2} \pi^2 (1 - \pi)^{n-2}$$

etc.

These $(n + 1)$ equations can be written in one general equation:

$$b(r;n,\pi) = \frac{n!}{r!(n - r)!} (\pi)^r (1 - \pi)^{n-r} \qquad \text{for } r = 0, 1, 2, \ldots, n \quad (4\text{-}21)$$

This is the frequency function of the binomial distribution with parameter $\pi$ and sample size $n$. Note that the sample size is critical in this distribution.

ASSUMPTIONS.  The population is assumed to be binomial (literally, two names; that is, there are only two kinds of population members). The sampling plan is, as ever, SIRS.

### 4-72  An Example

Consider the following model:

POPULATION.  All possible tosses of a given coin that is fair. Thus the population parameter is $\pi = \frac{1}{2} =$ proportion of heads.

SAMPLING PLAN.  Consider 5 tosses of the coin (which is another way of saying choose 5 from the population of tosses by SIRS).

STATISTIC.  For each sample of 5 tosses count the number of heads. This is the summary number of interest.

SAMPLING DISTRIBUTION. In this case the permissible values of the random variable ($n_H$) are 0, 1, 2, 3, 4, and 5. The probability function—Equation (4-21)—defined on these values yields

$$b(0;5,0.5) = \tfrac{1}{32} = \text{Pr[getting 0 heads]}$$
$$b(1;5,0.5) = \tfrac{5}{32} = \text{Pr[getting 1 head ]}$$
$$b(2;5,0.5) = \tfrac{10}{32} = \text{Pr[getting 2 heads]}$$
$$b(3;5,0.5) = \tfrac{10}{32} = \text{Pr[getting 3 heads]}$$
$$b(4;5,0.5) = \tfrac{5}{32} = \text{Pr[getting 4 heads]}$$
$$b(5;5,0.5) = \tfrac{1}{32} = \text{Pr[getting 5 heads]}$$

Figure 4-4 illustrates the binomial model for this example.

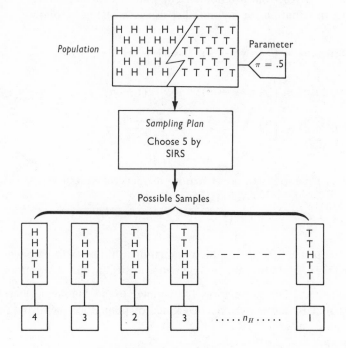

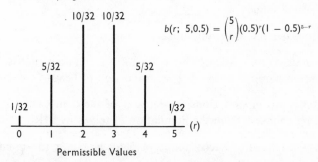

FIGURE 4-4. The binomial model: illustrated for the case of five values sampled by SIRS from a binomial population

## 4-73   Properties of the Binomial Distribution

We are dealing with a family of discrete sampling distributions, since for each value of $\pi$, the population parameter, and for each sample size $n$, we have a distinct distribution. The range of permissible values for the statistic, $n_H$, is 0 through $n$, that is, $(n + 1)$ distinct values.

EXPECTED VALUE (MEAN).   The mean of the sampling distribution is $n\pi$. In symbols

$$E(r) = \bar{r} = n\pi$$

STANDARD ERROR.   The standard deviation of the sampling distribution is $\sqrt{n\pi(1 - \pi)}$. In symbols

$$\mathrm{se}_r = E(r^2) - [E(r)]^2 = \sqrt{n\pi(1 - \pi)}$$

In the example above the mean of the sampling distribution of $b(r;5,0.5) = 5 * 0.5 = 2.5$, and the standard error is

$$\sqrt{(5)(0.5)(1 -- 0.5)} = \frac{\sqrt{5}}{2}$$

THE BINOMIAL EXPANSION.   In algebra a binomial is an expression having two terms. Consider the binomial expression $(p + q)$. If we insist that $p + q = 1$ and also that $p$ and $q$ must be nonnegative, then we can raise the binomial $(p + q)$ to any power, and the value of the expression will be unity:

$$\text{If } (p + q) = 1 \quad \text{then} \quad (p + q)^n = (1)^n = 1$$

If we now expand the expression $(p + q)^n$ for various values of $n$, we find that

$$(p + q)^1 = \qquad\qquad p + q$$
$$(p + q)^2 = \qquad\quad p^2 + 2pq + q^2$$
$$(p + q)^3 = \quad p^3 + 3p^2q + 3pq^2 + q^3$$
$$(p + q)^4 = p^4 + 4p^3q + 6p^2q^2 + 4pq^3 + q^4$$

and in the general case

$$(p + q)^n = \binom{n}{n}p^nq^0 + \binom{n}{n-1}p^{n-1}q^1 + \cdots + \binom{n}{r}p^rq^{(n-r)} + \cdots$$

Note now that these terms are identical with those given in Equation (4-21). The various terms in the expansion of $(p + q)^n$ give the probabilities of $r$ successes when $n$ values are sampled by SIRS from a population having parameter $p$. This situation, of course, occurs only when $p + q = 1$, and we assume $p$ to be the proportion of successes in the population.

## EXERCISES

1. Consider a binomial population consisting of $H$'s and $T$'s where $H$ is considered a success and the probability of $H$ in the population is $p$. For the following values of $n$ and $p$ compute (i) the sampling distribution for $n_H$, (ii) the mean of this distribution, and (iii) the standard error of this distribution:

   (a) $n = 2, p = 0.5$     (d) $n = 4, p = 0.5$
   (b) $n = 2, p = 0.2$     (e) $n = 4, p = 0.9$
   (c) $n = 4, p = 0.1$

2. The following tables give the number of heads $n_H$ obtained in a computer simulation of a coin-tossing experiment, where $n$, the sample size, and $p$, the population parameter, are as indicated:

   $n = 4, p = 0.1$     *Results of* 100 *simulations of* 4 *tosses* $(n_H)$

   ```
   0 1 1 1 0 1 0 0 0 1   2 0 0 0 0 0 0 0 0 1
   0 0 0 1 0 1 0 0 1 0   0 1 0 0 0 0 0 1 0 0
   0 1 2 1 1 0 0 0 1 1   0 0 0 1 1 0 0 0 1 0
   1 0 0 1 0 1 0 0 0 3   0 1 0 0 0 0 1 2 0 1
   0 0 2 0 0 0 0 0 0 1   0 0 0 0 0 1 0 0 0 0
   ```

   $n = 4, p = 0.5$     *Results of* 100 *simulations of* 4 *tosses* $(n_H)$

   ```
   2 3 2 1 2 1 2 4 4 3   2 0 3 1 1 1 1 2 2 3
   3 2 3 2 2 1 1 3 3 1   4 2 2 2 0 0 3 0 2 1
   1 2 3 2 2 2 1 3 3 2   3 3 2 1 2 2 1 2 2 1
   1 2 1 1 1 2 3 2 1 3   1 3 3 4 0 3 4 1 3 1
   2 1 2 0 2 3 1 2 3 2   2 2 1 3 2 1 2 2 3 2
   ```

   Plot these results in histogram form, and compare the relative frequencies of the $r$ successes with the actual probabilities computed from the sampling distribution of $r$.

3. Prove that the sum of the values $b(r;n,p)$ over all values of $r$ is unity. In other words, show that the equation for the binomial distribution is a probability function.

4. Consider the variable $X$, which has permissible values 1, 2, 3, and 4. Suppose that the frequencies of occurrence of these values in a sample size $N = 20$ are 4, 6, 9, and 1, respectively.
   (a) What is the mean value of this distribution?
   (b) Convert the frequencies of occurrence to relative frequencies of occurrence, and determine the formula for finding the mean when you are given distinct values and relative frequencies of occurrence.
   (c) For the binomial model with $n = 2$ and $p = 0.5$ compute the probabilities (relative frequencies, if you will) for each of the permissible outcomes (number of successes), and using the formula you developed in (b), compute the mean of the binomial distribution with $n = 2$ and $p = 0.5$.
   (d) See if you can use this method to derive the general formula for the mean $(= np)$ of a binomial variable.

5. As $n$, the sample size, increases, the range of permissible outcomes increases. Although the binomial distribution is a discrete distribution, it can be approximated by a normal distribution (which is continuous) and as $n$ increases, this

approximation gets better and better, even though $p$ is far from 0.5. Check this in the following way:

(a) Consider the binomial distribution with $n = 4$ and $p = 0.2$. Compute the binomial probabilities for $r = 0, 1, 2, 3$, and 4 successes. Compute the mean and the standard error for this distribution. Now convert the $r$-values (number of successes) to standard scores (or standardized values).

(b) On a piece of graph paper plot the binomial distribution on the standardized values.

(c) On the same piece of graph paper and the same abscissa, plot a few points of the standard normal distribution, ND(0,1).

(d) Now consider the binomial distribution with $n = 25$ and $p = 0.2$. Compute the mean and the standard error. Compute the values $b(r;n\ p)$ for $r = 0, 1, 2, 3, 5, 8, 10, 20, 25$. Standardize these values, and plot them on the same piece of graph paper. (If you feel strong, you should compute all the values of $b(r;n,p)$ for this exercise. It will make the graph clearer.)

6. Check the accuracy of the normal distribution approximation to the binomial in the following cases:

(a) $n = 25$, $p = 0.2$. On this binomial distribution the probability of at most three successes is the sum of the first four binomial probabilities. What would the probability be if we were to approximate this binomial with ND $(np, \sqrt{npq})$, where $q = 1 - p$?

(b) Repeat $a$, using $n = 4$ and $p = 0.2$.


## 4-8   THE MULTINOMIAL DISTRIBUTION

### 4-81   The Multinomial Model

POPULATION. Imagine an infinite population of members. Each member can be classified into one of $k$ types, which we identify as $C_1$, $C_2, \ldots, C_k$ ($C$ = class). The population parameters of interest are the summary numbers that indicate the probabilities of belonging to the various classes. Since these probabilities must sum to unity, we need to specify $(k - 1)$ of them, and the last one will be determined. Thus the parameters are $\pi_1, \pi_2, \pi_3, \ldots, \pi_{k-1}$. (Note that we use Greek symbols for parameters and Roman letters for statistics. In the literature, however, you will often see these multinomial probabilities and the binomial probability parameter in Section 4-7 written $p_1, p_2, \ldots, p_{k-1}$, and $p$.)

SAMPLING PLAN. Choose $n$ members from this population by SIRS.

STATISTICS. For the multinomial model we summarize the sample data in terms of $(k - 1)$ summary numbers, being the number of instances of class 1, class 2, class 3, . . . , class $(k - 1)$. Let us designate these summary numbers $n_1, n_2, n_3, \ldots, n_{k-1}$. Clearly if we know these $(k - 1)$ values, we also know $n_k$, the number of instances of class $k$ in the sample data.

SAMPLING DISTRIBUTION. We can think of the summary numbers as either $k$ distinct values or one $k$-tuple, $[n_1, n_2, \ldots, n_k]$. As far as the theory is concerned, it is more convenient to think of the latter as the summary of the sample data. Then the sampling distribution refers to (*i*) the set of permissible values of this *k*-tuple and (*ii*) the probability distribution defined on them. The sampling distribution in this case is discrete and more complicated than the binomial distribution. However, in order to use the same form as Equation (4-21), we define the probability for the outcome $[r_1, r_2, \ldots, r_k]$ as follows:

$$Pr([r_1, r_2, \cdots, r_k]; n, [\pi_1, \pi_2, \cdots, \pi_k])$$

$$= \frac{n!}{r_1! \, r_2! \cdots r_k!} (\pi_1)^{r_1}(\pi_2)^{r_2} \cdots (\pi_k)^{r_k} \cdot \quad (4\text{-}22)$$

ASSUMPTIONS. The population is assumed classifiable into *k* classes with known probabilities (or estimated probabilities), and the sampling plan is assumed to be SIRS.

### 4-82  An Example

A computer simulation of sampling from a multinomial population involving three classes with $p_1 = p_2 = p_3 = \frac{1}{3}$ and $n = 3$ produced the results shown in Table 4-7.

Table 4-7

| Sample | Class 1 | Class 2 | Class 3 |
|--------|---------|---------|---------|
| 1 | 1 | 2 | 0 |
| 2 | 2 | 0 | 1 |
| 3 | 1 | 1 | 1 |
| 4 | 3 | 0 | 0 |
| 5 | 1 | 1 | 1 |
| 6 | 0 | 2 | 1 |
| 7 | 1 | 1 | 1 |
| 8 | 1 | 0 | 2 |
| 9 | 2 | 0 | 1 |
| 10 | 0 | 0 | 3 |

The first thing to consider is how many different outcomes are possible when the sample size is 3. The permissible outcomes are

[3,0,0]  [0,3,0]  [0,0,3]  [2,0,1]  [2,1,0]
[0,2,1]  [1,2,0]  [0,1,2]  [1,0,2]  [1,1,1]

Using Equation (4-22), we may compute the probability for each of these 3-tuple outcomes as follows:

$$Pr\left([3,0,0];3,\left[\frac{1}{3},\frac{1}{3},\frac{1}{3}\right]\right) = \frac{3!}{3! \, 0! \, 0!} \left(\frac{1}{3}\right)^3 \left(\frac{1}{3}\right)^0 \left(\frac{1}{3}\right)^0 = \frac{1}{27}$$

which takes care of the first three permissible outcomes.

$$\Pr\left([2,0,1];3,\left[\frac{1}{3},\frac{1}{3},\frac{1}{3}\right]\right) = \frac{3!}{2!\,0!\,1!}\left(\frac{1}{3}\right)^2\left(\frac{1}{3}\right)^0\left(\frac{1}{3}\right)^1 = \frac{3}{27}$$

which takes care of the next six permissible outcomes.

$$\Pr\left([1,1,1];3,\left[\frac{1}{3},\frac{1}{3},\frac{1}{3}\right]\right) = \frac{3!}{1!\,1!\,1!}\left(\frac{1}{3}\right)^1\left(\frac{1}{3}\right)^1\left(\frac{1}{3}\right)^1 = \frac{6}{27}$$

which takes care of the last permissible outcome.

These probabilities tell us what to expect in a long series of repetitions of the experiment: Choose three values by SIRS and summarize the outcome in the form of a 3-tuple, $[n_1,n_2,n_3]$. For example, if we ask the computer to replicate this experiment 270 times, we shall be able to compare what actually occurred with what we expect (Table 4-8).

Table 4-8

| No. | Outcome type | Observed occurrences in 270 replications | Expected occurrence in 270 replications |
|---|---|---|---|
| 1 | [3,0,0] | 14 | 10 |
| 2 | [0,3,0] | 9 | 10 |
| 3 | [0,0,3] | 15 | 10 |
| 4 | [2,0,1] | 27 | 30 |
| 5 | [2,1,0] | 23 | 30 |
| 6 | [0,2,1] | 25 | 30 |
| 7 | [1,2,0] | 29 | 30 |
| 8 | [0,1,2] | 32 | 30 |
| 9 | [1,0,2] | 33 | 30 |
| 10 | [1,1,1] | 63 | 60 |

## 4-83  Properties of the Multinomial Distribution

The sum of the probabilities over all permissible $k$-tuple outcomes is equal to unity—this is a probability distribution. Given the population probability parameters, $p_1$ through $p_k$, and the sample size $n$, we can compute the expected number of cases per class—we expect $np_1$ in class 1, $np_2$ in class 2, etc. Other details of this distribution are beyond the scope of this text, and the interested reader is urged to browse in a mathematics library for more information.

## EXERCISES

1. Compute the multinomial probabilities for every permissible outcome for the following cases:
   (a) $n = 3$, $[p_1, p_2, p_3] = [0.5, 0.3, 0.2]$
   (b) $n = 4$, $[p_1, p_2, p_3, p_4] = [\frac{1}{4}, \frac{1}{4}, \frac{1}{4}, \frac{1}{4}]$
2. Draw a diagram to describe the multinomial model. Follow the outline of Figure 4-4. However, you will not be able to draw the sampling distribution for anything other than a trinomial, and this will have to be done carefully.
3. A computer-simulated replication of a multinomial sampling experiment ($n = 20$, $[p_1, p_2, p_3, p_4] = [0.5, 0.25, 0.15, 0.1]$) produced the following results over 20 replications. Total number of cases in the various classes over 20 replications of $n = 20$ sampled values were

   | Class | 1 | 2 | 3 | 4 |
   |---|---|---|---|---|
   | Frequency | 202 | 108 | 55 | 35 |

   How does this compare with what you would expect?
4. Does the multinomial distribution reduce to the binomial distribution when the number of classes $k = 2$?

# The t-Test

## 5-1 INTRODUCTION

In Chapters 5 through 8 we shall be learning how to make use of three important statistical models—the $t$-model, the $F$-model, and the $\chi^2$-model. From the experimenter's point of view, these models are useful for conducting *tests of significance*—the $t$-test (this chapter), the $F$-test (Chapters 6 and 7), and the $\chi^2$-test (Chapter 8).

We begin by discussing how to make use of the $t$-model. In general we wish to gain an understanding of the process of conducting a $t$-test on experimental data; we want to know how to perform the calculations with maximum efficiency; and we need to understand the theoretical foundations of the $t$-test.

This chapter is organized as follows. Section 5-2 considers Case 1, in which there is one measure for each of $n$ sample members. There is just one sample mean, $\overline{X}$, and the experimenter wishes to test the hypothesis that the population mean is some specified value, $\mu$. Section 5-3 considers Case 2, in which there are two measures per sample member (that is, an ordered two-tuple), and these measures are related in some way. The experimenter has two sample means, $\overline{X}$ and $\overline{Y}$, and he wishes to test the hypothesis that the difference between them is not significant. This is called the $t$-test for related measures. Section 5-4 considers Case 3, in which there are two independent samples. The experimenter has two sample means, $\overline{X}$ and $\overline{Y}$, and he wishes to test the hypothesis that the difference between them is not significant. This is called the $t$-test for independent measures. Section 5-5 considers some other applications of the $t$-model.

## 5-2 CASE 1: A SINGLE SAMPLE MEAN

### 5-21 An Example

An experimenter interested in reaction time devises the following experiment. A subject is required to stand erect on a small platform, and at the sound of a buzzer he must jump off the platform as fast as he can. As soon as the buzzer is sounded, an electric clock starts to record the time, and as soon as the subject jumps off the platform, the clock is switched off. The reading on the clock gives the jump reaction time. This measure is designated $RT_S$, reaction time to sound. After testing the reaction times of many college males, the experimenter reports that the mean jump reaction time to sound is 55.5 hundredths of a second.

An instructor in a laboratory course decides to replicate this experiment, making use of an available sample, namely, the 10 students in his course. For each of these 10 sample members he obtains a measure of $RT_S$ as follows:

| Subject | 1 | 2 | 3 | 4 | 5 | 6 | 7 | 8 | 9 | 10 |
|---------|---|---|---|---|---|---|---|---|---|----|
| $RT_S$* | 72 | 67 | 52 | 54 | 46 | 58 | 59 | 54 | 58 | 63 |

* In hundredths of a second.

## 5-22   Basic Calculations

As a matter of habit, the experimenter calculates the mean and the standard deviation of his data:

Mean $RT_S$:
$$\bar{X} = \frac{\sum_{i=1}^{10} X_i}{10} = 58.3$$

Standard deviation:
$$s_X = \sqrt{\frac{\sum X_i^2}{10} - \bar{X}^2} = 7.17$$

## 5-23   Making Use of the t-Model

The experimenter reported a mean of 55.5 hundredths of a second. The instructor obtained a sample mean of 58.3 hundredths of a second, and he wants to test the hypothesis that his mean is not significantly different from the reported mean.

The $t$-model involves three things: ($i$) a population assumption (that it is a ND($\mu,\sigma$)), ($ii$) a sampling-plan assumption (that it is an SIRS), and ($iii$) sampling distribution of a statistic $t$. In order to make use of the $t$-model, the instructor must decide whether he can accept the two basic assumptions—normality and SIRS. With respect to the population distribution of reaction times, $RT_S$, although he knows they can never be negative, he is prepared to believe that the distribution around the mean is essentially normal. His sample is simply an available sample, but again he feels there is no reason to believe it is biased in any peculiar way and so accepts the second assumption —an SIRS plan. In other words the instructor feels that the $t$-model describes the experimental setup adequately.

What about the two parameters of the normally distributed population? The mean is *hypothesized* to be 55.5. The standard deviation is *estimated* from the sample data. Referring to Section 4-34 and Equation (4-9), the experimenter estimates the population variance as follows:

$$\hat{s}_X^2 = \frac{\sum (X_i - \bar{X})^2}{(n - 1)} = 57.12$$

Hence $\qquad\qquad \hat{s}_X = 7.56$

Now for the one sample that is known to the instructor the data must be summarized in the form of a *t*-value. Thus, according to Equation (4-13),

$$t = \frac{(\bar{X} - \mu)}{\hat{s}/\sqrt{n}} = \frac{(58.3 - 55.5)}{7.56/\sqrt{10}} = 1.17$$

We are now ready to make use of the *t*-model. Figure 5-1 illustrates the total picture. Note that we are concerned here with a *t*-distribution with 9 degrees of freedom. The sampling plan calls for 10 independently and randomly chosen values, but we lose 1 degree of freedom for each parameter that is estimated from the sample data. Since we estimated the population variance $\sigma^2$, the *t*-distribution has $(10 - 1) = 9$ degrees of freedom. Note that we did not estimate $\mu$. The value of $\mu$ was hypothesized to be 55.5. Verbalizing Figure 5-1, we have the following situation:

| **Experimenter's knowledge** | **Statistician's *t*-model** |
|---|---|
| 1. Population | |
| Unknown except for rules for membership | $ND(\mu,\sigma)$, where $\mu = 55.5$ (hypothesized) and $\sigma = \hat{s}_X = 7.56$ (estimated) |
| 2. Sampling plan | |
| 10 available subjects | 10 values by **SIRS** |
| 3. Samples | |
| One sample of size 10 | Theoretically an infinite number of samples of size 10 |
| 4. Statistic | |
| One value of $t_9$: | Theoretically all values of $t_{(9)}$ |
| $t_{(9)} = 1.17$ | |

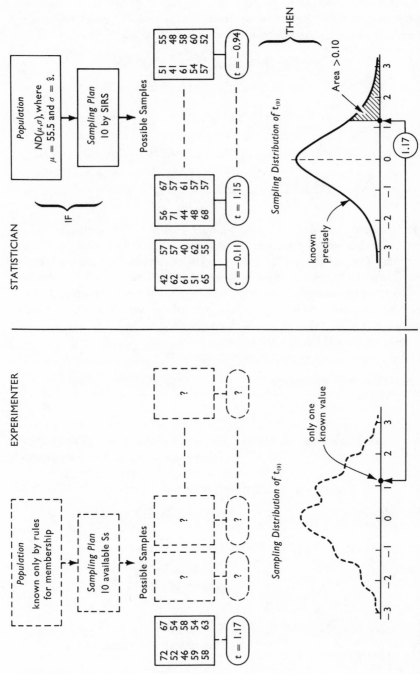

FIGURE 5-1. The use of the t-model: illustrated for the experiment involving reaction-time data (comparing a sample mean and a hypothesized mean)

### 5. Sampling distribution

Unknown                              Defined precisely as

$$f(t_9) = \frac{1}{\sqrt{9\pi}} \frac{\Gamma(5)}{\Gamma(4.5)} \left(1 + \frac{t^2}{9}\right)^{-5}$$

### 6. Question

What are the chances of getting $t_{(9)} \geq 1.17$ on this sampling distribution of $t_{(9)}$?

Looking up the $t$-tables in Appendix E, we find that the area to the right of $t_{(9)} = 1.17$ is more than 0.10. In other words, the chances of obtaining a $t$-value as large as 1.17 or larger are better than 1 in 10 under the conditions of the model. If the statistician did in fact obtain, say, 1,000 samples of size 10 and summarized each sample by means of the $t$-statistic, then more than 100 of these samples would yield $t$-values as large or larger than 1.17.

CONCLUSION. The instructor decides that his sample mean (58.3) does not differ significantly from the hypothesized mean (55.5), and he reports his findings as

$$t_{(9)} = 1.17 \qquad \text{(ns)}$$

where ns means not significant.

When does a $t$-value become significant? Usually the experimenter (or instructor, in this case) decides ahead of time what *significance level* to work with. By significance level we mean that probability (or area to the right under a $t$-distribution) which is small enough to make the experimenter begin to doubt the validity of the hypothesized mean. A common significance level in social science research is the *0.05 level*. If the probability of obtaining the sample $t$-value (or greater) is smaller than 0.05, then the experimenter will reject the hypothesized mean. In other words, when the probability of obtaining the sample $t$-value (or greater) is less than 5 in 100, the experimenter will begin to doubt whether the hypothesized mean can be accepted. His conclusion would then be that the sample mean and the hypothesized mean differ significantly beyond the 0.05 level, and he would report his findings as follows:

$$t_{(9)} = 2.80 \qquad (p < 0.05)$$

If the experimenter wishes to be more severe with himself, then he can decide to use the 0.01 level, and he will not say that a sample mean and hypothesized mean differ significantly unless $p < 0.01$.

### 5-24 Efficient Computation

As a general principle, it is more efficient to use the raw data than any transformation of it. In Case 1, where we have a single sample of size $n$ and therefore a single mean $\bar{X}$, all we need to do is to compute the two quantities $\sum X$ and $\sum X^2$. If we know these, we can easily compute

$$\bar{X} = \frac{\sum X}{n}$$

$$\hat{s}_X^2 = \frac{\sum X^2}{(n-1)} - \frac{(\sum X)^2}{n(n-1)} \tag{5-1}$$

and

$$t = \frac{(\bar{X} - \mu)}{\hat{s}_X/\sqrt{n}}$$

The instructor's problem can be handled as follows:

$$\sum X = 583 \quad \text{and} \quad \sum X^2 = 34{,}503$$

Therefore

$$\bar{X} = \frac{583}{10} = 58.3$$

$$\hat{s}_X^2 = \frac{34{,}503}{9} - \frac{(583)^2}{90}$$

$$= 57.12$$

$$\hat{s}_X = \sqrt{57.12} = 7.56$$

and

$$t_{(9)} = \frac{(58.3 - 55.5)}{7.56/\sqrt{10}} = 1.17$$

## 5-25  A Little Theory

STANDARD SCORE.  Consider $n$ numbers designated $X_1$ through $X_n$. Compute the mean $\bar{X}$ and the standard deviation $s_X$. Then if we want to convert one of the raw numbers, $X_i$, into its $z$-score form, we have

$$z_i = \frac{X_i - (\text{mean})}{(\text{standard deviation})} = \frac{X_i - \bar{X}}{s_X}$$

SAMPLING DISTRIBUTION OF A MEAN.  If we sample $n$ values by SIRS from $\text{ND}(\mu, \sigma)$, then the sampling distribution of the mean $\bar{X}$ is another normal distribution, with mean $= \mu$ and standard deviation $= \sigma/\sqrt{n}$. (See Sections 3-4 and 4-2.)

Now if we consider the complete set of means, designated $\bar{X}_1$, $\bar{X}_2$, $\bar{X}_3, \ldots, \bar{X}_n$, how may we convert any one of them (say, $\bar{X}_i$) into standard-score form? We simply subtract the mean (of the means), which is $\mu$, and divide by the standard deviation (of the means), which is $\sigma/\sqrt{n}$. Thus

$$z\text{-score for } \bar{X}_i = \frac{(\bar{X}_i - \mu)}{\sigma/\sqrt{n}} \tag{5-2}$$

The original set of means was distributed as $ND(\mu, \sigma/\sqrt{n})$. Thus the standardized means will be distributed as $ND(0,1)$.

SAMPLING DISTRIBUTION OF $t$.   The formula for $t$ is very much like that for standardizing a mean (above):

$$t = \frac{(\bar{X} - \mu)}{\hat{s}_X/\sqrt{n}} \tag{5-3}$$

Thus we should expect the sampling distribution of $t$ to be very much like that of the standardized means. This is the case. The only difference between Equations (5-2) and (5-3) is that the former makes use of the population parameter $\sigma$ and the latter the estimate $\hat{s}_X$. This estimate becomes better as the size of the sample increases; that is, as $n$ increases. Similarly, the sampling distribution of $t$ approximates the standard normal distribution, $ND(0,1)$, better as the sample size, $n$, increases. Alternatively, we say that the $t$-distribution approximates $ND(0,1)$ better as the degrees of freedom $(n - 1)$ increase.

## EXERCISES

(If you have not already done so, do the exercises for Section 4-5.)
1.  Consider the following two data sets:

> Set A $(n = 10)$:  5  5  6  5  4  5  5  6  4  5
> Set B $(n = 10)$:  4  5  6  3  4  5  6  7  4  5

(a) Compute the means for the two sets. Are they the same?
(b) Compute $s$ and $\hat{s}$ for each set. Are they the same?
(c) Compute the $t$-statistic when the population mean is hypothesized to be 6. Are the two $t$-values the same? If not, why not?
(d) Compute the mean, standard deviation, and $t$-value for a hypothesized population mean of 6 for this new data set:

> Set C $(n = 10)$:  3  4  5  6  7  3  4  5  6  7

(e) Thinking about the sampling fluctuation that would result when 10 values are sampled by SIRS from a normally distributed population, what would you say about the likelihood of getting sets of 10 values as indicated above?
2.  An experimenter is interested in the question of smoking behavior among college students. He believes that nonsmokers are more intelligent than normal and obtains a sample of 20 nonsmokers for his experiment. He obtains SAT-Math scores for these 20 sample members as follows:

> 598  627  673  559  631  650  562  373  512  564
> 668  753  583  619  596  527  460  585  582  352

Use the $t$-model to test the hypothesis that nonsmokers are not different from normal people (hypothesized mean = 500). Use a one-tailed test at the 0.05 level to see if the nonsmokers are more intelligent than normal people.
3.  Every year on the college campus thousands of students (male and female) go through rush week in an attempt to become pledged to a fraternity or sorority.

An experimenter believes that yea-sayers (those scoring high on the ARS—Agreement Response Scale) have a better chance of being pledged than nay-sayers (those scoring lower on the ARS). He obtains a sample of 15 women students who were just recently pledged and observes the following scores on the ARS:

55 45 44 57 65 39 58 51 66 65 51 69 64 47 57

(*a*) Compute the mean and standard deviation for these data.

(*b*) If the mean ARS score for women students is 54.5 (that is, the hypothesized population mean), test the hypothesis that these pledges are more yea-saying than usual.

(*c*) Draw a diagram for the experimenter's knowledge and the statistician's *t*-model for the experiment above. (Think carefully about rules for membership, $E$'s sampling plan as opposed to $S$'s sampling plan, $E$'s sample data as opposed to $S$'s potential knowledge, the parameters for $S$'s population, the particular *t*-distribution that is involved in this instance, and the scheme for rejecting the hypothesis of no difference.)

4. Consider the data used in Sections 5-21 to 5-24 (the reaction-time experiment), and follow this exercise through carefully.

(*a*) When we tested the observed mean (58.3 hundredths of a second) against a hypothesized mean (55.5), we found the difference to be not significant. What would the *t*-value have been if the hypothesized mean ($\mu$) had been (*i*) 55.0? (*ii*) 54.5? (*iii*) 54.0?

(*b*) If you succeeded with part (*a*), you noted that only the numerator in the equation for *t* has to be changed as we change the value of $\mu$. Working in reverse now, suppose that you have to compute the value of $\mu$ that will make the *t*-value (*i*) 2.0, (*ii*) 2.5, (*iii*) −1.0, (*iv*) −2.0. Do this.

(*c*) Now find the two values on the *t*-distribution with 9 df which cut off a total of 0.05 of the total area under the curve. We are thinking about values $t_L$ (lower value) and $t_U$ (upper value), where $t_L = -t_U$. The area to the right of $t_U$ is to be 0.025 and the area to the left of $t_L$ is to be 0.025, so that the sum of the areas in the two tails is 0.05. What are the values of $\mu$ that yield $t_L$ and $t_U$? Call these values $\mu_U$ and $\mu_L$, respectively.

(*d*) Refer now to Section 1-42 to verify that what you have just done is none other than the determination of the 95 percent confidence interval for the population parameter $\mu$.

5. Following Exercise 4, give the 90 percent confidence interval for the population mean reaction time to sound ($RT_S$).

## 5-3  CASE 2: THE *t*-TEST FOR RELATED MEASURES

### 5-31  An Example

An experimenter is interested in whether human beings respond more quickly to a sound signal than to a light signal? He is aware of physiological evidence that suggests that the answer is affirmative and decides to investigate the problem in connection with whole-body jumping, as in the example in Section 5-21. The apparatus consists of a jumping platform, a light source, a sound source, and an electric timer that records the reaction times to light or sound—$RT_L$ or $RT_S$. Rules for population membership are decided upon, and a sample of 10 subjects is selected in some stated manner. Each subject is made to jump in response to both the light source and the sound source, so that two measures, $RT_L$ and $RT_S$, are obtained for each subject. Clearly these two measures cannot be considered independent of each other. A heavy subject is likely to have a longer reaction time to both sound and light. An athletic subject is going to respond more quickly to both signals. The measures are related. We are dealing with an ordered two-tuple $(RT_S, RT_L)$ for each subject, where the order is a matter of arbitrary choice.

The results shown in Table 5-1 were obtained.

Table 5-1

| Subject | $RT_S{}^*$ | $RT_L{}^*$ | $(RT_L - RT_S)^*$ |
|---------|-----------|-----------|-------------------|
| 1 | 72 | 75 | 3 |
| 2 | 67 | 66 | −1 |
| 3 | 52 | 55 | 3 |
| 4 | 54 | 61 | 7 |
| 5 | 46 | 55 | 9 |
| 6 | 58 | 63 | 5 |
| 7 | 59 | 57 | −2 |
| 8 | 54 | 54 | 0 |
| 9 | 58 | 59 | 1 |
| 10 | 63 | 66 | 3 |

\* In hundredths of a second.

## 5-32 Basic Calculations

As a matter of habit, the experimenter calculates five statistics when his data consist of two measures per sample member (that is, ordered two-tuples.)

FOR REACTION TIMES TO SOUND $(RT_S)$

(1) $$\overline{S} = \frac{\sum S_i}{10} = 58.3$$

(2) $$s_S^2 = \frac{\sum S_i^2}{10} - (\overline{S})^2 = 51.41$$

Hence    $s_S = \sqrt{51.41} = 7.17.$

FOR REACTION TIMES TO LIGHT $(RT_L)$

(3) $\qquad \overline{L} = \dfrac{\sum L_i}{10} = 61.1$

(4) $\qquad s_L^2 = \dfrac{\sum L_i^2}{10} - (\overline{L})^2 = 39.09$

Hence $\quad s_L = \sqrt{30.09} = 6.25.$

CORRELATION BETWEEN $RT_S$ AND $RT_L$

(5) $\qquad r_{SL} = \dfrac{10(\sum [SL]) - (\sum S)(\sum L)}{\sqrt{10(\sum S^2) - (\sum S)^2}\,\sqrt{10(\sum L^2) - (\sum L)^2}} = 0.89$

This correlation coefficient gives some idea of the high degree of relatedness between the two measures.

## 5-33  Making Use of the *t*-Model

The experimenter has two means, $\overline{S} = 58.3$ and $\overline{L} = 61.1$, and he wants to know whether or not the difference between them is significant. He decides to test the hypothesis that there is no difference and calls this the null hypothesis, $H_0$. The alternative hypothesis, which he has reason to believe is more realistic, is that the mean jump reaction time to light should be longer than the mean jump reaction time to sound. He calls this hypothesis $H_1$.

Now, in order to test hypothesis $H_0$, the experimental situation must be put into the framework of a statistical model, in this case, the *t*-model. How shall we do this?

To start with, notice that the *t*-model handles only independent measures and the experimenter has related measures. If, however, for each subject a difference measure is obtained $(RT_L - RT_S)$, then the experimental data may be considered to be 10 independent difference measures. Then Case 2 (two related measures per sample member) is converted into Case 1 (a single sample) as follows:

Sample measures $(RT_L - RT_S)$: 3  −1  3  7  9  5  −2  0  1  3

Mean = 2.8

The whole problem may be rephrased as follows: The experimenter has one sample of size 10 and one sample mean, 2.8. He wishes to test a null hypothesis, $H_0$, which says that the population mean, $\mu$, is zero. The alternative hypothesis, $H_1$, says that the population mean is some positive value, not zero.

The *t*-model involves three things: (*i*) a population assumption (that it is $ND(\mu, \sigma)$), (*ii*) a sampling-plan assumption (that *n* values are selected by SIRS), and (*iii*) the sampling distribution of a statistic called *t*. The experimenter decides that the population of difference measures $(RT_L - RT_S)$ could well be normally distributed, and not knowing anything to the contrary, he accepts the SIRS assumption, too. What about the two parameters of the normally distributed population? The mean is hypothesized to be zero under $H_0$, and the variance, $\sigma^2$ is estimated from the sample data. If the sample data are now summarized in the form of a *t*-statistic, then we shall be dealing with a *t*-model with $(10 - 1) = 9$ degrees of freedom. Figure 5-1 can serve as the description of Case 2 as well as Case 1.

Designating the 10 difference measures as $D_1$ to $D_{10}$, we must make the following calculations—see Equations (5-1):

MEAN DIFFERENCE, $\bar{D}$

$$\bar{D} = \frac{\sum D_i}{10} = 2.8$$

ESTIMATED POPULATION VARIANCE, $\hat{s}_D^2$

$$\hat{s}_D^2 = \frac{\sum D_i^2}{9} - \frac{(\sum D_i)^2}{90} = 12.18$$

SAMPLE *t*-VALUE

$$t_{(9)} = \frac{(\bar{D} - \mu)}{\hat{s}_D/\sqrt{10}} = \frac{(2.8 - 0)}{\sqrt{12.18}/\sqrt{10}} = 2.54$$

We are now ready to make use of the *t*-model with 9 degrees of freedom. The model provides the sampling distribution of $t_{(9)}$, and the experimenter needs to find out what the chances are of obtaining a *t*-value such as $t_{(9)} = 2.54$. Looking up the *t*-tables (Appendix E), we find that the sample *t*-value, $t_{(9)} = 2.54$, falls between the 0.05 level and the 0.01 level. That is, if we repeatedly sample 10 values by SIRS from a normally distributed population (with mean zero and an estimated standard deviation 3.49) and summarize each sample by means of a *t*-value, then we expect that these *t* values will be as large as 2.54 or larger fewer than 5 times in 100 but more than 1 time in 100.

CONCLUSION.    Suppose that the experimenter had decided to work with the 0.05 level. Then his conclusion would be that the null hypothesis should be rejected, since $t_{(9)} = 2.54$ is significant beyond the 0.05 level:

$$t_{(9)} = 2.54 \qquad (p < 0.05).$$

In terms of the original problem, he would argue that the difference between the mean reaction time to sound and the mean reaction time to light is significant beyond the 0.05 level and that human beings do respond more quickly to sound than to light.

### 5-34 Efficient Computation

Consider $n$ sample members and two measures, $X$ and $Y$, on each member. The problem is to compute the following quantities efficiently: two means ($\bar{X}$ and $\bar{Y}$), two standard deviations ($s_X$ and $s_Y$), one correlation coefficient ($r_{XY}$), and the $t$-value for these related measures ($t_{n-1}$). The procedure is illustrated with the data from the example above.

For $n$ paired measures $(X_i, Y_i)$, for $i = 1, \ldots, n$, compute the following five basic quantities:

For the 10 paired measures $(S_i, L_i)$, for $i = 1, \ldots, 10$, compute:

(1)    $\sum X_i$          $\sum S_i = 583$

(2)    $\sum Y_i$          $\sum L_i = 611$

(3)    $\sum X_i^2$         $\sum S_i^2 = 34{,}503$

(4)    $\sum Y_i^2$         $\sum L_i^2 = 37{,}723$

(5)    $\sum (X_i Y_i)$       $\sum (S_i L_i) = 36{,}019$

All other computations are based on these five quantities.

#### 1. Two means

$$\bar{X} = \frac{\sum X_i}{n}$$

$$\bar{S} = \frac{583}{10} = 58.3$$

$$\bar{Y} = \frac{\sum Y_i}{n}$$

$$\bar{L} = \frac{611}{10} = 61.1$$

#### 2. Two standard deviations

$$s_X = \sqrt{\frac{\sum X^2}{n} - \bar{X}^2}$$

$$s_S = \sqrt{\frac{34{,}503}{10} - 58.3^2} = 7.17$$

$$s_Y = \sqrt{\frac{\sum Y^2}{n} - \bar{Y}^2}$$

$$s_L = \sqrt{\frac{37{,}723}{10} - 61.1^2} = 6.25$$

#### 3. Correlation coefficient

$$r_{XY} = \frac{n \sum XY - \sum X \sum Y}{\sqrt{n \sum X^2 - (\sum X)^2} \times \sqrt{n \sum Y^2 - (\sum Y)^2}}$$

$$r_{SL} = \frac{10(36{,}019) - (583)(611)}{\sqrt{5141}\,\sqrt{3909}}$$

$$= 0.89$$

### 4. The t-value

The $t$-value is computed from the difference measures:

$$D_i = (Y_i - X_i) \qquad\qquad D_i = (L_i - S_i)$$

and we need to know the sum of the differences and the sum of the squared differences:

$$\sum D = \sum Y - \sum X \qquad\qquad \sum D = 611 - 583 = 28$$

$$\sum D^2 = \sum Y^2 + \sum X^2 - 2 \sum XY \qquad \sum D^2 = 37{,}723 + 34{,}503$$

$$- 2(36{,}019)$$

$$= 188$$

Using these two quantities, we can compute the $t$-value by means of the following practical formula:

$$t_{(n-1)} = \frac{\sqrt{n-1} \sum D}{\sqrt{n \sum D - (\sum D)^2}} \qquad\qquad t_{(9)} = \frac{\sqrt{9}(28)}{\sqrt{10(188) - (28)(28)}}$$

$$= 2.54$$

If the experimenter is interested only in computing the $t$-value for a set of related measures on $n$ sample members, then the following flow chart summarizes an efficient computational procedure:

---

Read in $n$

---

Read in the data pairwise, $(X, Y)$, and compute
$D = Y - X$.
Cumulate the sum of the $D$'s, $\sum D$, and the sum of
squared $D$'s, $\sum D^2$.

---

Substitute in the formula

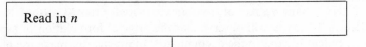

$$t_{(n-1)} = \frac{\sqrt{n-1} \sum D}{\sqrt{n \sum D^2 - (\sum D)^2}} \qquad (5\text{-}4)$$

to get the $t$-value with $(n-1)$ df.

## 5-35    A Little Theory

Since Case 2 (t-test for related measures) is in fact reduced to Case 1 (t-test for a single mean), the same theoretical notes apply to both cases. Reread Section 5-25. In this section we add some comments on the statistician's attitude to the t-statistic.

If the assumptions underlying the t-model are accepted (that is, the normality assumption and SIRS), then the statistician looks at the t-statistic as follows:

$$t = \frac{\text{(sample mean)} - \text{(hypothesized population mean)}}{\text{(independent estimate of standard error of means)}}$$

For simplicity suppose that the hypothesized population mean is zero. Then the numerator is simply one sample mean, and the denominator is an independent estimate of the standard error of the sample means. (Remember that "standard error" is another name for standard deviation of the sampling distribution.) Consider this standard error for a moment.

If we sample $n$ values from $ND(\mu,\sigma)$ by SIRS, then the sampling distribution of the sample means is $ND(\mu, \sigma/\sqrt{n})$. In other words, the standard error of the mean is $\sigma/\sqrt{n}$. When we use the t-model, the parameter $\sigma$ is not known. Hence we use $\hat{s}$ in place of $\sigma$. This gives us an estimate of the standard error—$\hat{s}/\sqrt{n}$. Two questions are of interest:

1. Is the numerator independent of the denominator? Is the sample mean $\bar{X}$ independent of the sample variance $s^2$ (or some function of it, like $\hat{s}/\sqrt{n}$)? The answer is affirmative.[1] In samples from a normal population, the sample mean and the sample variance are independent.

2. How many degrees of freedom are there for this t-statistic? Referring to Section 4-51, you will observe that the original formulation of $t$ involved $n$ independent squares in the denominator. In practice we make use of $\hat{s}$:

$$\hat{s} = \sqrt{\frac{\sum (X_i - \bar{X})^2}{(n - 1)}}$$

and although this summation is over the $n$ values of $X_i$ ($i = 1, 2, \ldots, n$), only $(n - 1)$ of the squares $(X_i - \bar{X})^2$ are independent. So we say that the estimate $\hat{s}$ is based on $(n - 1)$ independent squares, and hence the degrees of freedom for this t-statistic are $(n - 1)$.

### EXERCISES

1. Draw a diagram (experimenter's knowledge and statistician's model) for the example described in Section 5-3.

[1] M. G. Kendall and A. Stuart. *The advanced theory of statistics.* Vol. 1. New York. Hafner, 1958, p. 255.

2. A subject is seated in front of a visual field that is made to rotate very slowly. His task is to indicate when he just notices that the field is moving. The experimenter controls the speed of rotation (visual angle in seconds per second), and for each of six subjects he obtains two threshold measures for movement: (*i*) threshold for random black and white checks and (*ii*) checkerboard black and white checks. The results are as follows:

| Subject | 1 | 2 | 3 | 4 | 5 | 6 |
|---------|-----|-----|-----|----|-----|-----|
| (*i*)   | 81  | 90  | 107 | 56 | 78  | 100 |
| (*ii*)  | 89  | 110 | 141 | 68 | 121 | 130 |

For these data compute the *t*-statistic and the appropriate degrees of freedom. Test the hypothesis that the thresholds are significantly different for the two types of visual field (at the 0.01 level). Draw a diagram for this experiment.[2]

3. Ten hardy subjects participated in an experiment in which they were given increasingly painful electric shocks under two conditions: (*i*) vibration—concurrent vibratory stimulation—and (*ii*) nonvibration. The experimenter wanted to test a hunch that concurrent vibratory stimulation would increase the pain threshold (that is, make pain more bearable). The data were as follows:

| Subject | 1 | 2 | 3 | 4 | 5 | 6 | 7 | 8 | 9 | 10 |
|---------|------|------|------|------|------|------|------|------|------|------|
| Vibration | 98.2 | 71.7 | 78.6 | 87.0 | 61.0 | 83.8 | 80.3 | 88.2 | 77.8 | 72.2 |
| Nonvibration | 85.6 | 69.7 | 73.0 | 78.5 | 67.4 | 75.7 | 72.8 | 80.6 | 76.1 | 66.0 |

Define the null hypothesis, the alternative hypothesis, and the one-tail test of the experimenter's hunch, and draw a diagram of this experiment.[3]

4. Many standardized tests have several forms available so that the test may be administered at different times of the year to different (or the same) groups of subjects. The Miller Analogies Test has Forms K and T, and an experimenter is worried about practice effect for a subject who takes Form K and then within a year takes Form T. He decides to test his hypothesis that there is a practice effect (subjects are likely to improve if they take Form T within one year of taking Form K) and selects 16 subjects at random from the freshmen of a large state university, with the following results:

| Subject | 1 | 2 | 3 | 4 | 5 | 6 | 7 | 8 | 9 | 10 | 11 | 12 | 13 | 14 | 15 | 16 |
|---------|----|----|----|----|----|----|----|----|----|----|----|----|----|----|----|----|
| Form K | 60 | 24 | 61 | 38 | 27 | 42 | 39 | 51 | 48 | 43 | 38 | 45 | 33 | 31 | 39 | 52 |
| Form T | 70 | 21 | 62 | 45 | 23 | 48 | 45 | 61 | 59 | 57 | 46 | 44 | 40 | 34 | 53 | 54 |

[2] See N. F. Dixon. Effect of information content and size upon the absolute threshold for movement. *Perceptual Motor Skills*, 1967, **22**, 37–40.

[3] See B. Blitz et al. Attenuation of experimental pain by tactile stimulation. *Perceptual Motor Skills*, 1964, **19**, 311–316.

Perform a dependent *t*-test on these data, and see if the difference between the two means is significant at the 0.05 level. Draw a diagram for this experiment. In particular consider the assumptions of the *t*-model. Plot the differences (between scores on Forms K and T) in the form of a histogram, and ask yourself whether you are satisfied that the difference scores in the population could be assumed normally distributed.[4]

5. Attitudes may be changed experimentally. Consider a group of 15 pro-church people and a group of 15 neutral (as far as church is concerned) people. An experimenter asks each of these 30 subjects to read an anti-church paper to six friends and gets a measure of attitude change by administering a pre- and post-attitude test. The results are as follows:

Group I (pro-church)

| Subject | 1 | 2 | 3 | 4 | 5 | 6 | 7 | 8 | 9 | 10 | 11 | 12 | 13 | 14 | 15 |
|---|---|---|---|---|---|---|---|---|---|---|---|---|---|---|---|
| Pre- | 44 | 44 | 42 | 32 | 46 | 36 | 51 | 39 | 44 | 36 | 36 | 40 | 48 | 38 | 38 |
| Post- | 43 | 42 | 53 | 37 | 48 | 26 | 57 | 40 | 48 | 36 | 45 | 42 | 49 | 42 | 40 |

Group II (neutral)

| Subject | 1 | 2 | 3 | 4 | 5 | 6 | 7 | 8 | 9 | 10 | 11 | 12 | 13 | 14 | 15 |
|---|---|---|---|---|---|---|---|---|---|---|---|---|---|---|---|
| Pre- | 66 | 70 | 63 | 70 | 59 | 59 | 69 | 55 | 59 | 73 | 64 | 62 | 68 | 56 | 68 |
| Post- | 85 | 75 | 64 | 78 | 72 | 58 | 83 | 45 | 51 | 81 | 77 | 74 | 74 | 61 | 86 |

By inspection it is clear that the neutral group scores higher on the pre-attitude test scores, but we are interested in change. Perform a *t*-test for Group I to see if pro-church people changed their attitudes significantly (use the 0.05 level), and repeat the process for Group II. Can you reach a conclusion about which group changes most? Check the distribution of difference scores for each group separately to see if the assumption of normality is reasonable. Examine the mean and standard deviation of the difference scores for Groups I and II and state verbally what they indicate.[5]

6. The United States Navy is interested in the effects of nitrogen narcosis on performance of divers. An experiment was conducted to see if increased partial pressure of nitrogen (equivalent to 100 ft of seawater) impairs conceptual reasoning as measured by time taken to solve problems (taken from a problem-solving test). The data in Table 5-2 were obtained for 20 subjects.

Determine the two means, two standard deviations, correlation coefficient, mean of the difference scores, standard deviation of the difference scores, standard error of the mean difference, and *t*-value for these data. Does nitrogen narcosis affect conceptual reasoning adversely?[6]

[4] See R. G. Lane et al. Miller Analogies Test: A note on permissive retesting. *Journal of Applied Psychology*, 1966, **50**, 409–411.

[5] See E. McGinnies et al. Level of initial attitude, active rehearsal and instructional set as factors in attitude change. *Journal of Abnormal and Social Psychology*, 1964, **69**, 437–440.

[6] See R. J. Kissling. Performance impairment in nitrogen narcosis. *Journal of Applied Psychology*, 1962, **46**, 91–95.

Table 5-2

| Subject | Sea level* | 100 ft below* |
|---------|-----------|---------------|
| 1 | 6.2 | 7.5 |
| 2 | 7.9 | 8.8 |
| 3 | 5.5 | 12.2 |
| 4 | 5.4 | 9.5 |
| 5 | 5.4 | 9.9 |
| 6 | 5.0 | 4.0 |
| 7 | 8.0 | 13.8 |
| 8 | 4.8 | 7.5 |
| 9 | 10.3 | 16.4 |
| 10 | 8.3 | 10.8 |
| 11 | 7.2 | 9.0 |
| 12 | 8.2 | 6.7 |
| 13 | 6.8 | 12.3 |
| 14 | 9.7 | 7.8 |
| 15 | 9.6 | 12.9 |
| 16 | 9.0 | 14.5 |
| 17 | 8.4 | 9.3 |
| 18 | 8.4 | 11.9 |
| 19 | 6.7 | 10.2 |
| 20 | 8.6 | 9.2 |

\* In seconds per problem.

## 5-4   CASE 3: THE t-TEST FOR INDEPENDENT MEASURES

At the outset it should be pointed out that this case of the t-test can be handled as a special case of the F-test described in Chapter 6. This fact will be demonstrated later.

### 5-41   An Example

Instead of making use of another example, we shall use the data from Section 5-31 in a new context. The experimenter is still interested in the question of whether human beings jump more quickly in response to a sound or to a light. However, instead of choosing just one sample of size 10 and measuring each member under both conditions (light and sound), he now chooses two independent samples of size 10 each, using one sample to obtain 10 measures of $RT_S$ and the other to obtain 10 measures of $RT_L$. In other words, he chooses 20 subjects and uses 10 under the "sound" condition and 10 under the "light" condition. The measures are now unrelated. We do not have ordered two-tuples. For ease of reference the 10 measures of $RT_S$ will constitute Sample 1, and the 10 measures of $RT_L$ will constitute Sample 2. To make it quite clear that the 20 measures are in no way related to each other, we present the data from Section 5-31 in scrambled order as follows:

SAMPLE 1. Ten measures of $RT_S$ in hundredths of a second:

$$52 \quad 58 \quad 58 \quad 63 \quad 67 \quad 72 \quad 46 \quad 54 \quad 59 \quad 54$$

SAMPLE 2. Ten measures of $RT_L$ in hundredths of a second:

$$75 \quad 55 \quad 55 \quad 57 \quad 59 \quad 66 \quad 61 \quad 63 \quad 54 \quad 66$$

## 5-42 Basic Calculations

Mean reaction time to a sound signal $= \overline{S} = 58.3$
Mean reaction time to a light signal $= \overline{L} = 61.1$
Standard deviation of $RT_S$ measures $= s_S = 7.17$
Standard deviation of $RT_L$ measures $= s_L = 6.25$

(Note that there is no correlation coefficient, because the data are in no way paired.)

## 5-43 Making Use of the *t*-Model

The experimenter has two means, $\overline{S} = 58.3$ and $\overline{L} = 61.1$, and he wants to know whether the difference between them is significant or not. He decides to test the hypothesis that there is no difference and calls this the null hypothesis, $H_0$. His alternative hypothesis is $H_1$—that the mean jump reaction time to light is greater than the mean jump reaction time to sound.

How do we put this experimental situation into the framework of a *t*-model? First the assumptions underlying the *t*-model must be accepted. Under the null hypothesis we assume that the sampled values come from normal distributions having the same mean and the same variance, which is another way of saying that the population of reaction times, whether to light or sound, is assumed to be normally distributed. Furthermore, we assume that the two sets of 10 measures are drawn from this population by SIRS.

What about the two parameters, $\mu$ and $\sigma$, of the population? Well, whatever $\mu$ is, it is the same when we select Sample 1 as when we select Sample 2. The two samples are drawn from the same population under the null hypothesis, $H_0$. Thus we expect that the difference between Sample 1's mean and Sample 2's mean would be zero in the long run. But, of course, in any particular instance there might well be a difference between the two means. The question is how likely is such a difference under the null hypothesis.

There are two ways to estimate $\sigma$. We could use the data from Sample 1 and find $\hat{s}_S^2$, an unbiased estimate of $\sigma^2$. We could use the data from Sample 2 and find $\hat{s}_L^2$, an unbiased estimate of the same parameter, $\sigma^2$. Thus

$$\hat{s}_S^2 = 57.12 \quad \text{and} \quad \hat{s}_L^2 = 43.43$$

Which of these two values should we use as the estimate of $\sigma^2$? Neither. It is better to compute a *pooled estimate* of the population variance, according to the following formula:

$$\hat{s}^2 = \frac{(n_1 s_S^2 + n_2 s_L^2)}{(n_1 + n_2 - 2)} \tag{5-5}$$

where $n_1$ is the number of members in Sample 1 and $n_2$ is the number of members in Sample 2. The denominator expresses the degrees of freedom for the pooled estimate. There are $(n_1 + n_2)$ independently and randomly drawn sample values from the population. In order to compute $s_S^2$, we have to use the sample mean, $\overline{S}$, and this means that there are only $(n_1 - 1)$ independent squares of the form $(S_i - \overline{S})^2$. Similarly, in the case of $s_L^2$ there are only $(n_2 - 1)$ independent squares of the form $(L_j - \overline{L})^2$. Thus, altogether we are using $[(n_1 - 1) + (n_2 - 1)]$ independent squares in the estimation of the population variance. Hence there are $(n_1 + n_2 - 2)$ df.

Using Equation (5-5), we compute the pooled estimate of $\sigma^2$:

$$\hat{s}^2 = \frac{10(7.17)^2 + 10(6.25)^2}{(10 + 10 - 2)} = 50.28$$

Now in the computation of the *t*-statistic we deal with a formula of the following kind:

$$t = \frac{\text{(difference between means)} - \text{(hypothetical difference)}}{\text{(standard error of difference between means)}}$$

In order to determine the denominator here, we have to know something about the sampling distribution of the difference between two independent means. (Remember for the case of one mean the standard error of the sample mean was estimated as $\hat{s}/\sqrt{n}$. We need the equivalent form for the standard error estimate for differences between means.) Leaving the details to Section 5-45, we have the correct formula as

$$\text{se}_{(\overline{X}-\overline{Y})} = \hat{s}\sqrt{\frac{1}{n_1} + \frac{1}{n_2}}$$

$$= \sqrt{50.28}\sqrt{\tfrac{1}{10} + \tfrac{1}{10}} = 3.171$$

We are now in a position to define the (independent) *t*-statistic:

$$t_{(n_1+n_2-2)} = \frac{(\overline{X} - \overline{Y}) - \text{(hypothesized value)}}{\hat{s}\sqrt{1/n_1 + 1/n_2}} \tag{5-6}$$

In terms of the experimental problem,

$$t_{(10+10-2)} = \frac{(61.1 - 58.3) - (0)}{3.171} = 0.88$$

We are now ready to make use of the *t*-model with 18 degrees of freedom. Figure 5-2 illustrates the situation, and we verbalize the diagram on p. 149.

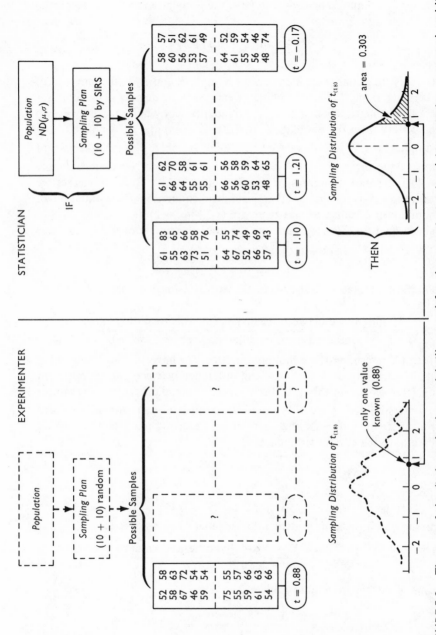

FIGURE 5-2. The use of the (independent) t-model: illustrated for the experiment involving reaction to sound and light (comparing two sample means)

| Experimenter's knowledge | Statistician's t-model |
|---|---|

## 1. Population

Unknown except for rules for membership

$ND(\mu,\sigma)$, where $\mu$ is of no consequence under $H_0$ and $\sigma$ = pooled estimate $\hat{s} = 7.09$

## 2. Sampling plan

20 available subjects split into two groups of 10

10 values by SIRS for Sample 1
10 values by SIRS for Sample 2

## 3. Samples

Two samples of size 10 each

Theoretically an infinite number of two-sample sets

## 4. Statistic

One value of $t_{(18)}$:

$$t_{(18)} = 0.88$$

Theoretically all values of $t_{(18)}$ defined according to Equation (5-6)

## 5. Sampling distribution

Unknown

Defined precisely as

$$f(t_{(18)}) = \frac{1}{\sqrt{18\pi}} \frac{\Gamma(9.5)}{\Gamma(9)} \left(1 + \frac{t}{18}\right)^{-19/2}$$

## 6. Question

What are the chances of getting $t_{(18)} \geq 0.88$ on this sampling distribution of $t_{(18)}$?

Looking up the t-tables in Appendix E, we find that the area to the right of $t_{(18)} = 0.88$ is obviously much larger than 0.05. Since the tables do not give enough values, we cannot say more than this, but you will note in Figure 5-2 that the exact area is given. This exact area was computed along with the simulated data that make up the statistician's side of Figure 5-2. Thus, in terms of the experimental problem, we can say that, *if* we accept a normally distributed population and *if* we think of the two samples as having been drawn from this normal population by SIRS, *then* the sampling distribution of the t-statistic with 18 df shows that the observed value of $t = 0.88$ falls well within the 0.05 acceptance region. For a one-tail test the 0.05 rejection region would be beyond $t = 1.734$.

CONCLUSION. The experimenter decides that the two sample means, $\bar{S}$ and $\bar{L}$ do not differ significantly, and he would report his test findings as follows:

$$t_{(18)} = 0.88 \qquad \text{(ns)}$$

In terms of the original problem, the experimenter would argue that the difference between $\bar{S} = 58.3$ and $\bar{L} = 61.1$ can easily be explained as sampling fluctuation under the null hypothesis and the $t$-model.

COMMENT. Note the following important fact: The data in Section 5-4 are the same as those in Section 5-3. The conditions of the experiment were different, however. When the 20 measures are considered as 10 ordered two-tuples (that is, dependent measures), $t_{(9)} = 2.54$ and is significant at the 0.05 level. When the measures are considered as two independent sets of 10 measures, $t_{(18)} = 0.88$ and is not significant. Clearly it is important to determine which test is appropriate for a particular experimental problem, since the use of an inappropriate test can lead to different conclusions. When you use the $t$-test, always state whether it is the $t$-test for dependent (or correlated) means or the $t$-test for independent means.

## 5-44   Efficient Computation

The general case is as follows: Draw $n_1$ values by SIRS from $ND(\mu,\sigma)$, and designate them $X_1$ to $X_{n_1}$. Draw $n_2$ values by SIRS from the same $ND(\mu,\sigma)$, and designate them $Y_1$ through $Y_{n_2}$. These $(n_1 + n_2)$ values have to be summarized according to the formula for $t$:

$$t_{(n_1+n_2-2)} = \frac{(\bar{X} - \bar{Y}) - (\text{expected value})}{\sqrt{\left[\frac{(n_1 s_X^2 + n_2 s_Y^2)}{(n_1 + n_2 - 2)}\right]\left(\frac{1}{n_1} + \frac{1}{n_2}\right)}} \tag{5-7}$$

An efficient computational procedure is given below and is illustrated with the data from Section 5-41.

Compute the following four basic quantities:

|     |              |                  |
|-----|--------------|------------------|
| (1) | $\sum X$     | $\sum S = 583$   |
| (2) | $\sum Y$     | $\sum L = 611$   |
| (3) | $\sum X^2$   | $\sum S^2 = 34{,}503$ |
| (4) | $\sum Y^2$   | $\sum L^2 = 37{,}723$ |

Then    $n_1 s_X^2 = \sum X^2 - \dfrac{(\sum X)^2}{n_1}$                $n_1 s_S^2 = 34{,}503 - \dfrac{(583)^2}{10}$

$\qquad\qquad\quad = A$                                      $\qquad\qquad = 514.1$

$\qquad n_2 s_Y^2 = \sum Y^2 - \dfrac{(\sum Y)^2}{n_2}$                $n_2 s_L^2 = 37{,}723 - \dfrac{(611)^2}{10}$

$\qquad\qquad\quad = B$                                      $\qquad\qquad = 390.9$

and

$$t = \frac{\sqrt{n_1 n_2 (n_1 + n_2 - 2)}(\bar{X} - \bar{Y})}{\sqrt{(n_1 + n_2)(A + B)}} \qquad\qquad t_{(18)} = \frac{\sqrt{100(18)}\,(2.8)}{\sqrt{20(514.1 + 390.9)}}$$

$$= 0.88$$

If a computer is going to be called upon to perform the computations, then the following flow chart summarizes an efficient procedure:

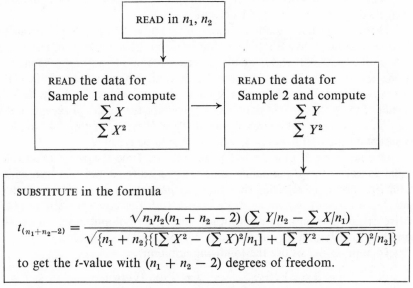

SUBSTITUTE in the formula

$$t_{(n_1+n_2-2)} = \frac{\sqrt{n_1 n_2(n_1 + n_2 - 2)}\, (\sum Y/n_2 - \sum X/n_1)}{\sqrt{\{n_1 + n_2\}\{[\sum X^2 - (\sum X)^2/n_1] + [\sum Y^2 - (\sum Y)^2/n_2]\}}}$$

to get the *t*-value with $(n_1 + n_2 - 2)$ degrees of freedom.

COMMENT. Although we have just indicated how the value of *t* may be computed most efficiently, it is to be emphasized that the *t*-statistic is merely a summary number. As such it does not describe all aspects of the experimental data. In fact, the only reason *t* is computed at all is that there is a statistical model for *t*. Therefore, you should develop the habit of computing all the appropriate statistics (summary numbers) for your experimental data. In the case of two samples of data that are independent, you should compute (*i*) two means, (*ii*) two standard deviations (preferably the estimates, $\hat{s}$), (*iii*) the difference between the two means, and if you plan to do a *t*-test, (*iv*) the pooled estimate of the population variance (or standard deviation), (*v*) the standard error of the difference between means, and (*vi*) the *t*-statistic.

### 5-45 A Little Theory

By now you should have performed several tests of significance. The typical procedure is to adopt a statistical model (the *t*-model in this chapter), estimate or hypothesize the population parameters, and then test to see if the value of the experimentally derived statistic could occur reasonably within the framework of the model. By reasonably we mean allowing for sampling fluctuation, and to make this concept precise, we typically choose the 0.05 level as the boundary between reasonable and unreasonable. In other words, when the probability of getting a value of the statistic under the assumptions of the model is less than 0.05, we reject the model. Now, what are we saying here? We are rejecting the model if it tells us that it is true with probability 0.05 or less. In other words, we are taking a risk. The risk is 0.05, or 5 percent, that we may be rejecting the null hypothesis when it is, in fact, true. This risk is known as *Type I error*. If we are working with the 0.01 level, then the Type 1 error is 1 percent.

There is a reverse argument as well. *If* we know the sampling distribution of some alternative hypothesis (an alternative to the hypothesis of the model —the null hypothesis) and *if* we do not reject the null hypothesis, we may be taking another risk. This risk is that the alternative hypothesis is, in fact, the true one. What we really have to know to determine this risk is the area in the tail of the alternative hypothesis that overlaps the region of acceptance of the null hypothesis. This area is called *Type II error*, or the risk involved in accepting the null hypothesis when it should be rejected.

One more bit of philosophy! If we call this Type II error $\beta$ (a conventional name), then we can define something called the *power* of a test, which is the probability of rejecting the null hypothesis when it should be rejected, and this is $(1 - \beta)$. Again we cannot work with this concept until an alternative hypothesis has been proposed and, more importantly, until the sampling distribution for the alternative hypothesis is available.

To sum up, let us use the following notation:

$$\alpha = \text{Type I error} \qquad \beta = \text{Type II error}$$
$$H_0 = \text{null hypothesis} \qquad H_1 = \text{alternative hypothesis}$$

Then
$$\alpha = \text{probability of rejecting } H_0 \text{ when } H_0 \text{ is true}$$
$$\beta = \text{probability of accepting } H_0 \text{ when } H_1 \text{ is true}$$
$$\beta = \text{probability of rejecting } H_1 \text{ when } H_1 \text{ is true}$$
$$1 - \beta = \text{power of the statistical test}$$

It is perhaps fortunate that the reason for studying statistics is that we have to settle for uncertain knowledge. With reference to the paragraphs above it may be remarked that since the "true" hypothesis is forever unknown, the experimenter can usually settle for an understanding of Type I error alone, and this means knowing about significance level. Thus, $\alpha$ is the familiar 0.05 level.

THE STANDARD ERROR OF A DIFFERENCE BETWEEN MEANS.    Consider two random variables $X$ and $Y$ with means $\mu_X$ and $\mu_Y$ and with variances $\sigma_X^2$ and $\sigma_Y^2$, respectively. Then if we consider choosing $n_1$ values from $X$ and $n_2$ values from $Y$ by SIRS, we know that the sampling distributions of $\bar{X}$ and $\bar{Y}$ (the sample means) will have means $\mu_X$ and $\mu_Y$ and variances $\sigma_X^2/n_1$ and $\sigma_Y^2/n_2$ respectively. Now consider the sampling distribution of $(\bar{X} - \bar{Y})$. First note that the variance of a sum is the sum of the variances when the variables are independent:

$$V_{(X+Y)} = V_X + V_Y \qquad \text{if } X \text{ and } Y \text{ are independent}$$

We can prove this by casting it the form of covariances:

$$V_{(X+Y)} = C_{(X+Y)(X+Y)} = C_{(XX+2XY+YY)} = C_{XX} + C_{YY} + 2C_{XY}$$
$$= V_X + V_Y + 0$$

Using the same procedure, can you prove that $V_{(X-Y)} = V_X + V_Y$ when $X$ and $Y$ are independent? Using this relationship, we can state that

$$V_{(\bar{X}-\bar{Y})} = V_{\bar{X}} + V_{\bar{Y}} \qquad \text{since } \bar{X} \text{ and } \bar{Y} \text{ are independent}$$
$$= \frac{\sigma_X^2}{n_1} + \frac{\sigma_Y^2}{n_2}$$

Now it is possible to conceive of a *t*-model for two independent samples where the null hypothesis says that the means are the same but that the variances need not be the same. Until now we have assumed that $\sigma_X^2$ and $\sigma_Y^2$ were identical. This is the equal-variance assumption. When we allow them to be different, we are making the unequal-variance assumption. Consider these two cases in turn.

UNEQUAL-VARIANCE ASSUMPTION.   The best estimate of $V_{(\bar{X}-\bar{Y})}$ for this case involves replacing $\sigma_X^2$ by $\hat{s}_X^2$ and $\sigma_Y^2$ by $\hat{s}_Y^2$ in the equation above. The only problem that remains concerns how many degrees of freedom are involved. A rather unpleasant formula is suggested for this:

$$df = \frac{1}{\left[\dfrac{k^2}{n_1 - 1} + \dfrac{(1 - k)^2}{n_2 - 1}\right]}$$

where

$$k = \frac{\hat{s}_X^2/n_1}{\hat{s}_X^2/n_1 + \hat{s}_Y^2/n_2}$$

In general, this formula will not give an integer value for degrees of freedom.

EQUAL-VARIANCE ASSUMPTION.   We replace $\sigma_X^2$ and $\sigma_Y^2$ with $\sigma^2$ and estimate this single population parameter using the pooled estimate $\hat{s}^2$. This assumption gives

$$V_{(\bar{X}-\bar{Y})} = \frac{\sigma^2}{n_1} + \frac{\sigma^2}{n_2} = \sigma^2\left(\frac{1}{n_1} + \frac{1}{n_2}\right)$$

and the estimate is

$$\hat{s}^2\left(\frac{1}{n_1} + \frac{1}{n_2}\right)$$

This is the form in which the standard error for the difference between means appears in Equation (5-6).

## EXERCISES

1. Consider the data in Exercise 5, Section 5-3. Obtain two sets of difference scores (one for the pro-church group and the other for the neutral group), and perform an independent $t$-test to see if the neutral group had greater attitude change than the pro-church group.
2. Referring to Exercise 3, Section 5-2, here are data concerning men students from two groups, rushees and nonrushees:

Rushees ($n_1 = 15$):  67  49  65  60  52  63  64  49  56  37  63  55  42
45  53

Nonrushees  ($n_2 = 20$):  47  54  62  53  45  68  58  67  53  38  50  52
42  66  41  51  51  49  56  50

Compute two means, two standard deviations, the difference between the two means, the standard error of the difference between means, and the independent $t$-statistic, and look in Appendix E to find the 0.05 and 0.01 levels for the $t$-distribution with the proper degrees of freedom. Test the significance of the difference between the means, and reach a conclusion about yea-sayers versus nay-sayers with respect to rushees versus nonrushees.[7]
3. It is conjectured that if a student-teacher's grade depends upon the improvement shown by his pupils while they are under his tutelage, then that teacher will do a better job of teaching. Two groups of student-teachers were obtained—one group whose grades depended on the grades of the students being taught, the other group a control group—and the differences between a pre- and post-test given to their pupils were as follows:

Experimental  ($n_1 = 20$):  9  9  3   3  13  9  12  1  0  31  4  1  13  12
2  4  9  14  19  10

Control ($n_2 = 30$):  0  2  10  $-2$   9   5   1  $-10$  16  $-3$  8  12  19
18  22  8   4  $-6$  $-6$  $-2$   0   3  $-8$  4  $-6$  $-9$
$-1$  20  6  17

Draw a diagram showing the use of the independent $t$-test for this experiment. Do the experimental teachers get better performance out of their students than the control teachers? Perform the independent $t$-test, and report your conclusions as you would for a journal article.[8]
4. An attempt to discriminate between delinquents and nondelinquents using the scores on the Ego Scale of the Arrow Dot Test produced the following results:

Delinquents  ($n_1 = 15$):  19  17  16  21  16  14  18  20  21  22  15  16
18  16  16

Nondelinquents ($n_2 = 14$):  20  21  22  21  29  20  21  17  18  16  18
21  17  14

Is there a significant difference between the means for these two groups on the Ego Scale of the Arrow Dot Test?[9]

[7] See I. Mahler. Yea-sayers and nay-sayers: A validating study. *Journal of Abnormal and Social Psychology*, 1962, **64**, 317–318.

[8] See M. C. Wittrock, Set applied to student teaching. *Journal of Educational Psychology*, 1962, **53**, 175–180.

[9] See R. J. Rankin and R. L. Wikoff. The IES Arrow Dot performance of delinquents and nondelinquents. *Perceptual and Motor Skills*, 1964, **18**, 207–210.

5. An experimenter developed a questionnaire that purported to measure "orality" on the basis of responses to food preference questions. In order to validate his questionnaire, he needed a group of subjects known to have high indices of "orality," and for this group he chose alcoholics. A second group of ordinary people served as a control group. These two groups provided the following data:

Alcoholics ($n_1 = 15$):   26   18   24   28   26   26   18   20   29   26   21   19
                            32   24   16
Normals   ($n_2 = 15$):   24   10   19   15   21   18   16   9   17   20   22   13   23
                          18   17

Draw a diagram, and perform an independent $t$-test to see if the experimenter's questionnaire was validated.[10]

6. In the following references check the assumptions of the $t$-model with particular reference to those indicated here.

   (a) Consider the paper "Ethnic and sex factors in classroom responsiveness" by S. Hutchinson et al. in *Journal of Social Psychology*, 1966, **69**, 321–325. How skewed is the distribution of responses if 55 out of 119 subjects gave no response and 77 percent of these no-response measures were within one group?

   (b) Consider the validity of the assumption of SIRS sampling in the study "Generality of response intensity following nonreinforcement" by G. Levine and R. Loesch in *Journal of Experimental Psychology*, 1967, **75**, 97–102.

   (c) In the study "Sequential patterns and maximizing" by C. R. Peterson and Z. J. Ulehla in *Journal of Experimental Psychology*, 1965, **69**, 1–4, what are the appropriate degrees of freedom for their $t$-test?

   (d) If your measure is mean recognition time for ambiguous pictures, what would you do if some subjects give up after trying to identify an object for a long time? What kind of distribution do you expect with mean recognition times? Can mean recognition times be negative? Consider these questions in conjunction with the paper "Concepts of set and availability and their relation to the reorganization of ambiguous pictorial stimuli" by G. J. Steinfeld in *Psychological Review*, 1967, **74**, 505–522, especially p. 518.

----

[10] See H. M. Wolowitz. Food preferences as an index of orality. *Journal of Abnormal and Social Psychology*, 1964, **69**, 650–654.

# The F-Test:
# One-way Analysis
# of Variance

## 6-1 INTRODUCTION

The reader should review Section 4-6 as an introduction to this chapter. The $F$-model, like the $t$-model, involves two basic assumptions: a normally distributed population and an SIRS plan. The $F$-statistic is defined as the ratio of two variance estimates, and these two estimates are independent of each other. Therefore, if an experimenter wishes to make use of the $F$-distribution, he has to satisfy himself that the population assumption (normally distributed) and the sampling-plan assumption (SIRS) are reasonable in the context of his experiment. When he comes to compute an $F$-statistic as a summary of his data, if he knows that the variance ratio involves variance estimates that are not independent, then he must reduce the degrees of freedom in the numerator and denominator until the estimates can be considered independent. A little practice in the use of the $F$-test will enable you to join a vast number of experimenters who like to use the $F$-model as the basis for reaching experimental conclusions.

1. If you obtain one sample mean and wish to test the hypothesis that the population mean is some specific value, then you might use the $t$-test.

2. If you obtain two sample means based on related measures, then you might use the $t$-test to test the hypothesis that the two means are not significantly different.

3. If you obtain two sample means based on independent measures, then you might use the $t$-test to test the hypothesis that the two means are not significantly different. (In this case you might also use the $F$-test, as we shall see in this chapter.)

4. If you obtain more than two sample means based on related measures, then you might take two means at a time and use a $t$-test to test the significance of the difference between the pair of means. In this circumstance you should

not think of the $F$-test, because the measures must be independent for the $F$-model to apply. (There is an exception to this statement that is accepted in practice—the *repeated-measures design*—but it will not be treated in this text, and the author urges you stay with the formal $F$-model until you are thoroughly familiar with it. At a later stage you might want to learn how to proceed when the requirements of the $F$-model are violated in certain respects.)

5. If you obtain more than two sample means based on independent measures, then you might take two means at a time and use a $t$-test for each pair. (This is known as *multiple t-testing*.) It is in this particular situation, however, that the $F$-test becomes most useful. In fact, if you have two or more sample means based on independent measures, then you might consider using the $F$-test to test the significance of the differences among all the means at once.

By way of illustration, suppose that an experimenter measured the jump reaction time to sound, $RT_S$, on each member of the following groups: (*i*) 25 boys age ten, (*ii*) 33 girls age ten, (*iii*) 17 men age thirty, and (*iv*) 21 women age thirty. He obtains four means: 57.1, 60.8, 58.2, and 63.4 hundredths of a second for groups *i*, *ii*, *iii*, and *iv*, respectively. He wants to know whether these differences are significant or not. The four groups of measures are independent of one another, so that he could apply multiple $t$-tests for independent measures as follows:

1. Test the difference between 57.1 and 60.8.
2. Test the difference between 57.1 and 58.2.
3. Test the difference between 57.1 and 63.4.
4. Test the difference between 60.8 and 58.2.
5. Test the difference between 60.8 and 63.4.
6. Test the difference between 58.2 and 63.4.

In other words, if we have four means, then there will be $(4 \times 3)/2 = 6$ separate $t$-tests. (If we have seven means, there will be $(7 \times 6)/2 = 21$ separate $t$-tests.)

In this situation it is appropriate to apply one $F$-test to test the significance of the differences among the four means. The experimenter summarizes his data—all the data for all four groups—in the form of one summary number, the $F$-statistic. In cooperation with a statistician, the appropriate $F$-model is examined, and the sampling distribution of the $F$-statistic yields the probability of obtaining an $F$-value such as the experimental $F$-value (or larger). If this probability is, say, less than 0.05, the experimenter concludes that the four means differ significantly. After obtaining a significant $F$-value, the experimenter might wish to perform a few $t$-tests to determine which of the four means differ significantly from which others.

If the experimental $F$-value turns out to be nonsignificant, then it is often advisable not to pursue separate $t$-tests. This is largely a matter of personal preference. In the opinion of this author, no harm is done if separate *t*-tests are applied after a nonsignificant *F*-value is obtained, as long as the assumptions underlying the *t*-test are acceptable to the experimenter for each such *t*-test.

We now turn to what is known as the *one-way analysis of variance*, which involves a simple use of the *F*-model. As the name suggests, we shall examine variance, and this is clearly appropriate when we are dealing with the *F*-statistic, which is a ratio of two variances. The word "one-way" implies one set of means. In Chapter 7 we shall consider *two-way analysis of variance*, in which there is more than one set of means.

## 6-2 ONE-WAY ANALYSIS OF VARIANCE

### 6-21 An Example

An experimenter has a hunch that performance is influenced by the amount of reward given. He designs an experiment[1] to examine this hunch.

POPULATION. The following explicit rules for membership are defined: (*i*) A member must be a male albino rat. (*ii*) A member must be naive with respect to the experimental situation. (*iii*) A member must be between 90 and 110 days old at the start of the experiment.

SAMPLE. An available sample of 15 rats (satisfying the rules for membership) is divided into three groups of five each. (Note, however, that one-way analysis of variance does not require equal numbers in each group.)

PERFORMANCE. The experimenter defines performance as the number of bar presses per minute in a Skinner Box. This constitutes the dependent measure.

REWARD. The experimenter defines amount of reward in terms of amount of food. The rats are placed on a 23-hour food-deprivation schedule so that food is an acceptable reward. The experimenter then allows one group of five rats to have a small reward (small amount of food), one group of five to have a large reward, and one group to have a medium reward.

DATA. After shaping the behavior of the rats until they press the bar to obtain food, the experimenter puts them through a number of test trials, with the results in Table 6-1.

---

[1] The example used here is an adaptation of an experiment reported by Paul J. Hutt in the *Journal of Comparative and Physiological Psychology*, 1954, **47**, 235–239: "The rate of bar pressing as a function of quality and quantity of reward."

Table 6-1    Bar Presses per Minute

| Amount of reward | | |
| --- | --- | --- |
| Small | Medium | Large |
| 3 | 10 | 13 |
| 5 | 8 | 11 |
| 6 | 5 | 7 |
| 3 | 7 | 11 |
| 3 | 5 | 8 |
| Means:    4 | 7 | 10 |

## 6-22   The Experimenter's Point of View

The three column means are different. In fact they seem different enough from one another to warrant the conclusion that amount of reward is directly related to performance. Within each column, however, there is also considerable variation, and the experimenter knows that a conclusion about between-column differences must take into account within-column differences. He argues that the greater the variability within the columns (known as *within-column variance*), the more difficult it will be to demonstrate significant differences between the column means (known as *between-column variance*). Thus, when he chooses a summary number (statistic) for these data, it is appropriate to find one that takes into account both the between-column variance and the within-column variance. Such a statistic is the $F$-statistic. It is a ratio of two variances, and in the case of a one-way analysis of variance (such as the present example),

$$F = \frac{\text{between-column variance}}{\text{within-column variance}}$$

The details concerning the computation of this summary number will be held until later. Suffice it to say that the experimenter finds for the data above that

$$F_{(2,12)} = 10.80$$

where the subscripts on $F$ indicate the degrees of freedom in the numerator and the denominator, respectively.

The experimenter has three sets of five measures each, has summarized all his data in the form of an $F$-statistic, and now wants to know whether this $F$-value is significant at, say, the 0.05 level or not. In order to know this, we must know the sampling distribution of $F_{(2,12)}$.

### 6-23   Making Use of the $F$-Model

The experimenter has obtained three means—4, 7, and 10—and his hunch is that they are significantly different from one another. In other words, he is inclined to believe that amount of reward does affect performance. Now this is tantamount to saying that the three samples (the three columns) were drawn from different populations. (Remember that when an experimenter says that there is a significant difference between his sample means, he is really saying that there is a significant difference between the population means.) When we set out to test a hypothesis, $H_0$, it is simpler to think of the three samples as having been drawn from the same population. In other words, if we choose three samples from the same population, then we expect that in the long run the three sample means will not be different. This is the null hypothesis, $H_0$. If we resort to symbols, we can describe the situation as follows:

1. $H_1$, "the three sample means are significantly different," means:
   (a) the five sample values in sample 1 (column 1) were drawn from a population with mean $\mu_1$,
   (b) the five sample values in sample 2 (column 2) were drawn from a population with mean $\mu_2$,
   (c) the five sample values in sample 3 (column 3) were drawn from a population with mean $\mu_3$,
   where $\mu_1$, $\mu_2$, and $\mu_3$ are not all the same.
2. $H_0$. "the three sample means are not significantly different," means that three samples were all drawn from the same population with mean $\mu$. Thus, $\mu_1 = \mu_2 = \mu_3 = \mu$.

How do we put this experimental situation into the framework of an $F$-model? First the assumptions underlying the $F$-model must be accepted. We have to assume that the population of performance measures (bar presses per minute) is normally distributed, ignoring the breakdown into three groups. We have to assume that three sets of five measures were sampled by SIRS from this population.

What about the parameters of the normally distributed population? Since we are considering three samples from this population, under $H_0$, we could estimate the population mean $\mu$ in three ways—the mean of Sample 1 is an unbiased estimate of the population mean $\mu$, the mean of Sample 2 is an unbiased estimate of $\mu$, and the mean of Sample 3 is an unbiased estimate of $\mu$. Which of these three shall we use? None of them. A better estimate is the *pooled* estimate, which we obtain by finding the total mean, or *grand mean*. Add up all 15 measures and divide by 15. This gives the grand mean, which is used as the estimate of the population mean, $\mu$.

The parameter $\sigma$ is a little more difficult to handle. We shall say simply that in the case of a one-way analysis of variance, there are two independent estimates of the population variance, $\sigma^2$. One is the variance between columns, and the other the variance within columns. If $H_0$ is true (that the three samples come from the same population), then these two estimates of $\sigma^2$ should be about the same. In other words, if we form the ratio of these two estimates (in the form of an $F$-statistic), then we should expect this ratio to be about one. (See Section 4-64 and note the mean of the $F$-distribution.) As this ratio departs from the expected value (close to unity), we begin to doubt the acceptability of the null hypothesis, $H_0$. If the three samples were not drawn from the same population, then the $F$-ratio will not have an expected value close to unity.

Figures 6-1 and 6-2 summarize the use of an $F$-model with (2,12) degrees of freedom (df), and a verbal description is given here.

| **Experimenter's knowledge** | **Statistician's $F$-model** |
|---|---|

### 1. Population

| | |
|---|---|
| Unknown except for rules for membership | $ND(\mu,\sigma)$, where $\mu$ is estimated by grand mean, $\sigma^2$ is estimated variously |

### 2. Sampling plan

| | |
|---|---|
| 15 available rats split into 3 groups of 5 | 5 values by SIRS for sample 1<br>5 values by SIRS for sample 2<br>5 values by SIRS for sample 3 |

### 3. Samples

| | |
|---|---|
| One set of 3 samples each of size 5 | Theoretically all sets of 3 samples each of size 5 |

### 4. Statistic

| | |
|---|---|
| One value of $F_{(2,12)} = 10.80$ | Theoretically all values of $F_{(2,12)}$ |

### 5. Sampling distribution

| | |
|---|---|
| Unknown | Defined precisely as |

$$Y = \frac{\Gamma(7)}{\Gamma(1)\Gamma(6)} 2^1 12^6 \frac{F^0}{(12 + 2F)^7}$$

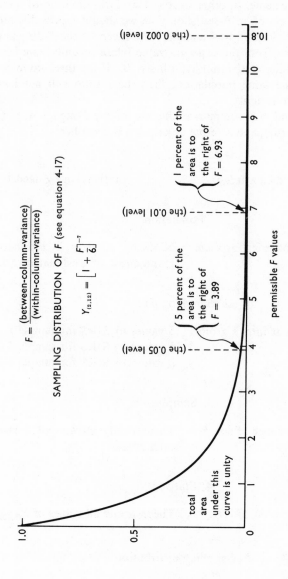

FIGURE 6-1. Details of the sampling distribution of the *F*-statistic with (2,12) df

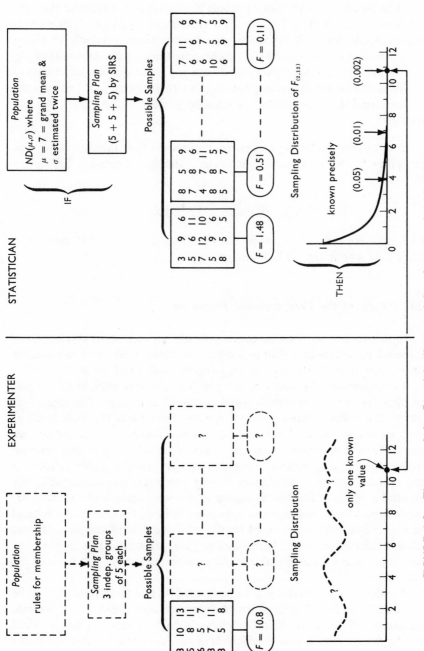

FIGURE 6-2. The use of the *F*-model: illustrated for the reward-performance study

Looking up the $F$-tables in Appendix F, we find that the area to the right of $F = 10.80$ is less than 0.01 on the $F$-distribution with (2,12) degrees of freedom. Under the null hypothesis $H_0$, if we repeatedly sample 15 values (3 samples of size 5 each), and if we summarize these 15 numbers in the form of an $F$-statistic, then we expect in the long run to find fewer than 1 case in 100 that shows an $F$-value as large as 10.8 or larger. Since this is less than the 0.05 level that the experimenter chooses to work with, he rejects the null hypothesis.

CONCLUSION. The experimenter concludes that there is a significant difference between his sample means, and he reports his findings as follows:

$$F_{(2,12)} = 10.80 \qquad (p < 0.01)$$

In terms of the original problem, the experimenter argues that amount of reward does significantly affect performance.

### 6-24  Details of the Computational Procedure

In this section we shall be concerned, not with the most efficient computational procedure but with a detailed examination of the computations that provide an understanding of the one-way analysis of variance.

The *experimental variable* in the problem above is amount of reward, and three *levels* are considered—small, medium, and large. The dependent measure is number of bar presses per minute. For each of the three levels of the experimental variable, we compute a mean number of bar presses per minute. Thus this problem concerns a set of means for one experimental variable. Since the appropriate summary number, the $F$-statistic, involves a ratio of variances and since there is only one experimental variable, the statistical analysis of the data is known as one-way analysis of variance, or, in abbreviated form, *one-way anova*. In what follows, the details of a general one-way anova will be presented on the left-hand side of the page, and at each step calculations will be performed on the experimental data given above. These calculations for a special case will appear on the right-hand side of the page.

The dependent measure will be designated $X$, and two subscripts will be appended. Thus $X_{ij}$ will refer to the $i$th dependent measure in the $j$th column. The number of entries in the $j$th column will be designated $n_j$, and we shall consider the one-way anova in which there are $c$ columns. In other words, we are considering $c$ samples, and the number of measures in each sample are given by $n_1, n_2, n_3, \ldots, n_c$.

## THE GENERAL LAYOUT

Let there be $c$ levels for one experimental variable (often known more simply as a *treatment*). Let there be $n_1$ measures in the first level, $n_2$ measures in the second level, . . . , $n_c$ measures in $c$th level. Let $N$ denote total number of measures, where

$$N = n_1 + n_2 + \cdots + n_c$$

Let $X_{ij}$ denote the $i$th entry in the $j$th level (column). Then the general layout for a one-way anova is

There are three levels (columns) for the treatment "amount of reward": small, medium, and large:

$n_1 = 5$ (small-reward group)

$n_2 = 5$ (medium-reward group)

$n_3 = 5$ (large-reward group)

$$N = 5 + 5 + 5 = 15$$

$X_{43}$ is the fourth entry in the third level (column), that is, 11. The layout for the special problem is

**Treatment levels**

| 1 | 2 | ... | $j$ | ... | $c$ |
|---|---|-----|-----|-----|-----|
| $X_{11}$ | $X_{12}$ | ... | $X_{1j}$ | ... | $X_{1c}$ |
| $X_{21}$ | $X_{22}$ | ... | $X_{2j}$ | ... | $X_{2c}$ |
| ... | ... | ... | ... | ... | ... |
| $X_{n_1 1}$ | ... | ... | ... | ... | $X_{n_c c}$ |
| | $X_{n^2 2}$ | | $X_{n_j j}$ | | |

**Amount of reward**

| Small | Medium | Large |
|-------|--------|-------|
| 3 | 10 | 13 |
| 5 | 8 | 11 |
| 6 | 5 | 7 |
| 3 | 7 | 11 |
| 3 | 5 | 8 |

(Note that there is no need for the number of entries in each column to be the same.)

## THE GRAND MEAN

The *grand mean* of all $N$ entries is the grand sum divided by $N$:

$$\bar{X}_{..} = \frac{\sum_j \sum_i X_{ij}}{N}$$

The grand mean is

$$\bar{X}_{..} = (3 + 5 + 6 + 3 + 3 + 10 + 8$$
$$+ 5 + 7 + 5 + 13 + 11 + 7$$
$$+ 11 + 8)/15$$
$$= 7$$

(The notation $\bar{X}_{..}$ becomes very useful and should be learned quickly. The bar always indicates a mean, and the two dots as subscripts indicate that the summation is over all values of $i$ and $j$.)

## THE COLUMN MEANS

Consider the $j$th column. To compute the mean for this column, we add up the $n_j$ entries and divide by $n_j$, as follows:

$$\bar{X}_{.j} = \frac{\sum_{i=1}^{n_j} X_{ij}}{n_j}$$

The set of column means is designated $\bar{X}_{.1}, \bar{X}_{.2}, \ldots, \bar{X}_{.c}$.

Consider the first column:

$$\bar{X}_{.1} = \frac{3 + 5 + 6 + 3 + 3}{5}$$

$$= 4$$

The other column means are

$$\bar{X}_{.2} = \frac{10 + 8 + 5 + 7 + 5}{5}$$

$$= 7$$

$$\bar{X}_{.3} = \frac{13 + 11 + 7 + 11 + 8}{5}$$

$$= 10$$

(Note here that the $j$th column mean is designated $\bar{X}_{.j}$. The bar indicates a mean. The dot in place of the subscript $i$ indicates that summation has occurred over all $i$-values, that is, over all entries in the $j$th column.)

## A PARTITION

We can consider the entry $X_{ij}$ to be made up of two parts:

$$X_{ij} = \bar{X}_{.j} + (X_{ij} - \bar{X}_{.j})$$

that is, the $j$th column mean plus the deviation from the column mean. We can also consider the column mean to be made up of two parts:

$$\bar{X}_{.j} = \bar{X}_{..} + (\bar{X}_{.j} - \bar{X}_{..})$$

that is, the grand mean plus the deviation of the column mean from the grand mean.

Consider the entry $X_{43} = 11$:

$$X_{43} = \bar{X}_{.3} + (X_{43} - \bar{X}_{.3})$$

$$= 10 + (11 - 10)$$

$$= 10 + 1$$

$$\bar{X}_{.3} = \bar{X}_{..} + (\bar{X}_{.3} - \bar{X}_{..})$$

$$= 7 + (10 - 7)$$

$$= 7 + 3$$

Putting these two partitions together, we have

$$\underset{\substack{\text{cell} \\ \text{entry}}}{X_{ij}} = \underset{\substack{\text{grand} \\ \text{mean}}}{\bar{X}_{..}} + \underset{\substack{\text{between-column} \\ \text{deviation}}}{(\bar{X}_{.j} - \bar{X}_{..})} + \underset{\substack{\text{within-column} \\ \text{deviation}}}{(X_{ij} - \bar{X}_{.j})}$$

$$X_{43} = \bar{X}_{..} + (\bar{X}_{.3} - \bar{X}_{..}) + (X_{43} - \bar{X}_{.3})$$

$$11 = 7 + (10 - 7) + (11 - 10)$$

Performing this partition for all cells in the layout, we have

$$
\begin{array}{|ccc|}
3 & 10 & 13 \\
5 & 8 & 11 \\
6 & 5 & 7 \\
3 & 7 & 11 \\
3 & 5 & 8
\end{array}
=
\begin{array}{|ccc|}
7 & 7 & 7 \\
7 & 7 & 7 \\
7 & 7 & 7 \\
7 & 7 & 7 \\
7 & 7 & 7
\end{array}
+
\begin{array}{|ccc|}
-3 & 0 & 3 \\
-3 & 0 & 3 \\
-3 & 0 & 3 \\
-3 & 0 & 3 \\
-3 & 0 & 3
\end{array}
+
\begin{array}{|ccc|}
-1 & 3 & 3 \\
1 & 1 & 1 \\
2 & -2 & -3 \\
-1 & 0 & 1 \\
-1 & -2 & -2
\end{array}
\quad (6\text{-}1)
$$

grand<br>means       between-column<br>deviations       within-column<br>deviations

For ease of reference, the partition (6-1) will be designated

$$\mathbf{D = M + B + W}$$

where $\mathbf{D}$ is the data array, $\mathbf{M}$ is the array of grand means, $\mathbf{B}$ is the array of between-column deviations, and $\mathbf{W}$ is the array of within-column deviations.

## PARTITIONING $SS_T$ INTO THE SUM OF $SS_B$ AND $SS_W$

In the next few divisions the aim is to show that the total variance—for all $N$ entries—may be partitioned into two separate variances—($i$) the between-column variance and ($ii$) the within-column variance. If there is really a significant difference between the treatments, then the between-column variance will be large relative to the within-column variance. Therefore, both these variances must be examined. Before proceeding to the variances per se, however, we examine the sums of squared deviations (known as SS). What we want to show is that

$$SS_T = SS_B + SS_W$$

where $SS_T$ is the total sum of squares (squared deviations, actually), $SS_B$ is the between sum of squares, and $SS_W$ is the within sum of squares.

Partition (6-1) was presented in the form $\mathbf{D = M + B + W}$. Clearly this may also be written $\mathbf{(D - M) = B + W}$, with the following results:

$$
\begin{array}{|ccc|}
-4 & 3 & 6 \\
-2 & 1 & 4 \\
-1 & -2 & 0 \\
-4 & 0 & 4 \\
-4 & -2 & 1
\end{array}
=
\begin{array}{|ccc|}
-3 & 0 & 3 \\
-3 & 0 & 3 \\
-3 & 0 & 3 \\
-3 & 0 & 3 \\
-3 & 0 & 3
\end{array}
+
\begin{array}{|ccc|}
-1 & 3 & 3 \\
1 & 1 & 1 \\
2 & -2 & -3 \\
-1 & 0 & 1 \\
-1 & -2 & -2
\end{array}
\quad (6\text{-}1')
$$

$\mathbf{(D - M)}$     $=$     $\mathbf{B}$     $+$     $\mathbf{W}$

In symbols the identity above expresses the relation

$$(X_{ij} - \bar{X}_{..}) = (\bar{X}_{.j} - \bar{X}_{..}) + (X_{ij} - \bar{X}_{.j}) \qquad (6\text{-}2)$$

In terms of this partition (6-1'), we can make the following identifications:

$$SS_T = \text{sum of squares of entries in } (\mathbf{D} - \mathbf{M})$$

$$SS_W = \text{sum of squares of entries in } \mathbf{W}$$

$$SS_B = \text{sum of squares of entries in } \mathbf{B}$$

And in terms of the symbols in Equation (6-2), we have

$$SS_T = \sum \sum (X_{ij} - \bar{X}_{..})^2$$
$$SS_B = \sum \sum (\bar{X}_{.j} - \bar{X}_{..})^2 \qquad (6\text{-}3)$$
$$SS_W = \sum \sum (X_{ij} - \bar{X}_{.j})^2$$

What has to be proved is that $SS_T = SS_B + SS_W$. This is one of the exercises below.

For the experimental data we can demonstrate that this partition is true:

$$SS_T = (16 + 4 + 1 + 16 + 16 + 9 + 1 + 4 + 0$$
$$+ 4 + 36 + 16 + 0 + 16 + 1) = 140$$

$$SS_B = (9 + 9 + 9 + 9 + 9 + 0 + 0 + 0 + 0 + 0$$
$$+ 9 + 9 + 9 + 9 + 9) = 90$$

$$SS_W = (1 + 1 + 4 + 1 + 1 + 9 + 1 + 4 + 0$$
$$+ 4 + 9 + 1 + 9 + 1 + 4) = 50$$

Thus, $SS_T = SS_B + SS_W$.

## CONVERTING SUMS OF SQUARES
## INTO VARIANCE ESTIMATES

To convert sums of squares into variance estimates, we simply divide by the degrees of freedom. We have three sums of squares, $SS_T$, $SS_B$, and $SS_W$, and we want to convert them into variance estimates, called *mean squares*, $MS_T$, $MS_B$, and $MS_W$. Thus we need to determine the degrees of freedom for each of these sums of squares.

### Consider $SS_T$

There are altogether $N$ independent values $X_{ij}$.

There are 15 measures in all.

There are $N$ deviations $(X_{ij} - \overline{X}_{..})$, but these are not all independent.

There are 15 deviations from the grand mean.

In fact, only $(N - 1)$ of these deviations are independent. The last one is constrained by the fact that the sum of these deviations is zero.

Only 14 of these deviations can be considered independent, since the sum of the 15 deviations must be zero.

Thus $SS_T$ is composed of $(N - 1)$ independent squares.

$SS_T$ is composed of $(15 - 1)$ independent squares.

The degrees of freedom for $SS_T$ are $(N - 1)$.

$SS_T$ has 14 df.

### Consider $SS_B$

The array **B** in partition (6-1) is used in the computation of $SS_B$. Since there are only $c$ column means involved and since the grand mean is a function of these, the degrees of freedom for $SS_B$ are $(c - 1)$.

There are 3 different column means. Thus degrees of freedom for $SS_B$ are $(3 - 1) = 2$.

### Consider $SS_W$

The array **W** in partition (6-1) is used in the computation of $SS_W$. Since the entries in every column sum to zero, there are $(n_1 - 1)$ degrees of freedom for column 1, $(n_2 - 1)$ for column 2, $(n_3 - 1)$ for column 3, and so on. Altogether then for $SS_W$ we have

In column 1 of **W** there are 5 entries which sum to zero. Thus

$$\text{df in column 1} = 5 - 1$$
$$\text{df in column 2} = 5 - 1$$
$$\text{df in column 3} = 5 - 1$$

giving a total

$$df_W = \sum_j (n_j - 1)$$
$$= (N - c)$$

$$df_W = 15 - 3$$
$$= 12$$

Now the mean squares (variance estimates) may be computed.

$$MS_T = \frac{SS_T}{df_T}$$

$$MS_T = \frac{140}{14} = 10$$

$$MS_B = \frac{SS_B}{df_B}$$

$$MS_B = \frac{90}{2} = 45$$

$$MS_W = \frac{SS_W}{df_W}$$

$$MS_W = \frac{50}{12} = 4.17$$

## THE COMPUTATION OF $F$ AND THE ANOVA TABLE

All that remains is the determination of an $F$-value. For a one-way anova this is simply the ratio of the between-column variance (which is estimated by $MS_B$) to the within-column variance (which is estimated by $MS_W$). Thus

$$F = \frac{MS_B}{MS_W}$$

and for the experimental problem

$$F = \frac{45}{4.17} = 10.80$$

Section 6-24 is rather long, and it is time to recapitulate. Conventionally, the results of an analysis of variance are presented in the form shown in Table 6-2.

Table 6-2    A One-way Analysis of Variance

| Source of variance | Sum of squares (SS) | Degrees of freedom (df) | Mean square (MS) | $F$ |
|---|---|---|---|---|
| Between-column differences | $SS_B = \sum\sum (\bar{X}_{.j} - \bar{X}_{..})^2$ | $(c - 1)$ | $MS_B = SS_B/(c - 1)$ | $\dfrac{MS_B}{MS_W}$ |
| Within-column differences | $SS_W = \sum\sum (X_{ij} - \bar{X}_{.j})^2$ | $(N - c)$ | $MS_W = SS_W/(N - c)$ | |
| Total | $SS_T = \sum\sum (X_{ij} - \bar{X}_{..})^2$ | $(N - 1)$ | | |

For the illustrative problem the table might appear in the literature as follows:

| Source | SS | df | MS | $F$ |
|---|---|---|---|---|
| Reward effects | 90 | 2 | 45 | 10.80 |
| Error | 50 | 12 | 4.17 | $(p < 0.01)$ |
| Total | 140 | 14 | | |

(Note that the within-column variance is often called *error variance*. Note also that the $MS_T$ serves no purpose in this table and is usually omitted.

Whereas it is true that $SS_T = SS_B + SS_W$ and that $df_T = df_B + df_W$, it is generally not true that $MS_T = MS_B + MS_W$.)

## 6-25   Efficient Computational Procedures

In practice the following formulas are used to evaluate $SS_T$, $SS_B$, and $SS_W$:

$$SS_T = \sum_j \sum_i X_{ij}^2 - \frac{\left(\sum_j \sum_i X_{ij}\right)^2}{N}$$

$$SS_B = \sum_j \left[\frac{\left(\sum_i X_{ij}\right)^2}{n_j}\right] - \frac{\left(\sum_j \sum_i X_{ij}\right)^2}{N} \qquad (6\text{-}4)$$

$$SS_W = SS_T - SS_B$$

These are merely rearrangements of the terms in Equation (6-3). (See Exercises 7–9 on page 178.) In order to use these efficient computational formulas, the experimenter must

1. Calculate the grand sum of all the entries in the data table

$$\sum_j \sum_i X_{ij} = 105$$

2. Calculate the grand sum of squared entries

$$\sum_j \sum_i X_{ij}^2 = 875$$

3. Calculate the column sums

$$\sum_i X_{i1} = 20$$

$$\sum_i X_{i2} = 35$$

$$\sum_i X_{i3} = 50$$

Then substitutions are made in the formulas (6-4) as follows:

$$SS_T = \sum \sum X^2 - \frac{\left(\sum \sum X_{ij}\right)^2}{N}$$

$$SS_T = 875 - \frac{105^2}{15} = 140$$

$$SS_B = \sum_j \left[\frac{\left(\sum X_{ij}\right)^2}{n_j}\right] - \frac{\left(\sum \sum X_{ij}\right)^2}{N}$$

$$SS_B = \left(\frac{20^2}{5} + \frac{35^2}{5} + \frac{50^2}{5}\right) - \frac{105^2}{15}$$

$$= 90$$

$$SS_W = SS_T - SS_B$$

$$SS_W = 140 - 90 = 50$$

If the computations are to be done on a computer, then the following flow chart might be used:

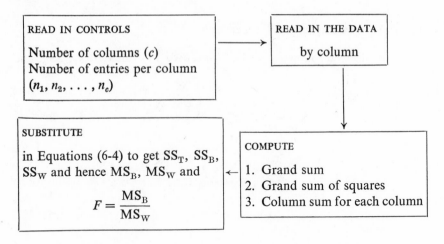

### 6-26   A Little Theory

The assumptions underlying the $F$-model are basically ($i$) a normally distributed population and ($ii$) an SIRS plan. From the experimenter's point of view, these assumptions are often expanded into the following considerations.

1. NORMALITY.   Can the population of measures be considered normally distributed?

2. HOMOSCEDASTICITY (EQUALITY OF VARIANCE).   If we are using an SIRS plan to sample from one population, then each sample so obtained should have more or less the same variance. Sampling fluctuation would make these variances differ from sample to sample, but within reason they should be within a factor of about 4 from one another. In the case of a one-way anova, the experimenter would ask whether the variances within each column were reasonably similar.

3. INDEPENDENCE.   The SIRS plan ensures independence of all the measures (sampled values). In practice the experimenter often has data that do not satisfy this independence assumption. This is particularly obvious in the case of repeated measures on the same subjects.

Considerations 1 and 3 must be decided on by the experimenter. In the case of consideration 2, it is possible to apply a test of significance to decide whether the equality-of-variance assumption is upheld. Suppose that an experimental setup involves six columns, or treatment levels. Each column has its own variance, and the experimenter wants to test whether the homoscedasticity assumption is upheld. He considers his largest column variance (let it be column 3, where $\hat{s}_3^2 = 17.3$, and there are 19 entries in that column) and his smallest column variance (let it be column 5, where $\hat{s}_5^2 = 9.9$, and there are 11 entries in that column). If the independence assumption is acceptable, then he can form an $F$-ratio using these two variances:

$$F_{(18,10)} = \frac{\text{maximum variance}}{\text{minimum variance}}$$

$$= \frac{17.3}{9.9} = 1.75$$

Looking up the $F$-tables (Appendix F), he notes that the 0.05 level on an $F$-distribution with (18,10) df is 2.41. Thus the obtained value of 1.75 is well within the 0.05 level, and he argues that the two variances do not differ significantly.

As a rule of thumb, it may be stated that if the ratio of the maximum and minimum variances is not greater than 4, little harm is done in using the $F$-test in a one-way anova.

THE ONE-WAY ANOVA MODEL.    The one-way anova design is a simple case of partitioning variance. All kinds of other anova designs are possible, and they tend to get complicated. A feature of all anova designs is that they make use of $F$-statistics, that is, ratios of independently estimated variances. But the theory underlying the appropriate use of the $F$-model becomes more obscure when the anova model becomes more complicated. We shall give only a glimpse of the procedure that is used to explicate these matters.

First a model (an equation) is propounded. In the case of a one-way anova, we argue that a dependent measure is made up of three parts—a grand mean, a column effect, and a random error. Thus

$$X_{ij} = \mu + C_j + e_{ij} \tag{6-5}$$

where $\mu$ is the (unknown) grand mean, $C_j$ is the column-$j$ effect, and $e_{ij}$ is a random-error effect. In other words, any given measure is partitioned into three components. (See partition 6-1.)

The next thing to do is to state the assumptions underlying this model. Consider what is known as a fixed-effects model. The population mean (grand mean) is a fixed constant. The column effect, $C_j$, is a constant for column $j$, and the sum of the column effects over all columns is zero. The random-error component, $e_{ij}$, is assumed to be a value obtained by SIRS from $ND(0,\sigma_e)$. This last assumption means that the error associated with any cell in the data table is independent of the error associated with any other cell, and the expected value of this error component is zero. It is this assumption which gives rise to the equality of variance assumption (that is, homoscedasticity).

Equation (6-5) plus the assumptions adhering to the components of the equation constitutes the one-way anova model.

*One-way anova model (fixed effects) is*

$$X_{ij} = \mu + C_j + e_{ij}$$

*where $\mu$ is a fixed constant*

$$C_j \text{ is a constant for all } j = 1, \ldots, c \text{ and } \sum_j C_j = 0$$

$$e_{ij} \text{ is obtained by SIRS from } ND(0, \sigma_e) \text{ for all } i \text{ and } j$$

Remember that only the measure $X_{ij}$ is known. The components $\mu$, $C_j$, and $e_{ij}$ are theoretical creations of the model.

When we have created the one-way anova model (fixed effects), the next step is to determine the expected values of the mean squares, $MS_B$ and $MS_W$. Without going into all the details, observe the following development:

$$\overline{X}_{\cdot j} = \frac{\sum_i X_{ij}}{n_j} = \frac{\sum_i (\mu + C_j + e_{ij})}{n_j} = \mu + C_j + \bar{e}_{\cdot j}$$

$$\overline{X}_{\cdot \cdot} = \frac{\sum_i \sum_j X_{ij}}{N} = \frac{\sum_i \sum_j (\mu + C_j + e_{ij})}{N} = \mu + 0 + \bar{e}_{\cdot \cdot}$$

Hence   $(\overline{X}_{\cdot j} - \overline{X}_{\cdot \cdot}) = (C_j + [\bar{e}_{\cdot j} - \bar{e}_{\cdot \cdot}])$

and   $(X_{ij} - \overline{X}_{\cdot j}) = (e_{ij} - \bar{e}_{\cdot j})$

These relations are a direct result of the assumptions of the model. Now consider the expressions for $MS_B$ and $MS_W$:

$$MS_B = \frac{\sum_i \sum_j (\overline{X}_{\cdot j} - \overline{X}_{\cdot \cdot})^2}{(c - 1)} = \frac{\sum_i \sum_j (C_j + [\bar{e}_{\cdot j} - \bar{e}_{\cdot \cdot}])^2}{(c - 1)}$$

$$MS_W = \frac{\sum_i \sum_j (X_{ij} - X_{\cdot j})^2}{(N - c)} = \frac{\sum_i \sum_j (e_{ij} - \bar{e}_{\cdot j})^2}{(N - c)}$$

The statistician now finds the expected values of these expressions, using only the assumptions of the model, and obtains

$$E(MS_B) = V_B + \sigma_e^2$$

$$E(MS_W) = \sigma_e^2$$

where   $V_B = \dfrac{\sum_j n_j C_j^2}{(c - 1)}$   is the variance of the column effects.

If we now look at the $F$-statistic, $F = MS_B/MS_W$, we note that the expected value of the numerator $E(MS_B)$ is composed of two parts: one is the error variance, $\sigma_e^2$, and the other is due to differences between column effects, $V_B$. The expected value of the denominator is simply the error variance, $\sigma_e^2$. Thus it is possible to see that, to the extent that the column effects are different from one another, to that extent will the $F$-ratio be expected to have a larger numerator than denominator. In other words, as $V_B$ becomes larger, the $F$-ratio becomes larger; and as the $F$-ratio becomes larger, the significance level becomes smaller (that is, the area in the right-hand tail of the $F$-distribution becomes smaller). And as the area in the right-hand tail becomes smaller, we argue more vehemently that there is a significant difference between the column effects.

This brief introduction to the process that is used by the statistician in deciding whether an $F$-ratio is appropriate or not will be repeated in the case of a two-way anova in Chapter 7. The interested student should know that the determination of expected values is actually very straightforward, involving no higher mathematics whatsoever. Some of the exercises below are intended to help you understand the very simple rules of expectation. If you master these problems, you should be able to prove the results given immediately above.

## EXERCISES

1. Consider the data used in Section 5-41 (for independent $t$-test), and treat it as a one-way anova problem involving two levels, $RT_S$ and $RT_L$.
   (a) Perform the partition (6-1) on these data.
   (b) Modify partition (6-1) into partition (6-1').
   (c) Compute $SS_T$, $SS_B$, and $SS_W$ by taking the sums of squares of the entries in $(D - M)$, $B$, and $W$, respectively.
   (d) Compute the $F$-ratio, and test the difference between the column effects for significance at the 0.05 level.
   (e) Check that $t^2 = F$ in this case, and identify the appropriate degrees of freedom for these two statistics.

2. When a subject is given the task of watching for interruptions in a continuous light source over a long period of time, his performance can be manipulated either by reward, by knowledge of results, or by both. An experimenter obtains four groups of subjects and assigns them to this vigilance task in the following manner: Group I is a control group, Group II is rewarded for success, Group III is told when they miss an interruption, and Group IV is both rewarded and told when they miss. The following data were obtained (measures are number of interruptions missed):

Group I ($n_1 = 5$):     10  24  21  16  25
Group II ($n_2 = 4$):    13   8  16  10
Group III ($n_3 = 6$):    9   6  12  11   7  14
Group IV ($n_4 = 6$):     3   6   4   8   4   5

(a) Draw a diagram of this experimental situation in conjunction with the use of the $F$-model.

(b) Using the most efficient computational procedure, develop the one-way anova table, and test the significance of the observed $F$-ratio.

(c) See the article "The effects of reward and knowledge of results on the performance of a simple vigilance task" by R. R. Sipowicz et al., *Journal of Experimental Psychology*, 1962, **64**, 58–61. In this article is a table showing the following means and standard deviations for the four groups:

| Group: | I | II | III | IV |
|---|---|---|---|---|
| Mean | 24.3 | 8.3 | 11.8 | 4.3 |
| Standard deviation | 12.1 | 7.1 | 10.5 | 2.4 |

If this was all you had to go on, what would be your conclusion concerning the assumption of homoscedasticity for this experiment? See page 60 to see how the authors handled the situation.

3. An experimenter studying problem-solving behavior decides to manipulate the conditions of a problem-solving task by defining three levels of instructions to his subjects: (*i*) no instructions are given, (*ii*) mild instructions are given to reduce overt responses during the performance of the task, and (*iii*) emphatic instructions are given that the number of overt responses is very important and that they should think before making any. He chooses a random sample of 30 men satisfying the rules for membership in a population of his making and randomly assigns them to the three treatment conditions, so that there are 10 in each condition. The dependent measure is number of overt responses over a series of problem-solving tasks, and the results are as follows:

Group I (no instr.): 168   144   136   128   145   109   143   142   170   120
Group II (mild): 147   145   136   155   106   136   124   94   124   104
Group III (emphatic): 82   96   64   72   86   77   83   87   86   60

(a) Find the means and standard deviations for each of these three groups of data.

(b) Perform a one-way anova to determine if there is a significant difference between the three means.

(c) In a follow-up study it is decided to test female subjects, and again 30 $S$s are chosen at random. However, a graduate student assistant makes the mistake of dividing the $S$s into three groups of unequal size: $n_1 = 9$, $n_2 = 11$, $n_3 = 10$. The results are as follows:

Group I (no instr.): 126   144   146   142   147   152   172   111   137
Group II (mild): 116   125   126   139   96   160   104   123   173   137
    131
Group III (emphatic): 120   95   102   93   120   93   91   72   93   86

Does the unequal $n$ make any difference? Perform a one-way anova to see if there is a significant difference between the effects of these three conditions on female subjects.[2]

[2] See C. P. Duncan. Effect of instructions and information on problem solving. *Journal of Experimental Psychology*, 1963, **65**, 321–327.

4. A stereograph is a set of two pictures which, when looked at with both eyes (one eye per picture), gives a superposed picture. An experimenter is aware that under these circumstances some parts of the original pictures may be suppressed (because of binocular rivalry, etc.), and so he sets out to examine the influence of various factors on suppression (measured in time units).[3] For each of five conditions the experimenter runs five subjects and comes up with the results in Table 6-3.

Table 6-3

| Condition: | 1 | 2 | 3 | 4 | 5 |
|---|---|---|---|---|---|
| | 24 | 18 | 1 | 17 | 4 |
| | 12 | 21 | 8 | 4 | 1 |
| | 17 | 9 | 3 | 6 | 3 |
| | 15 | 8 | 21 | 4 | 2 |
| | 21 | 12 | 11 | 11 | 6 |

(a) For each of these conditions compute $\bar{X}$ and $s$.

(b) Using efficient computational procedures, determine the one-way analysis-of-variance table for these data. Is the $F$-ratio significant beyond the 0.05 level? the 0.01 level?

(c) In the reference cited above, the experiment consisted of six conditions, and the following means and standard deviations were reported:

| Condition: | 1 | 2 | 3 | 4 | 5 | 6 |
|---|---|---|---|---|---|---|
| Mean | 18.24 | 12.38 | 9.25 | 1.44 | 9.88 | 1.88 |
| Standard deviation | 7.66 | 5.23 | 3.75 | 1.77 | 5.92 | 2.17 |

If you were faced with this table of data, what would you conclude about the assumption of normality (especially conditions 4 and 6) and the assumption of equal variance (homoscedasticity)?

5. Consider the following one-way anova table:

Between columns:  df = 3

Within columns:  df = 9

How many different experimental designs can you think of to yield this set of degrees of freedom?

(The following exercises are recommended by the council on statistical fitness!)

6. (a) Evaluate $\sum_{i=1}^{5} X_i$   if $X_i = 2^{(3i-1)}$.

(b) Evaluate $\sum_{i=1}^{3} (2X_i + 3)$   if $X_i = 2i$.

[3] See J. R. Law and H. Crovitz. Suppression in binocular vision. *American Journal of Psychology*, 1966, **79**, 623–627

(c) Evaluate $\sum\limits_{i=1}^{100} X_j$    if $X_j = 2j$.

(d) Evaluate $\sum\limits_{i=1}^{100} \sum\limits_{j=1}^{3} X_j$    if $X_j = 2j$.

(e) Evaluate $\sum\limits_{i=1}^{100} \sum\limits_{J=1}^{100} X_k$    if $X_k = 10^{-4}$.

7. (a) Expand $(A + B)^2$ and $(A - B)^2$.

   (b) Expand $(X_i - \bar{X})^2$.

   (c) Expand $\sum\limits_{i=1}^{n} (X_i - \bar{X})^2$, and show that it equals $\sum X_i^2 - (\sum X_i)^2/n$.

   (d) Expand $\sum\limits_{i=1}^{r} \sum\limits_{j=1}^{c} (X_{ij} - \bar{X}..)^2$.

   (e) In preparation for Chapter 7, expand $\sum\limits_{i=1}^{r} \sum\limits_{j=1}^{c} \sum\limits_{k=1}^{m} (X_{ijk} - \bar{X}...)^2$.

8. (a) Prove that $\dfrac{1}{c} \sum\limits_{j=1}^{c} \bar{X}._j = \bar{X}..$ .

   (b) Prove that $\dfrac{1}{r} \sum\limits_{i=1}^{r} \bar{X}_i. = \bar{X}..$ .

   (c) Evaluate $\sum\limits_{i=1}^{4} \sum\limits_{j=1}^{5} X_k$    if $X_k = 1$.

   (d) Evaluate $\sum\limits_{i=1}^{r} \sum\limits_{j=1}^{c} \bar{X}..$ .

   (e) Expand $\sum\limits_{i=1}^{r} \sum\limits_{j=1}^{c} (\bar{X}_i. - \bar{X}..)^2$, and simplify until you can see how this is like the formula for $SS_B$ (Equation 6-4), where we are thinking here about "between rows" and there are the same number of entries per row (namely, $c$).

9. (a) Refresh your memory of moments about zero. What is the special name given to $m_1'$? What is the value of the first moment about the mean for a set of data?

   (b) Consider partition (6-1'), or Equation (6-2), which is equivalent. The left-hand side is $(X_{ij} - \bar{X}..)$. Square this, and sum over all $i$ and $j$. (Exercise 7d above asks for the expanded form of this sum.) Now go over to the right-hand side of Equation (6-2), and expand and simplify the expression

$$\sum_i \sum_j (\bar{X}._j - \bar{X}..)^2 + \sum_i \sum_j (X_{ij} - \bar{X}._j)^2$$

   See if you can prove that these two expressions are the same.

   (c) Can you prove that the following cross-product term is zero?

$$2 \sum_{i=1}^{r} \sum_{j=1}^{c} (\bar{X}._j - \bar{X}..)(X_{ij} - \bar{X}._j)$$

   (d) Using the information in $a$ through $c$, show that $SS_T = SS_B + SS_W$.

10. This is an exercise in expectation for the interested student. (See Section 3-42 for a brief introduction.) If $X$ is a discrete random variable having permissible

values $X_i$ $(i = 1, \ldots, N)$ and probability distribution $p_i$ for $X_i$ $(i = 1, \ldots, N)$, then the expected value of $X$ is, by definition,

$$E(X) = \sum_{i=1}^{N} p_i X_i = m_1' = \text{mean}$$

Then, if $k$ is a constant, the following rules of expectation are true:

Rule 1:        $E(X + k) = E(X) + k$
Rule 2:        $E(kX) \quad = k*E(X)$
Rule 3:        $E(k) \quad\quad = k$

(a) Consider a binomial experiment (see Section 4-7): four tosses of a fair coin where $n_H$ = number of heads = number of successes. (i) What is the expected number of heads in four tosses? (ii) If you win \$5 for every head, what is the expected winning in four tosses? (You lose nothing for a tail.) (iii) A generous friend will pay \$3 for every time you toss four coins (or one coin four times) regardless of the outcome. His partner says he will take away \$2 for every head that turns up in four tosses. What are your expected winnings?

(b) $X$ is a random variable with mean $\mu$. We select one value, $X_i$, from this distribution. What is $E(X_i)$? Select another value, $X_j$. What is $E(X_j)$? What is $E(X_j - \mu)$?

(c) Rule 4: If $X$ and $Y$ are two random variables, then

$$E(X + Y) = E(X) + E(Y)$$

Consider a random variable $X$ with mean $\mu$. Select two values $X_1$ and $X_2$. What is $E(X_1 + X_2)$? Select $n$ values $X_1$ through $X_n$. What is the expected value of the sum of these $n$ values? Using Rules 2 and 4, determine the expected value of the mean of these $n$ values.

(d) What does the expression $E[X - E(X)]^2$ refer to?

## 6-3  TWO DEMONSTRATIONS

### 6-31  The Effect of Within-column Variation

It has been stated that the within-column variance can obscure the between-column variance. In other words, the larger the variation of the data within a column, the more difficult it is to demonstrate significant differences between column means. In order to make this point clear, consider the following two variations on the problem of amount of reward and performance introduced in Section 6-21.

EXAMPLE 1.   We keep the design of the experiment exactly as before. There are three columns and five entries per column. Furthermore, the column means are exactly the same—4, 7, and 10—and the grand mean is the same—7. The only difference is that the variation within a given column is greater than before. We expect therefore to obtain a much reduced $F$-value in spite of the fact that the between sum of squares, $SS_B$, is the same as before.

Table 6-4    Amount of Reward

| | Small | Medium | Large |
|---|---|---|---|
| | 9 | 8 | 15 |
| | 5 | 12 | 5 |
| | 1 | 3 | 15 |
| | 2 | 7 | 5 |
| | 3 | 5 | 10 |
| Means: | 4 | 7 | 10 |

The data for this demonstration are shown in Table 6-4. The summary one-way anova table for these data is as follows:

| Source | SS | df | MS | $F$ |
|---|---|---|---|---|
| Between | 90 | 2 | 45 | 2.9 |
| Within | 186 | 12 | 15.5 | |
| Total | 276 | 14 | | |

Under the hypothesis $H_0$ (the null hypothesis), the chances of obtaining an $F$-value as large as 2.9 or larger on the distribution of $F_{(2,12)}$ are about 1 in 10. In other words, the experimenter would conclude that the column means are not significantly different. These data do not support the hunch that amount of reward and performance are related positively.

EXAMPLE 2.    Once again consider the identical design—three columns and five entries per column. We now consider data that are conspicuous for having just two extreme entries. Thirteen of the rats seem to perform equivalently regardless of the reward condition, but one rat apparently gets excited about a medium reward and another about a large one (Table 6-5). Clearly the differences between the column means are due mainly to these two unusual rats. (Parenthetically, you may well argue that the $F$-model is not appropriate in this case, and you would be quite justified.)

The summary anova table for these data is as follows:

| Source | SS | df | MS | $F$ |
|---|---|---|---|---|
| Between | 90 | 2 | 45 | 0.915 |
| Within | 590 | 12 | 49.17 | |
| Total | 680 | 14 | | |

Table 6-5   Amount of Reward

| | Small | Medium | Large |
|---|---|---|---|
| | 3 | 15 | 30 |
| | 5 | 4 | 5 |
| | 6 | 5 | 5 |
| | 3 | 6 | 5 |
| | 3 | 5 | 5 |
| Means: | 4 | 7 | 10 |

Under hypothesis $H_0$ (the null hypothesis) the chances of obtaining an $F$-value as large as 0.915 or larger on the distribution of $F_{(2,12)}$ are about 1 in 2. Thus the experimenter would not reject the null hypothesis. Although this example patently violates the assumptions of the $F$-model, it is nevertheless comforting to find that the two peculiar rats do not sway the conclusion in favor of significant column differences.

These two examples illustrate the effect of within-column variance on the size of the $F$-statistic. The experimenter should be warned not to take differences between column means seriously until he has examined the within-column variation.

## 6-32   The Independent $t$-Test and the $F$-Test

It was pointed out in Chapter 5 that the $F$-test may be used in place of a $t$-test when the measures are independent. The reason for this is that the $F$-statistic with 1 df in the numerator and $n$ df in the denominator is defined exactly as the square of the $t$-statistic with $n$ df. Consider a population that is $ND(0,\sigma)$. Choose one value $X_0$, by SIRS, and then choose $n$ more by SIRS. Use these last $n$ to obtain an estimate of the variance $\sigma^2$. Then the ratio

$$t = \frac{X_0}{(\sum X_i^2/n)^{1/2}}$$

is, by definition, a $t$-statistic with $n$ df. Now consider the ratio

$$F = \frac{X_0^2}{\sum X_i^2/n}$$

which is by definition an $F$-statistic with 1 df in the numerator and $n$ df in the denominator. Clearly

$$t^2 = F$$

Let us rework the data in Section 5-41. There the data were analyzed according to the independent $t$-test, and a $t$-value of 0.88 was obtained, which for 18 df was not significant. We shall now consider the data to be arranged as a one-way anova having just two rows:

$$RT_S: \quad 52 \quad 58 \quad 58 \quad 63 \quad 67 \quad 72 \quad 46 \quad 54 \quad 59 \quad 54$$
$$RT_L: \quad 75 \quad 55 \quad 55 \quad 57 \quad 59 \quad 66 \quad 61 \quad 63 \quad 54 \quad 66$$

Remember that the data are in no way paired. We are considering 20 different subjects split into two groups of 10 each. Following the efficient computational procedures in Section 6-25, we obtain

The grand sum: $$\sum_i \sum_j X_{ij} = 1{,}194$$

The grand sum of squares: $$\sum_i \sum_j X_{ij}^2 = 72{,}226$$

Two-row sums: $$\sum_i X_{i1} = 583$$

$$\sum_i X_{i2} = 611$$

Substituting in the formulas (6-4), we get

$$SS_T = 72{,}226 - \frac{1{,}194^2}{20} = 944.2$$

$$SS_B = \frac{583^2}{10} + \frac{611^2}{10} - \frac{1{,}194^2}{20} = 39.2$$

$$SS_W = 944.2 - 39.2 = 905.0$$

Thus the summary table becomes

| Source | SS | df | MS | $F$ |
|--------|------|----|------|-------|
| Between | 39.2 | 1 | 39.2 | 0.779 |
| Within | 905.0 | 18 | 50.3 | |
| Total | 944.2 | 19 | | |

Note that this $F$-value is the same as the previously obtained $t$-value squared. Thus

$$F_{(1,18)} = 0.779 = (0.883)^2 = t^2_{(18)}$$

This $F$-value is well below the 0.05-level value on the distribution of $F_{(1,18)}$ and therefore indicates a nonsignificant difference between the column means 58.3 and 61.1.

In the case of two independent samples (and assuming normality and SIRS), which test should one use—the $F$-test or the $t$-test? Please yourself. As long as you remember that $t^2 = F$ in this special case, it is immaterial which you use.

## EXERCISES

1. In Section 6-31 modify the data in the small-, medium-, and large-reward conditions, keeping the column means the same, and perform the one-way anova to see what kind of table you get. As a further exercise, make up some data for this example (always keeping the column means the same) where the number of entries per column differs from column to column. For example, let $n_1 = 10$, $n_2 = 5$, $n_3 = 2$, and make up two sets of data, one showing small variation within column 1 and the other showing large variation within column 1. Will the within-column variation in column 1 be more important than in column 3?
2. Redo Exercise 2 in Section 5-4 as a one-way anova problem.
3. Redo Exercise 3 in Section 5-4 as a one-way anova problem.
4. Redo Exercise 4 in Section 5-4 as a one-way anova problem.
5. Redo Exercise 5 in Section 5-4 as a one-way anova problem.
6. This one is for the more mathematical student. Show that Equation (4-17), the $F$-distribution, reduces to (4-14), the $t$-distribution, when we replace $F$ by $t^2$. Check M. G. Kendall and A. Stuart, *The advanced theory of statistics* (New York: Hafner, 1958), Vol. 1, pp. 374, 377.

# 7

---

# The F-Test:
# Two-way Analysis
# of Variance

## 7-1  TWO-WAY ANOVA

### 7-11  An Example

Previous findings have hinted that the physiological arousal level of a frustrated person will be reduced if he is allowed to express aggression. An experimenter sets out to examine this prediction.[1]

POPULATION.  He creates the explicit rules for membership. A population member must be (*i*) an adult male, (*ii*) "normal," and (*iii*) of college age.

SAMPLE.  He selects a sample of 20 persons who satisfy these rules for membership.

DEPENDENT MEASURE.  He decides what will constitute the measure of physiological arousal. This is systolic blood pressure, or more accurately a difference in systolic blood pressure. The difference between pre- and post-experimental blood-pressure readings is to be recorded as the dependent measure.

TREATMENTS.  He decides what experimental variables (treatments) will be examined. For this study he chooses two treatments: (*i*) amount of frustration and (*ii*) amount of aggression allowed. For each treatment he designs two levels. In the case of frustration, a subject is to be either not frustrated ($F_1$) or frustrated ($F_2$). In the case of amount of aggression, a subject is to be either allowed no aggression ($A_1$) or allowed physical aggression ($A_2$).

---

[1] The example used here is adapted from an experiment reported by J. E. Hokanson and M. Burgess in the *Journal of Abnormal and Social Psychology*, 1962, **64**, 446–449: "The effects of three types of aggression on vascular processes."

DATA. The twenty subjects in the sample are allocated randomly to the four possible treatment conditions, as follows:

Amount of aggression
$A_1$: None        $A_2$: Physical

|  | $A_1$: None | $A_2$: Physical |
|---|---|---|
| $F_1$ | 5 subjects | 5 subjects |
| $F_2$ | 5 subjects | 5 subjects |

Frustration

The following results, showing differences between pre- and postexperimental systolic blood pressure, in millimeters of mercury, were obtained:

|  | $A_1$ | | | $A_2$ | | |
|---|---|---|---|---|---|---|
| $F_1$ | −1 | 4 | 4 | 4 | 6 | 2 |
|  | 3 | 0 | | 2 | 1 | |
| $F_2$ | 8 | 8 | 10 | 0 | 3 | 5 |
|  | 8 | 11 | | −1 | −2 | |

## 7-12  The Experimenter's Point of View

While conducting the experiment, the experimenter found that, on the average, a subject's blood pressure increased by about 10 mm of mercury when he became frustrated. If this subject was allowed to express physical aggression, his blood pressure returned to normal. If he was not allowed to express this aggression, the difference between pre- and post-readings remained high. Note that the data in cell (2,1) are large relative to the other cell entries.

There are several means of interest to the experimenter in this two-way anova design:

|  | $A_1$ | $A_2$ |  |
|---|---|---|---|
| $F_1$ | Cell (1,1) mean = 2 | Cell (1,2) mean = 3 | Row 1 mean = 2.5 |
| $F_2$ | Cell (2,1) mean = 9 | Cell (2,2) mean = 1 | Row 2 mean = 5.0 |
|  | Column 1 mean = 5.5 | Column 2 mean = 2.0 | Grand mean = 3.75 |

Note that (i) the two row means are different, (ii) the two column means are different, and (iii) the four cell means are different. The experimenter wants to know whether any of these differences are significant or not. In the language of anova, he asks whether there is (*i*) a significant *row effect*, (*ii*) a significant *column effect*, and (*iii*) a significant *interaction effect*? (The last effect will be explained more fully later in this chapter.) In other words, the experimenter wants to know whether sampling fluctuation can account for the observed differences between the means or whether it is safe to conclude that:

  1. The amount of frustration (called hereafter the *row effect*) has a significant effect on the dependent measure.

  2. The amount of aggression allowed (called hereafter the *column effect*) has a significant effect on the dependent measure.

  3. An interaction between frustration and allowed aggression (called hereafter the *interaction effect*) has a significant effect on the value of the dependent measure.

In choosing a summary number (statistic) to characterize each of these three effects, the experimenter is aware that within each cell there is considerable variation. It is clear that as this within-cell variance increases, it will become progressively more difficult to demonstrate significant row effects, column effects, and interaction effects. Thus, as in Chapter 6, the appropriate summary number in each case will be an *F*-value. There will be three *F*-values to consider:

  1. The row-effect *F*-value is the ratio of the between-row variance to within-cell variance.

  2. The column-effect *F*-value is the ratio of the between-column variance to within-cell variance.

  3. The interaction-effect *F*-value is the ratio of interaction variance to within-cell variance.

Estimates of these three variances are needed. The details will be given shortly, but in the meantime here are the values the experimenter obtains:

Row effect: $$F_{(1,16)} = \frac{\text{between-row variance}}{\text{within-cell variance}}$$
$$= 6.25$$

Column effect: $$F_{(1,16)} = \frac{\text{between-column variance}}{\text{within-cell variance}}$$
$$= 12.25$$

Interaction effect: $$F_{(1,16)} = \frac{\text{interaction variance}}{\text{within-cell variance}}$$
$$= 20.25$$

The experimenter designs his experiment as a two-way anova with five entries per cell (and note here that we must have equal entries per cell for this design—in contrast to the one-way design), summarizes all his data in the form of three $F$-ratios, and wants to know whether or not these $F$-ratios are significant at, say, the 0.05 level. In order to know this, we have to develop an acceptable $F$-model so that the sampling distribution of $F_{(1,16)}$ can be examined.

## 7-13   Making Use of the $F$-Model

The experimenter's design involves four cells with five measures in each. From a statistician's point of view, this situation is described simply as four samples of size 5. The experimenter has a hunch that these four cells are likely to contain different measures. At least he probably expects that not all the cells contain similar data. From the statistician's point of view, the easiest hypothesis to test is that all four samples were drawn from the same population. Thus we can define $H_0$, the statistician's null hypothesis, and $H_1$, the experimenter's hunch, as follows:

$H_0$: The four samples were drawn from the same population, and therefore the expected values of the cell means are all the same.

$H_1$: The sample in cell (1,1) was drawn from a population with mean $\mu_1$. The sample in cell (1,2) was drawn from a population with mean $\mu_2$. The sample in cell (2,1) was drawn from a population with mean $\mu_3$. The sample in cell (2,2) was drawn from a population with mean $\mu_4$. And not all these population means are the same.

Thus we might rephrase these two hypotheses as follows:

$H_0$:   $\mu_1 = \mu_2 = \mu_3 = \mu_4 = \mu$

$H_1$:   At least two of $\mu_1$, $\mu_2$, $\mu_3$, and $\mu_4$ are not the same.

How do we put this experimental situation into the framework of an $F$-model? First the assumptions underlying the $F$-model must be accepted. If we are going to use the $F$-model, we must assume that the population of blood-pressure differences is normally distributed (ignoring the breakdown into two treatments and two levels within each treatment). We must also assume that the four samples of size 5 were drawn from this normally distributed population by SIRS.

What about the two parameters—$\mu$ and $\sigma$—of the normal population? The null hypothesis, $H_0$, says that there is only one population mean, but since we have four samples of size 5, we have four sample means. Each of these cell means could be used to estimate the population mean. However, the best estimate is obtained by pooling the data and obtaining the *grand mean*, which is used as an estimate of the unknown population mean, $\mu$.

Once again the parameter $\sigma^2$ is a little more difficult to handle. We shall say simply that in the case of a two-way anova with multiple entries per cell,

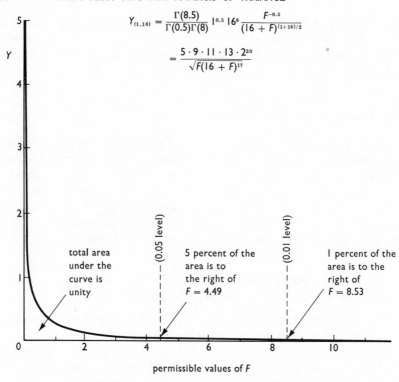

$$Y_{(1,16)} = \frac{\Gamma(8.5)}{\Gamma(0.5)\Gamma(8)} \, 1^{0.5} \, 16^8 \, \frac{F^{-0.5}}{(16 + F)^{(1+16)/2}}$$

$$= \frac{5 \cdot 9 \cdot 11 \cdot 13 \cdot 2^{20}}{\sqrt{F(16 + F)^{17}}}$$

total area under the curve is unity

(0.05 level)

5 percent of the area is to the right of $F = 4.49$

(0.01 level)

I percent of the area is to the right of $F = 8.53$

permissible values of F

FIGURE 7-1.   The sampling distribution of $F_{(1,16)}$

we can obtain four independent estimates—between-row variance, between-column variance, within-cell variance, and interaction variance. Making use of these four estimates, we can form the three $F$-ratios mentioned in Section 7-12. It happens that each of the three $F$-ratios has the same degrees of freedom, (1,16), but this occurrence is fortuitous.

Figure 7-1 and 7-2 summarize the use of an $F$-model with (1,16) df, and a verbal description is given here.

|  **Experimenter's knowledge**  |  **Statistician's F-model**  |
| --- | --- |

### 1. Population

| Unknown except for rules for membership | $ND(\mu,\sigma)$, where $\mu$ is estimated by grand mean, $\sigma^2$ is estimated variously |
| --- | --- |

### 2. Sampling plan

| 20 subjects at random, split into 4 groups of 5 each | 5 values by SIRS for sample 1 |
| --- | --- |
|  | 5 values by SIRS for sample 2 |
|  | 5 values by SIRS for sample 3 |
|  | 5 values by SIRS for sample 4 |

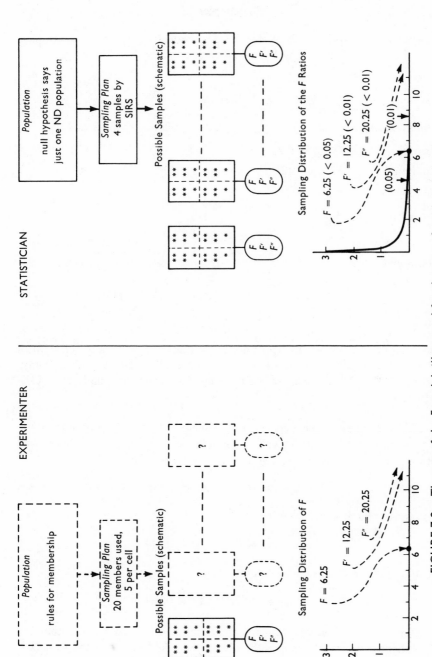

FIGURE 7-2. The use of the F-model: illustrated for the case of a two-way anova

### 3. Samples

One set of 4 samples, each of size 5    Theoretically all sets of 4 samples, each of size 5

### 4. Statistic

Three values of $F_{(1,16)}$:    Theoretically all values of $F_{(1,16)}$

| | |
|---|---|
| Rows: | $F_{(1,16)} = 6.25$ |
| Columns: | $F_{(1,16)} = 12.25$ |
| Interaction: | $F_{(1,16)} = 20.25$ |

### 5. Sampling distribution

Unknown    Defined precisely as an equation:

$$Y = \frac{\Gamma(8.5)}{\Gamma(0.5)\Gamma(8)} 1^{0.5} 16^8 \frac{F^{-0.5}}{(16 + F)^{8.5}}$$

Looking up the $F$-tables in Appendix F, we find that the area to the right of $F = 4.49$ is 0.05 and to the right of $F = 8.53$ is 0.01 on the $F$-distribution with (1,16) df. Thus, these are the $F$-values that define the 0.05 level and the 0.01 level.

CONCLUSIONS. The experimenter concludes that all three effects are significant beyond the 0.05 level, and indeed two of them are significant well beyond the 0.01 level. Thus, testing row effects, he reports

$$F_{(1,16)} = 6.25 \qquad (p < 0.05)$$

testing column effects, he reports

$$F_{(1,16)} = 12.25 \qquad (p < 0.01)$$

testing interaction effects, he reports

$$F_{(1,16)} = 20.25 \qquad (p < 0.01)$$

In terms of the original problem, the experimenter would argue that the dependent measure is significantly affected by whether or not the subject is frustrated and by whether the subject is allowed to express aggression or not and that there is a significant interaction between level of frustration and amount of aggression allowed.

## 7-14  Details of the Computational Procedure

As in Chapter 6, we shall go through the details of a computational procedure which is not the most efficient but which does provide some intuitive feeling for the analysis of a two-way design with multiple entries per cell.

There are two experimental variables—(*i*) amount of frustration and (*ii*) amount of aggression allowed—and there are two levels within each—$F_1$ = no frustration and $F_2$ = frustration, and $A_1$ = no aggression allowed and $A_2$ = physical aggression allowed. There are five measures per cell. The technical description of this experimental design is a two-way *factorial design* with multiple entries per cell. (Here the word "factorial" refers to factors, or what we have been calling treatments. There is no standardized language in this domain as yet, and so you should feel free to use either the word "factors" or the word "treatments.") When you perform the analysis of data obtained in such a design, you will be performing an analysis of variance. Thus it is probably most common to refer to the whole design as a two-way anova with multiple entries per cell.

The general dependent measure will be designated $X_{ijk}$, where the first subscript *i* refers to the row, the second subscript *j* to the column, and the third subscript *k* to the number of the cell entry. Thus $X_{ijk}$ is the *k*th measure in the cell (*i,j*), and the cell (*i,j*) is that cell in the *i*th row and *j*th column. We consider a general two-way anova with *m* entries per cell, in which there are *r* rows and *c* columns. As in Chapter 6, we shall illustrate the general case using the data from the example given above.

## THE GENERAL LAYOUT

Let the dependent measure be designated $X_{ijk}$, where

  $i = 1, 2, \ldots, r$ indicates row
  $j = 1, 2, \ldots, c$ indicates
    column
  $k = 1, 2, \ldots, m$ indicates which
    entry it is in (*i,j*)th cell

Thus we consider a general design in which there are *r* rows, *c* columns, and *m* entries per cell.
This makes a total of $N = rcm$ entries in all.
The general layout for this design has the following corner cells:

Columns

|  | | 1 | $\cdots$ | $c$ |
|---|---|---|---|---|
| Rows | 1 | $X_{111}$ <br> $X_{112}$ <br> $\cdots$ <br> $X_{11m}$ | $\cdots$ <br> $\cdots$ <br> $\cdots$ <br> $\cdots$ | $X_{1c1}$ <br> $X_{1c2}$ <br> $\cdots$ <br> $X_{1cm}$ |
|  |  | $\cdots$ | $\cdots$ | $\cdots$ |
|  | $r$ | $X_{r11}$ <br> $X_{r12}$ <br> $\cdots$ <br> $X_{r1m}$ | $\cdots$ <br> $\cdots$ <br> $\cdots$ <br> $\cdots$ | $X_{rc1}$ <br> $X_{rc2}$ <br> $\cdots$ <br> $X_{rcm}$ |

The experimental data are denoted $X_{ijk}$, where

$$i = 1, 2$$
$$j = 1, 2$$
$$k = 1, 2, 3, 4, 5$$

There are 2 rows ($F_1$ and $F_2$), 2 columns ($A_1$ and $A_2$), and 5 entries per cell.
This totals $20 = 2 \times 2 \times 5$ entries in all.
The experimental example has the following layout:

|  | $A_1$ | $A_2$ |
|---|---|---|
| $F_1$ | $X_{111} = -1$ <br> $X_{112} = 4$ <br> $X_{113} = 4$ <br> $X_{114} = 3$ <br> $X_{115} = 0$ | $X_{121} = 4$ <br> $X_{122} = 6$ <br> $X_{123} = 2$ <br> $X_{124} = 2$ <br> $X_{125} = 1$ |
| $F_2$ | $X_{211} = 8$ <br> $X_{212} = 8$ <br> $X_{213} = 10$ <br> $X_{214} = 8$ <br> $X_{215} = 11$ | $X_{221} = 0$ <br> $X_{222} = 3$ <br> $X_{223} = 5$ <br> $X_{224} = -1$ <br> $X_{225} = -2$ |

(Note that we require the same number of entries in every cell for the two-way design.)

## THE GRAND MEAN

The mean of all $rcm$ entries is

$$\bar{X}_{...} = \frac{\sum_i \sum_j \sum_k X_{ijk}}{N}$$

where $N = rcm$.

The grand mean is

$$\bar{X}_{...} = (-1 + 4 + 4 + 3 + 0 + 4$$
$$+ 6 + 2 + 2 + 1 + 8 + 8$$
$$+ 10 + 8 + 11 + 0 + 3 + 5$$
$$- 1 - 2)/20 = 3.75$$

(The grand mean now has three dots as subscripts to indicate summation over all values of $i, j$, and $k$. If the triple summation is to be performed on a computer, then there will be a triple loop.)

## THE ROW MEANS

Consider the $i$th row. There are $cm$ entries in this row. The mean is therefore

$$\bar{X}_{i..} = \frac{\sum_j \sum_k X_{ijk}}{cm}$$

Row 1: The mean is
$$\bar{X}_{1..} = (-1 + 4 + 4 + 3 + 0 + 4$$
$$+ 6 + 2 + 2 + 1)/10 = 2.5$$

Row 2: The mean is
$$\bar{X}_{2..} = (8 + 8 + 10 + 8 + 11 + 0$$
$$+ 3 + 5 - 1 - 2)/10 = 5.0$$

## THE COLUMN MEANS

Consider the $j$th column. There are $rm$ entries in this column. The mean is therefore

$$\bar{X}_{.j.} = \frac{\sum_i \sum_k X_{ijk}}{rm}$$

Column 1: The mean is
$$\bar{X}_{.1.} = (-1 + 4 + 4 + 3 + 0 + 8$$
$$+ 8 + 10 + 8 + 11)/10$$
$$= 5.5$$

Column 2: The mean is
$$\bar{X}_{.2.} = (4 + 6 + 2 + 2 + 1 + 0 + 3$$
$$+ 5 - 1 - 2)/10 = 2.0$$

## THE CELL MEANS

Consider the $(i,j)$th cell, that is, the cell in row $i$ and column $j$. There are $m$ entries in this cell. The cell mean is therefore

$$\bar{X}_{ij.} = \frac{\sum\limits_{k} X_{ijk}}{m}$$

The four cell means are

$$\bar{X}_{11.} = (-1 + 4 + 4 + 3 + 0)/5 = 2$$
$$\bar{X}_{12.} = (4 + 6 + 2 + 2 + 1)/5 = 3$$
$$\bar{X}_{21.} = (8 + 8 + 10 + 8 + 11)/5 = 9$$
$$\bar{X}_{22.} = (0 + 3 + 5 - 1 - 2)/5 = 1$$

## A PARTITION

As we showed in Section 6-24, it is possible, and also very useful, to consider any given measure as being made up of a number of components. In a one-way anova design the measure $X_{ij}$ was considered as being made up of a grand mean, the $j$th column effect, and a within-column effect (or error). In a two-way anova design with $m$ entries per cell, there are a few more components. Thus we consider $X_{ijk}$ to be made up of $(i)$ a grand mean, $(ii)$ the $i$th row effect, $(iii)$ the $j$th column effect, $(iv)$ the $(i,j)$th interaction effect, and $(v)$ a within-cell effect. In symbols the partition looks somewhat formidable but is actually quite straightforward.

Consider the entry $X_{ijk}$. This is the $k$th entry in cell $(i,j)$. We consider it to be made up of

Grand mean:

$$\bar{X}_{...}$$

$i$th row effect:

$$(\bar{X}_{i..} - \bar{X}_{...})$$

$j$th column effect:

$$(\bar{X}_{.j.} - \bar{X}_{...})$$

$(i,j)$th interaction effect:

$$(\bar{X}_{ij.} - \bar{X}_{i..} - \bar{X}_{.j.} + \bar{X}_{...})$$

Within-cell effect:

$$(X_{ijk} - \bar{X}_{ij.})$$

Consider the entry $X_{212} = 8$. This is the second entry in cell $(2,1)$. It is made up of

Grand mean:

$$\bar{X}_{...} = 3.75$$

2nd row effect:

$$(\bar{X}_{2..} - \bar{X}_{...}) = 5.0 - 3.75 = 1.25$$

1st column effect:

$$(\bar{X}_{.1.} - \bar{X}_{...}) = 5.5 - 3.75 = 1.75$$

(2,1)th interaction effect:

$$(\bar{X}_{21.} - \bar{X}_{2..} - \bar{X}_{.1.} - \bar{X}_{...})$$
$$= (9 - 5.0 - 5.5 + 3.75) = 2.25$$

Error effect:

$$(X_{212} - \bar{X}_{21.}) = 8 - 9 = -1$$

The reader should satisfy himself that the partition above is in fact always a true representation of $X_{ijk}$. In what follows we shall want to look at this partition in the following form:

$$(X_{ijk} - \bar{X}_{...}) = (\bar{X}_{i..} - \bar{X}_{...}) + (\bar{X}_{.j.} - \bar{X}_{...})$$
$$+ (\bar{X}_{ij.} - \bar{X}_{i..} - \bar{X}_{.j.} + \bar{X}_{...}) + (X_{ijk} - \bar{X}_{ij.}) \quad (7\text{-}1)$$

Here we are expressing the deviation from the grand mean in terms of (i) a row deviation, (ii) a column deviation, (iii) an interaction deviation, and (iv) a within-cell deviation. The special case of $X_{212}$ partitioned above demonstrates the accuracy of partition (7-1) for one particular dependent measure. Thus

$$(8 - 3.75) = (1.25) + (1.75) + (2.25) + (-1) = 4.25$$

If this partition is carried out for every entry in the two-way anova table, we shall have the following arrays:

$$\mathbf{D'} = \mathbf{R} + \mathbf{C} + \mathbf{I} + \mathbf{E} \quad (7\text{-}2)$$

where    $\mathbf{D'} =$

| | |
|---|---|
| −4.75 | 0.25 |
| 0.25 | 2.25 |
| 0.25 | −1.75 |
| −0.75 | −1.75 |
| −3.75 | −2.75 |
| 4.25 | −3.75 |
| 4.25 | −0.75 |
| 6.25 | 1.25 |
| 4.25 | −4.75 |
| 7.25 | −5.75 |

(Note that $\mathbf{D'} = \mathbf{D} - \mathbf{M}$, where $\mathbf{D}$ is the original data matrix and $\mathbf{M}$ a matrix of grand means.)

$\mathbf{R} =$

| | |
|---|---|
| −1.25 | −1.25 |
| −1.25 | −1.25 |
| −1.25 | −1.25 |
| −1.25 | −1.25 |
| −1.25 | −1.25 |
| 1.25 | 1.25 |
| 1.25 | 1.25 |
| 1.25 | 1.25 |
| 1.25 | 1.25 |
| 1.25 | 1.25 |

$\mathbf{C} =$

| | |
|---|---|
| 1.75 | −1.75 |
| 1.75 | −1.75 |
| 1.75 | −1.75 |
| 1.75 | −1.75 |
| 1.75 | −1.75 |
| 1.75 | −1.75 |
| 1.75 | −1.75 |
| 1.75 | −1.75 |
| 1.75 | −1.75 |
| 1.75 | −1.75 |

$$I = \begin{array}{|cc|} \hline -2.25 & 2.25 \\ -2.25 & 2.25 \\ -2.25 & 2.25 \\ -2.25 & 2.25 \\ -2.25 & 2.25 \\ \hline 2.25 & -2.25 \\ 2.25 & -2.25 \\ 2.25 & -2.25 \\ 2.25 & -2.25 \\ 2.25 & -2.25 \\ \hline \end{array} \qquad E = \begin{array}{|cc|} \hline -3 & 1 \\ 2 & 3 \\ 2 & -1 \\ 1 & -1 \\ -2 & -2 \\ \hline -1 & -1 \\ -1 & 2 \\ 1 & 4 \\ -1 & -2 \\ 2 & -3 \\ \hline \end{array}$$

These partitioned data tables will be used in the following sections.

## $SS_T$: THE TOTAL SUM OF SQUARES

(In the next few sections we aim to show that the total variance, for all $N = rcm$ entries, may be partitioned into four separate variances: (*i*) the between-row variance, (*ii*) the between-column variance, (*iii*) the interaction variance, and (*iv*) the within-cell variance, or error variance. However, before proceeding to estimates of these variances *per se*, we examine the sums of squared deviations. It will be shown that

$$SS_T = SS_R + SS_C + SS_I + SS_E$$

where $SS_R$ is the row sum of squares, $SS_C$ is the column sum of squares, $SS_I$ is the interaction sum of squares, and $SS_E$ is the error sum of squares.)

To get the total sum of squares, $SS_T$, we subtract the grand mean from each $X_{ijk}$ to get a deviation, square each of these deviations, and add them all up. Thus

In terms of the partition (7-2), the deviations we are considering for $SS_T$ are the entries in **D'**. Squaring and adding, we have

$$SS_T = \sum_i \sum_j \sum_k (X_{ijk} - \bar{X}_{...})^2 \qquad SS_T = 273.75$$

## PARTITIONING $SS_T$ INTO $(SS_R + SS_C + SS_I + SS_E)$

Partition (7-1) expresses the following identity:

$$(X_{ijk} - \bar{X}_{...}) = (\bar{X}_{i..} - \bar{X}_{...}) + (\bar{X}_{.j.} - \bar{X}_{...})$$
$$+ (\bar{X}_{ij.} - \bar{X}_{i..} - \bar{X}_{.j.} + \bar{X}_{...}) + (X_{ijk} - \bar{X}_{ij.})$$

Now it can be shown (see Exercise 7 below) that the following relation is also true:

$$\sum_i \sum_j \sum_k (X_{ijk} - \bar{X}_{...})^2 = \sum_i \sum_j \sum_k (\bar{X}_{i..} - \bar{X}_{...})^2 + \sum_i \sum_j \sum_k (\bar{X}_{.j.} - \bar{X}_{...})^2$$

$$+ \sum_i \sum_j \sum_k (\bar{X}_{ij.} - \bar{X}_{i..} - \bar{X}_{.j.} + \bar{X}_{...})^2$$

$$+ \sum_i \sum_j \sum_k (X_{ijk} - \bar{X}_{ij.})^2 \qquad (7\text{-}3)$$

or, in brief,

$$SS_T = SS_R + SS_C + SS_I + SS_E$$

In terms of Equation (7-2) (the partition of the whole data table), we may say that the sum of the squared entries in $\mathbf{D}'$ is equal to the sum of the squared entries in $\mathbf{R}$ plus the sum of the squared entries in $\mathbf{C}$ plus the sum of the squared entries in $\mathbf{I}$ plus the sum of the squared entries in $\mathbf{E}$. To illustrate, we have

$$SS_T = \sum \sum \sum (X_{ijk} - \bar{X}_{...})^2 \qquad SS_T = 273.75 \ \text{(sum of squares in } \mathbf{D}')$$

$$SS_R = \sum \sum \sum (\bar{X}_{i..} - \bar{X}_{...})^2 \qquad SS_R = 31.25 \quad \text{(sum of squares in } \mathbf{R})$$

$$SS_C = \sum \sum \sum (\bar{X}_{.j.} - \bar{X}_{...})^2 \qquad SS_C = 61.25 \quad \text{(sum of squares in } \mathbf{C})$$

$$SS_I = \sum \sum \sum (\bar{X}_{ij.} - \bar{X}_{i..} - \bar{X}_{.j.} + \bar{X}_{...})^2 \qquad SS_I = 101.25 \quad \text{(sum of squares in } \mathbf{I})$$

$$SS_E = \sum \sum \sum (X_{ijk} - \bar{X}_{ij.})^2 \qquad SS_E = 80.00 \quad \text{(sum of squares in } \mathbf{E})$$

And clearly, for the data on the right, $SS_T = SS_R + SS_C + SS_I + SS_E$.

## CONVERTING SUMS OF SQUARES INTO VARIANCE ESTIMATES

To convert sums of squares into variance estimates, we simply divide by the degrees of freedom. We have five sums of squares above, and we aim to convert each of them into a variance estimate, called a mean square. Thus we want $MS_T$, $MS_R$, $MS_C$, $MS_I$, and $MS_E$. How many degrees of freedom are associated with each of these?

## Consider $SS_T$

In partition (7-2) the matrix $\mathbf{D}'$ has $N = rcm$ entries in the general case. But the sum of these entries must be zero. Therefore, only $(N - 1)$ of these entries may be considered independent. Thus, in the general case, $SS_T$ has $(rcm - 1)$ df, or

$$df_T = rcm - 1$$

There are $20 = 2 \times 2 \times 5$ entries in $\mathbf{D}'$, and the sum of these 20 entries is zero. Therefore, only $(20 - 1) = 19$ entries can be considered independent.

$$df_T = 20 - 1 = 19$$

## Consider $SS_R$

The partition $\mathbf{R}$ in the general case involves only $r$ distinct values (the $r$ row deviations), and every column in $\mathbf{R}$ sums to zero. Thus we consider $SS_R$ to be made up of only $(r - 1)$ independent squares of the form

$$(\bar{X}_{i..} - \bar{X}_{...})^2$$

Hence $\quad df_R = r - 1$

There are only $r = 2$ distinct values in $\mathbf{R}$, and each column sums to zero. Therefore, we can consider only $(r - 1) = 1$ value in $\mathbf{R}$ to be an independent value. All the rest are constrained. Hence the degrees of freedom for $SS_R$ are

$$df_R = 2 - 1 = 1$$

## Consider $SS_C$

The partition $\mathbf{C}$ in the general case involves only $c$ distinct values (the $c$ column deviations), and every row sums to zero. Thus we consider $SS_c$ to be made up of only $(c - 1)$ independent squares of the form

$$(\bar{X}_{.j.} - \bar{X}_{...})^2$$

Hence $\quad df_C = c - 1$

There are only $c = 2$ distinct values in $\mathbf{C}$, and each row sums to zero. Therefore, we can consider only $(c - 1) = 1$ value in $\mathbf{C}$ to be an independent value. All other values are constrained. Hence the degrees of freedom for $SS_C$ are

$$df_C = 2 - 1 = 1$$

## Consider $SS_I$

There are $rc$ deviations in $\mathbf{I}$, but they are such that across any row they must sum to zero, down any column they must sum to zero, and over all cells they sum to zero. In fact, there are only $(r - 1)$ independent interaction deviations in any row and only $(c - 1)$ in any column. All told, therefore, there are $(r - 1) \times (c - 1)$ independent interaction deviations. Hence for $SS_I$

$$df_I = (r - 1)(c - 1)$$

There are 4 cells, and within each the interaction deviations are all the same (see $\mathbf{I}$). But these deviations are such that across both rows they sum to zero and down both columns they sum to zero. Hence, if we know just one of these deviations, all the others will be known. There are $(2 - 1) \times (2 - 1)$ independent values. Hence

$$df_I = (2 - 1)(2 - 1) = 1$$

Consider $SS_E$

There are $rc$ cells in **E**, and within each cell the entries sum to zero. Hence, within each cell there are only $(m - 1)$ entries that can be considered independent. All told, therefore, there are $rc(m - 1)$ independent entries:

$$df_E = rc(m - 1)$$

There are 4 cells in **E**, and within each cell the entries sum to zero. Hence, within each cell there are only $(5 - 1)$ entries that can be considered independent. All told, therefore, there are $4(5 - 1)$ independent entries:

$$df_E = 2 \times 2(5 - 1) = 16$$

Having now determined the degrees of freedom for each of the sums of squares, we can compute the mean squares (variance estimates) as follows:

$$MS_T = \frac{SS_T}{df_T} \qquad\qquad MS_T = \frac{273.75}{19} = 14.41$$

$$MS_R = \frac{SS_R}{df_R} \qquad\qquad MS_R = \frac{31.25}{1} = 31.25$$

$$MS_C = \frac{SS_C}{df_C} \qquad\qquad MS_C = \frac{61.25}{1} = 61.25$$

$$MS_I = \frac{SS_I}{df_I} \qquad\qquad MS_I = \frac{101.25}{1} = 101.25$$

$$MS_E = \frac{SS_E}{df_E} \qquad\qquad MS_E = \frac{80.00}{16} = 5.00$$

## THE COMPUTATION OF THE THREE *F*-RATIOS

All that remains is the computation of the three *F*-ratios that were initially discussed. The row-effect *F*-ratio is

$$F_{(1,16)} = \frac{MS_R}{MS_E} = 6.25$$

The column-effect *F*-ratio is

$$F_{(1,16)} = \frac{MS_C}{MS_E} = 12.25$$

The interaction-effect $F$-ratio is

$$F_{(1,16)} = \frac{MS_I}{MS_E} = 20.25$$

Again, as in Chapter 6, the computational details have been spelled out at some length in the interest of clarifying the steps involved in partitioning the total variance into various mean squares. Conventionally the results of an analysis of variance are presented in tabular form (Table 7-1).

The experimental data would be presented as in Table 7-2.

## 7-15  Efficient Computation

In practice the following formulas are used to evaluate $SS_T$, $SS_R$, $SS_C$, $SS_I$, and $SS_E$:

$$SS_T = \left(\sum_i \sum_j \sum_k X_{ijk}^2\right) - \frac{\left(\sum_i \sum_j \sum_k X_{ijk}\right)^2}{rcm}$$

$$= (\text{grand sum of squares}) - \frac{(\text{grand sum})^2}{rcm}$$

$$SS_R = \sum_i \left[\frac{\left(\sum_j \sum_k X_{ijk}\right)^2}{cm}\right] - \frac{\left(\sum_i \sum_j \sum_k X_{ijk}\right)^2}{rcm}$$

$$= \frac{\sum_{\text{rows}} (\text{row sum})^2}{cm} - \frac{(\text{grand sum})^2}{rcm}$$

$$SS_C = \sum_j \left[\frac{\left(\sum_i \sum_k X_{ijk}\right)^2}{rm}\right] - \frac{\left(\sum_i \sum_j \sum_k X_{ijk}\right)^2}{rcm} \qquad (7\text{-}4)$$

$$= \frac{\sum_{\text{cols}} (\text{col sum})^2}{rm} - \frac{(\text{grand sum})^2}{rcm}$$

$$SS_E = \left(\sum_i \sum_j \sum_k X_{ijk}^2\right) - \sum_i \sum_j \left\{\frac{\left(\sum_k X_{ijk}\right)^2}{m}\right\}$$

$$= (\text{grand sum of squares}) - \frac{\sum_{\text{cells}} \sum (\text{cell sum})^2}{m}$$

$$SS_I = SS_T - SS_R - SS_C - SS_E$$

These are merely rearrangements of the terms shown in Equation (7-3). See Exercise 8 below. In order to use these efficient computational formulas,

Table 7-1    Two-way Analysis of Variance with $m$ Entries per Cell

| Source of variance | Sum of squares (SS) | df | Mean sq. (MS) | F-ratio |
|---|---|---|---|---|
| Row effects | $SS_R = \sum \sum \sum (\bar{X}_{i..} - \bar{X}_{...})^2$ | $(r - 1)$ | $MS_R$ | $MS_R/MS_E$ |
| Column effects | $SS_C = \sum \sum \sum (\bar{X}_{.j.} - \bar{X}_{...})^2$ | $(c - 1)$ | $MS_C$ | $MS_C/MS_E$ |
| Interaction | $SS_I = SS_T - SS_R - SS_C - SS_E$ | $(r - 1)$ $\times (c - 1)$ | $MS_I$ | $MS_I/MS_E$ |
| Error | $SS_E = \sum \sum \sum (X_{ijk} - \bar{X}_{ij.})^2$ | $rc(m - 1)$ | $MS_E$ | |
| Total | $SS_T = \sum \sum \sum (X_{ijk} - \bar{X}_{...})^2$ | $rcm - 1$ | | |

the experimenter must

1. Calculate the grand sum of all the entries in the data table.

$$\sum_i \sum_j \sum_k X_{ijk} = 75$$

2. Calculate the grand sum of squared entries.

$$\sum_i \sum_j \sum_k X_{ijk}^2 = 555$$

3. Calculate the $r$ row sums.

$$\sum_j \sum_k X_{1jk} = 25 \qquad \text{row 1}$$

$$\sum_j \sum_k X_{2jk} = 50 \qquad \text{row 2}$$

4. Calculate the $c$ column sums.

$$\sum_i \sum_k X_{i1k} = 55 \qquad \text{col 1}$$

$$\sum_i \sum_k X_{i2k} = 20 \qquad \text{col 2}$$

5. Calculate the $rc$ cell sums.

$$\sum_k X_{11k} = 10 \qquad \text{cell (1,1)}$$

$$\sum_k X_{12k} = 15 \qquad \text{cell (1,2)}$$

$$\sum_k X_{21k} = 45 \qquad \text{cell (2,1)}$$

$$\sum_k X_{22k} = 5 \qquad \text{cell (2,2)}$$

Table 7-2

| Source | SS | df | MS | F |
|---|---|---|---|---|
| Frustration | 31.25 | 1 | 31.25 | 6.25  ($p < 0.05$) |
| Aggression | 61.25 | 1 | 61.25 | 12.25  ($p < 0.01$) |
| (Frustration) × (Aggression) | 101.25 | 1 | 101.25 | 20.25  ($p < 0.01$) |
| Error | 80.00 | 16 | 5.00 | |
| Total | 273.75 | 19 | | |

Then substitutions are made in the formulas (7-4) as follows:

$$SS_T = \sum \sum \sum X_{ijk}^2 - \frac{(\sum \sum \sum X_{ijk})^2}{rcm} \qquad SS_T = 555 - \frac{75^2}{20} = 273.75$$

$$SS_R = \sum_i \frac{(\sum \sum X_{ijk})^2}{cm} - \frac{(\sum \sum \sum X_{ijk})^2}{rcm} \qquad SS_R = \left(\frac{25^2}{10} + \frac{50^2}{10}\right) - \frac{75^2}{20} = 31.25$$

$$SS_C = \sum_j \frac{(\sum \sum X_{ijk})^2}{rm} - \frac{(\sum \sum \sum X_{ijk})^2}{rcm} \qquad SS_C = \left(\frac{55^2}{10} + \frac{20^2}{10}\right) - \frac{75^2}{20} = 61.25$$

$$SS_E = \sum \sum \sum X_{ijk}^2 - \sum_i \sum_j \frac{(\sum X_{ijk})^2}{m} \qquad SS_E = 555 - \frac{(10^2 + 15^2 + 45^2 + 5^2)}{5}$$

$$= 80.00$$

$$SS_I = SS_T - SS_R - SS_C - SS_E \qquad SS_I = 273.75 - 31.25 - 61.25$$

$$- 80.00 = 101.25$$

These values can then be used in conjunction with the degrees of freedom to determine the mean squares and the three $F$-ratios.

If the computations are to be done on a computer, then the flow chart in Table 7-3 might be used.

### 7-16   A Little Theory

The introductory remarks in Section 6-26 apply here too. We present here a two-way anova with multiple entries per cell in the form of a *fixed-effects model*. The development is similar to that given for the fixed-effects model of a one-way anova.

THE TWO-WAY (MULTIPLE-ENTRY) ANOVA MODEL.    First we propound the model in the form of an equation:

$$X_{ijk} = \mu + R_i + C_j + I_{ij} + e_{ijk} \qquad (7-5)$$

where $\mu$ = true mean
   $R_i$ = $i$th row effect
   $C_j$ = $j$th column effect
   $I_{ij}$ = interaction effect in $(i,j)$th cell
   $e_{ijk}$ = random-error effect attached to $k$th entry in $(i,j)$th cell

What we are saying here is that, given any dependent measure $X_{ijk}$, we consider it to be made up of underlying components—a grand mean, an effect due to being in the $i$th row, an effect due to being in the $j$th column, an effect

Table 7-3    Flow Chart for Two-way Analysis of Variance with $m$ Entries per Cell

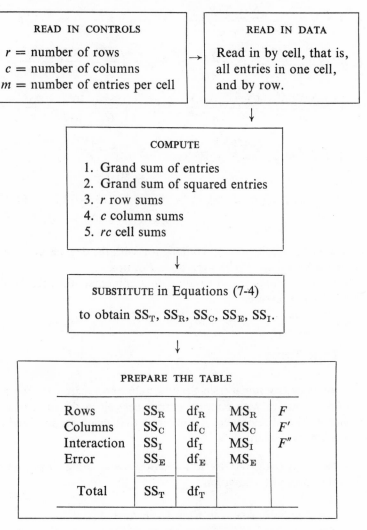

that depends on the interaction of row $i$ and column $j$—whatever is not accounted for by these components is considered a random error. In a *fixed-effects model*, the error component, $e_{ijk}$, is the only one that is a random variable. All other components are considered fixed effects.

Equation (7-5) specifies the underlying components. Now we must state the assumptions that are attached to each component. Perhaps the best way to explain them is to perform a partition, very like partition (7-1), for a particular two-way anova design. Consider a $2 \times 3$ design with 3 entries per cell. The data table would look like this:

$$\mathbf{X} = \begin{array}{|ccc|}
\hline
X_{111} & X_{121} & X_{131} \\
X_{112} & X_{122} & X_{132} \\
X_{113} & X_{123} & X_{133} \\
\hline
X_{211} & X_{221} & X_{231} \\
X_{212} & X_{222} & X_{232} \\
X_{213} & X_{223} & X_{233} \\
\hline
\end{array}$$

In terms of the model (7-5), we partition this matrix of data into the following matrices:

$$\mathbf{M} = \begin{array}{|ccc|}
\hline
\mu & \mu & \mu \\
\mu & \mu & \mu \\
\mu & \mu & \mu \\
\hline
\mu & \mu & \mu \\
\mu & \mu & \mu \\
\mu & \mu & \mu \\
\hline
\end{array}
\qquad
\mathbf{R} = \begin{array}{|ccc|}
\hline
R_1 & R_1 & R_1 \\
R_1 & R_1 & R_1 \\
R_1 & R_1 & R_1 \\
\hline
R_2 & R_2 & R_2 \\
R_2 & R_2 & R_2 \\
R_2 & R_2 & R_2 \\
\hline
\end{array}
\qquad
\mathbf{C} = \begin{array}{|ccc|}
\hline
C_1 & C_2 & C_3 \\
C_1 & C_2 & C_3 \\
C_1 & C_2 & C_3 \\
\hline
C_1 & C_2 & C_3 \\
C_1 & C_2 & C_3 \\
C_1 & C_2 & C_3 \\
\hline
\end{array}$$

$$\mathbf{I} = \begin{array}{|ccc|}
\hline
I_{11} & I_{12} & I_{13} \\
I_{11} & I_{12} & I_{13} \\
I_{11} & I_{12} & I_{13} \\
\hline
I_{21} & I_{22} & I_{23} \\
I_{21} & I_{22} & I_{23} \\
I_{22} & I_{22} & I_{23} \\
\hline
\end{array}
\qquad
\mathbf{E} = \begin{array}{|ccc|}
\hline
e_{111} & e_{121} & e_{131} \\
e_{112} & e_{122} & e_{132} \\
e_{113} & e_{123} & e_{133} \\
\hline
e_{211} & e_{221} & e_{231} \\
e_{212} & e_{222} & e_{232} \\
e_{213} & e_{223} & e_{233} \\
\hline
\end{array}$$

Remember that only the measure $X_{ijk}$ is known. The partitioning due to the model is theoretical, but the following assumptions are made:

1. The true mean is a fixed constant, the same for all entries in all cells.
2. The row effects are constants—within a given row the row effect is the same for all entries in that row—but the sum of all the row effects $(R_1 + R_2)$ is required to be zero.
3. The column effects are constants—within a given column the column effect is the same for all entries in that column—but the sum of all the column effects $(C_1 + C_2 + C_3)$ is required to be zero.

4. The interaction effects are constants—within a given cell the interaction effect is the same for all entries in that cell—but the sum of the interaction effects is required to be zero across any row and down any column. For example, $I_{21} + I_{22} + I_{23} = 0$ and $I_{11} + I_{21} = 0$.

5. The error effects are, in general, different for every dependent measure, but they are required to have an expected value of zero, and they are thought of as having been obtained by SIRS from a normal distribution $\text{ND}(0,\sigma_e)$. It is this assumption concerning the error effect that gives rise to what is known as *homoscedasticity* (the equal-variance assumption of anova models).

Equation (7-5), plus the assumptions adhering to the components in the equation, constitutes the two-way multiple-entry anova model (fixed-effects case).

*Two-way multiple-entry anova model (fixed effects) is*

$$X_{ijk} = \mu + R_i + C_j + I_{ij} + e_{ijk}$$

*where* $\mu$    *is a fixed constant*

$R_i$  *is a constant for each i and* $\sum_i R_i = 0$
$C_j$  *is a constant for each j and* $\sum_j C_j = 0$
$I_{ij}$  *is a constant for each* $(i,j)$ *and* $\sum_j I_{ij} = \sum_i I_{ij} = 0$
$e_{ijk}$ *is obtained by SIRS from* $\text{ND}(0,\sigma_e)$ *for all i, j, and k*

INTERPRETING THE MEANS.    Consider the general case of $r$ rows and $c$ columns and $m$ entries per cell. The $k$th dependent measure in cell $(i,j)$ is $X_{ijk}$. In Section 7-14 extensive use was made of the following means: $\bar{X}_{...}$, $\bar{X}_{i..}$, $\bar{X}_{.j.}$, and $\bar{X}_{ij.}$ (the grand mean, the $i$th row mean, the $j$th column mean, and the $(i,j)$th cell mean, respectively). In terms of the model above, how shall we express these means? 

Consider the grand mean $\bar{X}_{...}$:

$$\bar{X}_{...} = \frac{\sum_i \sum_j \sum_k X_{ijk}}{rcm}$$

$$= \frac{\sum_i \sum_j \sum_k [\mu + R_i + C_j + I_{ij} + e_{ijk}]}{rcm}$$

Taking into account the assumptions of the model, we reduce this to

$$\bar{X}_{...} = \mu + 0 + 0 + 0 + \bar{e}_{...}$$

Similarly we may show that

$$\bar{X}_{i..} = \mu + R_i + 0 + 0 + \bar{e}_{i..}$$
$$\bar{X}_{.j.} = \mu + 0 + C_j + 0 + \bar{e}_{.j.}$$
$$\bar{X}_{ij.} = \mu + R_i + C_j + I_{ij} + \bar{e}_{ij.}$$

INTERPRETING THE MEAN SQUARES.    Having expressed the various means in terms of the components of the model, we now proceed to express the mean squares in terms of these components:

$$MS_R = \frac{\sum \sum \sum (\bar{X}_{i..} - \bar{X}_{...})^2}{(r-1)}$$

$$= \frac{\sum \sum \sum [R_i - (\bar{e}_{i..} - \bar{e}_{...})]^2}{(r-1)}$$

Similarly    $$MS_C = \frac{\sum \sum \sum [C_j + (\bar{e}_{.j.} - \bar{e}_{...})]^2}{(c-1)}$$

$$MS_I = \frac{\sum \sum \sum [I_{ij} + (\bar{e}_{ij.} - \bar{e}_{i..} - \bar{e}_{.j.} + \bar{e}_{...})]^2}{(r-1)(c-1)}$$

$$MS_E = \frac{\sum \sum \sum (e_{ijk} - \bar{e}_{ij.})^2}{rc(m-1)}$$

EXPECTED MEAN SQUARES.    The statistician now determines the expected values of these mean squares, using only the assumptions of the model, and comes up with

$$E(MS_R) = V_R + \sigma_e^2 \quad \text{where} \quad V_R = \frac{cm \sum_i R_i^2}{(r-1)}$$

$$E(MS_C) = V_C + \sigma_e^2 \quad \text{where} \quad V_C = \frac{rm \sum_j C_j^2}{(c-1)}$$

$$E(MS_I) = V_I + \sigma_e^2 \quad \text{where} \quad V_I = \frac{m \sum_i \sum_j I_{ij}^2}{(r-1)(c-1)}$$

$$E(MS_E) = \sigma_e^2$$

Why does he do this? His main interest is in the three $F$-ratios discussed earlier. The statistician asks: If I want to test the significance of the row effects, what is the appropriate $F$-ratio to use? He can answer this question only if (*i*) he defines a model precisely (as was done above) and (*ii*) uses the assumptions of the model to determine the expected mean squares.

1.  Consider the row effect. The $F$-ratio used earlier was

$$F_{rows} = \frac{MS_R}{MS_E}$$

Having obtained the expected mean squares, the statistician examines

$$\frac{E(MS_R)}{E(MS_E)} = \frac{V_R + \sigma_e^2}{\sigma_e^2}$$

Clearly this is an appropriate $F$-ratio to use to test the row effects. As the variance of the row effects, $V_R$, gets larger, so this $F$-ratio will become larger and hence more significant.

2. Consider the column effect. The statistician examines

$$\frac{E(MS_C)}{E(MS_E)} = \frac{V_C + \sigma_e^2}{\sigma_e^2}$$

Again this is an appropriate $F$-ratio, since its size depends on the variance of the column effects $V_C$.

3. Consider the interaction effect. The statistician examines

$$\frac{E(MS_I)}{E(MS_E)} = \frac{V_I + \sigma_e^2}{\sigma_e^2}$$

Again this ratio depends fundamentally on the variance of the interaction effects, $V_I$, and thus is an appropriate $F$-ratio to use to test the significance of interaction effects.

This brief look at the theory underlying a fixed-effects model for a two-way anova design may seem formidable when you first read it. The interested student should know, however, that everything depends on being able to obtain expected values of random variables, and this is a straightforward process. Some of the exercises in Section 6-2 were designed to familiarize you with the essentials of expectation, and below you will find further exercises. The effort you make to understand expectation of random variables will be valuable because it will enable you to bridge the gap between a statistics text written for social scientists (experimenters) and a text written for mathematicians.

### EXERCISES

1. An experimenter divided 40 subjects (selected at random) into four equal groups of 10 each and assigned these groups randomly to the cells of a 2-by-2 factorial design, as follows:

|  |  | Motivation | |
|---|---|---|---|
|  |  | High | Low |
|  | Fast | 10 | 10 |
| Rate | | | |
|  | Slow | 10 | 10 |

His interest was in the ability of subjects to estimate time intervals. Thus, after performing a 15-min task, the subjects were asked to estimate the time interval for it, and the experimenter manipulated motivation (two levels) and rate of progress on the task (two levels). The data were as follows:

Motivation

|  |  | High |  |  |  |  | Low |  |  |  |  |
|---|---|---|---|---|---|---|---|---|---|---|---|
| Rate | Fast | 16 | 11 | 6 | 13 | 11 | 18 | 15 | 22 | 22 | 20 |
|  |  | 14 | 14 | 9 | 11 | 13 | 15 | 19 | 18 | 20 | 17 |
|  | Slow | 16 | 20 | 11 | 17 | 19 | 15 | 15 | 22 | 13 | 22 |
|  |  | 19 | 14 | 16 | 16 | 12 | 19 | 14 | 15 | 17 | 12 |

(a) Determine the two row means, the two column means, and the four cell means.

(b) Determine the four within-cell variances, and consider the validity of the assumption of homoscedasticity.

(c) Using efficient computational procedures, prepare a two-way anova table, and test the significance of the row effects, column effects, and interaction effects in this experiment.[2]

2. Conceptual ability is considered to be directly related to intelligence. An experimenter wishes to demonstrate this hypothesis and at the same time is interested in a hunch that personality adjustment affects conceptual ability. He sets up a 2 × 3 factorial design as follows:

IQ

|  | High | Average | Low |
|---|---|---|---|
| Adjusted | 6 | 6 | 6 |
| Maladjusted | 6 | 6 | 6 |

(a) Consider very carefully what problems are involved in selecting a sample of subjects to fit this design. Since a two-way design requires equal entries per cell, can this assignment of subjects be considered representative?

(b) The following data were obtained:

|  | High | Average | Low |
|---|---|---|---|
| Adjusted | 4 7 4 5 7 8 | 3 8 9 6 7 6 | 2 4 7 5 9 4 |
| Maladjusted | 6 6 4 2 5 6 | 3 4 2 7 5 3 | 3 2 4 4 3 4 |

Determine the cell means, the row means, the column means, and the grand mean, and develop the partition (7-2) for these data. By summing the squares of the matrices in partition (7-2), make up the two-way anova table for this experiment. What conclusions would you draw?[3]

---

[2] When you have reached your conclusions, check R. D. Meade. Effect of motivation and progress on the estimation of longer time intervals. *Journal of Experimental Psychology*, 1963, **65**, 564–567.

[3] See K. Kennedy and S. L. Kates. Conceptual sorting and personality adjustment in children. *Journal of Abnormal and Social Psychology*, 1964, **68**, 211–214.

3. In a bargaining situation, consider a buyer and a seller trying to reach agreement on a price. Let the seller be one of four possible types:

|  | Yielding | Demanding |
|---|---|---|
| White | Type 1 | Type 2 |
| Negro | Type 3 | Type 4 |

Replicating this design 10 times for each cell and using as dependent measure the agreed-upon price, the following data were obtained:

|  | Yielding | Demanding |
|---|---|---|
| White | 92 108 99 99 111<br>117 107 109 121 122 | 119 107 126 116 126<br>106 103 100 126 116 |
| Negro | 112 119 123 116 104<br>121 97 119 121 96 | 105 99 101 104 103<br>110 100 104 104 99 |

(a) Obtain the cell means, the row means, the column means, and the within-cell variances. Is the equal-variance assumption justified?

(b) Perform a two-way analysis of variance on these data, and state your experimental conclusions.[4]

4. In the following two articles, check the equality of cell entries in the factorial designs used:

   (a) J. Jecker et al. Teacher accuracy in assessing cognitive visual feedback from students. *Journal of Applied Psychology*, 1964, **48**, 393–397.

   (b) W. F. Patton and C. C. Cleland. Birth order, sex and achievement gain of institutionalized retardates. *Psychological Reports*, 1966, **19**, 327–330.

5. In discussing the utility of a model for psychotherapy, an investigator designed an experiment to test the effect of set (empathy versus personal problems) and awareness (aware versus unaware) on the subjects' responses to verbal conditioning. Using seven subjects per cell in this 2-by-2 design, the following data were obtained:

|  | Unaware | Aware |
|---|---|---|
| Empathy | −5 −5 6 15<br>3 15 −11 | 15 16 5 24<br>10 10 6 |
| Personal problems | 7 4 11 −2<br>−4 23 13 | 9 12 −1 10<br>−10 −8 15 |

Perform a two-way anova on these data, and reach your own experimental conclusions. Check the following reference to see what kind of dependent measure was employed and draw a diagram of the experiment: P. Ekman et al. Interaction of set and awareness as determinants of response to verbal conditioning. *Journal of Abnormal and Social Psychology*, 1963, **66**, 387–389. Check the results in this paper, and see if you agree with the authors' conclusion.

[4] See J. M. Hatton. Reactions of Negroes in biracial bargaining situations. *Journal of Personality and Social Psychology*, 1967, **7**, 301–306.

6. Factory supervisors are said to overestimate the morale of the workers they supervise. In an attempt to study this possibility, an experimenter identified three factory plants, five supervisors, and five men under each supervisor. A given supervisor predicted the morale score for his group, and the observed morale score was obtained by administering a test to the five workers. The data in Table 7-4 were obtained.

Table 7-4

| Plant 1: | | | | | |
|---|---|---|---|---|---|
| Supervisor's prediction | 50 | 45 | 50 | 46 | 49 |
| Worker's observed score | 52 | 46 | 48 | 44 | 46 |
| Plant 2: | | | | | |
| Supervisor's prediction | 52 | 53 | 56 | 49 | 53 |
| Worker's observed score | 46 | 49 | 51 | 50 | 50 |
| Plant 3: | | | | | |
| Supervisor's prediction | 59 | 54 | 53 | 52 | 52 |
| Worker's observed score | 45 | 47 | 47 | 49 | 44 |

(a) Now if these data were analyzed as a two-way anova, what would the table be? What conclusions would you reach?

(b) Should the data above have been analyzed as a two-way anova? Consider the pairwise nature of the data. What alternative analysis should have been performed? Do this alternative analysis and state your conclusions.[5]

7. Equation (7-1) shows the partition of $(X_{ijk} - \bar{X}_{..})$ into four components. Identify these four components verbally.

(a) If $A = B + C + D + E$, expand $A^2$.

(b) Now identify the letters $A$, $B$, $C$, $D$, and $E$ with the five parts of Equation (7-1), and expand $A^2$.

(c) If we now sum over all entries in the cell and over rows and over columns, show that the cross-product terms are equal to zero. In other words, try to establish the identity $SS_T = SS_R + SS_C + SS_I + SS_E$. (*Hint:* Make use of the fact that $m_1 = 0$ for any set of numbers.)

8. (a) Consider $SS_T$ as defined on the left-hand side of Equation (7-3). Show that it can be expanded into the form shown for $SS_T$ in Equation (7-4). See Exercise 7 in Section 6-2 as a warm-up exercise for this one.

(b) Repeat part *a* for the error sum of squares $SS_E$.

9. Try to write down the partition, equivalent to Equation (7-1), for a three-way anova with $M$ entries per cell. (There should be eight terms on the right-hand side of the equation: three main effects, three first-order interactions, one second-order interaction, and one error effect—the within-cell variation.)

10. If you have succeeded with Exercise 9, try to develop the formulas for $SS_T$, $SS_R$, $SS_C$, $SS_B$, $SS_{RC}$, $SS_{RB}$, $SS_{CB}$, $SS_{RCB}$, and $SS_E$, where we are thinking of rows (R), columns (C), and blocks (B); three first-order interactions—rows-by-columns (RC), rows-by-blocks (RB), columns-by-blocks (CB); the second-order interaction—rows-by-columns-by-blocks (RCB); and the error term (E).

11. Exercise 10 in Section 6-2 contained a number of exercises in expectation and ended with $E[(X_i - E(X_i))^2]$.

(a) Show that $E[(X_i - E(X_i))^2] = E(X_i^2) - [E(X_i)]^2$. In words this says that the expected value of the squares minus the square of the expected value equals the variance. Compare this with the most efficient formula for computing variance—see Equation (2-7).

(b) We have previously seen that, if $X$ is a random variable with variance $V_X$, then $kX$ will have variance $k^2 V_X$, where $k$ is a constant. Prove this, using the expectation formula for variance.

(c) If $X$ is a random variable with variance $V_X$, then we know that the random variable $(aX + b)$ has variance $a^2 V_X$. Prove this, using the expectation form for variance.

(d) If you succeed with the above parts of this exercise, then you are in a position to go back to the section "A Little Theory" in Sections 6-26 and 7-16. Using the information available in the models for one-way and two-way fixed-effects designs, see if you can arrive at one or more of the expected-mean-square results in those sections.

## 7-2  SPECIAL CASE: TWO-WAY ANOVA WITH JUST ONE ENTRY PER CELL

In the special case where $m = 1$, that is, where there is only one entry per cell, it is not possible to estimate a separate variance for interaction and a separate variance for error. In other words, given $r$ rows and $c$ columns and $rc$ entries (one per cell), it will be possible only to estimate (i) a between-row variance, (ii) a between-column variance, and (iii) a residual or error variance. The reason for this situation can best be explained by referring to the degrees-of-freedom column in the general two-way anova table given in Section 7-14. Note that the degrees of freedom for the interaction effect are

$$df_I = rc(m - 1)$$

Clearly, if $m = 1$, then $df_I = 0$. In order to get a variance estimate, we have to divide $SS_I$ by $df_I$, but if $df_I = 0$, then we cannot do so.

The principle is straightforward. For a general two-way anova with $r$ rows, $c$ columns, and $m$ entries per cell, there are $rcm$ entries in all. Since we use all these entries to estimate the population mean (the grand mean), the total degrees of freedom are $(rcm - 1)$. Now we plan to partition the total sum of squares, $SS_T$, into independent sums of squares. (They have to be independent if we are going to use $F$-ratios because the $F$-model requires it.) We can think of this partition in terms of the total degrees of freedom $df_T$ as well. We found earlier that

$$df_T = df_R + df_C + df_I + df_E$$

In the case of a two-way anova with $m = 1$ entry per cell, we can determine only three partitions of $SS_T$—$SS_R$, $SS_C$, and $SS_E$—and we find that

$$df_T = df_R + df_C + df_E.$$

Table 7-5   Two-way Anova with One Entry per Cell

| Source | Sum of squares | df | Mean square | $F$ |
|--------|----------------|-----|-------------|-----|
| Rows | $SS_R = \sum_i \sum_j (\bar{X}_{i.} - \bar{X}_{..})^2$ | $(r-1)$ | $MS_R$ | $MS_R/MS_E$ |
| Columns | $SS_C = \sum_i \sum_j (\bar{X}_{.j} - \bar{X}_{..})^2$ | $(c-1)$ | $MS_C$ | $MS_C/MS_E$ |
| Error | $SS_E = SS_T - SS_R - SS_C$ | $(r-1)(c-1)$ | $MS_E$ | |
| Total | $SS_T = \sum_i \sum_j (X_{ij} - \bar{X}_{..})^2$ | $(rc-1)$ | | |

The summary for this special case is shown in Table 7-5. (*Note*: There is no need for a third subscript on $X$ in this case.)

The efficient computational formulas for $SS_T$, $SS_R$, and $SS_C$ are the same as before, with $m$ now set equal to unity, and $SS_E$ is obtained by subtraction. Thus

$$SS_T = \sum_i \sum_j X_{ij}^2 - \frac{\left(\sum_i \sum_j X_{ij}\right)^2}{rc}$$

$$SS_R = \sum_i \frac{\left(\sum_j X_{ij}\right)^2}{c} - \frac{\left(\sum_i \sum_j X_{ij}\right)^2}{rc}$$

$$SS_C = \sum_j \frac{\left(\sum_i X_{ij}\right)^2}{r} - \frac{\left(\sum_i \sum_j X_{ij}\right)^2}{rc}$$

$$SS_E = SS_T - SS_R - SS_C$$

In order to perform the analysis,

1. Compute the grand sum of the $rc$ entries, $\sum_i \sum_j X_{ij}$.
2. Compute the grand sum of the $rc$ squared entries, $\sum_i \sum_j X_{ij}^2$.
3. Compute the $r$ row sums, $\sum_j X_{ij}$, for $i = 1, \ldots, r$.
4. Compute the $c$ column sums, $\sum_i X_{ij}$, for $j = 1, \ldots, c$.

Then proceed by substituting these quantities in the efficient computational formulas above.

Only two $F$-values are possible here. One is for the row effect, and the other for the column effect. Thus

$$F = \frac{MS_R}{MS_E} \quad \text{for row effect}$$

and $\quad\quad\quad\quad F = \frac{MS_C}{MS_E} \quad \text{for column effect}$

The only conclusions that can be reached by the experimenter are whether or not there are a significant (*i*) row effect and (*ii*) column effect.

## EXERCISES

1. For the data in the illustrative example (Section 7-11), imagine that the only information you had available was the cell means. Thus the data were

|       | $A_1$ | $A_2$ |
|-------|-------|-------|
| $F_1$ | 2     | 3     |
| $F_2$ | 9     | 1     |

   Perform a one-way anova with one entry per cell, and present the results in the form of the summary table. Are the row and column effects significant?
2. If you performed an experiment according to a 4 × 5 factorial design with one entry per cell, what would the degrees of freedom be in the summary anova table?
3. If you consider a 2 × 2 factorial design with one entry per cell, then the $F$-ratio for testing the row effect will have (1,1) df. The 0.05 level for a random variable with an $F_{(1,1)}$ distribution is 161.40. Can you generate four numbers for the four cells that will give rise to such a large $F$-ratio for rows?

## 7-3  THREE DEMONSTRATIONS

The following demonstrations are intended to show the role of the error term in the analysis of row effects, column effects, and interaction effects for a two-way anova with multiple entries per cell. The design is exactly the same as the illustrative problem in this chapter. The cell means, the row means, the column means, and the grand mean are the same. Only the within-cell variation (the error variance) is varied, so that the effect on the $F$-ratios can be observed.

DEMONSTRATION 1. First we use data that show considerable variation within each cell, and we expect that this within-cell variation will obscure the differences between row means, column means, and cell means. Here are the data:

|  | $A_1$ | $A_2$ |
|---|---|---|
| $F_1$ | −4 | 10 |
|  | 0 | 1 |
|  | 4 | 1 |
|  | 2 | −3 |
|  | 8 | 6 |
| $F_2$ | 17 | −3 |
|  | 10 | −1 |
|  | 12 | 6 |
|  | 2 | 1 |
|  | 4 | 2 |

The analysis of these data is shown in Table 7-6. None of the $F$-values reaches the 0.05 level, which is $F = 4.49$ for an $F$-distribution with (1,16) df. The experimenter concludes that none of the observed differences between row effects, column effects, and interaction effects are significant at the 0.05 level. The within-cell variation is too large relative to the observed differences between means to allow rejection of the null hypothesis.

DEMONSTRATION 2. The artificial data used here are intended to show the effect of a few unique subjects on the outcome of an experimental analysis. Most of the entries show a dependent measure of 4 mm of mercury (difference in systolic blood pressure). The data are as follows:

|  | $A_1$ | $A_2$ |
|---|---|---|
| $F_1$ | 4 | 4 |
|  | 4 | 4 |
|  | 4 | 4 |
|  | 4 | 4 |
|  | −6 | −1 |
| $F_2$ | 4 | 4 |
|  | 4 | 4 |
|  | 4 | 4 |
|  | 16 | −4 |
|  | 17 | −3 |

The analysis of these data is shown in Table 7-7. The fact that the most extreme results (the measures 16 and 17) fall in the same cell gives rise to an interaction effect that is significant at the 0.05 level. However, the so-called

Table 7-6

| Source | SS | df | MS | F | |
|--------|-----|-----|-----|------|------|
| Rows | 31.25 | 1 | 31.25 | 1.33 | (ns) |
| Columns | 61.25 | 1 | 61.25 | 2.61 | (ns) |
| Interaction | 101.25 | 1 | 101.25 | 4.31 | (ns) |
| Error | 376.00 | 16 | 23.50 | | |
| Total | 569.75 | 19 | | | |

main effects (the row effect and the column effect) are not significant. What should the experimenter conclude under these circumstances? The F-model has produced an F-value that is significant beyond the 0.05 level. The experimenter, however, need not accept this as a blind injunction to accept the significance of the interaction effect. Knowing what the data table looks like (that is, taking cognizance of the fact that there are two very peculiar dependent measures), the experimenter would do well to argue that the significance of the interaction effect is due largely to these two extreme results. He should conclude that further experimentation is in order before he can be confident that this interaction effect is a feature of this study.

If this seems like an arbitrary use of an F-test, the reader should remind himself that the experimenter should not be a slave to any statistical test. He should be the master of any such test. The fundamental principle is: Experimenter, know your data!

DEMONSTRATION 3. If an experimenter is concerned about exposing significant row and column effects (and possibly interaction effects as well), he should strive to reduce the within-cell variation as much as possible. Just how he goes about this is a matter of expertise in the substantive field, in equipment design, and in operational skill—topics that do not concern us

Table 7-7

| Source | SS | df | MS | F | |
|--------|-----|-----|-----|------|------------|
| Rows | 31.25 | 1 | 31.25 | 1.40 | (ns) |
| Columns | 61.25 | 1 | 61.25 | 2.75 | (ns) |
| Interaction | 101.25 | 1 | 101.25 | 4.55 | ($p < 0.05$) |
| Error | 356.00 | 16 | 22.25 | | |
| Total | 549.75 | 19 | | | |

directly here—but to show the effect of small within-cell variation, here is a demonstration that uses the following data:

|       |       | $A_1$ | $A_2$ |
|-------|-------|-------|-------|
|       |       | 3     | 4     |
|       |       | 1     | 3     |
| $F_1$ |       | 3     | 2     |
|       |       | 1     | 3     |
|       |       | 2     | 3     |
|       |       | 9     | 0     |
|       |       | 9     | 1     |
| $F_2$ |       | 9     | 2     |
|       |       | 9     | 1     |
|       |       | 9     | 1     |

The analysis of these data is shown in Table 7-8. The various $F$-values are now very large, and the experimenter would have no qualms about rejecting the null hypothesis of no differences between means.

These three demonstrations were presented to show the effects of within-cell variation on the size of the $F$-values. Whether or not the assumptions underlying the $F$-model are satisfied is of less importance here than the points established, namely,

1. If the within-cell variation is large, it will be difficult to obtain significant main effects.

2. If the within-cell variation is small, it will be easier to obtain significant main effects.

3. If there are some unique, extreme results, the experimenter should use his common sense to decide whether or not further experimentation is necessary to establish the validity of an interaction effect (or any other effect, for that matter).

Table 7-8

| Source      | SS     | df | MS    | F                      |
|-------------|--------|----|-------|------------------------|
| Rows        | 31.25  | 1  | 31.25 | 62.5  ($p < 0.01$)     |
| Columns     | 61.25  | 1  | 61.25 | 122.5  ($p < 0.01$)    |
| Interaction | 101.25 | 1  | 101.25| 202.5  ($p < 0.01$)    |
| Error       | 8.00   | 16 | 0.50  |                        |
| Total       | 201.75 | 19 |       |                        |

## EXERCISES

1. (a) Consider the data in demonstration 1 in Section 7-3. Partition the original data matrix according to Equation (7-1) or partition (7-2).

   (b) Using efficient computational procedures, produce the two-way anova table for these data. Check that they match the results given above.

2. Recompute the anova table for demonstration 2.

3. Recompute the anova table for demonstration 3.

4. Put all the data from demonstrations 1, 2, and 3 together to make a 2 × 2 table with 15 entries per cell. Perform the anova for these data. What are the significance levels for the three $F$-ratios now?

5. Section 7-3 sought to demonstrate the effect of within-cell variation on the size of the $F$-ratios. There is another factor affecting the size of the $F$-ratio, namely, the number of entries per cell. When you use a very large number of entries per cell, the $F$-ratios can get very large.[6] To demonstrate this effect, the following computer simulation was conducted. A 2 × 3 factorial design was envisaged in which the cell means were

|   |   |   |
|---|---|---|
| 4 | 5 | 6 |
| 5 | 6 | 7 |

The cell standard deviations were all made equal to 2. By means of an algorithm, the computer program generated $m$ entries per cell from normally distributed populations with means as indicated and standard deviation equal to 2. The number of entries per cell ($m$) was varied. Some of the results are given in Table 7-9.

Table 7-9

| Experiment | $F$-ratio for rows | Columns | Interaction |
|:---:|:---:|:---:|:---:|
| 1 | 2.543<br>df (1,18) | 3.219<br>(2,18) | 0.159<br>(2,18) |
| 2 | 4.147<br>df (1,18) | 0.235<br>(2,18) | 1.100<br>(2,18) |
| 3 | 4.839<br>df (1,54) | 16.038<br>(2,54) | 1.790<br>(2,54) |
| 4 | 44.188<br>df (1,594) | 51.617<br>(2,594) | 0.096<br>(2,594) |
| 5 | 306.074<br>df (1,5994) | 509.115<br>(2,5994) | 2.708<br>(2,5994) |

Notice how with increasing degrees of freedom for the error term, the size of the $F$-ratios increases dramatically. For each of the experiments above, determine how many entries per cell. Can you understand why increasing $m$ should lead to such large $F$-values? (Ask yourself where the sampling distribution of the mean fits into this discussion.)

[6] See H. A. Grace. Hostility, communication and international tension: I. The hostility inventory. *Journal of Social Psychology*, 1951, **34**, 31–40.

# 8

---

# The Chi-square
# Goodness-of-fit Test

## 8-1 INTRODUCTION

The $\chi^2$-distribution was introduced in Section 4-4 (see Figure 4-1 for a summary). There it was shown that:

1. *If* the population distribution is the standard normal distribution ND(0,1)
2. And *if* the sampling plan is choose $n$ values from this population by SIRS,
3. *Then* the sampling distribution of the $\chi^2$-statistic, defined as the sum of squares of these $n$ values, can be specified precisely in the form of an equation.

There is a separate equation for each value of $n$, where $n$ is known as degrees of freedom. Thus we talk about a random variable which has a $\chi^2$-distribution with $n$ degrees of freedom (df).

In this chapter we shall consider a statistic whose sampling distribution is only *approximately* a $\chi^2$-distribution.

At the outset let us understand that a thorough acquaintance with the theory underlying the $\chi^2$-statistic in Section 4-4 is not all that difficult, but to understand the theory underlying this approximate $\chi^2$-statistic requires considerable sophistication—well beyond the scope of this text. Paradoxically, from the experimenter's point of view, the use of the approximate $\chi^2$-statistic is quite straightforward. It is the justification that is difficult.

The general approach in this chapter is as follows. An experimenter is interested in populations that are categorical in nature. For example, if the experiment is to toss a coin, then the population of outcomes will consist of just two categories—heads ($H$) and tails ($T$)—and the only population parameter (summary number) of interest will be $p$ = Probability (heads). Knowing this value $p$, the experimenter will also know $q$ = Probability (tails) $= 1 - p$. We can represent such a population as follows:

$$
\boxed{
\begin{array}{l}
H\ H\ H\ H\ H\ \Big/ \ T\ T\ T\ T \\
\quad H\ H\ H\ H\ \diagup\ T\ T\ T\ T \\
\cdots\cdots\cdots\cdots\diagup\cdots\cdots \\
\qquad H\ H\ H\ \diagup\ \ T\ T\ T
\end{array}
}
\quad \text{Parameter} \longrightarrow \boxed{p = \Pr(H)}
$$

Consider another example, in which the experimenter asks a subject to write down a sequence of 100 random numbers from 0 through 9. If we are interested in how many times a 0 is used, a 1, a 2, a 3, etc., then the population will consist of 10 categories—labeled 0, 1, 2, 3, ... , 9. The parameters (population summary numbers) of interest will then be

$$p_0 = \Pr(0); \quad p_1 = \Pr(1); \quad \ldots ; \quad p_9 = \Pr(9)$$

These ten parameters must sum to unity, so that we will need to specify only nine of them; the tenth would be determined.

Under these circumstances the sample data consist of frequencies of occurrence in the given categories, and we shall call them *observed frequencies*. In the case of the coin-tossing experiment, we might sample 60 tosses, and the observed frequencies might be

$$n_H = \text{number of heads} = 24$$
$$n_T = \text{number of tails} = 36$$

These observed frequencies are compared with *expected frequencies*, that is, those which we would expect if we knew the population parameter $p = \Pr(H)$. Suppose that $p = 0.5$ (the coin is fair). Then how many heads would you expect in 60 tosses? The expected frequencies would be

$$n_H = 60 \times (0.5) = 30$$
$$n_T = 60 \times (1 - 0.5) = 30$$

It is convenient to use the following notation:

Observed frequencies: $\qquad O_H = 24 \qquad O_T = 36$

Expected frequencies: $\qquad E_H = 30 \qquad E_T = 30$

where $O =$ observed and $E =$ expected.

How do we summarize these sample data? The statistic of interest in this chapter is defined as follows:

$$\chi^2 = \sum_i \frac{(O_i - E_i)^2}{E_i} \tag{8-1}$$

which for the example above yields

$$\chi^2 = \frac{(24 - 30)^2}{30} + \frac{(36 - 30)^2}{30} = 2.4$$

In general, verbalizing Equation (8-1), we see that for each category of interest we must obtain an observed frequency and an expected frequency and then compute

$$\frac{(\text{Observed frequency} - \text{expected frequency})^2}{(\text{Expected frequency})}$$

and sum these quantities across all categories.

This statistic, $\chi^2$, in some ways gives us a measure of the goodness of fit between the observed frequencies and the expected frequencies, and so it is often called the $\chi^2$ goodness-of-fit statistic. And the experimenter is concerned about the shape of the sampling distribution of this $\chi^2$ goodness-of-fit statistic. As we have already indicated, the sampling distribution is approximately a chi-square distribution with a specified number of degrees of freedom.

How many degrees of freedom are there for the coin-tossing experiment? There are only two categories—$H$ and $T$—and if we know how many heads were obtained, we know all we need to know about the sample data. In general, for the case of $m$ categories, the number of degrees of freedom is calculated according to the rule

(Number of categories $- 1$) $-$ (number of parameters estimated)

Since no parameters (population summary numbers) were estimated from the sample data, the coin-tossing experiment yields

$$\text{df} = (2 - 1) - (0) = 1$$

Thus the $\chi^2$ goodness-of-fit statistic is distributed approximately as a $\chi^2$-distribution with 1 df.

Finally, then, we ask how the experimenter makes use of the $\chi^2$-model. For his one sample of 60 tosses the experimenter obtains a summary number $\chi^2 = 2.4$. The statistician argues that, *if* the population is assumed to consist of two categories with probability parameters $p$ and $q = 1 - p$ and *if* the sampling plan is to choose 60 members (or toss a coin 60 times) by SIRS, *then* the sampling distribution of the summary number $\chi^2$ (as defined in Equation 8-1) is approximately a $\chi^2$-distribution with 1 df. Looking up the $\chi^2$-tables (Appendix D), the experimenter notes that a value of 2.4 or greater for a $\chi^2$-distribution with 1 df can occur more than 10 times in 100. In other words, the experimenter argues that there is not enough evidence to say that his coin is biased. If a fair coin can yield results such as his sample data more than 10 times in 100, then it is quite possible that his own coin is a fair one.

Figure 8-1 summarizes the coin-tossing experiment as an illustration of the use of the chi-square goodness-of-fit test.

## 8-2  COMPARING SAMPLE DISTRIBUTIONS WITH POPULATION DISTRIBUTIONS

### 8-21  Example 1: A Rectangular (or Uniform) Distribution

THE PROBLEM.  An experimenter makes use of a table of random numbers (or a random-number generator on a computer) and selects the first 100 digits (0 through 9). The results are as follows:

| Digit | Observed frequency in first 100 digits |
|:-----:|:--------------------------------------:|
| 0 | 7 |
| 1 | 11 |
| 2 | 13 |
| 3 | 6 |
| 4 | 9 |
| 5 | 10 |
| 6 | 6 |
| 7 | 12 |
| 8 | 14 |
| 9 | 12 |
| Total | 100 |

He is interested in testing the hypothesis that these first 100 digits were generated by SIRS from a population in which the permissible digits appeared with equal probability; that is, the population distribution is a uniform (or rectangular) distribution over the permissible values.

EXPECTED FREQUENCIES.  The hypothesis dictates that each of the 10 digits, 0 to 9, can occur with probability $p = \frac{1}{10}$.  In the framework of the chi-square goodness-of-fit test, we would say that there are $m = 10$ categories in the population, that there are 10 parameters of interest (the probabilities of an element falling into a given category), and that they are all the same:

$$p_0 = p_1 = p_2 = \cdots = p_8 = p_9 = \tfrac{1}{10}$$

Thus, if we selected 100 elements from this population by SIRS, then we

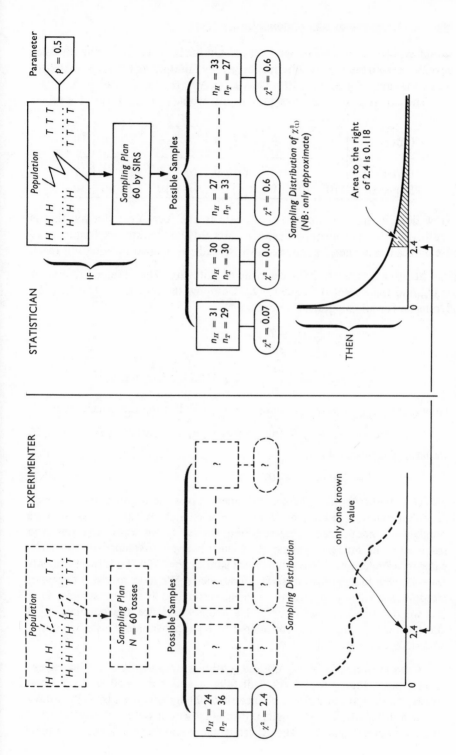

FIGURE 8-I. The use of the chi-square goodness-of-fit model: the case of two categories

would expect ten 0s, ten 1s, ten 2s, . . . , ten 9s. In general, for the $i$th category, we obtain the expected frequency, $E_i$, by multiplying the $i$th probability, $p_i$, by the sample size, $N = 100$. Thus $E_i = Np_i$, for $i = 0$ through 9.

The experimenter can now present his problem in the form of a table:

| Category: | 0 | 1 | 2 | 3 | 4 | 5 | 6 | 7 | 8 | 9 |
|---|---|---|---|---|---|---|---|---|---|---|
| Observed | 7 | 11 | 13 | 6 | 9 | 10 | 6 | 12 | 14 | 12 |
| Expected | 10 | 10 | 10 | 10 | 10 | 10 | 10 | 10 | 10 | 10 |

How does he now summarize these data in the form of a statistic that is sensitive to the agreement between the observed and the expected frequencies? He makes use of the $\chi^2$ goodness-of-fit statistic as defined in Equation (8-1).

SUMMARY NUMBER.  Consider the $i$th category. The observed frequency is $O_i$, and the expected frequency $E_i$. Compute the quantity $(O_i - E_i)^2 / E_i$. Doing so for all categories, we obtain

$$\chi^2 = \sum_{i=0}^{9} \frac{(O_i - E_i)^2}{E_i}$$

$$= \frac{(7 - 10)^2}{10} + \cdots + \frac{(12 - 10)^2}{10} = 7.6$$

How many degrees of freedom are involved? Following the general rule

$$df = (m - 1) - \text{(number of parameters estimated)}$$

we have, for this problem,

$$df = (10 - 1) - (0) = 9$$

Notice that the degrees of freedom depend upon the number of categories, $m$, rather than on the number of sample elements, $N$. We are interested in the number of independent observed frequencies. If we know the observed frequencies in nine categories, then the observed frequency in the tenth category is determined, since they must sum to $N = 100$. Thus there are only $(m - 1) = 9$ independent observed frequencies. We have to lose a degree of freedom for each population parameter estimated from the sample data, but we did not estimate any in this example. Hence the goodness-of-fit statistic for this problem is considered to be approximately distributed as a $\chi^2$-distribution with 9 df.

CONCLUSION.  Looking up the $\chi^2$-tables (Appendix D), the experimenter notes that $\chi^2 = 7.6$ for 9 df falls at about the 0.50 level. In other words, there is about a 50:50 chance that 100 digits chosen by SIRS from a uniform distribution of the digits 0 through 9 would yield a chi-square value as large or larger than 7.6. The experimenter would feel confidence that these first 100 digits from the random-number tables did indeed come from a uniform distribution by SIRS.

This example is summarized in Figure 8-2.

## 8-22 Important Commentary

It has been stated that the formal justification for the appropriate use of the chi-square goodness-of-fit statistic is difficult, but at the very least you should note that the following conditions must be satisfied:

1. Each sample observation must fall in one and only one of the $m$ categories.

2. All sample observations must be independent of one another.

3. The *expected* frequencies must all be reasonably large, say, at least 5 and preferably much larger than that. (This condition can be taken as a rule of thumb. The larger the expected frequencies, the better will be the approximation to a chi-square distribution.)

Note that each of these conditions is fulfilled in the problem above.

## 8-23 Example 2: A Normally Distributed Population

THE PROBLEM. An experimenter reading Section 3-3 of this text learns of the existence of an algorithm that allegedly produces values sampled by SIRS from a normal distribution, $ND(\mu,\sigma)$. He makes use of the algorithm to produce 1,000 values and decides to test whether these values can indeed be considered an SIRS sample from a normal distribution. (An equivalent problem that sometimes occurs in practice is the following: An experimenter obtains a set of data and wants to know whether or not he can consider these data as normally distributed.

ESTIMATING THE PARAMETERS $\mu$ AND $\sigma$.   Let us assume that we do not know what values of $\mu$ and $\sigma$ were used in the production of the 1,000 values. Under these circumstances the first thing we must do is estimate them. Normal distributions are two-parameter distributions, and so if we plan to test the normality of a set of data, we must know what normal distribution we are talking about. Using the 1,000 sample values, we estimate $\mu$ and $\sigma$ as follows:

Estimate of $\mu$:   $\bar{X} = -1.1$     (sample mean)

Estimate of $\sigma$:   $\hat{s}_x = 2.3$     (sample standard deviation—see Section 4-33)

The problem is now rephrased. Can the 1,000 sampled values be considered an SIRS sample from the normal distribution, $ND(-1.1,2.3)$? (For later reference we must remember that we have estimated two population parameters and shall therefore have to lose two degrees of freedom.)

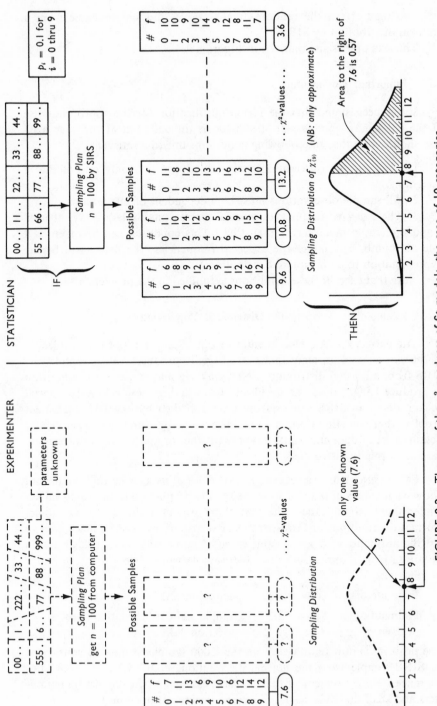

FIGURE 8-2. The use of the $\chi^2$ goodness-of-fit model: the case of 10 categories

MAKING USE OF THE GOODNESS-OF-FIT TEST. The experimenter must create $m$ categories, determine how many of the 1,000 sampled values fall into each of them, and, according to some model, determine how many would be expected to fall in each category.

The best way to create the categories is the following. Looking up the tables for the standard normal distribution ND(0,1), the experimenter creates categories that split the distribution into equal parts (referring to equal area). For example, supppose that he wishes to create 10 categories. Then the normal distribution is split so that the area under the curve within each category is as close to $\frac{1}{10}$ as possible. The divisions in Table 8-1 are suitable.

Table 8-1

| Category | Interval on ND(0,1) | Area under curve |
|:---:|:---:|:---:|
| 1 | $-\infty < z \le -1.28$ | $\simeq 0.1$ |
| 2 | $-1.28 < z \le -0.84$ | $\simeq 0.1$ |
| 3 | $-0.84 < z \le -0.52$ | $\simeq 0.1$ |
| 4 | $-0.52 < z \le -0.25$ | $\simeq 0.1$ |
| 5 | $-0.25 < z \le 0.00$ | $\simeq 0.1$ |
| 6 | $0.00 < z \le 0.25$ | $\simeq 0.1$ |
| 7 | $0.25 < z \le 0.52$ | $\simeq 0.1$ |
| 8 | $0.52 < z \le 0.84$ | $\simeq 0.1$ |
| 9 | $0.84 < z \le 1.28$ | $\simeq 0.1$ |
| 10 | $1.28 < z < +\infty$ | $\simeq 0.1$ |

Now it is important to remember that these divisions were created for ND(0,1). What are the appropriate divisions for the normal distribution of interest to the experimenter, namely, ND($-1.1$,2.3)? The best way to handle this is to convert all observed values into standard scores (see Section 2-3), using the formula

$$z_i = \frac{(X - \bar{X})}{\hat{s}_X} = \frac{(X + 1.1)}{2.3}$$

If we do so, then we have effectively changed the original problem into the following: Can the 1,000 standard scores, $z_i$ ($z$-scores), be considered an SIRS sample from ND(0,1)? There is no need to choose separate categories for ND($-1.1$,2.3).

When we have done this preliminary work, the problem is quite simple. Table 8-2 presents the sample data. The observed frequencies are obtained by finding out how many $z$-scores fall into each of the categories. The expected frequencies are obtained by multiplying the population probabilities ($\frac{1}{10}$ for each category) by the sample size ($N = 1,000$).

Table 8-2

| Category | Observed frequency | Expected frequency |
|----------|--------------------|--------------------|
| 1 | 92 | 100 |
| 2 | 105 | 100 |
| 3 | 111 | 100 |
| 4 | 105 | 100 |
| 5 | 113 | 100 |
| 6 | 110 | 100 |
| 7 | 90 | 100 |
| 8 | 98 | 100 |
| 9 | 88 | 100 |
| 10 | 88 | 100 |
| Total | 1,000 | 1,000 |

THE SUMMARY NUMBER. All that remains is the computation of the $\chi^2$ goodness-of-fit statistic according to Equation (8-1). Thus

$$\chi^2 = \sum_{i=1}^{10} \frac{(O_i - E_i)^2}{E_i}$$

$$= \frac{(92 - 100)^2}{100} + \frac{(105 - 100)^2}{100} + \cdots + \frac{(88 - 100)^2}{100}$$

$$= 8.96$$

DEGREES OF FREEDOM. According to the rule given earlier, the correct number of degrees of freedom is

$$(m - 1) - (\text{number of parameters estimated}) = (10 - 1) - (2) = 7$$

CONCLUSION. Looking up the chi-square tables (Appendix D), we find that the value $\chi^2 = 8.96$ for 7 df falls at about the 0.25 level. In other words, *if* the population is a 10-category population with equal probabilities for each category and *if* the sampling plan is to select $N = 1,000$ members by SIRS, then the probability of obtaining a chi-square goodness-of-fit value of 8.96 or larger is 0.25. Sampling fluctuation could account for the discrepancy between observed and expected frequencies about 25 times in 100. The experimenter would accept the hypothesis that his 1,000 values did indeed represent an SIRS sample from a normal distribution with mean $= -1.1$ and standard deviation $= 2.3$.

CAUTION. This test alone is not sufficient to verify that the sampled values were in fact, normally distributed. We should also consider the skewness of the observed data and maybe also the kurtosis and some other features—the number of categories used, whether the categories were of equal width, and so on. We shall not belabor the example with such finesse. Instead we note simply that one test of normality yields positive results. The goodness-of-fit test as applied above increases our confidence in the normality assumption.

## 8-24 A Little Theory

To some readers it may seem unnecessary to use the chi-square goodness-of-fit test in the case of the coin-tossing experiment, since such experiments are commonly used to illustrate the binomial distribution (see Section 4-7). As a matter of fact, these two are related in theory. In a nutshell, the relationship is as follows. As $N$ tends to infinity, the binomial probability distribution tends to the normal distribution; and as $m$ (the number of categories) tends to infinity, the chi-square distribution tends to the normal distribution. Of course, in practice, things do not reach infinity, but the following illustration will show that the approximations are reasonable even for very small $N$ and $m$.

Consider the experiment of tossing a coin 10 times and recording the number of heads $n_H$. Suppose that the outcome is

$$n_H = 8$$

We shall now consider three ways to determine the probability of at least 8 heads in 10 tosses for a fair coin. In other words, given the hypothesis that $p = \Pr(H) = \frac{1}{2}$, what is the probability of obtaining 8 or more heads in 10 tosses?

THE BINOMIAL PROBABILITY. Following Equations (4-21), we want the following probabilities:

$$b(8;10,0.5) = \frac{10!}{8!\,2!}\,(0.5)^8(1 - 0.5)^2 = \frac{45}{2^{10}}$$

$$b(9;10,0.5) = \frac{10!}{9!\,1!}\,(0.5)^9(1 - 0.5)^1 = \frac{10}{2^{10}}$$

$$b(10;10,0.5) = \frac{10!}{10!\,0!}\,(0.5)^{10}(1 - 0.5)^0 = \frac{1}{2^{10}}$$

The probability of at least 8 heads is the sum of these three quantities (see Section 3-13, especially the addition law on p. 72):

$$\Pr(\text{at least 8 heads in 10 tosses}) = \frac{56}{2^{10}} = 0.0547$$

THE NORMAL APPROXIMATION. For the binomial distribution above,

$$\text{Mean} = Np = 10 \times (0.5) = 5$$

$$\text{Standard deviation} = \sqrt{Npq} = \sqrt{10 \times (0.5) \times (0.5)} = \frac{\sqrt{10}}{2}$$

Thus, converting the number $r = 8$ successes to standard-score form, we have

$$\frac{8 - \text{mean}}{\text{standard deviation}} = \frac{8 - 5}{\sqrt{10}/2} = 1.90$$

Treating this as a $z$-score on the standard normal distribution, ND(0,1), and looking up the normal tables (Appendix C), we find that the area under the curve to the right of $z = 1.90$ is 0.029 approximately. Thus, if we were to (unwisely) use the normal approximation to the binomial in this case (where $N$ is as small as 10), the probability of at least 8 heads would come out as 0.029.

The central-limit theorem states that as $N$ tends to infinity, the binomial distribution approximates the normal distribution. In the case considered here, $N = 10$ is certainly not close to infinity.

THE CHI-SQUARE GOODNESS-OF-FIT APPROXIMATION. For this approximation we consider just two categories—heads and tails—and the observed frequencies are $n_H = 8$ and $n_T = 2$. The expected frequencies are computed to be

$$E_H = Np = 10 \times (0.5) = 5 \qquad \text{and} \qquad E_T = Nq = 5$$

Thus the tabled values would be

|  | H | T |
|---|---|---|
| Observed | 8 | 2 |
| Expected | 5 | 5 |

and the chi-square value would be computed as

$$\chi^2 = \frac{(8 - 5)^2}{5} + \frac{(2 - 5)^2}{5} = 3.6$$

The degrees of freedom are $(m - 1) = 2 - 1 = 1$, and looking up the chi-square tables (Appendix D), we find that a value as large or larger than 3.6 can occur with a probability of about 0.06. Note that this probability is much closer to the exact value of 0.0547 given by the binomial probability. Recall that the rule of thumb for using the chi-square goodness-of-fit test requires the expected values in each category to be at least 5 and preferably more. In this case the expected values in both categories were 5, and the approximation is fairly good.

COMMENT. In the comparison among the true binomial probability, the normal approximation, and the chi-square approximation, we have been a little unfair to the normal approximation. There is a very simple correction that may be applied to make the normal approximation much better. We wanted to find the probability of at least 8 heads. This means the sum of the probabilities of 8 heads, 9 heads, and 10 heads. Now since the binomial distribution is discrete, the boundary between 7 heads and 8 heads can be chosen as 7.5 when we apply the normal approximation. Thus, if we convert 7.5 heads into standard-score form, we obtain

$$\frac{(7.5 - Np)}{\sqrt{Npq}} = \frac{(7.5 - 5)}{\sqrt{10/2}} = 1.58$$

Looking up this value on the ND(0,1), we find that the area to the right of 1.58 is 0.057, which is a much better approximation.

## EXERCISES

1. Check the values obtained for the chi-square goodness-of-fit statistic in (a) Section 8-21 and (b) Section 8-23.
2. Check the values obtained for the chi-square goodness-of-fit statistic in (a) Figure 8-1 and (b) Figure 8-2.
3. In Examples 1 and 2 (Sections 8-21 and 8-23), would the value of the chi-square goodness-of-fit statistic have been any different if the observed values had been shuffled around among the 10 categories? Give your reasons. Under what circumstances would such a shuffle (i) change or (ii) not change the value of the statistic?
4. An experimenter wanted to learn whether human subjects would prefer immediate shock (IS) to variably delayed shock (VDS). Given a panel containing two buttons, the subject was free to push one button for IS and another for VDS. The experimenter decided that, if a subject gave more than 25 out of 40 responses to IS (or VDS), then he would be classified as preferring the IS condition (or the VDS condition). If the split was more nearly even, the subject would be classified as having no preference. Forty subjects were run, with the following results:

| IS preference | VDS preference | No preference |
| --- | --- | --- |
| 14 | 6 | 20 |

Test the hypothesis that these data can reasonably be considered an SIRS sample from a population having three categories with parameters $p_1 = p_2 = p_3 = \frac{1}{3}$.[1]
5. An experimenter had a hunch that superior and average college students come from different backgrounds. He conducted a large-scale survey to find out what kinds of parental occupation were represented among average college

[1] See P. Badia et al. Preference behavior in an immediate versus variably delayed shock situation. *Journal of Experimental Psychology*, 1966, **72**, 847–852. Check the values of the chi-square goodness-of-fit statistic given in this article.

students and came up with the results in the middle two columns of Table 8-3. Using these data as expected percentages of parental occupation, the experimenter then studied 155 superior college students and found their data to be as indicated in the last column of Table 8-3. Perform a chi-square goodness-of-fit test to see whether the superior students (the sample) match the unselected survey group (the population). Draw a diagram for this study, and identify the population parameters. Are these parameters estimated or hypothesized?[2]

Table 8-3

| Parental occupation | Survey group | | Superior |
| --- | --- | --- | --- |
| | No. | Percent | |
| Professional | 454 | 12.1 | 32 |
| Business | 184 | 4.9 | 28 |
| Clerical | 190 | 5.0 | 22 |
| Skilled | 630 | 16.8 | 19 |
| Personal | 758 | 20.2 | 7 |
| Farming | 763 | 20.3 | 17 |
| Semiskilled | 381 | 10.1 | 20 |
| Unskilled | 398 | 10.6 | 10 |

6. Examine the article by R. G. Smart. Alcoholism, birth order and family size. *Journal of Abnormal and Social Psychology*, 1963, **66**, 17–23. Note in particular how categories are combined when the expected frequencies are less than 5. Note also how the expected frequencies are determined according to some assumptions made by the experimenter. Always be aware of the fact that expected frequencies come from some model. This model might be the most direct one— all categories are equally likely—or it might be quite complicated, having experimenter assumptions to add to more conventional assumptions. In Exercise 5 above, the experimenter did a large-scale survey to develop his model of expected frequencies.

7. Imagine a task in which you see a series of erratic lines arranged in a zigzag pattern and directed more or less toward nine target objects. The experimenter asks you to tell him which three targets a particular line will intersect (if projected). By carefully arranging the lines and targets, the experimenter can introduce more or less uncertainty and more or less target probability (that is, probability that a target is involved in the intersection of chosen lines). For a series of low-uncertainty paths (lines), the experimenter obtains the following results:

| | Observed frequency | Expected frequency |
| --- | --- | --- |
| High target probability | 681 | 562 |
| Low target probability | 1,023 | 1,142 |

[2] The data for this example came from an article by M. D. Jenkins and C. M. Randall. Differential characteristics of superior and unselected Negro college students. *Journal of Social Psychology*, 1948, **27**, 187–202.

Do these data depart significantly from the expected results? What effect does the large $N$ (total frequency) have on a chi-square goodness-of-fit test?[3]

8. Do you think that you could tell the difference between Coca Cola, Pepsi Cola, and Royal Crown Cola by taste alone? Suppose that you were presented with 12 glasses of cola (4 of each kind and completely unidentifiable visually) and that your judgments were as follows:

| | |
|---|---|
| Coca Cola | 3 out of 4 correct |
| Pepsi Cola | 2 out of 4 correct |
| Royal Crown | 1 out of 4 correct |

If this experiment were repeated for a total of 50 subjects, then we could present the results as in Table 8-4.

(a) Assuming chance judgments, what are the population parameters for getting 0 correct out of 4, 1 out of 4, 2 out of 4, and at least 3 out of 4? (Use the binomial model.)

(b) Given $N = 50$, what would the expected frequencies be for the categories 0, 1, 2, and 3 or 4?

(c) Test the hypothesis that the judgments for Coca Cola were chance judgments. What are the appropriate degrees of freedom?

(d) Is the assumption of independence valid in this experimental setup? Think carefully about this.

(e) Repeat c for each of the other two brands.[4]

Table 8-4

| Brand name | Number of correct identifications | | | |
|---|---|---|---|---|
| | 0 | 1 | 2 | 3 or 4 |
| Coca Cola | 10 | 15 | 15 | 10 |
| Pepsi Cola | 12 | 16 | 11 | 11 |
| Royal Crown | 17 | 25 | 5 | 3 |

9. If the number of cases is small in certain categories, then the expected frequencies are likely to be less than 5. What should you do in such cases? Pool categories. For example, an experimenter wanted to find out whether neuropsychiatric patients are worse (or better) drivers than a random sample of California automobile drivers. He determined how many auto accidents each driver had had in a stated period of time and used the data from a random sample of California drivers to obtain the expected frequencies for the 165 patients. The results are shown in Table 8-5. How would you test the goodness of fit for these data?[5]

[3] See J. O. Morrissette and W. H. Pearson. Prediction of behavior under conditions of uncertainty. *Journal of Experimental Psychology*, 1963, **65**, 391–397. Recompute some of the chi-square values mentioned in this article.

[4] See F. J. Thumin. Identification of cola beverages. *Journal of Applied Psychology*, 1962, **46**, 358–360.

[5] See M. W. Buttiglieri and M. Guenette. Driving record of neuropsychiatric patients. *Journal of Applied Psychology*, 1967, **51**, 96–100.

Table 8-5

| Accidents | Patient frequency | Expected frequency |
|-----------|-------------------|--------------------|
| 0 | 133 | 129.79 |
| 1 | 31 | 28.85 |
| 2 | 1 | 5.28 |
| 3 | 0 | 0.87 |
| 4 | 0 | 0.17 |
| 5 | 0 | 0.02 |
| 6+ | 0 | 0.02 |

## 8-3   TESTING INDEPENDENCE

### 8-31   Recapitulation

We have seen how the chi-square goodness-of-fit statistic (Equation 8-1) can be used to evaluate the fit between observed frequencies and expected frequencies over a set of categories. Given $m$ categories and $N$ observations that are independent and have to fall into one and only one of the categories, the sample data consist of the observed frequencies in each category. To obtain the expected frequencies, we have to know (or estimate) the population parameters, $p_1$ through $p_m$, which are the probabilities of occurrence of each category. Given these probabilities, the expected frequencies are simply

$$Np_1, Np_2, \ldots, Np_m$$

Now let us consider a set of categories arranged in the form of a two-way table. For example, consider two kinds of voters—D for Democrat and R for Republican—and two kinds of behavior—smoking and nonsmoking (S and NS). The two-way table would be as follows:

In other words, we are thinking here about four categories, but they are arranged in the form of a $2 \times 2$ *contingency table*. In general, we might think of a contingency table with $r$ rows and $c$ columns, making a total of $rc$ categories (or cells). Suppose that we interview $N = 100$ voters (assuming they are either Democrats or Republicans) and find out whether they are smokers or nonsmokers. Each voter will fall into one and only one cell of the contingency table, and we shall assume that they behave independently of one another. It is thus a simple matter to obtain observed frequencies in the cells of a contingency table. What about the expected frequencies?

## 8-32   The Expected Frequencies

First consider the notion of independence. In Section 3-14 joint probabilities and conditional probabilities were introduced. Equation (3-5) defines the notion of independence. If $X$ and $Y$ are independent of each other, then

$$p(XY) = p(X)p(Y)$$

Note that $p(XY)$ is a joint probability.

In the case of a contingency table, say, the $2 \times 2$ case, let us assume that the marginal probabilities are known, as follows:

|   | S | NS |   |
|---|---|----|---|
| D |   |    | $p_1$ |
| R |   |    | $q_1$ |
|   | $p_2$ | $q_2$ | |

where $p_1 = \text{Pr(Democrat)}$
$q_1 = \text{Pr(Republican)} = 1 - p_1$
$p_2 = \text{Pr(smoker)}$
$q_2 = \text{Pr(nonsmoker)} = 1 - p_2$

What is the probability that a voter is both a Democrat and a smoker? That is, we want the joint probability $\text{Pr(D} \cdot \text{S)}$. We can answer this question very simply if we are prepared to accept the independence of political party and smoking behavior. Under this assumption we have

$$p(\text{D} \cdot \text{S}) \quad = p(\text{D})p(\text{S}) \quad = p_1 p_2$$

Similarly
$$p(\text{D} \cdot \text{NS}) = p(\text{D})p(\text{NS}) = p_1 q_2$$

$$p(\text{R} \cdot \text{S}) \quad = p(\text{R})p(\text{S}) \quad = q_1 p_2$$

$$p(\text{R} \cdot \text{NS}) = p(\text{R})p(\text{NS}) = q_1 q_2$$

At this point we can compute the expected frequencies in the four cells. All we have to do is to multiply the joint probabilities by $N$ (the size of the sample), as follows:

|   |   | S | NS |
|---|---|---|----|
| Expected frequencies | D | $Np_1 p_2$ | $Np_1 q_2$ |
|   | R | $Nq_1 p_2$ | $Nq_1 q_2$ |

*Do not forget that these frequencies depend upon the assumption of independence.*

By way of illustration, consider the following values for $p_1, q_1, p_2,$ and $q_2$:

|   | S | NS |   |
|---|---|----|---|
| D |   |    | $p_1 = 0.5$ |
| R |   |    | $q_1 = 0.5$ |

$p_2 = 0.7 \quad q_2 = 0.3$

Using these marginal probabilities and assuming the independence of the attributes of political party and smoking behavior, the joint probabilities would be as follows:

|   | S | NS |
|---|---|----|
| D | 0.35 | 0.15 |
| R | 0.35 | 0.15 |

Now suppose that $N = 100$; that is, 100 voters were sampled by SIRS and assigned to an appropriate cell in the 2 × 2 contingency table. The expected frequencies in each cell would simply be the joint probabilities multipled by $N = 100$:

|   | S | NS |
|---|---|----|
| D | 35 | 15 |
| R | 35 | 15 |

At this point the problem can be evaluated as before. We need to summarize the observed frequencies together with the expected frequencies in such a way as to evaluate the fit. The chi-square goodness-of-fit statistic is used as before.

To conclude the problem, let the observed data be

|   | S | NS |
|---|---|----|
| D | 50 | 10 |
| R | 20 | 20 |

Then, applying Equation (8-1), we have

$$\chi^2 = \frac{(50 - 35)^2}{35} + \frac{(10 - 15)^2}{15} + \frac{(20 - 35)^2}{35} + \frac{(20 - 15)^2}{15}$$

$$= 16.19$$

The degrees of freedom in this case depend upon whether or not the marginal probabilities were estimated from the sample data. Let us assume that they were not. Then the degrees of freedom equal $(m - 1)$, where $m$ is the number of categories; that is,

$$df = 4 - 1 = 3$$

Looking up this value of chi-square in the $\chi^2$-tables (Appendix D), we note that a value as large or larger than 16.19 can occur with probability less than .01. Conclusion? The tenability of the independence hypothesis (that smoking behavior and party affiliation are independent) is suspect. There appears to be some relationship between what party you belong to and whether you smoke or not, and the experimenter would reject the hypothesis of independence at beyond the 0.01 level.

## EXERCISES

1. Reread Section 3-14. Then consider a fourfold contingency table (another name for the 2 × 2 table) with row and column labels as follows:

$$
\begin{array}{c|c|c|}
 & \text{C} & \text{D} \\
\hline
\text{A} & & \\
\hline
\text{B} & & \\
\hline
\end{array}
$$

   (a) If $p(A) = 0.4$, $p(D) = 0.2$, define the rest of the marginal probabilities.
   (b) What are the four joint probabilities under the assumption of independence of rows and columns?
   (c) What would the four joint probabilities be in general, that is, if the rows and columns were not necessarily independent?
   (d) If you add up the four joint probabilities under the assumption of independence, what will the answer be?
   (e) If you add up the four joint probabilities in general, what will the answer be? (*Hint:* What will $[p(C \mid A) + p(D \mid A)]$ be?)
2. Consider an experiment involving a 3 × 3 contingency table and $N = 60$ observations. The marginal probabilities are

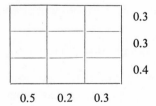

   (a) Compute the joint probabilities under the assumption of independence.

(b) Compute the expected frequencies under the assumption of independence.
(c) The experimental data were

| 9 | 9 | 9 |
|---|---|---|
| 7 | 7 | 7 |
| 4 | 4 | 4 |

Compute the value of the chi-square goodness-of-fit statistic.
(d) Consult Section 8-22 to see if any of the conditions have been violated in this exercise.


## 8-4  TWO-BY-TWO CONTINGENCY TABLES

### 8-41  An Example[6]

An experimenter has a hunch that individuals with complex cognitive systems are likely to attribute interpersonal conflict to imaginary people more often than do individuals with simple cognitive systems. Sixty subjects are chosen as the sample members, and each subject is classified according to two variables: (A) cognitive system—complex or simple; and (B) degree of conflict attributed—high or low. The data obtained are shown in the form of a contingency table (any two-way classification of objects gives rise to a contingency table):

|  | | (A) Cognitive system | | |
|---|---|---|---|---|
|  | | $A_1 =$ complex | $A_2 =$ simple | |
| (B) Conflict | $B_1 =$ high | 18 | 6 | 24 |
|  | $B_2 =$ low | 17 | 19 | 36 |
|  | | 35 | 25 | 60 |

The row totals, column totals, and grand total are also shown. Given these data, the experimenter wants to know whether there is any association between cognitive system and attribution of conflict.

### 8-42  Making Use of the Chi-square Goodness-of-fit Model

From the experimenter's point of view, there are two variables, $A$ and $B$, having two categories each, and he has obtained frequency data for this

---

[6] Adapted from an article by T. Tripodi and J. Bieri in *Journal of Personality*, 1966, **34**, 144–153: "Cognitive complexity, perceived conflict, and certainty."

fourfold contingency table. If he wants to test the goodness of fit of his experimental data to some expected frequencies, then there must be some hypothesis that gives rise to the expected frequencies. What is this hypothesis? It is the hypothesis that variables $A$ and $B$ are independent. Let us call this hypothesis $H_0$.

Under $H_0$, the statistician sees the problem as follows:

POPULATION.   There is an infinite population of members classified according to a $2 \times 2$ contingency table. The parameters of interest are the marginal probabilities, as shown here:

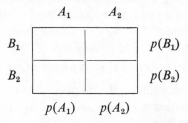

Actually we need to know only two of these (one of the row parameters and one of the column parameters), and then the other two will be determined.

SAMPLING PLAN.   $N = 60$ members are chosen by SIRS from this population.

STATISTIC.   There are two parts to the determination of the statistic (summary number) of interest.

(a) *The observed frequencies.*   Every sample size $N = 60$ will consist of four numbers—the frequencies in the four cells of the table. We shall call these the observed frequencies and shall designate them $O_{ij}$, the observed frequency in the $(i,j)$th cell (row $i$ and column $j$). Thus for any given sample we have

| | |
|---|---|
| $O_{11}$ | $O_{12}$ |
| $O_{21}$ | $O_{22}$ |

(b) *The expected frequencies.*   Under $H_0$, the independence hypothesis, the statistician computes expected frequencies, as indicated in Section 8-3: (i) determine the joint probabilities by multiplying marginal probabilities together, and (ii) multiply joint probabilities by $N = 60$, the sample size. Thus

$$\begin{array}{|c|c|} \hline E_{11} & E_{12} \\ \hline E_{21} & E_{22} \\ \hline \end{array} = \begin{array}{|c|c|} \hline Np(A_1)p(B_1) & Np(A_2)p(B_1) \\ \hline Np(A_1)p(B_2) & Np(A_2)p(B_2) \\ \hline \end{array}$$

where $E_{ij}$ designates the expected frequency in the $(i,j)$th cell.

Now the statistic of interest can be computed:

$$\chi^2 = \sum_{i=1}^{r} \sum_{j=1}^{c} \frac{(O_{ij} - E_{ij})^2}{E_{ij}} \tag{8-1$'$}$$

Note that this has the same form as Equation (8-1). The only difference is that we now sum over rows and columns of the contingency table.

SAMPLING DISTRIBUTION. This goodness-of-fit statistic is designated $\chi^2$, that is, chi-square, but it should never be forgotten that this is the goodness-of-fit chi-square statistic. It is not distributed exactly as a chi-square distribution. Its sampling distribution is only approximately a chi-square distribution. Remembering this, we must ask how many degrees of freedom there are so as to define which member of the family of chi-square distributions we are talking about. The general rule is

df = (number of categories − 1) − (number of parameters estimated)

In the case of contingency tables, the number of categories is the number of cells, but how many parameters were estimated from the data? This varies. Consider the following cases:

(a) *When the population parameters are known.* Section 8-3 shows how we determine expected frequencies when the population parameters are known prior to the gathering of data. Since we estimate no parameters from the data, df = (4 − 1) − (0) = 3.

(b) *When the population parameters are estimated.* We need to estimate two parameters, say, $p(A_1)$ and $p(B_1)$. Then the other two will be determined. The long-run relative-frequency interpretation of probability allows us to use a relative frequency as an estimate of the required probability. What is the relative frequency of $A_1$? There are 35 cases of $A_1$ out of a total of $N = 60$, so that the estimate of $p(A_1)$ is 35/60. Similarly, the estimate of $p(B_1)$ is 24/60. From this point on, the determination of the expected frequencies is as indicated in Section 8-3. But how many degrees of freedom are involved? Following the rule, df = (4 − 1) − (2) = 1. Thus the sampling distribution of the chi-square goodness-of-fit statistic is approximately a $\chi^2$-distribution with 1 df.

ASSUMPTIONS. Refer to Section 8-22 to refresh your memory of the assumptions underlying goodness-of-fit models in general, and add to these the assumption of independence in the case of contingency tables.

Now the experimenter and the statistician are in a position to cooperate. The experimenter summarizes his observed data in the form of the chi-square goodness-of-fit statistic, $\chi^2 = 4.57$, and since he had to use his sample data to estimate two population parameters, he regards this summary number as having (approximately) a chi-square distribution with 1 df. The statistician can tell him (from Appendix D) that this value is significant beyond the 0.05 level, and the experimenter interprets this by saying that since the chances of getting a chi-square value as large or larger than 4.57 are less than 5 in 100, he will reject the hypothesis of independence. He will report that there is a significant association between cognitive system and attributed conflict.

## 8-43   Details of the Computational Procedure

### THE GENERAL LAYOUT

Let us designate the general $2 \times 2$ contingency table as:

| | | |
|---|---|---|
| $O_{11}$ | $O_{12}$ | $R_1$ |
| $O_{21}$ | $O_{22}$ | $R_2$ |
| $C_1$ | $C_2$ | $N$ |

| | | |
|---|---|---|
| 18 | 6 | 24 |
| 17 | 19 | 36 |
| 35 | 25 | 60 |

where $R_1$, $R_2$ = row totals
$C_1$, $C_2$ = column totals
$N$ = total frequency

### ESTIMATING THE POPULATION PROBABILITIES

Since this is a case in which the population parameters must be estimated from the data, we proceed as follows:

Relative frequencies in each row are $R_1/N$ and $R_2/N$, and relative frequencies in each column are $C_1/N$ and $C_2/N$. These are taken to be the estimates of the population parameters.

$R_1/N = 24/60$

$R_2/N = 36/60$

$C_1/N = 35/60$

$C_2/N = 25/60$

### DETERMINING THE JOINT PROBABILITIES

Under the assumption of independence, the joint probabilities in the four cells are obtained by multiplying the marginal probabilities together appropriately, as follows:

The joint probabilities are

| | |
|---|---|
| $\left[\dfrac{R_1}{N}\right]\left[\dfrac{C_1}{N}\right]$ | $\left[\dfrac{R_1}{N}\right]\left[\dfrac{C_2}{N}\right]$ |
| $\left[\dfrac{R_2}{N}\right]\left[\dfrac{C_1}{N}\right]$ | $\left[\dfrac{R_2}{N}\right]\left[\dfrac{C_2}{N}\right]$ |

| | |
|---|---|
| $\left[\dfrac{24}{60}\right]\left[\dfrac{35}{60}\right]$ | $\left[\dfrac{24}{60}\right]\left[\dfrac{25}{60}\right]$ |
| $\left[\dfrac{36}{60}\right]\left[\dfrac{35}{60}\right]$ | $\left[\dfrac{36}{60}\right]\left[\dfrac{25}{60}\right]$ |

## DETERMINING THE EXPECTED FREQUENCIES

The expected frequencies are obtained by multiplying the joint probabilities by the sample size, $N$, as follows:

| $\dfrac{(R_1)(C_1)}{N}$ | $\dfrac{(R_1)(C_2)}{N}$ |
|---|---|
| $\dfrac{(R_2)(C_1)}{N}$ | $\dfrac{(R_2)(C_2)}{N}$ |

| $\dfrac{24 * 35}{60}$ | $\dfrac{24 * 25}{60}$ |
|---|---|
| $\dfrac{36 * 35}{60}$ | $\dfrac{36 * 25}{60}$ |

$=$

| 14 | 10 |
|---|---|
| 21 | 15 |

## COMPUTING THE SUMMARY NUMBER

All that remains is the use of Equation (8-1') to compute the value of the chi-square goodness-of-fit statistic:

$$\chi^2 = \frac{(18 - 14)^2}{14} + \frac{(6 - 10)^2}{10} + \frac{(17 - 21)^2}{21} + \frac{(19 - 15)^2}{15}$$

$$= 4.57$$

and the degrees of freedom:

$$df = (4 - 1) - (2) = 1$$

### 8-44  Efficient Computation

The computations are quite straightforward, however you look at them. The following steps may be distinguished:

1. Compute the row sums and the column sums.
2. For each cell multiply the appropriate row sum and column sum together, and divide by $N$. (This gives the expected frequencies for the case in which population probabilities must be estimated from the data; for the other case see Section 8-3.)
3. Compute the chi-square goodness-of-fit statistic from Equation (8-1').

See Exercise 1 below for the special case of fourfold tables.

### 8-45  A Little Theory

The assumptions underlying the theoretical justification for the use of the chi-square goodness-of-fit model are complicated and well beyond the scope of this text. We should be aware, however, that somewhere along the line we make the switch from a discrete problem (a multinomial problem—see

Section 4-8) to a continuous problem (the chi-square distribution). This switch involves the use of the famous Central Limit Theorem, which requires that $N$ tend to infinity. In Section 8-22 we made one concession to this asymptotic requirement by saying that the expected values must not be less than 5 and should be larger for better approximations. Now we consider another concession that is known as *Yates' correction for continuity* in fourfold contingency tables. At the end of Section 8-24, we noted that the normal approximation to the binomial distribution could be made closer if we used a 0.5 adjustment. We do a similar 0.5 adjustment to make the use of the chi-square goodness-of-fit model more appropriate in the case of $2 \times 2$ contingency tables. Instead of using Equation (8-1′) to compute $\chi^2$, we use

$$\chi^2 = \sum_{i=1}^{r} \sum_{j=1}^{c} \frac{(|O_{ij} - E_{ij}| - 0.5)^2}{E_{ij}} \tag{8-1''}$$

where $|O_{ij} - E_{ij}|$ means the absolute (positive) value of the difference between observed and expected frequencies in cell $(i, j)$.

Note that this correction for continuity is applied only to situations involving 1 df.

## EXERCISES

1. Show that Equation (8-1′) can be reduced to the following form for the special case of a fourfold contingency table:

$$\chi^2 = \frac{N(O_{11}O_{22} - O_{12}O_{21})^2}{R_1 R_2 C_1 C_2}$$

Demonstrate that this is so for the example in Section 8-41.
2. (a) Recompute the value of the chi-square goodness-of-fit statistic for the example in Section 8-41, using the formula in Equation (8-1″), that is, using the correction for continuity.
   (b) Show that Equation (8-1″) can be reduced to the following form for the special case of a fourfold contingency table:

$$\chi^2 = \frac{N(|O_{11}O_{22} - O_{12}O_{21}| - N/2)^2}{R_1 R_2 C_1 C_2}$$

   (c) Use this new version of Equation (8-1″) to demonstrate that it is true for the example in Section (8-41).
3. Consider the following fourfold contingency table:

| 6 | 14 |
|----|----|
| 13 | 7 |

   (a) Compute the chi-square goodness-of-fit statistic, using Equations (8-1′) and (8-1″). Which is more conservative?

(b) See the article by L. Weinstein. Social schemata of emotionally disturbed boys. *Journal of Abnormal and Social Psychology*, 1965, **70**, 457–461. Did this author use the corrected or the uncorrected formula for chi-square? Check the other chi-square values given in this article.

4. An experimenter believes that students' responses to instructors are related to these students' attitude toward their fathers. He obtains a sample of students, asks them to evaluate their instructors in terms of permissiveness, and finds out whether or not these students are critical of their fathers. The results are presented in the form of a 2 × 2 contingency table:

|  | Critical | Not critical |
|---|---|---|
| Permissive | 13 | 20 |
| Not permissive | 23 | 13 |

(a) Use the chi-square goodness-of-fit model to test the hypothesis that instructor ratings and father ratings are independent.

(b) Draw a diagram for this experiment.

(c) See the article by L. T. Orchus and W. J. Gnagey. Factors related to the shift of professional attitudes of students in teacher education. *Journal of Educational Psychology*, 1963, **54**, 149–154. Did these authors use corrected or uncorrected chi-square values?

5. Are girls who live in "row dorms" more authoritarian than girls who live in "nonrow dorms"? An experimenter studied 100 subjects (30 from nonrow dorms and 70 from row dorms) by giving them a test (to get authoritarian scores) and presenting the data in the form of a contingency table:

|  | Nonrow dorm | Row dorm |
|---|---|---|
| High authoritarian | 10 | 40 |
| Low authoritarian | 20 | 30 |

(a) Estimate the marginal probabilities.

(b) What are the expected frequencies under the hypothesis of independence?

(c) Compute $\chi^2$, using the formula in Exercise 1 above.

(d) Compute $\chi^2$, using the formula in Exercise 2 above.

(e) Which formula did the authors use in the following article? A. E. Siegel and S. Siegel. Reference groups, membership groups, and attitude change. *Journal of Abnormal and Social Psychology*, 1957, **55**, 360–364.

6. If you tell a child not to play with a certain toy and you threaten him with dire consequences if he disobeys, what are the long-term effects? An experimenter designs a fourfold contingency table as follows:

|  | Low threat | High threat |
|---|---|---|
| Played with toy | 6 | 14 |
| Did not play with toy | 15 | 7 |

where the children are originally told under low and high threats not to play with the toy but are later given the opportunity to do so.

   (a) Is there any significant relationship between original threat and later behavior?

   (b) See J. L. Freedman. Long term behavioral effects of cognitive dissonance. *Journal of Experimental Social Psychology*, 1965, **1**, 145–155. Did this author correct for continuity?

7. Sometimes in the literature you will find fourfold contingency tables presented differently. Consider:

   (a) R. W. Pace. Oral communication and sales effectiveness. *Journal of Applied Psychology*, 1962, **46**, 321–324. Here we find results presented as in Table 8-6.

Table 8-6

| Impression | High | | Low | | $\chi^2$ |
|---|---|---|---|---|---|
| | Yes | No | Yes | No | |
| 1. Overall | 13 | 7 | 3 | 14 | 6.577 |
| 8. Initial | 16 | 4 | 9 | 8 | 1.960 |

Check these values, and decide whether the author used the correction for continuity.

   (b) H. G. Furth. The influence of language on the development of concept formation in deaf children. *Journal of Abnormal and Social Psychology*, 1961, **63**, 386–389. Here you will have to read the article more carefully to interpret the table showing chi-square values. Table 1 on page 388 of the article shows entries like those in Table 8-7. Read the article to find out what sort of analysis

Table 8-7

| Age | Sameness | | $\chi^2$ |
|---|---|---|---|
| | Hearing | Deaf | |
| 7 | 4 | 7 | 0.44 |
| 12 | 22 | 15 | 2.54 |

yielded the chi-square values reported in this table.

   (c) C. C. Seltzer. Occupation and smoking in college graduates. *Journal of Applied Psychology*, 1964, **48**, 1–6. In this article is a table like Table 8-8:

Table 8-8

| Group | Nonsmokers | | Smokers | | $\chi^2$ |
|---|---|---|---|---|---|
| | No. | Percent | No. | Percent | |
| Organization | 56 | 24.9 | 220 | 32.8 | 4.99 |
| Arts | 7 | 3.1 | 24 | 5.6 | 0.11 |

Here each chi square is actually based on a 2 × 2 table, where two of the four entries are given in the table and the other two are obtained by subtracting from the total number of nonsmokers and smokers, respectively.

8. Sometimes in the literature you will be hard put to discover how the reported chi-square value was obtained. By way of illustration use Equations (8-1′) and (8-1″) on the following contingency-table data:

| | |
|---|---|
| 6 | 10 |
| 15 | 5 |

Now look up J. E. Gordon and F. Cohn. Effect of fantasy arousal of affiliation drive on doll play. *Journal of Abnormal and Social Psychology*, 1963, **66**, 301–307, and see if you can "arouse the appropriate fantasy" to come up with a chi-square value of 6.89.

## 8-5    R-BY-C CONTINGENCY TABLES

### 8-51    An Example[7]

An experimenter interested in eye dominance and handedness classifies 400 subjects according to these two variables. His data are as follows:

|   |   | $B_1$ = left | $B_2$ = both | $B_3$ = right |   |
|---|---|---|---|---|---|
|   | $A_1$ = left | 37 | 61 | 27 | 125 |
| $A$: Handedness | $A_2$ = both | 30 | 27 | 18 | 75 |
|   | $A_3$ = right | 61 | 104 | 35 | 200 |
|   |   | 128 | 192 | 80 | 400 |

*B*: Eye dominance

The row totals, column totals, and grand total are also shown. The experimenter wants to know whether there is any association between eye dominance and handedness.

### 8-52    Making Use of the Chi-square Goodness-of-fit Model

As an exercise, go through Section 8-42, and try to extend the conversation to the general $R \times C$ table. No new concepts are involved. There are $R$ row probabilities (parameters) to be hypothesized or estimated, and only

[7] Adapted from an article by T. L. Woo in *Biometrika*, 1928, **20A**, 125: "Eye dominance and handedness."

$(R - 1)$ of them are independent. There are $C$ column probabilities (parameters) to be hypothesized or estimated, and only $(C - 1)$ are independent. The degrees of freedom for the general case of $R \times S$ tables are

$$df = (\text{number of cells} - 1) - (\text{number of parameters estimated})$$

In the case where the sample data are used to estimate the parameters, the degrees of freedom are

$$df = (RC - 1) - (R - 1) - (C - 1)$$

### 8-53 Details of the Computational Procedure

### THE GENERAL LAYOUT

The observed data are designated

| $O_{11}$ | $O_{12}$ | $\cdots$ | $O_{1C}$ | $R_1$ |
|---|---|---|---|---|
| $O_{21}$ | $O_{22}$ | $\cdots$ | $O_{2C}$ | $R_2$ |
| $\cdots$ | $\cdots$ | $\cdots$ | $\cdots$ | $\cdots$ |
| $O_{R1}$ | $O_{R2}$ | $\cdots$ | $O_{RC}$ | $R_R$ |
| $C_1$ | $C_2$ | $\cdots$ | $C_C$ | $N$ |

| 37 | 61 | 27 | 125 |
|---|---|---|---|
| 30 | 27 | 18 | 75 |
| 61 | 104 | 35 | 200 |
| 128 | 192 | 80 | 400 |

Here $R = 3$ and $C = 3$.

### ESTIMATING THE POPULATION PARAMETERS

For this example we use the sample data to estimate the parameters of the population. We need $R$ row parameters (probabilities) and $C$ column parameters (probabilities).

For the $i$th row, the relative frequency is $R_i/N$, which is used to estimate the unknown parameter for the $i$th row. For the $j$th column, the relative frequency is $C_j/N$, which is used to estimate the unknown parameter for the $j$th column.

The estimates are

Row 1: 125/400
Row 2: 75/400
Row 3: 200/400
Col. 1: 128/400
Col. 2: 192/400
Col. 3: 80/400

## DETERMINING THE JOINT PROBABILITIES

Under the assumption of independence, the joint probability for cell $(i,j)$ is

$$\left(\frac{R_i}{N}\right)\left(\frac{C_j}{N}\right)$$

Joint probabilities are

| | | |
|---|---|---|
| $\dfrac{125}{400} * \dfrac{128}{400}$ | $\dfrac{125}{400} * \dfrac{192}{400}$ | $\dfrac{125}{400} * \dfrac{80}{400}$ |
| $\dfrac{75}{400} * \dfrac{128}{400}$ | $\dfrac{75}{400} * \dfrac{192}{400}$ | $\dfrac{75}{400} * \dfrac{80}{400}$ |
| $\dfrac{200}{400} * \dfrac{128}{400}$ | $\dfrac{200}{400} * \dfrac{192}{400}$ | $\dfrac{200}{400} * \dfrac{80}{400}$ |

## DETERMINING EXPECTED FREQUENCIES

Under the assumption of independence, expected frequencies are obtained by multiplying joint probabilities by sample size $N$. Thus for cell $(i,j)$ the expected frequency is

$$E_{ij} = N * \frac{R_i}{N} * \frac{C_j}{N} = \frac{R_i * C_j}{N}$$

Expected frequencies are

| | | |
|---|---|---|
| $\dfrac{125 * 128}{400}$ | $\dfrac{125 * 192}{400}$ | $\dfrac{125 * 80}{400}$ |
| $\dfrac{75 * 128}{400}$ | $\dfrac{75 * 192}{400}$ | $\dfrac{75 * 80}{400}$ |
| $\dfrac{200 * 128}{400}$ | $\dfrac{200 * 192}{400}$ | $\dfrac{200 * 80}{400}$ |

## COMPUTING THE SUMMARY NUMBER

All that remains is the use of Equation (8-1') to compute the value of the chi-square goodness-of-fit statistic. Since the table of expected values reduces to

| | | |
|---|---|---|
| 40 | 60 | 25 |
| 24 | 36 | 15 |
| 64 | 96 | 40 |

the required value is

$$\chi^2 = \frac{(37-40)^2}{40} + \frac{(61-60)^2}{60} + \frac{(27-25)^2}{25} + \frac{(30-24)^2}{24} + \frac{(27-36)^2}{36}$$

$$+ \frac{(18-15)^2}{15} + \frac{(61-64)^2}{64} + \frac{(104-96)^2}{96} + \frac{(35-40)^2}{40}$$

$$= 6.185$$

The degrees of freedom for this problem are

$$df = (3*3-1) - (3-1) - (3-1) = 4$$

## CONCLUSION

The summary number $\chi^2$ fluctuates from sample to sample, and its sampling distribution is approximately a chi-square distribution with 4 df. Looking up the value 6.185 in Appendix D, we find that the probability of getting a value not less than 6.185 on $\chi^2_{(4)}$ is about 0.20. The experimenter would conclude that the data in the contingency table do not show significant association between eye dominance and handedness. In terms of the goodness-of-fit model, we should say that the assumption of independence fits the data reasonably well.

### 8-54  A Little Theory

In Sections 8-3 through 8-5 we have been concerned with testing an independence hypothesis. If we reject the hypothesis of independence, then we are implying that there is some dependence (or association) between the attributes that define the contingency table. There are a number of measures that purport to measure the degree of association between the attributes, and, of course, each of these measures is a statistic. As such, each must have a sampling distribution. The most commonly used measures of association are related to the chi-square goodness-of-fit statistic and therefore have sampling distributions that are related to the chi-square distribution.

THE COEFFICIENT OF CONTINGENCY.    Pearson's $C$ is defined as

$$C = \sqrt{\frac{\chi^2}{N + \chi^2}} \tag{8-2}$$

Now if you use $C$ as a measure of association, then you might also want to ask if the obtained value of $C$ is significantly different from zero. How can you test for this? The test is nothing other than the chi-square goodness-of-fit test for independence in an $R \times C$ contingency table, as discussed in Sections 8-51 through 8-53, or Sections 8-41 through 8-44 if $R = C = 2$. If you reject the hypothesis of independence, then the measure of assocation is significant, by implication.

THE PHI COEFFICIENT.    When the table is fourfold, a very common measure of association is the phi coefficient, also known as the *fourfold point correlation*, defined as

$$\phi = \sqrt{\frac{\chi^2}{N}} \tag{8-3}$$

Here, too, if you determine the value of $\phi$ for a given fourfold contingency table, you might wish to test whether it is significantly different from zero.

And here, too, if the chi-square goodness-of-fit test of independence is negative (that is, we reject the hypothesis of independence), then by implication the measure of association is significant.

The interested student is urged to consult the following authoritative articles by L. A. Goodman and W. H. Kruskal:

Measures of association for cross classifications. *Journal of the American Statistical Association*, 1954, **49**, 732–764.

Measures of association for cross classifications: II. Further discussion and references. *Journal of the American Statistical Association*, 1959, **54**, 123–163.

Measures of association for cross classifications: III. Approximate sample theory. *Journal of the American Statistical Association*, 1963, **58**, 310–364.

## EXERCISES

1. An experimenter defined a sample of undergraduate unmarried males for the purpose of studying deviant sexual behavior. Classifying the subjects into aggressive and nonaggressive types, he obtained frequencies for each of the categories of pressure exerted by friends for new sexual experience. (See Table 8-9.)

Table 8-9

| Degree of pressure | Nonaggressive | Aggressive |
|---|---|---|
| Great deal | 6 | 4 |
| Considerable | 9 | 16 |
| Moderate | 52 | 26 |
| Little | 80 | 29 |
| None | 107 | 12 |

(a) Under the hypothesis of independence, determine the estimates of the population parameters (marginal probabilities) and the joint probabilities.

(b) Using Equation (8-1'), compute the value of the chi-square goodness-of-fit statistic for these data. Is there a significant association between felt pressure and aggressive rating?

(c) Are the expected values in all cells adequately large? Combine the first two rows, and recompute $\chi^2$. Check this value with that obtained in E. J. Kanin. Reference groups and sex conduct norm violations. *Sociological Quarterly*, 1967, **8**, 495–504.

2. A mother's behavior relative to her son can have an effect on the later behavior of the son. An experimenter designs an experiment to evaluate this assertion, classifies a sample of boys into aggressive, assertive, and nonaggressive, classifies the mothers into categories of overcontrolled, normal control, and subnormal control, and obtains observed frequency data as in Table 8-10.

(a) Obtain the joint probabilities under the assumption of independence. What is the sum of the nine joint probabilities?

Table 8-10

| Control | Aggressive | Assertive | Nonaggressive |
|---------|-----------|-----------|---------------|
| Over | 10 | 26 | 27 |
| Normal | 4 | 39 | 16 |
| Subnormal | 11 | 33 | 8 |

(b) Compute the chi-square goodness-of-fit statistic, and decide whether or not to reject the hypothesis of independence at the 0.05 level.

(c) Compute the value of $C$ (Equation 8-2) and $\phi$ (Equation 8-3).

(d) Check the value of chi-square obtained in W. McCord et al. Familial correlates of aggression in nondelinquent male children. *Journal of Abnormal and Social Psychology*, 1961, **62**, 79–93.

3. The Goodenough Draw-a-Man Test was given to three groups of Jamaican children to determine whether skin color and scores on the test were associated. The data are shown in Table 8-11.

(a) Determine the expected frequencies under the assumption of independence and using the sample data.

(b) Determine the value of the chi-square goodness-of-fit statistic, and reach a conclusion concerning the independence of Draw-a-Man scores and skin color.

(c) Check the other chi-square values reported in R. E. Grinder et al. Relationships between Goodenough Draw-a-Man Test performance and skin color among preadolescent Jamaican children. *Journal of Social Psychology*, 1964, **62**, 181–188.

Table 8-11

| Skin color | Low scores | High scores |
|------------|-----------|-------------|
| Light | 29 | 77 |
| Mixed | 89 | 108 |
| Dark | 387 | 251 |

4. Among female schizophrenics there are many more last-born than first-born individuals. Does this hold equally among Protestant, Catholic, and Jewish schizophrenics? An experiment is conducted to see if there is any association between birth rank and religion, with the results shown in Table 8-12.

(a) Determine the expected frequencies under the hypothesis of independence, and compute the chi-square goodness-of-fit statistic for these data.

(b) What conclusion do you reach concerning the hypothesis of independence? If there does seem to be a relationship between birth order and religion of female schizophrenics, what kind of relationship is it? (Examine Table 8-12 to answer this question.)

Table 8-12

| Birth rank | Protestant | Catholic | Jewish |
|------------|-----------|----------|--------|
| First-born | 63 | 19 | 3 |
| Last-born | 78 | 54 | 10 |

(c) Examine the article by C. Schooler. Birth order and hospitalization for schizophrenia. *Journal of Abnormal and Social Psychology*, 1964, **69**, 574–579. Compare your conclusions with those given in the article.

5. Sometimes an experimenter makes categories out of nearly continuous data for the purpose of evaluating the association between two variables. For example, if a subject is required to engage in serial-list learning under various kinds of conditioning, then the dependent measure may be time-to-success in learning the serial list. This time measure may be categorized into short, medium, and long and the data converted into frequencies within these categories. Consider Table 8-13 for such an experiment.

Table 8-13

| Number of conditioned GSRs | Total time | | |
|---|---|---|---|
| | Short | Medium | Long |
| 0–3 | 15 | 40 | 39 |
| 4–7 | 16 | 19 | 5 |
| 8–11 | 9 | 11 | 4 |

(a) Determine the expected frequencies under the hypothesis of independence, and obtain the value of chi square.

(b) Should the hypothesis of independence be rejected?

(c) Compute the values of C—Equation (8-2)—and $\phi$—Equation (8-3). Are these measures of association significantly different from zero? Is the association positive or negative? Check the article by I. C. Murphy. Serial learning, conditionability and the choice of an independent measure of anxiety. *Journal of Abnormal and Social Psychology*, 1964, **69**, 614–619.

6. Is there a relationship between neuroses and psychoses and social class? Table 8-14 gives some data relevant to this question.

Table 8-14

| Social class | Neuroses | Psychoses |
|---|---|---|
| I | 10 | 9 |
| II | 88 | 43 |
| III | 115 | 145 |
| IV | 175 | 583 |
| V | 61 | 662 |

(a) Determine the estimated population parameters (row marginal probabilities), the expected frequencies in the 10 cells according to the hypothesis of independence, and the value of the chi-square goodness-of-fit statistic.

(b) What conclusion do you reach on the basis of using the chi-square goodness-of-fit model to test the hypothesis of independence?

(c) Check the article by A. B. Hollingshead and F. C. Redlich. Social stratification and psychiatric disorders. *American Sociological Review*, 1953, **18**, 163–169. Check the value of chi square obtained for Table I in this article.

# Correlation and Regression

## 9-1 THE CORRELATION COEFFICIENT[1]

### 9-11 An Example

Twenty-five twelfth-graders were administered a test designated A, and a year later their grade-point averages (GPA) were obtained from the colleges they attended. The (fictitious) results are shown in Table 9-1. The question of interest is whether there is a significant relationship between the scores on test A and the later GPA (designated B, for convenience). Implicit in this

Table 9-1

| Subject | Score ($A_i$) | GPA ($B_i$) | Subject | Score ($A_i$) | GPA ($B_i$) |
|---------|---------------|-------------|---------|---------------|-------------|
| 1 | 18 | 3.3 | 14 | 13 | 1.9 |
| 2 | 17 | 2.8 | 15 | 19 | 3.9 |
| 3 | 12 | 2.1 | 16 | 18 | 2.5 |
| 4 | 11 | 1.9 | 17 | 19 | 2.9 |
| 5 | 15 | 2.6 | 18 | 19 | 2.8 |
| 6 | 15 | 2.5 | 19 | 23 | 3.6 |
| 7 | 10 | 1.6 | 20 | 20 | 3.2 |
| 8 | 10 | 1.7 | 21 | 20 | 3.5 |
| 9 | 11 | 1.9 | 22 | 18 | 3.7 |
| 10 | 11 | 2.3 | 23 | 16 | 2.6 |
| 11 | 14 | 2.1 | 24 | 15 | 2.7 |
| 12 | 13 | 2.4 | 25 | 15 | 2.3 |
| 13 | 12 | 2.2 | | | |

[1] Reread Section 2-4 as an introduction to this chapter.

interest is the hope that, if there is a significant relationship, then the scores on test A may be used to predict the GPA at the end of the freshman year at college.

## 9-12  Basic Calculations

Whenever an experimenter obtains $N$ two-tuples as his dependent measures, there should be a natural tendency to compute five basic quantities:

$$\sum A = 384 \qquad \sum B = 65.0$$
$$\sum A^2 = 6214 \qquad \sum AB = 1{,}047.9 \qquad \sum B^2 = 178.92$$

Substituting these values in equations for computing the means, variances (Equation 2-7), and correlation coefficient (Equation 2-14), he will obtain:

Two means: $\qquad\qquad\qquad \bar{A} = 15.36 \qquad$ and $\qquad \bar{B} = 2.60$

Two standard deviations: $\qquad s_A = 3.55 \qquad$ and $\qquad s_B = 0.63$

One correlation: $\qquad\qquad\qquad\qquad r_{AB} = 0.884$

These are the basic summary numbers for the experimental data.

## 9-13  Defining a Statistical Model

From the experimenter's point of view, he knows now that the correlation coefficient is 0.884. This suggests to him that there is a definite positive relationship between the scores on test A and the grade-point average a year later. But he also knows about sampling fluctuation and wonders what the chances are of getting a correlation coefficient as large or larger than 0.884 when the true population parameter (the correlation coefficient for the population) is zero. In other words, the experimenter would like to know what kind of sampling distribution this correlation coefficient has.

From the statistician's point of view, it is not possible to talk about a sampling distribution until some assumptions are made about the population distribution and the sampling plan. In order to make things precise, he offers the following model.

POPULATION.  Let the population be a *bivariate normal distribution.* What does this mean? Imagine a three-dimensional plot of the distribution, as in Figure 9-1. Then we are talking about a random variable that is an ordered two-tuple $(X, Y)$. The permissible values for this ordered two-tuple are all points in the plane of the $X$ and $Y$ axes. The probability function defined on these permissible values gives rise to the surface shown in the figure.

How many parameters are necessary to define a bivariate normal distribution? Five. As with all bivariate (two-tuple) sets of numbers the five most

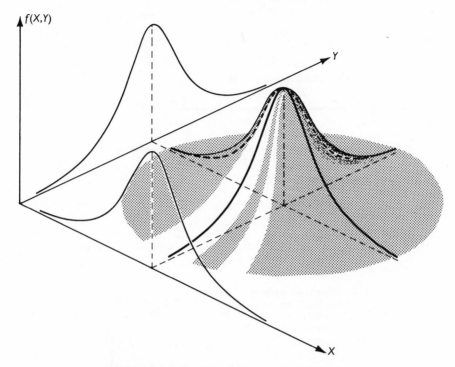

FIGURE 9-1. The bivariate normal distribution

important summary numbers are two means, two standard deviations, and one correlation coefficient. These five parameters define the bivariate normal distribution completely, and we shall designate them $\mu_X, \mu_Y, \sigma_X, \sigma_Y, \rho_{XY}$. (The sample statistics corresponding to these parameters are $\overline{X}, \overline{Y}, s_X, s_Y, r_{XY}$.) For the record, the equation of the bivariate normal distribution in standard form (that is, when the variables $X$ and $Y$ have been standardized) is

$$f(X,Y) = \frac{1}{2\pi\sqrt{1-\rho^2}} e^{-(x^2-2\rho xy+y^2)/[2(1-\rho^2)]} \tag{9-1}$$

(If you enter a value for the standard score $x$ and a value for the standard score $y$, then Equation 9-1 tells you the height of the three-dimensional surface. What is the height of the surface when $x = y = 0$?)

SAMPLING PLAN. Choose $N$ two-tuples by SIRS.

SAMPLES. Repeated application of this sampling plan will produce as many samples of size $N$ as we please. Theoretically we imagine the statistician to be able to generate every possible sample.

SUMMARY NUMBER. Each sample of $N$ ordered two-tuples is summarized in the form of Pearson's product-moment correlation coefficient, $r$.

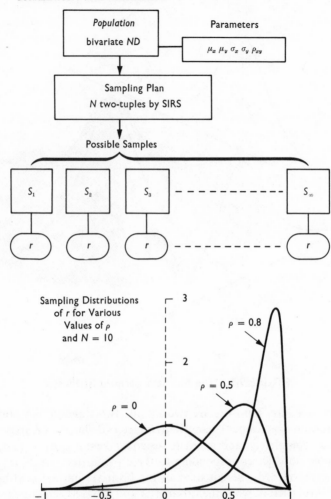

FIGURE 9-2.   The sampling distribution of the correlation coefficient ($r$)

SAMPLING DISTRIBUTION.   It was Fisher who discovered the equation for the sampling distribution of $r$. The equation is complicated[2] and is not given here, but the interesting thing about it is that, although the population distribution is a five-parameter distribution, the sampling distribution of $r$ depends on only two quantities: ($i$) $N$, the size of the sample, and ($ii$) $\rho$, the population correlation coefficient. The equation for the sampling distribution of $r$ describes a *family* of distributions, since for each combination of $N$ and $\rho$ there is a distinct sampling distribution.

[2] Harald Cramer, *Mathematical methods of statistics.* Princeton, N.J.: Princeton University Press, 1946. P. 398. M. G. Kendall and A. Stuart. *The advanced theory of statistics.* Vol. 1. New York: Hafner, 1958. P. 255.

PROPERTIES OF THE SAMPLING DISTRIBUTION OF $r$.    Figure 9-2 illustrates the shape of several sampling distributions of $r$. If the population parameter, $\rho$, is zero, the sampling distribution of $r$ is symmetrical about zero, but in all other cases (when $\rho \neq 0$) the sampling distributions are skew. This skewness becomes pronounced as the value of $\rho$ approaches $+1$ or $-1$, even when the sample is reasonably large (like $N = 100$). The way the statistician describes the situation is as follows: The sampling distribution of $r$ approaches normality very slowly when the parameter $\rho$ is not close to zero.

This skewness poses something of a problem for the experimenter. Suppose that he obtains a sample correlation coefficient of $r = 0.56$ and wants to test the hypothesis that the population correlation coefficient is $\rho = 0.70$. There are no tables to consult, and he knows that the sampling distribution of $r$ is complicated and skewed. He also knows that his sample is small ($N$ being 25, say). What is he to do?

Before answering this question, let us examine briefly the sampling distribution of $r$ when the population parameter $\rho = 0$. This is the only symmetrical distribution, and for the record, we present the equation of this special sampling distribution:

$$f(r) = \frac{1}{\sqrt{\pi}} \frac{\Gamma[(N-1)/2]}{\Gamma[(N-2)/2]} (1 - r^2)^{(N-4)/2} \tag{9-2}$$

Now this frequency function could be tabled (and it has been), but we can go one step further and save ourselves the trouble of including another table in the Appendix.

If we summarize the $N$ ordered two-tuples of the sample in the form of

$$t = \sqrt{N-2} \, \frac{r}{\sqrt{1-r^2}} \tag{9-3}$$

where $r$ is the sample correlation coefficient, then it can be proved that this new statistic, $t$, is distributed as a $t$-statistic with $(N-2)$ df.

## 9-14   Making Use of the Model to Test the Hypothesis $\rho = 0$

This section is brief, since we plan to supersede it in Section 9-15 with a more flexible model.

The experimenter obtained 25 ordered two-tuples as his sample and observed that the correlation between the scores on test A and the grade-point averages (B) was 0.884. Is this significantly different from zero? (We hope so!)

The statistician suggests that the data be summarized in the form of $t$ (Equation 9-3), and the experimenter does this:

$$t = \sqrt{25 - 2} \, \frac{0.884}{\sqrt{1 - 0.884^2}} = 9.069$$

Looking up the $t$-tables (Appendix E) with $(N - 2) = 23$ df, he notes that this value of $t$ is well beyond the 0.01 level, and so he confidently rejects the hypothesis that the population parameter (correlation coefficient) was zero. There is a significant correlation between the scores on test A and the GPA. (*Note:* This test is performed only when we are testing the significance of the difference from zero. In other words, *if* the population is bivariate normal with parameter $\rho = 0$ and *if* the sampling plan is SIRS, *then* the summary number $t$—Equation (9-3)— is distributed as a $t$-distribution with $(N - 2)$ df.)

### 9-15   Fisher's *r*-to-*z* Transformation

Because of the skewness of the sampling distributions of $r$ whenever the population correlation is different from zero and because of the complicated equations involved, Fisher developed the following very useful transformations of correlation coefficients:

Sample correlation $r$:
$$z = \frac{1}{2} \ln \frac{(1 + r)}{(1 - r)} \tag{9-4}$$

Population correlation $\rho$:
$$\zeta = \frac{1}{2} \ln \frac{(1 + \rho)}{(1 - \rho)} \tag{9-5}$$

where "ln" stands for the natural logarithm to the base $e$. These transformations are known as the *r-to-z transformation* and the *rho-to-zeta transformation*, respectively. For ready reference see Appendices G and H, which give *r*-to-*z* and *z*-to-*r* transformations.

Now, why are these transformations useful? The reason is that the sampling distribution of $z$ (for various values of $N$ and $\rho$) is very nearly normal even when the sample size is very small (like $N = 10$). This property is important because it means that we no longer have to deal with skewed distributions having complicated equations, and we do not have to restrict ourselves to testing the hypothesis that $\rho = 0$.

*For given N and $\rho$, the sampling distribution of z is approximately normally distributed with mean and standard deviation as follows:*

$$Mean = \zeta + \frac{\rho}{2(N - 1)}$$
$$Standard\ deviation = \frac{1}{\sqrt{N - 3}} \tag{9-6}$$

Let us now use this property of $z$-distributions to test the hypotheses (*i*) that $\rho = 0$ and (*ii*) that $\rho \neq 0$ but rather some fixed value other than zero.

EXAMPLE 1: TEST THE HYPOTHESIS THAT $\rho = 0$. The experimenter obtained a sample value of $r = 0.884$. Making use of the $r$-to-$z$ transformation, test the hypothesis that the population correlation coefficient was zero. What is the statistical model being used? See Figure 9-3 for a diagrammatic representation. Note that $z$ is the summary number of interest, and in order to specify its (approximate) sampling distribution, we have to have $\zeta$ and $\rho$ and $N$. The computations are as follows: (i) Given that $N = 25$, $r = 0.884$, and $\rho = 0$, we compute (ii) $z$, $\zeta$, the mean (expected value) of $z$, and the standard error of $z$ (from Equation 9-6):

$$z = \frac{1}{2} \ln \frac{(1 + 0.884)}{(1 - 0.884)} = 1.394 \qquad \text{Equation (9-4)}$$

$$\zeta = \frac{1}{2} \ln \frac{(1 + 0)}{(1 - 0)} = 0 \qquad \text{Equation (9-5)}$$

$$E(z) = \left[ 0 + \frac{0}{2(25 - 1)} \right] = 0 \qquad \text{Equation (9-6)}$$

$$\text{se}_z = \frac{1}{\sqrt{25 - 3}} = 0.213 \qquad \text{Equation (9-6)}$$

At this point we know that the summary number $z$ is distributed approximately as a normal distribution with a mean of 0 and a standard deviation of 0.213. Forming the standard normal deviate for the value $z = 1.394$, we have

$$\text{Standard form of } z = \frac{z - E(z)}{\text{se}_z}$$

$$= \frac{1.394 - 0}{0.213}$$

$$= 6.537$$

By now you should not even have to look this one up in the ND(0,1) tables. This value is obviously well beyond the 0.01 level on the standard normal distribution, and the conclusion is, as before, that this sample correlation coefficient is significantly different from zero.

COMMENT. It may be somewhat confusing to see an expression like "standard form of $z$" when it was previously asserted that the symbol $z$ was conventionally used to designate a standard form. Unfortunately, in Fisher's $r$-to-$z$ transformation, the variable $z$ is not in standard form so that you should be careful to distinguish these cases. Remember that (i) Fisher's

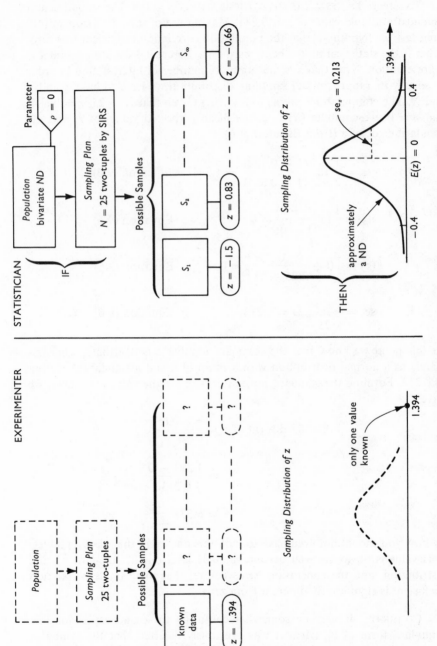

FIGURE 9-3. Making use of the statistical model for testing correlation coefficients

$z$ is approximately distributed as

$$\mathrm{ND}\left(\left[\zeta + \frac{\rho}{2(N-1)}\right], \left[\frac{1}{\sqrt{N-3}}\right]\right)$$

so that (ii), $\qquad \dfrac{z - [\zeta + \rho/2(N-1)]}{1/\sqrt{N-3}} = \dfrac{z - E(z)}{\mathrm{se}_z}$

is distributed approximately as $\mathrm{ND}(0,1)$.

EXAMPLE 2: TEST THE HYPOTHESIS THAT $\rho = 0.70$. Given that $N = 25$, $r = 0.884$, and $\rho = 0.7$, we compute $z$, $\zeta$, the mean (expected value) of $z$, and the standard error of $z$:

$$z = 1.394 \qquad \text{as before in Example 1}$$

$$\zeta = \frac{1}{2} \ln \frac{(1 + 0.7)}{(1 - 0.7)} = 0.867$$

$$E(z) = 0.867 + \frac{0.7}{2(25 - 1)} = 0.882$$

$$\mathrm{se}_z = 0.213 \qquad \text{as before in Example 1}$$

The standard form for $z$ is therefore

$$\frac{(1.394 - 0.882)}{0.213} = 2.401$$

This is one value of a random variable that is approximately distributed as $\mathrm{ND}(0,1)$, and the probability of obtaining values as large as this or larger is about 0.008. If we are testing the hypothesis that the observed $r = 0.884$ is significantly larger than 0.7, then a one-tail test shows that this is indeed so ($r = 0.884$ is significantly larger than 0.7) at the 0.01 level.

EXAMPLE 3: FIND THE 95 PERCENT CONFIDENCE INTERVAL FOR $r = 0.884$. In Example 1 we tested to see if $r = 0.884$ was significantly different from zero, and it was. In Example 2 we tested to see if $r = 0.884$ was significantly different from 0.7, and it was. Clearly there must be some value of $\rho$ (the population parameter) that is not significantly different from $r = 0.884$. In fact we are interested in two critical values which we shall designate $\rho_L$ and $\rho_U$. The range from $\rho_L$ to $\rho_U$ must be the 95 percent confidence region, which means that the area in each tail of the sampling distribution must be 0.025. Looking up the $\mathrm{ND}(0,1)$ tables, we note that if the standard normal deviate is $+1.96$, then there will be about 0.025 unit of area in the right tail; and if the standard normal deviate is $-1.96$, there will be about 0.025 unit of area in the left tail. Study Figure 9-4. What we really have to look for first

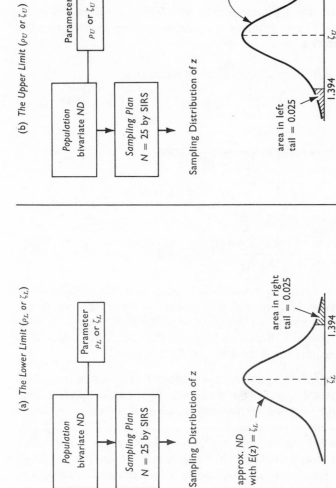

**FIGURE 9-4.** Finding the 95 percent confidence limits for a sample correlation coefficient

*Note:* We work backward to find confidence intervals. Knowing the shape of the sampling distribution and knowing the sample value z = 1.394, we look for $\zeta_L$ and $\zeta_U$.

is two values of $E(z)$ that satisfy the following equations:

$$\frac{1.394 - E(z)}{0.213} = 1.96 \tag{9-7}$$

and
$$\frac{1.394 - E(z)}{0.213} = -1.96 \tag{9-8}$$

The solutions to these two equations are straightforward:

For Equation (9-7):        $E(z) = 0.977$

For Equation (9-8):        $E(z) = 1.811$

Now, to convert these values of $E(z)$ into values of $\rho$ through the medium of Equation (9-6) is a difficult problem unless we make one simplifying assumption: ignore the term $[\rho/2(N - 1)]$. Under this assumption, $E(z) = \zeta$, and so we can use the $z$-to-$r$ tables (Appendix H) to convert $E(z)$ into $\zeta$-values. Doing so, we have

For Equation (9-7):        $\rho_L = 0.752$

For Equation (9-8):        $\rho_U = 0.948$

These are the approximate boundaries of the 95 percent confidence interval for the population correlation coefficient, based on an observed value, $r = 0.884$.

COMMENT. Note that the only value you have to change if you want to determine some other confidence interval is 1.96. For example, if you look up the tables for $ND(0,1)$, you will find that the 99 percent confidence region refers to plus and minus 2.57. In general, then, the confidence interval for the population correlation coefficient is given by

$$[z - k(\text{se}_z)] \le \zeta \le [z + k(\text{se}_z)]$$

after these boundaries have been converted into values of $\rho$. The constant $k$ refers to the critical points on the $ND(0,1)$ and will vary according to what confidence interval is being sought.

Note that, in order to compute boundaries for confidence intervals, we had to make a simplifying assumption, that $E(z) = \zeta$, rather than the definition in Equation (9-6). This approximation is good if $N$ is moderate (not less than 50, say) and $\rho$ is small (not more than $|0.5|$, say).

## EXERCISES

1. Compute the correlation coefficient for the following sample of two-tuples:

| | | | |
|---|---|---|---|
| (5,12) | (8,14) | (10,17) | (9,10) |
| (10,10) | (12,20) | (11,13) | (4,21) |
| (13,13) | (3,19) | (9,8) | (9,18) |
| (12,8) | (10,20) | (6,17) | (10,6) |
| (4,21) | (3,16) | (3,17) | (9,9) |

(a) Draw a graph of these two-tuples.

(b) Use Equation (9-3) to test whether the sample $r$ is significantly different from zero.

(c) Use the $r$-to-$z$ transformation to see whether the sample $r$ is significantly different from zero.

(d) Use the $r$-to-$z$ transformation to see whether the sample $r$ is significantly different from $-0.25$.

2. From Table 2-4 plot the ordered two-tuples $(A,D)$, that is, scores on Number Series versus scores on Word Recognition. Is the correlation between these two tests significantly different from zero? After you have made your decision, ask yourself how you were able to do so. Consider the assumptions of the model, the risk involved in rejecting or accepting the hypothesis of zero correlation, and so on.

3. Consider a sample correlation coefficient $r = 0.50$ based on a sample size $N = 52$. Using the $r$-to-$z$ transformation, decide whether this $r$ value is significantly different from (a) $\rho = 0$, (b) $\rho = 0.1$, (c) $\rho = 0.3$, (d) $\rho = 0.4$, (e) $\rho = 0.6$, (f) $\rho = 0.8$. (g) Making use of the simplification (namely, $E(z) = \zeta$) introduced in Example 3 in Section 9-15, determine the 95 percent confidence interval for $\rho$.

4. Convert $r = 0.46$ into its corresponding $z$-value. What would be the $z$-value for $r = -0.46$? Can you show in general that if $+r$ is converted into $+z$, then $-r$ is converted into $-z$?

5. The following computer simulation was performed to check the statement that the sampling distribution of $r$ is skewed for values of the population parameter $\rho$ other than zero. A computer program was written to perform SIRS sampling

Table 9-2

| Midpoint of interval | Frequency |
|---|---|
| 0.00 | 2 |
| 0.05 | 0 |
| 0.10 | 4 |
| 0.15 | 7 |
| 0.20 | 17 |
| 0.25 | 23 |
| 0.30 | 20 |
| 0.35 | 32 |
| 0.40 | 48 |
| 0.45 | 61 |
| 0.50 | 62 |
| 0.55 | 57 |
| 0.60 | 71 |
| 0.65 | 52 |
| 0.70 | 28 |
| 0.75 | 10 |
| 0.80 | 5 |
| 0.85 | 1 |
| 0.90 | 0 |
| 0.95 | 0 |

Total    500

from a bivariate normal distribution with known parameters (that is, the five parameters had to be fed into the computer). The sampling plan was to choose 25 two-tuples from this defined population. For each sample the value of $r$ was computed, and in 59.09 sec the computer managed to produce 500 such samples. Intervals were made on the range of permissible values for $r$ (namely, from $-1$ to $+1$), and the frequencies in Table 9-2 were obtained for a population with $\mu_X = 5$, $\mu_Y = 4$, $\sigma_X = 2$, $\sigma_Y = 2$, and $\rho_{XY} = 0.5$. Make a histogram out of these data, and compute the mean, standard deviation, and coefficient of skewness.

6. The same computer program used to obtain the results in Exercise 5 produced the following results (Table 9-3) for the bivariate normal population with parameters $\mu_X = 5$, $\mu_Y = 4$, $\sigma_X = 2$, $\sigma_Y = 2$, and $\rho_{XY} = 0.8$. The sample size was again $N = 25$.

Table 9-3

| Midpoint of interval | Frequency |
|---|---|
| 0.50 | 2 |
| 0.55 | 6 |
| 0.60 | 13 |
| 0.65 | 25 |
| 0.70 | 44 |
| 0.75 | 85 |
| 0.80 | 125 |
| 0.85 | 143 |
| 0.90 | 54 |
| 0.95 | 3 |
| Total | 500 |

(a) Plot a histogram for these data.

(b) Determine the mean, standard deviation, and skewness for this distribution of sample correlation coefficients.

(c) What would happen to the skewness coefficient if the sample size were $N = 1,000$? if it were $N = 10$?

7. Using the values tabled in Appendix G, plot a graph showing how to convert $r$-values to $z$-values. Can you see from this chart why the $z$-values are likely to be more symmetrically distributed than the $r$-values? Consider the data in Exercise 5, and imagine that you had every one of the 500 sample $r$-values in front of you. You have already seen that the distribution of the $r$-values is skew. If you used your graph from this exercise, would the skewness tend to disappear?

## 9-2  SIMPLE REGRESSION

### 9-21  An Example

Return to Table 9-1 in Section 9-11. There are 25 two-tuples of the form (score on test A; GPA at the end of freshman year), and we designate the two-tuple for the $i$th subject $(A_i, B_i)$. For ready reference we repeat Table 9-1 here.

Table 9-1

| Subject | Score ($A_i$) | GPA ($B_i$) | Subject | Score ($A_i$) | GPA ($B_i$) |
|---------|---------------|-------------|---------|---------------|-------------|
| 1 | 18 | 3.3 | 14 | 13 | 1.9 |
| 2 | 17 | 2.8 | 15 | 19 | 3.9 |
| 3 | 12 | 2.1 | 16 | 18 | 2.5 |
| 4 | 11 | 1.9 | 17 | 19 | 2.9 |
| 5 | 15 | 2.6 | 18 | 19 | 2.8 |
| 6 | 15 | 2.5 | 19 | 23 | 3.6 |
| 7 | 10 | 1.6 | 20 | 20 | 3.2 |
| 8 | 10 | 1.7 | 21 | 20 | 3.5 |
| 9 | 11 | 1.9 | 22 | 18 | 3.7 |
| 10 | 11 | 2.3 | 23 | 16 | 2.6 |
| 11 | 14 | 2.1 | 24 | 15 | 2.7 |
| 12 | 13 | 2.4 | 25 | 15 | 2.3 |
| 13 | 12 | 2.2 | | | |

The question of interest is to what extent the experimenter could have predicted the grade-point averages on the basis of knowing the scores on test A (for ability, say)? Clearly this question is not unrelated to that posed in Section 9-11. Is there a significant relationship between $A$ and $B$? If there is, then we are likely to be able to predict significantly better than chance.

## 9-22 Basic Calculations

These are just the same as in Section 9-12. We compute two means ($\bar{A} = 15.36$, $\bar{B} = 2.60$), two standard deviations ($s_A = 3.55$, $s_B = 0.63$), and one correlation coefficient ($r_{AB} = 0.884$).

## 9-23 The Experimenter's Viewpoint

The experimenter observes that subject 1 obtains an ability score of $A_1 = 18$, and at the end of his freshman year he has a grade-point average of $B_1 = 3.3$. What he would like to have is some rule (function) that converts a value of $A$ into some predicted value of $B$ so that this value $B$ and the true value of $B$ are as close as possible. Now what kind of function would this be? The experimenter can lay down certain requirements for this function: that it should be (*i*) a simple function and (*ii*) as accurate as possible. As a concession to requirement (*i*), he might restrict his attention to *linear* functions (that is, straight-line functions). In other words, given a score $A_i$, he looks for a function that has the following form:

$$\hat{B}_i = c_0 + c_1 A_i \tag{9-9}$$

where $\hat{B}_i$ is the predicted value (function value) of $B$ for the $i$th subject and $c_0$ and $c_1$ are constants defining the intercept and slope of the straight line, respectively. These constants $c_0$ and $c_1$ can be chosen as you wish, but of course you will want to do so wisely. Equation (9-9) defines a linear function (or rule) that assigns to each distinct value of $A$ a particular value of $\hat{B}$. It is known as the *linear regression of B on A* when we think about it in a statistical context. Note that we could also define the linear regression of $A$ on $B$, as follows:

$$\hat{A}_j = d_0 + d_1 B_j \qquad (9\text{-}10)$$

How shall we choose the constants $c_0$ and $c_1$ (or $d_0$ and $d_1$)? Requirement (*ii*) says that the function should be as accurate as possible. We take this to mean that the predicted value of $B_i$ (namely, $\hat{B}_i$) should be as close as possible to the actual value $B_i$. And what do we mean by as close as possible? For each subject we define an error of prediction, as follows:

$$\begin{aligned} e_i &= [B_i - \hat{B}_i] \\ &= [B_i - (c_0 + c_1 A_i)] \end{aligned} \qquad (9\text{-}11)$$

and we compute a summary number that we call $\theta$ (theta):

$$\theta = \sum e_i^2 = \sum (B_i - \hat{B}_i)^2 \qquad (9\text{-}12)$$

Then the problem is defined as follows. Find $c_0$ and $c_1$ such that $\theta$ (the sum of the squares of the errors of prediction) is as small as possible. This is a well-defined problem with a well-defined solution. Leaving the details until Section 9-25, note that the experimenter chooses the following values:

$$c_0 = 0.1921 \quad \text{and} \quad c_1 = 0.1568$$

Thus the simple linear regression equation for predicting $B$ from $A$ (that is, the regression of $B$ on $A$) is

$$\hat{B}_i = 0.1921 + 0.1568 A_i \qquad (9\text{-}13)$$

How does the experimenter make use of this regression equation? For each subject he enters an observed score, $A_i$, and obtains a predicted score, $\hat{B}_i$. For example,

For subject 1:     $\hat{B}_1 = 0.1921 + 0.1568(18) = 3.01$

Doing this for all students and writing down the original score for comparison, we have Table 9-4.

Another way of visualizing this process of regression is by means of a scatterplot. Figure 9-5 shows the scatterplot of the original scores and the position of the regression line (Equation 9-13). To obtain the predicted score for any given value of $A$, proceed vertically to the regression line and then horizontally to the $B$ axis. This gives the value of $\hat{B}$.

From the experimenter's point of view, this is the kind of thing he wants to do—but there is something more. The coefficient $c_1$ is known as the *regression coefficient*, and it is a statistic. Hence, it fluctuates from sample to

Table 9-4

| Subject | $B$ | $\hat{B}$ | $e$ | Subject | $B$ | $\hat{B}$ | $e$ |
|---|---|---|---|---|---|---|---|
| 1 | 3.3 | 3.01 | 0.29 | 14 | 1.9 | 2.23 | −0.33 |
| 2 | 2.8 | 2.86 | −0.06 | 15 | 3.9 | 3.17 | 0.73 |
| 3 | 2.1 | 2.07 | 0.03 | 16 | 2.5 | 3.01 | −0.51 |
| 4 | 1.9 | 1.92 | −0.02 | 17 | 2.9 | 3.17 | −0.27 |
| 5 | 2.6 | 2.54 | 0.06 | 18 | 2.8 | 3.17 | −0.37 |
| 6 | 2.5 | 2.54 | −0.04 | 19 | 3.6 | 3.80 | −0.20 |
| 7 | 1.6 | 1.76 | −0.16 | 20 | 3.2 | 3.33 | −0.13 |
| 8 | 1.7 | 1.76 | −0.06 | 21 | 3.5 | 3.33 | 0.17 |
| 9 | 1.9 | 1.92 | −0.02 | 22 | 3.7 | 3.01 | 0.69 |
| 10 | 2.3 | 1.92 | 0.42 | 23 | 2.6 | 2.70 | −0.10 |
| 11 | 2.1 | 2.39 | −0.29 | 24 | 2.7 | 2.54 | 0.16 |
| 12 | 2.4 | 2.23 | 0.17 | 25 | 2.3 | 2.54 | −0.24 |
| 13 | 2.2 | 2.07 | 0.13 | | | | |

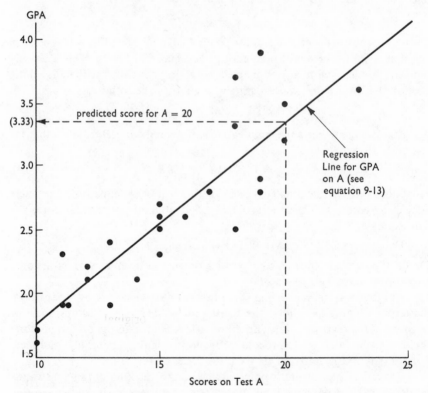

FIGURE 9-5.   Linear regression: illustrated for the case of grade-point average regressed on scores on Test A

sample. What kind of sampling distribution does it have? At this point the experimenter must turn to the statistician for help.

## 9-24   The Statistician's Viewpoint

The following model defines the statistician's viewpoint concerning the regression of one variable, $Y$, on another, $X$.

POPULATION.   Let the population be a bivariate normal distribution with parameters $\mu_X$, $\mu_Y$, $\sigma_X$, $\sigma_Y$, and $\rho_{XY}$. (Note at this point that the regression coefficient for $Y$ on $X$ will be shown to be equal to $\rho_{XY}\sigma_Y/\sigma_X$ and will be designated $\beta_{YX}$, the parameter value.)

SAMPLING PLAN.   Choose $N$ two-tuples by SIRS from this population. Identify these sampled values as $(X_i, Y_i)$ for $i = 1$ through $N$.

STATISTIC.   For each sample compute the value of the regression coefficient, $b_{YX} = r_{XY}s_Y/s_X$.

SAMPLING DISTRIBUTION.   *If* the population is bivariate normal and *if* the sampling plan is SIRS, *then* it is possible to determine some characteristics of the shape of the sampling distribution of this statistic $b_{YX}$. However, the mathematics is difficult, and the resulting equations are so complicated as to be of little practical value. Instead it can be shown that if we compute the summary number

$$t' = \frac{s_X\sqrt{N-2}}{s_Y\sqrt{1 - r_{XY}^2}}\ (b_{YX} - \beta_{YX}) \tag{9-14}$$

where $\beta_{YX}$ is the hypothesized parameter (population) value, then $t'$ is distributed as a $t$ statistic with $(N-2)$ df.

ASSUMPTIONS.   The basic assumptions are (*i*) a bivariate normal population and (*ii*) an SIRS sampling plan.

## 9-25   Details of the Computational Procedure

Given $N$ ordered two-tuples of the form $(X_i, Y_i)$ for $i = 1 - N$, compute the five basic quantities:

$N = 25$ for the experimental data above, and the basic quantities are

$$\sum X$$
$$\sum Y$$
$$\sum X^2$$
$$\sum Y^2$$
$$\sum XY$$

$$\sum A = 384.00$$
$$\sum B = 65.00$$
$$\sum A^2 = 6{,}214.00$$
$$\sum B^2 = 178.92$$
$$\sum AB = 1{,}047.90$$

As will be shown in Section 9-27, when we set up the linear regression equation,

$$\hat{Y}_i = b_0 + b_1 X_i \qquad\qquad \hat{B}_i = c_0 + c_1 A_i$$

and seek to determine the two constants in such a way as to minimize

$$\theta = \sum (Y_i - \hat{Y}_i)^2 \qquad\qquad \theta = \sum (B_i - \hat{B}_i)^2$$

then the solutions are

$$b_0 = \frac{(\sum X^2)(\sum Y) - (\sum XY)(\sum X)}{N(\sum X^2) - (\sum X)^2}$$

$$c_0 = \frac{(6{,}214)(65) - (1{,}047.9)(384)}{25(6{,}214) - (384)^2}$$

$$= 0.1921 \qquad\qquad (9\text{-}15)$$

and

$$b_1 = \frac{N(\sum XY) - (\sum X)(\sum Y)}{N(\sum X^2) - (\sum X)^2}$$

$$c_1 = \frac{25(1{,}047.9) - (384)(65)}{25(6{,}214) - (384)^2}$$

$$= b_{YX}$$

$$= 0.1568 \qquad\qquad (9\text{-}16)$$

(Note that these are the efficient formulas for computing the constants of the regression equation. We do not need a special section on "Efficient computational procedures.")

At this point we have determined the regression of $Y$ on $X$:

$$\hat{Y}_i = b_0 + b_{YX} X_i \qquad\qquad \hat{B}_i = 0.1921 + 0.1568 A_i$$

*Test the difference between a sample value ($b_{YX}$) and a population parameter ($\beta_{YX}$).* Compute the summary number:

$$t' = \frac{s_X \sqrt{N-2}}{s_Y \sqrt{1 - r_{XY}^2}} (b_{YX} - \beta_{YX})$$

$$t' = \frac{3.55 \sqrt{25-2}}{0.63 \sqrt{1 - 0.884^2}} (0.1568 - \beta_{BA})$$

$$= 1.84 \qquad \text{when } \beta_{BA} = 0.125$$

Then this statistic is distributed as a $t$ statistic with $(N-2)$ df. If we are testing to see whether $b_{YX}$ is larger than $\beta_{YX}$, then we consider the area in one tail of the $t$ distribution and decide on a significance level.

Look up this value in the $t$ tables with 23 df. Is $b_{BA} = 0.1568$ significantly larger than $\beta_{BA} = 0.125$? The area to the right of $t' = 1.84$ with 23 df is $<0.05$, and we reject the hypothesis that $\beta_{BA} = 0.125$.

## 9-26   Confidence Intervals for the Regression Lines

In the formula for $t'$ the only quantity that does not come from the sample data is the parameter $\beta_{YX}$. Abbreviating this to $\beta$ (but not forgetting that we are thinking about regressing $Y$ on $X$), let us try to determine an upper value and a lower value ($\beta_U$ and $\beta_L$) such that we can claim to have found the 95 percent confidence interval for the regression coefficient. Let us illustrate the problem for the experimental data being used in this section.

First, rearrange the formula for $t'$. Let

$$Q = \frac{s_X\sqrt{N-2}}{s_Y\sqrt{1-r_{XY}^2}} \qquad\qquad Q = \frac{3.55\sqrt{25-2}}{0.63\sqrt{1-0.884^2}}$$

$$= 57.954$$

Then $\quad t' = Q(b_{YX} - \beta) \qquad\qquad t' = 57.954(0.1568 - \beta)$

Thus $\quad \beta = b_{YX} - t'\left(\dfrac{1}{Q}\right) \qquad\qquad \beta = 0.1568 - t'\left(\dfrac{1}{57.954}\right)$

Now what value shall be chosen for $t'$? This depends on what confidence interval we are talking about. If we want the 95 percent confidence interval, then we should look up the $t$ tables for a $t$ distribution with $(25 - 2) = 23$ df and find out what values of $t$ leave 0.025 of the area in each tail. The appropriate values are $t = 2.069$ (leaves 0.025 in the right-hand tail) and $t = -2.069$ (leaves 0.025 in the left-hand tail). Substituting these values for $t'$, we obtain the required values for $\beta_L$ and $\beta_U$:

$$\beta_L = (0.1568) - (+2.069)\left(\frac{1}{57.954}\right) = 0.1211$$

and $\quad \beta_U = (0.1568) - (-2.069)\left(\frac{1}{57.954}\right) = 0.1925$

We have found the upper and lower limits for the slope of the regression line (with 95 percent confidence). What about the position of the line? There are an infinite number of straight lines having slope 0.1211, for example. Which among them are legitimate in the context of this problem concerning scores on test A and grade-point average? To answer this question, we first note that the regression line (Equation 9-13 and others) passes through the point $(\bar{X}, \bar{Y})$, that is, the two means. In fact, it is useful to know that with a little juggling the regression line can be written in the following easily remembered form:

$$\frac{(\hat{Y}_i - \bar{Y})}{s_Y} = r_{XY}\frac{(X_i - \bar{X})}{s_X} \qquad\qquad (9\text{-}17)$$

In words this equation shows that if you write down the standard score for $Y_i$ on the left-hand side and the standard score for $X_i$ on the right-hand side, then the regression equation for $Y$ on $X$ can be obtained simply by multiplying by $r_{XY}$ on the right-hand side and changing $Y_i$ to $\hat{Y}_i$. (What would be the form for regressing $X$ on $Y$?) Now it should be clear from Equation (9-17) that the point $(\bar{X}, \bar{Y})$ satisfies the equation. Substitute $\bar{X}$ for $X_i$ and $\bar{Y}$ for $Y_i$, and satisfy yourself that this is so.

Returning to the problem of locating a family of regression lines that can be conceived of as constituting a 95 percent confidence set, let us find a 95 percent confidence region for the mean of the predicted $Y$ values, that is, for the mean of the $\hat{Y}_i$ values. In the sample data, the mean of $\hat{Y}$ is exactly the same as that of $Y$, and the sampling distribution of $\bar{Y}$ would be $ND(\mu, \sigma/\sqrt{N})$ if we knew $\mu$ and $\sigma$. Since we do not know these parameter values, we estimate the first as $\bar{Y}$ and the second as $\hat{s}_Y$. Then the sampling distribution of the mean, $\bar{Y}$, has the $t$ distribution with $(N - 1)$ df. Looking up the 95 percent values on this $t$ distribution with $(25 - 1) = 24$ df, we find that the limits of the 95 percent confidence region are $+2.064$ and $-2.064$. Hence the 95 percent confidence limits for the mean of the $Y$ values are defined by the endpoints:

$$\bar{Y}_L = \bar{Y} - (t)\left(\frac{\hat{s}_Y}{\sqrt{N}}\right) \qquad \bar{B}_L = 2.60 - (2.064)(0.127)$$
$$= 2.34$$
$$\bar{Y}_U = \bar{Y} + (t)\left(\frac{\hat{s}_Y}{\sqrt{N}}\right) \qquad \bar{B}_U = 2.60 + (2.064)(0.127)$$
$$= 2.86$$

Now we have found the 95 percent confidence interval for the slope of the regression line and the 95 percent confidence for the positioning of the line. Putting this information together in the form of a chart, we have Figure 9-6.

### 9-27   A Little Theory

Consider $N$ two-tuples $(X_i, Y_i)$, $i = 1, \ldots, N$. Let us concentrate on regressing $Y$ on $X$ in this section. First we make the assumption that

$$Y_i = \hat{Y}_i + e_i$$

We are saying that any given $Y$-value is made up of two parts: a predictable part, $\hat{Y}_i$, and a random error, $e_i$, which is not predictable. The predictable part is determined by means of the linear regression equation:

$$\hat{Y}_i = b_0 + b_{YX}X_i$$

The predictable part, $\hat{Y}_i$, and the unpredictable part, $e_i$, are independent of each other. Hence we can write the equation

$$V_Y = V_{\hat{Y}} + V_e$$

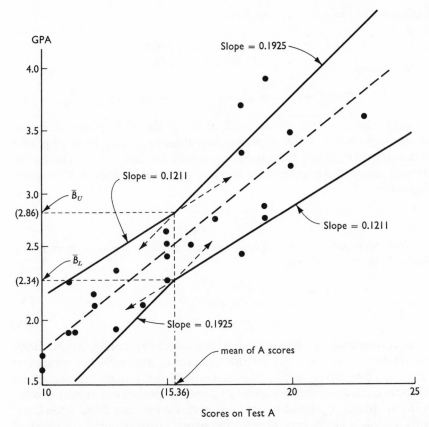

FIGURE 9-6. Scatterplot showing the region within which the regression lines for GPA on A lie: the 95 percent confidence family of regression lines

where $V$ denotes variance. In other words, we can partition the variance of $Y$ into two independent parts. Let us evaluate the two parts $V_{\hat{Y}}$ and $V_e$.

THE VARIANCE OF THE PREDICTED $\hat{Y}$ VALUES.  For simplicity we shall drop the subscripts on $b_{YX}$ and ignore $b_0$ because the variance of a set of values is unaffected by the addition of a constant, namely, $b_0$. (We are saying that $V_{\hat{Y}} = V_{(b_0+bX)} = V_{(bX)}.$)

$$V_{\hat{Y}} = V_{bX} = b^2 V_X$$

using the regression equation and the rule for variance of $bX$, where $b$ is a constant.

At this point let us show that $b_{YX} = b = r_{XY}(s_Y/s_X)$. Consider Equation (9-16). You should recognize this as having the following form:

$$(b_1) = b = \frac{C_{XY}}{C_{XX}}$$

and since $C_{XY} = r_{XY}s_X s_Y$, we have

$$b = \frac{r_{XY}s_X s_Y}{s_X^2} = r_{XY}\left(\frac{s_Y}{s_X}\right)$$

Finally, then,

$$V_{\hat{Y}} = b^2 V_X = r_{XY}^2 \left(\frac{s_Y^2}{s_X^2}\right)s_X^2 = r_{XY}^2 V_Y \qquad (9\text{-}18)$$

In words this says that the variance of the predicted $\hat{Y}$ values cannot be greater than that of the original $Y$ values (because $r^2$ can never be greater than unity). Or, stated the other way round, the squared correlation coefficient tells us the proportion of variance in $Y$ that is predictable by linear regression:

$$r_{XY}^2 = \frac{V_{\hat{Y}}}{V_Y}$$

THE VARIANCE OF THE ERRORS OF PREDICTION.   We now turn to $V_e$. Since $V_Y = V_{\hat{Y}} + V_e$, we have

$$\begin{aligned} V_e &= V_Y - V_{\hat{Y}} \\ &= V_Y - r_{XY}^2 V_Y \\ &= V_Y(1 - r_{XY}^2) \end{aligned} \qquad (9\text{-}19)$$

From this equation we can see that as the correlation coefficient gets closer and closer to $+1$ (or $-1$), so the variance of the errors of prediction decreases. This agrees with common sense. If the variables $X$ and $Y$ are perfectly correlated, then we should be able to predict one from the other perfectly; that is, $V_e$ should be zero, which it is in this case. Often when linear regression is used in experiments, the experimenter reports the standard error of prediction. For the example used in Section 9-2, it would be as follows:

$$se_{B \cdot A} = s_B \sqrt{1 - r_{BA}^2} = 0.294$$

(Note that this standard error occurs in Equation 9-14.) The subscript $B \cdot A$ is conventional and is read "$B$ on $A$."

How to solve for $b_0$ and $b_1$.   For the interested student the following procedure may be used to derive Equations (9-15) and (9-16). The problem is one of finding a minimum value for a function defined as follows:

$$\theta = \sum (Y_i - \hat{Y}_i)^2 = \sum (Y_i - b_0 - b_1 X_i)^2$$

Differentiating with respect to $b_0$ and $b_1$, we obtain

$$\frac{\partial \theta}{\partial b_0} = \sum (Y_i - b_0 - b_1 X_i)(-2)$$

$$\frac{\partial \theta}{\partial b_1} = \sum (Y_i - b_0 - b_1 X_i)(-2X_i)$$

where $\partial$ is the symbol for the partial derivative.

Setting these derivatives equal to zero (at the minimum value the derivatives must be zero) and expanding, we have

$$\sum Y_i - Nb_0 - b_1 \sum X_i = 0$$

$$\sum X_i Y_i - b_0 \sum X_i - b_1 \sum X_i^2 = 0$$

Solving these two equations for $b_0$ and $b_1$ yields Equations (9-15) and (9-16).

Note what happens to these two equations when we are dealing with standardized scores. See if you can show that they reduce to

$$b_0 = 0 \qquad \text{and} \qquad b_1 = r_{XY}$$

In other words, when the variables $X$ and $Y$ are standardized, the regression of $Y$ on $X$ is simply $\hat{Y} = r_{XY}X$. (What will be the regression of $X$ on $Y$ in this case?)

## EXERCISES

1. For the data in Section 9-21 do the following:
   (a) Find the regression line for $A$ on $B$.
   (b) Compute the 95 percent confidence interval for the regression coefficient in this case.
   (c) Compute the 95 percent confidence interval for the mean of $A$.
   (d) Draw a graph showing the original points, the regression of $A$ on $B$, and the 95 percent confidence region for this regression line.
2. Draw a diagram of the experiment discussed in Section 9-21. (Note well that whenever an experimenter determines a regression line, he has to have ordered two-tuples to obtain the regression coefficient and the confidence intervals, etc, In a situation like the present, however, where grades on a test are being used to predict grade-point averages later on, it is clear that we are not interested in predicting the grades for the sample whose grade-point averages we already have! We might use the regression line obtained for one completed study for a set of subjects who have at this time had only test A. Under these circumstances, sampling-fluctuation considerations are a little more complicated. Think about this problem.)
3. Using the data for tests $C$ (Mechanical Comprehension) and $G$ (Paper Form Board) in Table 2-1, regress $G$ on $C$.
   (a) Compute the basic statistics.
   (b) Compute the variance of the errors of prediction, $V_{G \cdot C}$.
   (c) Compute the variance of the predicted $G$ scores.
   (d) Compute the 90 percent confidence interval for the slope of the regression line.
   (e) Compute the 90 percent confidence interval for the mean of $G$.
4. Consider the data in Table 2-2 for tests $C$ and $G$.
   (a) Using Equations (9-15) and (9-16), compute the values of $b_0$ and $b_1$. Is $b_0 = 0$? Should it be? (Regress $G$ on $C$.)
   (b) Draw a graph of the standard scores for $C$ and $G$.
   (c) Superimpose the regression line for $G$ on $C$. Does this regression line pass through the origin of coordinates? Should it?
   (d) What is the standard error of prediction for $G$ on $C$?
   (e) What is the standard error of prediction for $C$ on $G$?

($f$) What is the regression coefficient for $G$ on $C$?

($g$) What is the regression coefficient for $C$ on $G$?

($h$) What is the product of the two regression coefficients?

5. Rewrite Equation (9-17) in the form $Y = b_0 + b_1 X$, and show that the values are the same in Equations (9-15) and (9-16).

6. In Table 9-4 is a list of the observed $B$ values and the predicted $B$ values and also the difference between them, $e$.

   ($a$) Compute the mean of these errors.

   ($b$) Compute the variance and standard deviation of these errors.

   ($c$) Compute $V_{B \cdot A}$ according to Equation (9-19). Does this match your answer to $b$?

   ($d$) For the $B$ values compute $\sum B$ and $\sum B^2$, and use these basic quantities to compute $V_B$.

   ($e$) Compute $V_B$ according to Equation (9-18). Does this match your answer to $d$?

7. (Everybody should do this one!) Consider the following two-tuple data:

| $X$ | 1 | 4 | 7 | 7 | 2 | 4 | 4 | 4 | 4 | 4 | 1 | 7 | 1 | 3 | 1 | 7 | 1 | 4 | 7 | 7 | 1 | 7 | 1 |
|---|---|---|---|---|---|---|---|---|---|---|---|---|---|---|---|---|---|---|---|---|---|---|---|
| $Y$ | 2 | 7 | 3 | 6 | 4 | 3 | 1 | 4 | 5 | 2 | 1 | 2 | 3 | 4 | 7 | 1 | 6 | 6 | 7 | 5 | 5 | 4 | 4 |

   ($a$) Compute the five basic quantities.

   ($b$) Compute the five vital statistics.

   ($c$) Using these five statistics, compute the regression coefficients $b_{YX}$ and $b_{XY}$.

   ($d$) Draw a graph (scatterplot) of these data, and discuss the assertion that pictorial representations of data can often guide us as to how much computation is necessary.

*two*

---

# THE BAYESIAN
# APPROACH

# INTRODUCTION TO PART TWO

ORIENTATION. At present there is still considerable stereotypy in the kinds of statistical analyses that are acceptable among social scientists. Although terms like "decision theory," "information theory," and "theory of games" are well known and although various books and articles have addressed themselves to the pros and cons of introducing these notions into the field of social science, there really has not been much change in experimental design as reported in the standard social science literature. This conservatism may speak well for the satisfactory status of the traditional ways, but it might also be time to reflect on how an experimenter goes about his task of experimenting and reporting conclusions.

The author had for some years felt the need to consider alternatives to setting up a null hypothesis in order to reject it and, having considered the position of the Bayesians, was a ready convert at an intensive summer session in information theory.[1] Perhaps the major attraction was the constant emphasis on the encoding of the experimenter's knowledge—the relentless introspection by the experimenter in order to encode all he knew of the situation. The idea of an experimenter approaching a statistician with the request "I want to reject the null hypothesis" was totally out of place. The Bayesian orientation is threefold:

1. Encode all you know about a problem area—and this means defining a mutually exclusive and exhaustive set of hypotheses, assigning prior probabilities on each of them, and assigning probabilities to the measures of interest under each hypothesis.

2. Having set up the premises (prior information), make use of Bayes' theorem in some form to arrive at conclusions (posterior information).

3. Use the posterior information to make inductive inferences.

PREPARATION. You will find many conditional probabilities mentioned in this part of the text. In fact, you should never find a probability that is not a conditional probability, since everything is conditional upon what we know. The evidence form of Bayes' theorem makes use of logarithms to base 10, and the uncertainty measure, entropy, makes use of logarithms to base 2. The solution for maximum-entropy priors is beyond the level of preparation expected for this text and so is not included. Mostly, however,

---

[1] "Information Theory," a summer program at Dartmouth College's Thayer School of Engineering offered by Myron Tribus and P. T. Shannon, 1965.

you will find that the qualitative correspondence with common sense (which is a desideratum for plausible reasoning in the Bayesian approach) is compelling, and mathematical preparation *per se* is inconsequential.

ORGANIZATION.   Chapter 10 discusses foundations for a model of plausible reasoning and ends with three useful forms for Bayes' theorem. Chapter 11 considers the major problems of (*i*) how to assign prior probabilities (or how to encode your prior knowledge) and (*ii*) how to comprehend new information. Section 11-4 gives some examples worked out in detail.

REFERENCES.   The author owes a considerable debt (in terms of the material presented here), to the text by Myron Tribus and an unpublished manuscript by E. T. Jaynes. The references are:

Tribus, Myron. *Rational descriptions, decisions, and designs.* New York: Pergamon Press, 1969.
Jaynes, E. T. *Probability theory in science and engineering.* Unpublished manuscript, Physics Department, Washington University, St. Louis, Mo.

One other reference of significance to the Bayesian approach, but written before the introduction of maximum entropy priors, is:

Edwards, W., Lindman, H., and Savage, L. J. Bayesian statistical inference for psychological research. *Psychological Review*, 1963, **70**, 193–242.

The interested reader is urged to consult abstracts of the literature for more on this general approach.

# Foundations of
# Plausible Reasoning

## 10-1  INTRODUCTION

### 10-11  Uncertainty

The weatherman predicts the weather for tomorrow, and he is not always correct. His prediction is based upon (*i*) the latest meteorological data and (*ii*) certain premises which in turn are based upon (*iii*) past experience. Whether or not his prediction is correct is one matter. Whether or not he reasoned rationally from the known data and the accepted premises through to a conclusion is another matter. In the face of uncertainty, we are concerned about reasoning from incomplete information, and we want to be sure that this reasoning is in some sense rational or plausible.

A clinical psychologist administers a personality test to a college freshman and on the basis of the results decides that the freshman is maladjusted. He may be right, and he may be wrong. Whether he is right or wrong is one matter. How he reasoned from the test results through to his conclusion is another matter. The point is that the psychologist is faced with a situation of uncertainty and cannot therefore be expected to arrive at foolproof inferences. He does not know everything about this college freshman, but given what he does know and given the premises that past experience has led him to accept, he attempts to arrive at a plausible inference. In the face of uncertainty we want to know how to reason from partial information through to a conclusion or inference.

Note that it is convenient to think of all experimental situations as situations of uncertainty and, further, that we may consider three aspects of such situations:

1. The premises and past experience in general
2. The reasoning process from premises to conclusions in the face of new data
3. The correctness of the conclusion or inference

We wish to make the point here that our fundamental concern should be with the second aspect, and we argue our case as follows. If we had to be sure that the premises were correct before starting an experiment, we should simply never be able to begin at all. Whether or not we accept the premises of another investigator is one matter, but we are more interested in whether this investigator reasoned rationally from his premises to his conclusion. In the face of uncertainty, premises cannot be correct or incorrect. They are either acceptable or unacceptable.

With respect to the third aspect, namely, the correctness of the conclusion or inference, we argue that the plausibility of the reasoning process should be examined independently of the correctness of the outcome. To establish this point, consider the following situation. You are invited to take any coin and toss it 10 times. If the coin does not land heads on every toss, you will win $1,000. If the coin does land heads on every toss, you lose $1. Should you play the game? You say, "Sure"—and lose! Would you then say that your reasoning process had been at fault because it happened that you lost? Clearly not. The odds were heavily in your favor, 1,023 to 1, and nobody would consider that your reasoning process had been irrational.

Naturally, the correctness of the outcome is stored as past experience, and the next time you are faced with the same game, you will take into account your previous successes or failures, but the point remains that the plausibility of the reasoning process in a particular instance is independent of the correctness of the conclusion in that instance.

## 10-12   Deductive Logic

We are concerned with the logic of the reasoning process. Traditionally, deductive logic has been explained with the aid of syllogisms, such as this one:

SYLLOGISM 1  *If A* is true, *then B* is true.
       *A* is true.
       _____
       *Therefore B* is true.

or its inverse:

SYLLOGISM 2  *If A* is true, *then B* is true.
       *B* is false.
       _____
       *Therefore A* is false.

Perhaps the easiest way to examine these syllogisms is by means of Venn diagrams, and by way of illustration consider a colony of rats divided into three groups. For the first group the following proposition is true for all members:

$$A \equiv \text{"I have not been given food for 48 hours."}$$

For the second group the following proposition is true for all members:

$B \equiv$ "I have not been given food for 24 hours."

All other rats are in the third group and have had food in their cages at all times. A Venn diagram of this situation can be drawn as follows:

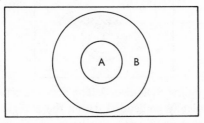

Notice that all members of the first group are embedded within the circle for proposition $B$, since it will be true that if a rat has not been given food for 48 hours, it has also not been given food for 24 hours. We can interpret the two syllogisms above as follows:

SYLLOGISM 1'    *If* "I have not been given food for 48 hours,"
    *then* "I have not been given food for 24 hours."
    "I have not been given food for 48 hours."

    *Therefore* "I have not been given food for 24 hours."

SYLLOGISM 2'    *If* "I have not been given food for 48 hours,"
    *then* "I have not been given food for 24 hours."
    "I have not been given food for 24 hours" is false.

    *Therefore* "I have not been given food for 48 hours" is false.

In order to gain a little facility with Venn diagrams, let us consider Syllogism 2 somewhat more closely. First let us shade the region in which $A$ is true:

(*i*)

The unshaded region is therefore the region in which $A$ is false. Similarly, let us shade in the region in which $B$ is true.

(*ii*)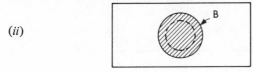

The unshaded region is the region in which *B* is false. Looking at these two diagrams, notice that wherever *B* is false, *A* is also false but not the other way around. In the following diagram the shaded region is a region in which *A* is false but *B* is true.

(*iii*)

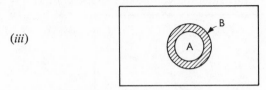

Now return to the original Syllogism 2. The first line establishes the fact that the *A* region is completely embedded within the *B* region because it says in effect, "Wherever *A* is true, *B* must also be true." The second line says *B* is false. The unshaded region in diagram (*ii*) shows where *B* is false. Since this region is also a region in which *A* is false, the syllogism is complete.

### 10-13  Plausible Reasoning

Very seldom do we have the right kind of information to allow deductive reasoning as illustrated in Section 10-12. More commonly our reasoning is as follows:

SYLLOGISM 3    *If A is true, then B is true.*
*B* is true.
_____

*Therefore A becomes more plausible.*

or

SYLLOGISM 4    *If A is true, then B becomes more plausible.*
*B* is true.
_____

*Therefore A becomes more plausible.*

To understand Syllogism 3, examine diagram (*ii*) above. The region where *B* is true covers two subregions—one in which *A* is true and one in which *A* is not true. Thus, if we know *B* is true, we do know that *A* *might* be true. *A* becomes more plausible.

We might attempt to draw a Venn diagram for Syllogism 4 as follows:

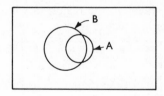

Here, most of the time that $A$ is true, $B$ will also be true, but there are exceptions. So that when we say, "$A$ is true," we feel, "$B$ is more plausible." The syllogism says, "$B$ is true." Where $B$ is true, $A$ can be either true or false; but we cannot escape the conclusion that when $B$ is true, $A$ becomes more plausible.

The following illustration serves to clarify Syllogism 4. Consider a set of adult males aged twenty and the following two propositions:

$A \equiv$ "My waist measures 6 inches more than my chest."
$B \equiv$ "I am unathletic."

Clearly, if $A$ is true, then $B$ becomes more plausible; and if $B$ is true, we would also feel that $A$ becomes more plausible.

## 10-14   A Model for Plausible Reasoning

"The brain, in doing plausible reasoning, not only decides whether something becomes more plausible or less plausible, but it evaluates the degree of plausibility in some way. And it does it in some way that makes use of our past experience as well as the specific data of the problem we're reasoning on. Is it possible to reduce this process of plausible reasoning to quantitative terms?"[1]

The answer is affirmative. In 1812 Laplace developed what was known as the *calculus of inductive inference* (which we shall refer to as the *model for plausible reasoning*), and we argue here that his development expresses what we as experimenters want to know about reasoning plausibly from premises to conclusions. Before going into this straightforward model, let us consider certain desiderata for plausible reasoning. What kinds of conditions would you impose to ensure that a person's reasoning process could be called rational or plausible? There are bound to be some differences of opinion in setting up the desiderata, but we believe the following to be essential:

1. UNAMBIGUITY.   When an experimenter describes the experimental situation, he must do so in the form of statements that are unambiguous. One way to ensure this is to compose propositions that have *denials*, or alternatives.

2. UNIVERSAL COMPARABILITY.   No matter what the problem area is, we want to be able to apply the model for plausible reasoning. In other words, we must be able to decide whether the reasoning process is plausible or not, regardless of the problem area. One way to accomplish this is to make use of the real-number system when we assign degrees of plausibility to propositions.

[1] E. T. Jaynes, unpublished manuscript, Physics Department, Washington University, St. Louis, Mo. Secs. 1–15 and 1–16.

3. CONSISTENCY. If there are several ways of handling a problem, we want to be sure that all ways lead to the same conclusion. The model of plausible reasoning must have this property. The process of plausible reasoning must also be consistent with all that we know about the problem.

4. CORRESPONDENCE WITH COMMON SENSE. The experimenter always brings to his problem a certain amount of common sense, and a model for plausible reasoning must have some kind of qualitative correspondence with this common sense.

It is a remarkable fact that, given the desiderata above, we can develop a model for plausible reasoning which is (*i*) unique (in that it is the only model that seems to satisfy the four requirements listed above), (*ii*) very simple to understand, (*iii*) comprehensive (in that it contains deductive reasoning as a special case and is not limited to any particular class of problems), and (*iv*) flexible (in that new information can be introduced into the conversation at any time).

Since the mainstay of this model is Bayes' theorem in one form or another, we have chosen to designate this general approach the *Bayesian approach*, and we contrast it to what we call the traditional approach, which was developed in Chapters 1 to 9.

## EXERCISES

1. Consider the following commonly used syllogism:

    *If* "Rat *X* is not given food for 24 hours," *then* "Rat *X* is hungry."
    "Rat *X* is not given food for 24 hours."
    _____
    *Therefore* "Rat *X* is hungry."

    (*a*) First consider whether the first line (the major premise) is a reasonable operational statement of  hunger"; that is, does it have a qualitative correspondence with common sense?
    (*b*) What is the inverse of this syllogism? Does the inverse have qualitative correspondence with common sense? (Are there exceptions?)
    (*c*) Consider Syllogisms 3 and 4 in connection with the syllogism above. Phrase it in the form of types 3 and 4. Do these have correspondence with common sense?

2. Repeat parts *a* through *c* of Exercise 1 for the following syllogism:

    *If* "Subject *S* scores high on the Taylor Manifest Anxiety test," *then* "Subject *S* is anxious."
    "Subject *S* scores high on the Taylor Manifest Anxiety test."
    _____
    *Therefore* "Subject *S* is anxious."

3. What is the inverse of Syllogism 3?
4. What is the inverse of Syllogism 4?

5. For each of the following syllogisms, (*i*) draw a Venn diagram to describe the situation, (*ii*) state the inverse of the syllogism, and (*iii*) decide whether the original and the inverse both have qualitative correspondence with common sense. (We identify the *A* and the *B* and the syllogism type—1, 2, 3, or 4):

   (*a*) Syllogism 1, where
   *A* ≡ "Subject *S* hears a 1,000-cps tone at 0.0002 dyne/cm²."
   *B* ≡ "Subject *S* has acute hearing ability."

   (*b*) Syllogism 1, where
   *A* ≡ "Subject *S* reports that he hears a 1,000-cps tone at 0.0002 dynes/cm²."
   *B* ≡ "Subject *S* has acute hearing ability."

   (*c*) Syllogism 3 with *A* and *B* as in *b*.

   (*d*) Syllogism 1, where
   *A* ≡ "Subject *S* has acute hearing ability."
   *B* ≡ "Subject *S* reports that he hears a 1,000-cps tone at 0.0002 dyne/cm²."

   (*e*) Syllogism 4, where *A* and *B* are as in *d*.

   (*f*) Syllogism 2, where
   *A* ≡ "Rat *Y* has been on an intermittent reinforcement schedule."
   *B* ≡ "Response *R* of rat *Y* will extinguish slowly."

   (*g*) Syllogism 4, where *A* and *B* are as in *f*.

6. Consider the first desideratum (for a model of plausible reasoning). If the null hypothesis ($H_0$: "There is no difference between reaction time to sound and reaction time to light") is to be considered unambiguous, what is its denial? How many alternatives are there to the null hypothesis? In the real world of experimentation how many alternative hypotheses can one handle?*

7. Consider the third desideratum. If the experimenter has reason to believe that reaction time (RT) to sound is shorter than RT to light, is it consistent with all he knows to set up the null hypothesis that there is no difference?*

8. Consider the syllogism of type 1, where
   *A* ≡ "Under the assumptions of the null hypothesis the probability of getting $t > 1.9$ for 10 df is $<0.05$."
   *B* ≡ "The null hypothesis should be rejected."

   (*a*) Consider the inverse of the syllogism. Does it correspond qualitatively with common sense?

   (*b*) Consider a syllogism of type 5, as follows:

   *Syllogism 5*: *If A is true, then B becomes more plausible.*
   *A is true.*
   _____
   *Therefore B becomes more plausible.*

   For the *A* and *B* of this exercise, state Syllogism 5. Does this correspond qualitatively with common sense?

   (*c*) What would be the inverse of syllogism 5? Draw a Venn diagram to explain your answer. Does statement *A* have a denial?*

* This exercise and some of the others for this section are intended to make you think hard about the traditional approach to hypothesis testing. Every time an experimenter reaches an experimental conclusion, he must have used some kind of logic to get there. It is a valuable exercise to attempt to make up syllogistic summaries of the process. This author does not wish to denounce traditional hypothesis testing categorically. However, to avoid misuse of traditional tests and to minimize the occasions in which you set up null hypotheses (which you have reason to believe are not true) in order to reject them (in favor of an infinite number of alternatives), you should seriously reflect on the procedure of testing as almost universally practiced in the social sciences.

## 10-2  THE MODEL FOR PLAUSIBLE REASONING

### 10-21  Symbolic Logic

The first desideratum for a model of plausible reasoning is that statements be unambiguous. We can accomplish this goal by using only propositions that are capable of being demonstrated true or false; that is, every proposition must have a denial. If we develop a set of symbols to handle such propositions, we shall be in a position to discuss symbolic logic.

An uppercase letter will be used to designate a proposition, and a lowercase letter its denial. Thus

$$C \equiv \text{"My IQ exceeds 83."}$$
$$c \equiv \text{"My IQ does not exceed 83."}$$

If we have two propositions, $A$ and $B$, then the two letters written together, $AB$, will define *conjunction* as follows:

$A \equiv$ "I am over 6 feet tall."

$B \equiv$ "I am less than 150 pounds in weight."

$AB \equiv$ "I am over 6 feet tall, *and* I am less than 150 pounds in weight."

In terms of a Venn diagram, the region of conjunction is as shown:

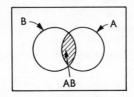

The shaded region is the region of conjunction, $AB$.

We define *disjunction* (using a plus sign) as follows:

$A + B \equiv$ "I am over 6 feet tall, *or* I am less than 150 pounds in weight, *or* both are true."

This is called *inclusive* disjunction because it includes the possibility that both statements are true. If we wish to indicate $A$ *or* $B$ strictly, that is, not allowing both to be true, then we talk about *exclusive* disjunction. The following Venn diagrams illustrate the difference between these two cases of disjunction:

INCLUSIVE DISJUNCTION

**A + B**

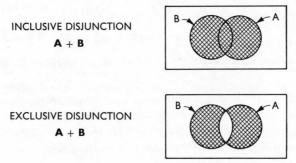

EXCLUSIVE DISJUNCTION

**A + B**

We shall not make a distinction between these two cases in the terminology (we shall always use a plus sign), but where necessary we shall qualify which case we are dealing with. In the above diagrams the shaded portions indicate the regions of disjunction for each case.

Conjunctions and disjunctions can be formed with more than two statements. For example,

$ABc \equiv$ "I am over 6 feet tall, *and* I am less than 150 pounds in weight, *and* my IQ does not exceed 83."

$A + b + C \equiv$ "I am over 6 feet tall, *or* I am not less than 150 pounds in weight, *or* my IQ exceeds 83, *or* any combination of these three statements is true."

(This is a case of *inclusive* disjunction.)

$A + BC \equiv$ "I am over 6 feet tall *or* (I am less than 150 pounds in weight *and* my IQ exceeds 83), but not both."

(This is a case of *exclusive* disjunction.)

Note the following points:

1. The order in which the symbols occur is of no consequence. Thus $ABDGC = DBACG = GDCBA = \cdots$ etc.

2. The equals sign does not indicate anything about the meaning of the statements. To say that $A = B$ means only that whenever $A$ is true, $B$ is true, and vice versa.

3. Compound statements satisfy the ordinary rules of algebra, but there is one qualification of importance. For example,

$$(A + B)(C + D) = AC + AD + BC + BD$$

but $$AAAA = A^4 = A$$

since the statement $A$ said four times does not alter its truth value. Similarly, there is no place for numerical coefficients. For example,

$$(A + B)(A + B) = AA + AB + BA + BB$$
$$= AA + 2AB + BB = A + AB + B$$

Remember, we are concerned only about whether a proposition (be it simple or compound) is true or false.

TRUTH TABLES. It is a simple matter to develop what is known as a *truth table* for any compound proposition. For example, suppose that we wish to demonstrate that the denial of $AB$ is $a + b$. Consider the four combinations of true and false pertaining to propositions $A$ and $B$:

|   | A | B |
|---|---|---|
| 1 | T | T |
| 2 | T | F |
| 3 | F | T |
| 4 | F | F |

Now for each of these four combinations we want to know what the truth value is for the compound statements $AB$ and $a + b$:

|   | A | B | AB | $a + b$ |
|---|---|---|----|---------|
| 1 | T | T | T | F |
| 2 | T | F | F | T |
| 3 | F | T | F | T |
| 4 | F | F | F | T |

Consider line 1. If $A$ is true and $B$ is true, then certainly $AB$ is true (both $A$ and $B$ are true); but since $a$ is false and $b$ is false, $a + b$ is false (neither $a$ nor $b$ is true).

It takes very little practice to be able to write truth tables for all kinds of compound statements. Suffice it for now to state that the above truth table demonstrates that the denial of $AB$ is $a + b$. Wherever $AB$ is true, $a + b$ is false, and vice versa. This is the definition of denial. We could spend a lot of time doing exercises with symbolic logic, but that would obscure the main line. We merely want to argue that the statements that are handled in a model of plausible reasoning must be unambiguous. We conclude this brief survey with an example.

AN EXAMPLE. A principal calls in two teachers to get their opinions about a difficult child in the fourth grade. The first teacher reports:

"Either this child is not too bright, or else the IQ test results rate him too low and he is bright."

The second teacher reports:

"Either the IQ test results rate him too low and he is bright or else the IQ test results do not rate him too low."

The principal wants to know whether these two reports are different or not. He first reduces the problem to statements that have denials, as follows:

$A \equiv$ "The child is bright."

$a \equiv$ "The child is not bright."

$B \equiv$ "The IQ test results are spuriously low."

$b \equiv$ "The IQ test results are not spuriously low."

In terms of these statements, the principal represents the first teacher's comments by means of the following compound statement:

$$a + BA$$

and the second teacher's statement by means of the following compound statement:

$$BA + b$$

Developing the truth table for this situation, we have

| $A$ | $B$ | $AB$ | $a$ | $b$ | $a + BA$ | $BA + b$ |
|-----|-----|------|-----|-----|----------|----------|
| T | T | T | F | F | T | T |
| T | F | F | F | T | F | T |
| F | T | F | T | F | T | F |
| F | F | F | T | T | T | T |

Note that the last two columns do not match perfectly. In other words, the truth values for the first teacher's opinion do not match those for the second teacher's opinion. This difference is sufficient to show that the two statements are not the same.

### 10-22 Use of the Real-number System

The second desideratum for our model of plausible reasoning is that of universal comparability—or, in simpler language, the ability to comprehend all kinds of problems. When we are faced with propositions that are neither true nor false but rather are more or less plausible, we want to have some measure of this degree of plausibility. We need a universal scale on which the extreme points represent true and false and the points between represent varying degrees of plausibility. The real-number system suggests itself for this scale, but you should note well that we are perfectly free to make use of it as we please. As a matter of convenience, we shall stipulate that the real-number scale representing plausibility must (*i*) be continuous, (*ii*) be directly related to the degree of plausibility (that is, the larger the degree of plausibility, the larger is the real number used to represent that plausibility) (*iii*) have an upper limit of unity (corresponding to "certainty" or "truth"), (*iv*) have a lower limit of zero, corresponding to "impossibility or "falsity"). Now, such a scale looks very much like a probability scale, and from now on we shall use the word "probability" when we talk about this scale. You should, however, clearly understand this one thing: we are under no obligation to use the word "probability." We are not bound to any definition of probability (such as the long-run relative-frequency definition in Chapter 3). In the Bayesian approach *probability is an encoding of knowledge*, or "common sense reduced to calculation," to use a phrase from Jaynes. We do not care to theorize about repetitions of random experiments (which are the basis of the long-run relative-frequency approach). Given any proposition, we want to know right now: "What is the state of our knowledge about this proposition? What degree of plausibility shall we attach to it?" According to whatever relevant information is available, we encode our knowledge in the form of a plausibility measure.

Let us designate the plausibility of proposition $A$ given knowledge $B$ by the real number $x$, as follows:

$$x = [A \mid B]$$

Here $x$ is a real number that represents (on our universal scale) the plausibility of $A$ if we know $B$ to be true.

Now consider three propositions, $A$, $B$, and $C$. Suppose that we know $C$ to be true. In other words, our state of knowledge at this moment is described in proposition $C$. Then we shall want to know at least the following plausibility measures:

$$\begin{aligned}
u &= [A \mid C] \\
v &= [B \mid C] \\
w &= [AB \mid C] \\
y &= [A \mid BC] \\
z &= [B \mid AC]
\end{aligned} \qquad (10\text{-}1)$$

These five real numbers are the plausibilities of the five possible statements we might make about $A$ and $B$ if we know $C$ to be true.

Now there has to be some kind of relationship among these various plausibility measures, and this is where the other two desiderata come in. The third desideratum was that of consistency. If a problem can be solved in more than one way, then each way must lead to the same result. We do not want to have to change the line of reasoning because the problem is framed in a slightly different way. It is also desirable to be able to comprehend all that we know. The model of plausible reasoning must be consistent with all that we know. We do not ignore information that violates a pet theory. This requirement leads easily into the fourth desideratum, namely, qualitative correspondence with common sense.

Consider the number $w = [AB \mid C]$. This number cannot be assigned independently of the number $u = [A \mid C]$ or the number $v = [B \mid C]$. Common sense tells us that if we know the plausibility of $A$ given $C$ and of $B$ given $C$, then the plausibility of $AB$ given $C$ is in some sense constrained. Common sense also tells us that $w$ cannot be independent of $y = [A \mid BC]$ or $z = [B \mid AC]$. Indeed, there must be some kind of relationship among the numbers $u$, $v$, $w$, $y$, and $z$. What is this relationship?

The arguments leading to an answer to this question are given elsewhere,[2] but for our purposes it is enough to note that the following equations define the relationships we are looking for:

$$[AB \mid C] = [A \mid BC] \cdot [B \mid C] = [B \mid AC] \cdot [A \mid C] \qquad (10\text{-}2)$$

At this point you should examine Equation (3-4). Equation (10-2) is identical in form to the multiplication law of the relative-frequency probability approach. They are identical but were reached by completely different routes. Since we have agreed to restrict the plausibility measures to the interval 0 through 1 and since we have agreed to using the word "probability" in place of "plausibility," we shall dispense with the brackets and write

$$p(AB \mid C) = p(A \mid BC)p(B \mid C) = p(B \mid AC)p(A \mid C) \qquad (10\text{-}3)$$

It will also follow that

$$p(A \mid C) + p(a \mid C) = 1 \qquad (10\text{-}4)$$

*We may look on Equations (10-3) and (10-4) as defining the elementary properties of a system of plausible reasoning, especially designed for coping with uncertainty.*

The model is as simple as that.

Note, however, that we have not indicated how to assign the real numbers to the various statements. Equations (10-3) and (10-4) tell us only whether or not the numbers we assign are consistent with our desiderata for plausible reasoning. If we assign plausibility measures $u$, $v$, $w$, $y$, and $z$ in such a way that they do not satisfy Equations (10-3), then we have violated one or more of the desiderata. According to the Bayesian approach, there is no alternative to Equations (10-3) and (10-4).

SUMMARY.   We have set up four desiderata for a system of plausible reasoning, and following them through, we have arrived at a very simple quantitative model for plausible reasoning. The quantitative model involves essentially just one major rule:

*Rule* 1:        $p(AB \mid C) = p(A \mid BC)p(B \mid C) = p(B \mid AC)p(A \mid C)$

[2] Myron Tribus. *Rational descriptions, decisions, and designs.* New York: Pergamon Press, 1969.

and one other equation that establishes the relationship between a statement and its denial:

*Rule* 2:  $$p(A \mid C) + p(a \mid C) = 1$$

These are the basic rules for deciding whether the reasoning process is rational (plausible) or not.

## EXERCISES

1. Let $A$ and $B$ be as follows:

$$A \equiv \text{"I scored more than 700 on the SAT-V."}$$
$$B \equiv \text{"I scored more than 700 on the SAT-M."}$$

   (a) Rewrite Syllogism 4 using these statements. If you knew nothing about the SAT-V and SAT-M tests, would this syllogism correspond qualitatively with common sense? If you knew that the correlation between scores on SAT-V and SAT-M was 0.70 would that make a difference?
   (b) State the proposition $A + B$.
   (c) State the proposition $AB$.
   (d) State the proposition $Ab$.
   (e) Draw up a truth table to find out whether $(a + B)$ is the denial of $Ab$.
   (f) What is the denial of $ab$? Does this denial involve inclusive or exclusive disjunction?

2. Let

$$A \equiv \text{"The null hypothesis } H_0 \text{ is true."}$$
$$B \equiv \text{"An alternative hypothesis } H_1 \text{ is true."}$$

   (a) State the proposition $(A + B)$. What kind of disjunction is this?
   (b) If you were to consider the statement $AB$, what problems would it give rise to?
   (c) If you now consider the kinds of data that would result if $H_0$ were true and the kinds of data that would result if $H_1$ were true, how reasonable is the statement $CD$, where

$$C \equiv \text{"Data obtained if } H_0 \text{ is true is 46.3."}$$
$$D \equiv \text{"Data obtained if } H_1 \text{ is true is 46.3."}$$

   (d) To illustrate part $c$, consider a binomial experiment as follows:

   Experiment:   Toss a coin three times and record the number of heads.
   Hypotheses:   $H_0 \equiv$ "The probability of a head is 0.5."
   $H_1 \equiv$ "The probability of a head is 0.7."

   Are these two hypotheses mutually exclusive? Are the data from each mutually exclusive?

3. To illustrate the third desideratum (consistency), consider a manufacturer of Skinner Boxes and a psychologist interested in buying several. An engineer makes public the fact that in the manufacturing process one of two things can happen. If $P$ happens, then the number of defective bar-press-yields-food-pellet mechanisms is one-third of the boxes produced. If $Q$ happens, then the proportion of defectives is one-ninth. Thus two hypotheses are before the floor:

$$H_0 \equiv \text{"The proportion of defectives is one-third."}$$
$$H_1 \equiv \text{"The proportion of defectives is one-ninth."}$$

The manufacturer, defending himself, says that the probability of $H_0$ being true is 0.1, and the cautious and suspicious psychologist evaluates all he knows and says that the probability of $H_0$ being true is 0.6. If these two individuals now watch the assembly line and study the output of Skinner Boxes—whether they are defective or not—then they should both arrive at the same final conclusion regardless of their prior difference of opinion. (This assumes that they both want to operate within the framework of a model for plausible reasoning.)

(a) If the first Skinner Box on the assembly line is defective, what will the new (posterior) probabilities be for hypothesis $H_0$ for the manufacturer and the psychologist? Use Rule 1 in the form of Bayes' theorem. See Section 3-15 and Equation (3-7).

(b) What will happen if the next one is also defective?

(c) Compute the posterior probability for the manufacturer and the psychologist for the following two sequences of defective ($D$) and good ($G$) Skinner Boxes on the assembly line:

$$(i)\ D\ D\ G\ G\ G\ D\ D\ G\ G\ D\ D\ G\ G\ G\ G$$
$$(ii)\ G\ G\ G\ D\ D\ G\ G\ D\ D\ G\ G\ G\ G\ G$$

After each datum compute the posterior probability for $H_0$, and let this be the prior probability when you go to the next datum.

4. Rule 1 says that $p(AB \mid C) = p(A \mid C)p(B \mid AC) = p(B \mid C)p(A \mid BC)$.

(a) If you think of $A$ as a conjunction $DE$, see if you can expand $p(DEB \mid C)$ (or if you prefer, $p(ABC \mid D)$).

(b) What would the expansion of $p(ABCD \mid E)$ be? Can you generalize?

(c) The expansion of $p(ABC \mid D)$ involves six possible expressions on the right-hand side of the equation. (Compare this with the two expressions on the right-hand side of Rule 1.) If you take two of these six possible expressions, having a factor in common, show that Bayes' theorem results when you set them equal to each other.

5. In the Bayesian approach all probabilities (or plausibilities) are conditional. Why is this so in a model of plausible reasoning? To get a feeling for this important point, consider the plausible reasoning behind a baseball manager's decision to substitute Hugh Go as a pinch hitter for Joe Blow.

## 10-3  BAYES' THEOREM

### 10-31  The Standard Form

We have already introduced Bayes' theorem in Section 3-15. The reader is urged to reread that section before continuing. The essence of Bayes' theorem is contained in Rule 1 in Section 10-22. Consider

$$p(A \mid BC)p(B \mid C) = p(B \mid AC)p(A \mid C)$$

Dividing both sides by $p(B \mid C)$, we get Bayes' theorem:

$$p(A \mid BC) = p(A \mid C)\frac{p(B \mid AC)}{p(B \mid C)}$$

Rephrasing the theorem in terms of other symbols (as we did in Section 3-15), let us consider two mutually exclusive and exhaustive hypotheses, $H_1$ and $H_2$.

An experimenter is conducting an experiment in which he believes that either $H_1$ or $H_2$ is true. We shall designate everything he knows about the experiment (his past experience, hunches, etc.) by the symbol $X$, and we shall designate the data he obtains in his current experiment by the symbol $D$. Now consider the following stages in his reasoning:

1. What is his state of knowledge about $H_1$ before he obtains the new data? We call this his *prior knowledge*, and we require the experimenter to state the plausibility of $H_1$ prior to conducting the experiment. What is the *prior probability* of $H_1$, given all that you know? From the experimenter's point of view, this means specifying $p(H_1 \mid X)$, and since $H_2$ is the denial of $H_1$, we can use Rule 2 to obtain

$$p(H_2 \mid X) = 1 - p(H_1 \mid X)$$

2. The experimenter then obtains new data, $D$, which affects the plausibility of hypothesis $H_1$. He reasons as follows. First, what are the chances of obtaining the data, $D$, if hypothesis $H_1$ is, in fact, true? This requires him to specify $p(D \mid H_1X)$. Next he wants to compare this probability with the probability of getting the data, $D$, under any hypothesis whatsoever. The latter probability is $p(D \mid X)$. The ratio of these two probabilities,

$$\frac{p(D \mid H_1X)}{p(D \mid X)}$$

gives him some feeling for how likely hypothesis $H_1$ is when data such as $D$ are obtained. We call this the *likelihood ratio*.

3. Finally, having established his prior probabilities and the likelihood ratio, how may the experimenter reason rationally to obtain the *posterior probability* of $H_1$ being true? The model for plausible reasoning requires the use of Bayes' theorem to produce the posterior probability $p(H_1 \mid DX)$.

We write Bayes' theorem for this problem as follows:

$$p(H_1 \mid DX) = p(H_1 \mid X) \frac{p(D \mid H_1X)}{p(D \mid X)} \qquad (10\text{-}5)$$

posterior         prior        likelihood
probability     probability      ratio

AN EXAMPLE.    The following instructive example is taken from Tribus' book:

$H_1 \equiv$ "Mr. Q can always foretell the future correctly and will do so when asked about a specific event."

$H_2 \equiv h_1$, that is, the denial of $H_1$.

$D \equiv$ "The sun will rise tomorrow."

$X \equiv$ "The various things we know."

Suppose that Mr. Q, having been asked whether the sun will rise tomorrow, makes statement $D$. How does this affect the plausibility of $H_1$? The likelihood ratio in this case is

$$\frac{p(D \mid H_1X)}{p(D \mid X)}$$

Now the numerator must be unity because we are asking about the plausibility of statement $D$ if we know $H_1$ to be true. We do not say, "$H_1$ is true" but simply, "*If* $H_1$ is true." Thus, if we accept $H_1$ as true, then $p(D \mid H_1X)= 1$ because $H_1$ says that whatever Mr. Q tells us is correct. The denominator is $p(D \mid X)$, or the probability that the sun will rise tomorrow, given the various things we know. Again this is unity. We do not need a Mr. Q to tell us this. So $p(D \mid X) = 1$, and the likelihood ratio is also unity.

What does this tell us? It tells us very directly that the model of plausible reasoning demands no change in the plausibility of hypothesis $H_1$ when Mr. Q makes statement $D$. The posterior probability of $H_1$, $p(H_1 \mid DX)$, is no different from the prior probability of $H_1$, $p(H_1 \mid X)$. This conclusion agrees with common sense.

Suppose that Mr. Q, having been asked to do so, makes statement $D'$:

$D' =$ "The detailed information about the contents of the front page of the *New York Times* three weeks from now will be as indicated on this sheet of paper."

Imagine that three weeks later you discover that what Mr. Q stated was indeed true. "Even without the benefit of mathematics it should be obvious that the next time Mr. Q makes a prediction it will pay to listen a bit more attentively!"[3]

Consider Bayes' equation in this case.

1. PRIOR PROBABILITY.  Let us assign to $p(H_1 \mid X)$ an extremely small number, such as 0.0000001. (The fact that we assign any nonzero number at all is a tribute to our open-mindedness.)

2. LIKELIHOOD RATIO.  The numerator, $p(D' \mid H_1X)$, must again be unity, since we are asking about the plausibility of $D'$ if we know $H_1$ to be true. If $H_1$ is true, then $D'$ will be true. The denominator, $p(D' \mid X)$, is now a very small number. We are asking about the plausibility of a correct prediction, such as $D'$, given the various things we know. Well, the various things we know make it very unlikely that anybody could foretell the contents of the front page of the *New York Times* three weeks hence. Suppose that we assign the value 0.000001 to the denominator.

[3] Tribus, pp. 74–76.

3. POSTERIOR PROBABILITY.    Using Bayes' equation, we have

$$p(H_1 \mid D'X) = p(H_1 \mid X) \frac{p(D' \mid H_1X)}{p(D' \mid X)}$$

$$= 0.0000001 \frac{1}{0.000001}$$

$$= 0.1$$

This time the statement $D'$ makes a considerable difference to the posterior probability. Once again the model for plausible reasoning, namely, Bayes' theorem, produces results that are compatible with common sense.

COMMENT.    The term $p(D \mid X)$ in Equation (10-5) can be evaluated as shown in Equation (3-7), and we shall see later (Section 11-32) how to derive the form

$$p(D \mid X) = \sum_{i=1}^{k} p(H_i \mid X)p(D \mid H_iX)$$

**10-32    The Odds Form**

If we divide the probability of a statement by the probability of its denial, we have defined the *odds* on the statement. Thus

$$O(A \mid B) = \frac{p(A \mid B)}{p(a \mid B)} \tag{10-6}$$

where we use the symbol $O$ to designate odds.

Consider two mutually exclusive and exhaustive hypotheses $H_1$ and $H_2$. Then $H_2$ is the denial of $H_1$, and vice versa. Given data $D$, we can write the following *odds ratio:*

$$\frac{p(H_1 \mid DX)}{p(H_2 \mid DX)} = O(H_1 \mid DX)$$

In the terminology of Section 10-31 we shall call this a *posterior odds*. It is the odds ratio for $H_1$, given data $D$ and everything else we know, $X$. Now the numerator and the denominator can be expanded, using Bayes' equation, as follows:

$$O(H_1 \mid DX) = \frac{p(H_1 \mid DX)}{p(H_2 \mid DX)}$$

$$= \frac{p(H_1 \mid X)}{p(H_2 \mid X)} \frac{p(D \mid H_1X)/p(D \mid X)}{p(D \mid H_2X)/p(D \mid X)}$$

$$= O(H_1 \mid X) \frac{p(D \mid H_1X)}{p(D \mid H_2X)} \tag{10-7}$$

$$\underset{\substack{\text{posterior} \\ \text{odds}}}{\phantom{O(H_1 \mid X)}} \quad \underset{\substack{\text{prior} \\ \text{odds}}}{\phantom{\frac{p}{p}}} \quad \underset{\substack{\text{likelihood} \\ \text{ratio}}}{\phantom{\frac{p}{p}}}$$

This we call the *odds form* of Bayes' equation.

AN EXAMPLE.   Consider the case of a student trying to make up his mind whether to go to College A (a highly competitive school with a limited enrollment) or to College Z (a low-grade college with an enormous enrollment). He considers two hypotheses:

$$H_1 \equiv \text{``I am a brilliant student.''}$$

$$H_2 \equiv \text{``I am an ordinary student.''}$$

These are the only two hypotheses he allows himself to think about, so that we may regard them as mutually exclusive and exhaustive. He imagines himself going through the first semester, taking just one course, and wants to figure out the posterior odds on $H_1$ if he were to get an A in the course. Thus the data in this example is the statement

$$D \equiv \text{``I get an A on the course.''}$$

We designate his background knowledge as follows:

$$X \equiv \text{``The various things I know about College A.''}$$

$$X' \equiv \text{``The various things I know about College Z.''}$$

COLLEGE A.   The student establishes prior probabilities as follows:

$$p(H_1 \mid X) = 0.5 \quad \text{and} \quad p(H_2 \mid X) = 0.5$$

In other words, he gives himself only a 50:50 chance of being considered a brilliant student at College A. However, knowing of the fierce competition and the reluctance of professors to award A's, he establishes the following probabilities for the likelihood ratio:

$$p(D \mid H_1 X) = 0.8 \quad \text{and} \quad p(D \mid H_2 X) = 0.1$$

In other words, he figures that people who are not brilliant do not stand much chance of getting an A in the course. Putting this problem into the framework of the odds form of Bayes' equation, we have

$$O(H_1 \mid DX) = O(H_1 \mid X) \frac{p(D \mid H_1 X)}{p(D \mid H_2 X)}$$

$$= \left(\frac{0.5}{0.5}\right)\left(\frac{0.8}{0.1}\right) = 8$$

He concludes that if he went to College A and got an A in the course, the posterior odds in favor of $H_1$ (8:1) would be dramatically different from the prior odds (1:1), and he would have cause for rejoicing.

COLLEGE Z.   Knowing what he does about College Z, he establishes prior probabilities, as follows:

$$p(H_1 \mid X') = 0.75 \quad \text{and} \quad p(H_2 \mid X') = 0.25$$

In other words, he reasons that he has a much better chance of looking like a brilliant student at College Z than at College A. This time, however, he knows that A's are awarded more freely, and there is a good chance that an ordinary student could get an A in the course. Thus he establishes the following probabilities for the likelihood ratio:

$$P(D \mid H_1 X') = 0.9 \quad \text{and} \quad p(D \mid H_2 X') = 0.45$$

Putting this problem into the framework of the odds form of Bayes' equation, we have

$$O(H_1 \mid DX') = O(H_1 \mid X') \frac{p(D \mid H_1 X')}{p(D \mid H_2 X')}$$

$$= \left(\frac{0.75}{0.25}\right)\left(\frac{0.90}{0.45}\right) = 6$$

He concludes that, if he went to College Z and got an A in the course, the posterior odds (6:1) would not be so dramatically different from the prior odds (3:1) as in the case of College A. Going to College Z and getting an A would not be so flattering to his ego as going to College A and getting an A.

### 10-33   The Evidence Form

One other version of the Bayes' equation is the *evidence form*. This has perhaps the most general utility and will be used extensively later. We take the logarithm of the odds form, as follows:

$$10 \log_{10} O(H_1 \mid DX) = 10 \log_{10} \left[ O(H_1 \mid X) \frac{p(D \mid H_1 X)}{p(D \mid H_2 X)} \right]$$

$$= 10 \log_{10} O(H_1 \mid X) + 10 \log_{10} \frac{p(D \mid H_1 X)}{p(D \mid H_2 X)}$$

and if we designate $10 \log_{10} O(H_1 \mid DX)$ by means of the shorthand $\mathrm{ev}(H_1 \mid DX)$, where "ev" is read "evidence," we have the evidence form of Bayes' equation:

$$\mathrm{ev}(H_1 \mid DX) = \mathrm{ev}(H_1 \mid X) + 10 \log_{10} \frac{p(D \mid H_1 X)}{p(D \mid H_2 X)} \tag{10-8}$$

| posterior evidence | prior evidence | increment or decrement in evidence |
|---|---|---|

This is a useful form to work with, since the last term indicates whether the evidence in favor of $H_1$ is increased or decreased when the new data $D$ are taken into account. In particular this form is useful for performing *sequential* analysis of data, as illustrated in the following example.

AN EXAMPLE.  The school year in the Southern Hemisphere runs over the calendar year, whereas in the Northern Hemisphere it runs from September to June. A student completes half of his third grade in the Southern Hemisphere, and then has to go to school in the Northern Hemisphere. The question is whether he should go into third or fourth grade in the Northern Hemisphere school. A rational-thinking admissions officer decides to administer a number of test items in sequence to this student in order to decide whether to assign him to a third- or a fourth-grade class. The test items are all equally difficult, and in the past it has been found that 60 percent of the fourth-graders can answer the items correctly, whereas only 30 percent of the third-graders can. The two hypotheses of interest are

$$H_1 \equiv \text{"This student is third-grade material."}$$

$$H_2 \equiv \text{"This student is fourth-grade material."}$$

The data $D$ are considered sequentially. Given the first item, the student may get it right $(R)$ or wrong $(W)$. Similarly for the second item, the third, and so on, until the admissions officer is confident about which assignment to make. Suppose that the student performs as follows:

$$W \quad W \quad R \quad W \quad R \quad W \quad W \quad W \quad R \quad W \quad W \quad W$$

How may the admissions officer use these data sequentially to reach his decision?

PRIOR EVIDENCE.  To establish the prior evidence, $\mathrm{ev}(H_1 \mid X)$, where $X = $ all that he knows about the problem, the officer argues that he has no information to favor $H_1$ over $H_2$, or vice versa. In other words,

$$p(H_1 \mid X) = p(H_2 \mid X) = 0.5$$

This means that

$$\mathrm{ev}(H_1 \mid X) = 10 \log_{10}\left(\frac{0.5}{0.5}\right) = 0$$

The prior evidence in favor of $H_1$ ("This student is third-grade material") is zero.

INCREMENT OR DECREMENT IN EVIDENCE.  The data are of two kinds— $R$ or $W$. We need to calculate the change in evidence for each kind of datum.

1. If an item is answered right $(R)$, we compute

$$10 \log_{10} \frac{p(R \mid H_1 X)}{p(R \mid H_2 X)} = 10 \log_{10} \frac{0.30}{0.60} = -3.01$$

In other words, every time this student answers an item correctly $(R)$, the evidence for hypothesis $H_1$ decreases by 3.01 decibels.[4]

[4] The engineers who first worked seriously with the evidence form of Bayes' theorem have dubbed the units *decibels* (db), since they found the "$10 \log_{10}$" form analogous to the sound measure of the same name.

2. If an item is answered wrong $(W)$, we compute

$$10 \log_{10} \frac{p(W \mid H_1 X)}{p(W \mid H_2 X)} = 10 \log_{10} \frac{0.70}{0.40} = +2.43 \text{ db}$$

In other words, every time this student answers an item incorrectly, the evidence for hypothesis $H_1$ increases by 2.43 db.

POSTERIOR EVIDENCE.   Let us consider the posterior evidence sequentially.

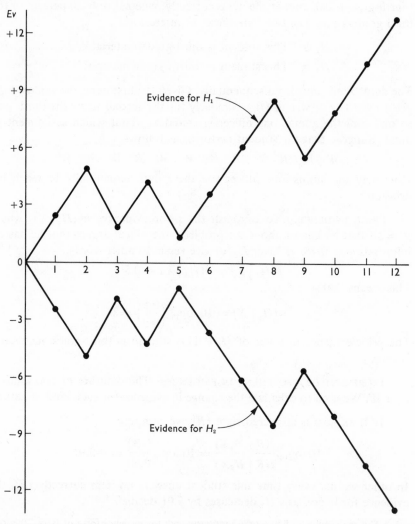

FIGURE 10-1.   Sequential study of the evidence for two hypotheses, $H_1$ and $H_2$: illustrating the example discussed in Section 10.33

1. After item 1 was answered $W$,

$$ev(H_1 \mid WX) = 0 + 2.43 = 2.43 \text{ db}$$

2. After item 2 was answered $W$,

$$ev(H_1 \mid WWX) = 2.43 + 2.43 = 4.86 \text{ db}$$

3. After item 3 was answered $R$,

$$ev(H_1 \mid RWWX) = 4.86 - 3.01 = 1.85 \text{ db}$$

4. After item 4 was answered $W$,

$$ev(H_1 \mid WRWWX) = 1.85 + 2.43 = 4.28 \text{ db}$$

And so on. Figure 10-1 shows graphically what is happening to both hypotheses. Notice that when we deal with just two mutually exclusive and exhaustive hypotheses, the evidence lines for $H_1$ and $H_2$ are mirror images of each other. Notice also that in this figure the evidence lines start at zero on the left. The reason is that the experimenter had no relevant prior information to prefer $H_1$ over $H_2$ or vice versa. Hence he had to settle for equal priors. If the priors for $H_1$ and $H_2$ had been different, the evidence lines would not have started at zero. Remember, too, that the evidence scale can easily be interpreted in probability terms or as odds ratios (by using Appendix I).

By the time this student has answered 12 items as shown, the admissions officer finds that the evidence for $H_1$ stands at 12.84 db (odds better than 19:1, probability greater than 0.95), and so with 95 percent confidence he concludes that the student should be placed in the third grade.

## 10-34  Relationship among Probability, Odds, and Evidence

It is useful to draw up a table for converting probabilities into odds and evidence, and vice versa. The procedure is quite simple. For example, if $p(A \mid X) = 0.6$, what are the values to assign to $O(A \mid X)$ and $ev(A \mid X)$? They are as follows:

$$O(A \mid X) = \frac{p(A \mid X)}{p(a \mid X)} = \frac{p(A \mid X)}{1 - p(A \mid X)} = \frac{0.6}{0.4} = 1.5$$

and        $$ev(A \mid X) = 10 \log_{10} O(A \mid X) = 10 \log_{10} (1.5) = 1.761$$

Proceeding in this manner, we may develop the table shown in Appendix I.

### EXERCISES

1. Using Appendix I, convert the following odds ratios into evidence: (a) 1:1, (b) 1:2, (c) 2:1, (d) 1:3, (e) 3:1, (f) 1:$\infty$, (g) $\infty$:1.
2. Using Appendix I, convert the following evidence measures (in decibels) to both probabilities and odds ratios: (a) 1 db, (b) −1 db, (c) 5 db, (d) −5 db, (e) 10 db, (f) −10 db, (g) 20 db, (h) −20 db.

3. Examine the evidence form of Bayes' theorem (Equation 10-8). The increment or decrement is a term of the form $10 \log_{10} (Q)$, where $Q$ is $p(D \mid HX)/p(D \mid hX)$. Although $Q$ is not an odds ratio, show that Appendix I may be used to evaluate $10 \log_{10} (Q)$, where (a) $Q = 1$, (b) $Q = 10$, (c) $Q = 20$, (d) $Q = 0.25$.

4. Consider Exercise 3 of Section 10-2.
   (a) Compute the prior probability, prior odds, and prior evidence for $H_0$ and $H_1$ for the manufacturer.
   (b) Repeat part a for the psychologist.
   (c) Compute the increment or decrement in evidence for $H_0$ if the first Skinner Box on the assembly line is defective ($D$) for (i) the manufacturer and (ii) the psychologist. Are these two quantities the same?
   (d) Compute the increment or decrement in evidence for $H_0$ if the first Skinner Box on the assembly line is good ($G$) for (i) the manufacturer and (ii) the psychologist. Are these two quantities the same?
   (e) Repeat part c for the hypothesis $H_1$.
   (f) Repeat part d for the hypothesis $H_1$.
   (g) Now repeat part c of Exercise 3 for Section 10-2, using the evidence form of Bayes' theorem. (Note: You should discover that the increment or decrement in evidence is the same for both manufacturer and psychologist in this example. The probabilities $p(D \mid H_0X)$ and $p(D \mid H_1X)$ were not assigned by either the manufacturer or the psychologist but rather by an independent agent, the engineer. Can you think of a situation in which these would not be the same for the manufacturer and the psychologist?)

5. When you deal with continuous distributions (like the ND(0,1), for example), it is not possible to assign a finite probability to the occurrence of any one of the permissible values. (Since the range of $z$ is minus infinity to plus infinity, you would find yourself in the position of assigning finite probabilities to an infinite number of $z$ values, and then of course the sum of the probabilities would not be unity.) Instead of saying that the height of the curve at any particular point is the probability of occurrence of that point, the mathematician says the probability density at that point, say, $z_p$ (particular value of $z$), is $f(z_p) \, dz$ where $f(z_p)$ is the height of the curve at $z_p$ (see Appendix C) and $dz$ is the differential (of differential calculus). To illustrate the usage of this probability density, consider the following problem. You are told that the computer will perform SIRS sampling from either ND(0,1) or ND(1,1). The first value that comes out is 0.5. Identify $H_0 \equiv$ "Population is ND(0,1)," $H_1 \equiv$ "Population is ND(1,1)," and $D \equiv$ "Outcome is 0.5."
   (a) Define $p(D \mid H_0X)$ as a probability density.
   (b) Define $p(D \mid H_1X)$ as a probability density.
   (c) Consider the last term in the evidence form of Bayes' theorem. Compute the increment or decrement in evidence for $H_0$, given $D$.
   (d) Compute the increment or decrement in evidence for $H_1$.
   (e) Compute the increment or decrement in evidence for $H_0$ if the next value produced by the computer is $-0.5$.

6. Following on from Exercise 5 above, consider the data in Appendix B (SIRS values from ND(0,1)). Starting anywhere in the table, see how many values it takes to convince Mr. Q that these tables were derived from ND(0,1) rather than ND(1,1) if (i) Mr. Q establishes priors as

$$p(H_0 \mid X) = 0.5 \quad \text{and} \quad p(H_1 \mid X) = 0.5$$

or (ii) Mr. Q establishes priors as follows:

$$p(H_0 \mid X) = 0.8 \quad \text{and} \quad p(H_1 \mid X) = 0.2$$

7. Write the equation for the standard normal distribution, ND(0,1), and write the equation for the general ND($\mu,\sigma$).
   (a) What is the relationship between the ordinate on ND(0,1) and the ordinate on ND($\mu,\sigma$)?
   (b) Consider the hypotheses $H_0$ and $H_1$, where

   $H_0 \equiv$ "The numbers in Appendix B are SIRS values from ND(0,1)."
   $H_1 \equiv$ "The numbers in Appendix B are SIRS values from ND(0,2)."

   Working from the top of column 1 and going down the column, how many values would it take to convince yourself that one of these hypotheses has overwhelming plausibility (as measured, say, by an odds ratio of better than 100 to 1)?
8. Consider Appendix A, ostensibly SIRS values from a rectangular distribution on the range (0,1). Using the notion of probability density (see Exercise 5 above), how many values would it take to distinguish between the following two hypotheses?

   $H_0 \equiv$ "Values in Appendix A are SIRS values from a ND(0.5,0.5)."
   $H_1 \equiv$ "Values in Appendix A are SIRS values from a rectangular distribution on the interval (0,1)."

# *How to Proceed Rationally*

## 11-1 INTRODUCTION

### 11-11 On Being Rational

In Chapter 10 we explored the foundations of plausible reasoning and reached the conclusion that, in the face of uncertainty, being rational means being true to the four desiderata for plausible reasoning, namely,

1. Making use of unambiguous statements (each statement must have a denial)

2. Allowing for universal comparability (making use of the real-number system to assign plausibilities or probabilities)

3. Being consistent with all we know (encoding all the relevant information and making sure that all permissible solutions lead to the same result)

4. Ensuring a qualitative correspondence with common sense (we do not knowingly make decisions or probability assignments that are contrary to our better judgment)

It was shown that such a system of plausible reasoning could be quantified very simply and uniquely in the form of two rules:

Rule 1: $\qquad p(AB \mid C) = p(A \mid BC)p(B \mid C) = p(B \mid AC)p(A \mid C)$

Rule 2: $\qquad\qquad p(A \mid C) + p(a \mid C) = 1$

If a set of probability assignments satisfies these two rules, then we argue that the encoding of knowledge has been done rationally. These rules tell us when a set of probability assignments are consistent with the model for plausible reasoning, but they do not tell us how to assign the probability measures. In this chapter we shall consider the latter question in detail.

In order to discuss the problem of how to assign probabilities, we have to specify what we mean by probability, and we have to determine a rational measure of uncertainty.

## 11-12   What Is Probability?

An astronaut sitting in his capsule on top of the booster rocket asks himself, "What is the probability of success of this mission?" A student, having just completed his final examinations, asks himself, "What is the probability of obtaining a distinction in these examinations?" An experimenter, interested in finding out whether reaction time is shorter when responding to sound than to light, asks himself, "What is the probability of my hunch being true?"

These three situations are real-world situations, each of which involves uncertainty. Each situation also involves some relevant prior information. The astronaut knows about the previous successes and failures of the booster rocket, about the previous successes and failures of unmanned test flights, about the care and attention given the preparation of his own flight plan. But he does not know whether his own flight will be a success or not. There is no such thing as long-run relative frequency in connection with his own mission. It has never been run before; it will never be run again. When he asks, "What is the probability of success of my mission?" he is forced to encode all the relevant prior information, and if he obeys the desiderata for plausible reasoning, he will encode this information in the form of a real number between 0 and 1.

The student also has prior information to consider. He knows how well he has done in the past. He has some awareness of the attitude of his professors to his work. He has a feeling about how well he did in the finals. But, again, there is no such thing as long-run relative-frequency probability of a distinction. It makes no sense to him to say, "If I repeat this final examination over and over again, independently, then in the long run my chances of obtaining a distinction are about 70 in 100." When he asks, "What is the probability of gaining a distinction?" he is forced to work only with the relevant prior information, and if he follows the rules for plausible reasoning, he will encode his prior knowledge in the form of a number between 0 and 1.

The experimenter has a hunch that reaction time to sound is shorter than reaction time to light. Where did he get this hunch? Clearly it is based on some prior knowledge. If he knows about the physiology of the situation, he has some relevant prior information in favor of the hunch. He knows too, however, that measurements of reaction time in experimental settings depend upon the quality of the equipment, the quality of the subjects used (whether they obey instructions, for example), and so on. Given all this prior information, together with previously published data in the specific problem area, he might encode his knowledge as follows: "Given the experimental conditions, I expect my hunch to have a plausibility (probability) measure of 0.75."

How shall we interpret a probability assignment? The astronaut, for example, says, "According to all my relevant knowledge, I say the probability of success of this mission is 0.60." Does this mean that this mission will succeed 60 out of 100 times? No. This cannot be, because his mission happens only once. Instead it is better to interpret this encoding of knowledge as a *fair bet*. If the astronaut were to split a dollar on success and failure, consistent with all he knows about the situation, then he would give 60 cents for a success and 40 cents for a failure.

If the student says, "The probability of my obtaining a distinction is 0.7," then we interpret this as splitting a dollar 70:30 in favor of a distinction. If it is a fair bet, it will be consistent with the four desiderata for plausible reasoning. Similarly, the experimenter has split a dollar 75:25 in favor of his hunch. He has encoded his relevant knowledge, using a code that satisfies the desiderata for plausible inductive inference.

### 11-13    A Rational Measure of Uncertainty—Entropy

Consider a fair coin and the following mutually exclusive and exhaustive set of hypotheses:

$$H_1 \equiv \text{"The outcome of the next toss is a head."}$$

$$H_2 \equiv \text{"The outcome of the next toss is a tail."}$$

You are invited to play the following game. Toss the coin just once, and bet on the outcome. Before you toss the coin, you are in a situation of uncertainty. You know that it can land heads or tails. Knowing all you do about the situation, you encode your knowledge by splitting a dollar on the outcome to yield

$$p(H_1 \mid X) = 0.5$$
$$p(H_2 \mid X) = 0.5$$

where $X \equiv$ "all you know about the situation." In other words, in the absence of any information to the contrary, you would place even money on the two possible outcomes. Can we define a measure of the uncertainty of this situation? Yes, and we do so without derivation here. The quantity, $H$, defined as follows,

$$H = -p(H_1 \mid X) \log_2 p(H_1 \mid X) - p(H_2 \mid X) \log_2 p(H_2 \mid X)$$
$$= -0.5 \log_2 0.5 - 0.5 \log_2 0.5 = -0.5 \log_2 0.25 = 0.5 \log_2 4.0 = 1$$

is known as the *uncertainty*, or *entropy*, of the situation. Its units are called *bits* (binary digits), and we say that the toss of a fair coin is a situation involving one bit of uncertainty, or the entropy is one bit.

| Before the toss of a fair coin | After the toss of a fair coin |
|---|---|
| Uncertainty, or entropy, is $H = 1$ bit. | Uncertainty, or entropy, is $H = 0$ bits. After a toss, the uncertainty is removed, and we say that one bit of *information* has been added to our knowledge. |

Now consider the following situation. Before you is a panel on which appear two light bulbs—one green and one red. I tell you that the green light comes on three times as often as the red light. Now you have to bet on the outcome of the next trial, during which one light will come on. You consult all you know, and encode your knowledge as follows:

$$p_1 = p(\text{outcome is green light} \mid X) = 0.75$$
$$p_2 = p(\text{outcome is red light} \mid X) \;\;\; = 0.25$$

What is the uncertainty of this situation? The entropy measure, $H$, is defined as

$$H = -p_1 \log_2 p_1 - p_2 \log_2 p_2$$
$$= -0.75 \log_2 0.75 - 0.25 \log_2 0.25$$
$$= -0.75(-0.415) - 0.25(-2) = 0.811$$

Notice that now the uncertainty of the situation is less than the coin-tossing situation. Why? The coin-tossing case is a situation of maximum uncertainty, since we have no information which would make heads more likely than tails, or vice versa. The red-and-green-light problem does not involve so much uncertainty, because we have information telling us that one light is more likely than another. Thus we conclude that in situations involving two mutually exclusive and exhaustive hypotheses, the maximum uncertainty is 1 bit. Any information that makes one hypothesis more likely than the other reduces the uncertainty.

| Before the light came on | After the light came on |
|---|---|
| Entropy, or uncertainty, is $H = 0.811$ bit. | Entropy, or uncertainty, is $H = 0$ bits. There is no uncertainty after the light shines, and we say that 0.811 bit of information has been added. |

SUMMARY. In general, if we are faced with an uncertain situation involving $k$ mutually exclusive and exhaustive hypotheses (or possible outcomes), we first encode our knowledge with respect to each of these hypotheses:

$$p_1 = \Pr(\text{outcome is } H_1 \mid X)$$
$$p_2 = \Pr(\text{outcome is } H_2 \mid X)$$
.
.
.
$$p_k = \Pr(\text{outcome is } H_k \mid X)$$

and define

*A rational measure of uncertainty: the entropy of the total situation is H, where*

$$H = -\sum_{i=1}^{k} p_i \log_2 p_i$$

The situation will be maximally uncertain when all the outcomes (or hypotheses) are equally likely. Under these circumstances the entropy measure reduces to $H = \log_2 k$, that is, the logarithm to base 2 of the number of alternatives. For example, when $k = 2$, maximum entropy is $\log_2 2 = 1$ bit. When $k = 8$, maximum entropy is $\log_2 8 = 3$.

## EXERCISES

1. The following exercise is designed to give flexibility in the process of assigning prior probabilities. For each of the cases mentioned define (*i*) the set of permissible values (the mutually exclusive and exhaustive set of outcomes, or hypotheses, if you like) and (*ii*) the prior probabilities that you would assign to these permissible outcomes.
   (*a*) You are feeling unwell (but not too seriously unwell), and you are interested in the question, "What is my body temperature?"
   (*b*) In a laboratory course you plan to find that frequency at which a flickering light is perceived to be fused (nonflickering). This is the CFF (critical fusion frequency). If you were about to perform an experiment, what assignment would you make over what range of frequencies?
   (*c*) You are at a baseball game, and a new player comes up to bat. Consider the question of his batting average by the end of the season.
   (*d*) What salary do you think you'll be earning five years from now?
   (*e*) What will the weather be like a week from now?
2. Given a numerical grading system where $5 = A$, $4 = B$, $3 = C$, $2 = D$, and $1 = E$, what would you mean (in the way of a probability assignment over these grade possibilities) if you said: "I expect a $B$"?
3. Referring to Exercise 2, what would the statistician mean if he stated that $E(X) = 4$ (in words, "Expected value of $X$, the grade, equals 4").
4. Appendix J gives values for $(-p \log_2 p)$. Compute the entropy for the following situations:

(a) A fair coin is about to be tossed.

(b) A biased coin is about to be tossed.

(c) A coin having $p$(heads) = 0.3 is about to be tossed.

(d) A die is about to be thrown.

(e) A die with the following probability assignment is about to be thrown: $p(1) = 0.5, p(2) = 0.2, p(3) = 0.1, p(4) = 0.1, p(5) = 0.05, p(6) = 0.05$.

5. What is the maximum entropy for situations involving $k$ possible outcomes where (a) $k = 3$? (b) $k = 10$? (c) $k = 20$?

6. (a) Think of a rat going through a training period in a $T$-maze. During the whole process, what is happening to the entropy of its responses (turn to the right or turn to the left) as the rat learns that the right side is consistently rewarded?

(b) Think of the first trial from the rat's point of view. What hypotheses should it entertain at the choice point? What assignment of priors would you expect from a rat with a left-turning bias?

(c) Thinking of the rat as a rational Bayesian, would you expect a rat with a left-turning bias to take longer to accumulate enough evidence to settle on the appropriate response (to the right for reward) than a rat with a right-turning bias?

## 11-2   HOW TO ASSIGN PROBABILITIES

### 11-21   Introduction

In the controversy that has raged between the traditional approach and the Bayesian approach, the major issue seems to be the assignment of prior probabilities. Bayes' equation tells us how to proceed from prior information to posterior information or how to reason from premises to conclusions, but it does not tell us how to encode our knowledge. Since we have to encode our prior knowledge before using Bayes' equation, it is of central importance to consider just how we do encode it.

But there is one point that should be made promptly and emphatically. If we are to be true to the desiderata for plausible reasoning, there is no escape from this initial (prior) encoding of our knowledge; and although the antagonists of the Bayesian approach often criticize the "arbitrary assignment of prior probabilities," they are in no way free of this problem themselves. In the traditional approach we look for a statistical model that is an adequate representation of the real-world experimental situation. Do we avoid the problem of assigning prior probabilities in this approach? Certainly not. The typical assumptions of a traditional statistical model are (i) a normally distributed population and (ii) an SIRS plan. These assumptions take the place of assigning priors.[1] The question that faces the experimenter after he accepts a traditional statistical model is, "Are the assumptions of this model consistent with all I know?" The rational-thinking experimenter can never escape this question.

[1] We shall refer to prior probabilities as priors.

Thus we argue that the assignment of priors has to be done one way or the other. In the case of a traditional test, such as the $t$-test, the $F$-test, or the $\chi^2$-test, the experimenter is saying, "I will allow my knowledge of the situation to be encoded in the form of the normality assumption and the SIRS plan." In the case of the Bayesian approach, the experimenter will designate the set of mutually exclusive and exhaustive hypotheses and will encode his knowledge about each in the form of a probability measure. If necessary, he will also have to encode a number of conditional probabilities. For example, if he is considering three hypotheses, $H_1$, $H_2$, and $H_3$, and plans to obtain data, $D$, he will need to establish the following priors:

$$p(H_1 \mid X) \qquad p(H_2 \mid X) \qquad p(H_3 \mid X)$$
$$p(D \mid H_1 X) \qquad p(D \mid H_2 X) \qquad p(D \mid H_3 X)$$

As you become more familiar with the Bayesian approach, you will notice that the formulation of your problem in Bayesian terms makes you concentrate more and more on your experimental problem and less and less on "satisfying assumptions." Or, to make the point another way, the traditional approach (significance testing in particular) tends to generate stereotyped experimental designs, whereas the Bayesian approach is at the command of the innovative experimenter.

### 11-22  Uniform Priors

Consider an experimental situation in which there are $k$ mutually exclusive and exhaustive hypotheses ($H_1$ through $H_k$) of interest to the experimenter. If the experimenter considers all he knows about the situation and concludes that there is nothing to suggest one hypothesis as being more likely than another, then he will assign *uniform priors*, as follows:

$$p(H_i \mid X) = \frac{1}{k} \qquad \text{for all } i = 1, \ldots, k$$

This corresponds to a rectangular distribution on the $k$ permissible hypotheses:

Prior probability distribution

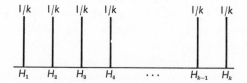

Such a probability assignment has been called by various names, including uniform priors, minimally informed priors, priors established according to the principle of insufficient reason, and rectangular priors.

Some examples of situations that require this kind of prior probability assignment are as follows:

1. A fair coin is tossed, and you are to assign priors to the two hypotheses $H_1 \equiv$ "outcome is a head" and $H_2 \equiv$ "outcome is a tail." The uniform prior is given as

$$p(H_i \mid X) = 0.5 \qquad \text{for} \qquad i = 1, 2$$

2. An honest die is thrown, and you are to assign priors to the six possible outcomes—1, 2, 3, 4, 5, or 6. Based on your previous experience with honest dice and your current knowledge, you would assign minimally informed priors as follows:

$$p(H_i \mid X) = \tfrac{1}{6} \qquad \text{for} \qquad i = 1, 2, 3, 4, 5, 6$$

where $H_i \equiv$ "the outcome is $i$."

3. A student is asked to decide between two mutually exclusive and exhaustive hypotheses:

$H_1 \equiv$ "Reaction time to sound is shorter than reaction time to light."

$H_2 \equiv$ "Reaction time to sound is not shorter than reaction time to light."

If this student is not well-read in the area and has no relevant information concerning which hypothesis is more likely to be true, then he will have to assign priors according to the principle of insufficient reason, as follows:

$$p(H_1 \mid X) = 0.5 \qquad \text{and} \qquad p(H_2 \mid X) = 0.5$$

MAXIMUM ENTROPY PRIOR.   We conclude this section by introducing yet another name for the uniform prior—the *maximum entropy prior*. It was shown in Section 11-13 that the uncertainty of a situation could be measured in the form of $H$, the entropy measure. It was also stated there that when all the alternatives were equally likely, the situation involved maximum entropy. It was a maximally uncertain situation. Thus, in the absence of any relevant information, the experimenter assigns maximum entropy priors.

This concept is very useful both here and in what follows. If the experimenter wishes to be true to the desiderata for plausible reasoning, then he must be consistent with all he knows. But, having considered all he knows, he must not go beyond the facts. Hence we propound the following rule for assigning priors:

> *Priors must be assigned in such a way as to be consistent with all that is known, but beyond that they must be maximally noncommittal.*

If all that is known is insufficient reason to prefer one hypothesis over another, then the maximally noncommittal priors will be the maximum entropy priors. However, we also use the term "maximum entropy prior" for situations in which we do have reason to favor some hypotheses over others. The point is that if you are uncertain, then you do not know everything. Making use of all you *do* know, how can you assign priors in such a way that you will be maximally noncommittal with respect to what you *do not* know? With respect to whatever uncertainty exists, we want to maximize entropy. In the next few sections we shall lead up to a consideration of how to maximize entropy subject to all you know. For now, simply remember that the term "maximum entropy prior" is the name we use for the distribution of prior probabilities that is (*i*) consistent with all that is known but beyond that is (*ii*) maximally noncommittal.

## 11-23   Expectation

We have discussed situations in which there is no relevant prior information to prefer one hypothesis over another. In real life such situations are not so common as other situations in which we do have some knowledge which makes us feel that the assignment of uniform priors is not consistent with all we know. How shall we handle these cases?

Consider the following example: I tell you that the coin that is about to be tossed is biased, but I tell you no more. If you now had to split a dollar on the outcomes heads and tails, how would you do it? In spite of the fact that you know the coin to be biased, since you do not know which way the bias is, you will have to split the dollar 50:50 for a rational bet. You do know, however, that this prior assignment,

$$p(\text{heads} \mid X) = 0.5$$

$$p(\text{tails} \mid X) = 0.5$$

can be improved upon. As you become more familiar with the results of tossing this coin, you will be assigning new priors each time you toss it.

Now suppose I told you that heads appear 60 percent of the time. If this information is correct, then the rational thing for you to do is to assign the following priors:

$$p(\text{heads} \mid X) = 0.6$$

$$p(\text{tails} \mid X) = 0.4$$

In a situation like this one, involving only two hypotheses, there is only 1 degree of freedom, since knowing one of the priors means knowing the other.

Now consider this situation. A student is contemplating the grade he expects to obtain at the end of the semester. Knowing all he does about himself, the institution, and the instructors (let us designate all this knowledge $X$), he must assign priors over the set of possible grades—A, B, C, D, and E. Let these priors be designated as follows:

$$p_1 = \Pr[\text{my grade will be } A \mid X]$$
$$p_2 = \Pr[\text{my grade will be } B \mid X]$$
$$p_3 = \Pr[\text{my grade will be } C \mid X]$$
$$p_4 = \Pr[\text{my grade will be } D \mid X]$$
$$p_5 = \Pr[\text{my grade will be } E \mid X]$$

Now, in this situation it is a rare student who would argue that uniform priors should be assigned, so let us consider a student who is reasonably competent and whose expectation is a B. This expectation is part of $X$ (all that is known about the situation). Although he expects a B, however, he is well aware that he could end up with an A or a C, and there is even a remote chance that he could get a D or an E. How shall he assign priors ($p_1$ through $p_5$) in such a way as to be consistent with all he knows?

For the ensuing discussion we need to define a variable $Y$ that takes on five distinct values corresponding to the grades A, B, C, D, and E. We do so as follows:

$$Y_1 = 1 \quad (= A)$$
$$Y_2 = 2 \quad (= B)$$
$$Y_3 = 3 \quad (= C)$$
$$Y_4 = 4 \quad (= D)$$
$$Y_5 = 5 \quad (= E)$$

The particular values we use are arbitrary, of course. We also need to define quantitatively what we mean by expectation, and we do so as follows, using the symbol $E$ for expectation:

$$E(Y) = p_1 Y_1 + p_2 Y_2 + p_3 Y_3 + p_4 Y_4 + p_5 Y_5$$
$$= \sum_{i=1}^{5} \{p_i Y_i\}$$

If you return to Chapter 2, you will note that this is equivalent to the definition of a mean for a discrete random variable.

Returning now to the problem of assigning priors in this grading problem, the situation may be characterized as follows:

1. We know that the variable $Y$ can take on one of five values, but we do not know which one it will in fact be in the forthcoming examination.

2. We expect the value of $Y$ to be 2 (corresponding to a B), or we may state this as follows: the expected value of $Y$ is 2.

3. We want to assign priors (that is, we want to define a probability distribution over the five permissible values of $Y$) which are consistent with all we know but beyond that are maximally noncommittal (or minimally prejudiced).

To demonstrate the freedom we have to choose these priors (assuming that we are ignoring the requirements of plausible reasoning for the moment), consider the following possible assignments:

ASSIGNMENT 1

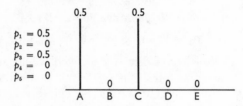

$$p_1 = 0.5$$
$$p_2 = 0$$
$$p_3 = 0.5$$
$$p_4 = 0$$
$$p_5 = 0$$

These priors satisfy rule 2 (they sum to unity), and their expected value is

$$E(Y) = \sum_{i=1}^{5} (p_i Y_i) = (0.5)1 + (0)2 + (0.5)3 + (0)4 + (0)5$$
$$= 2 \quad \text{(equivalent to a } B)$$

ASSIGNMENT 2

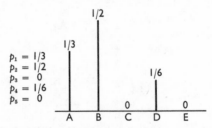

$$p_1 = 1/3$$
$$p_2 = 1/2$$
$$p_3 = 0$$
$$p_4 = 1/6$$
$$p_5 = 0$$

These priors also satisfy rule 2 (they sum to unity), and their expected value is

$$E(Y) = (\tfrac{1}{3})1 + (\tfrac{1}{2})2 + (0)3 + (\tfrac{1}{6})4 + (0)5$$
$$= 2 \quad \text{(equivalent to a } B)$$

In other words, both the assignments above satisfy Rule 2 and the expected value requirement. What makes them unsatisfactory? They are not maximally noncommittal. You might simply ask yourself whether assignment 1 fits with common sense. Is it reasonable to assume that the grade is going to be either an A or a C but nothing else? Or in the case of assignment 2, is it reasonable to believe that there is a chance of getting a D but no chance at all of getting a C?

At this time we shall not discuss how to go about assigning maximally noncommittal priors for this problem (this will be done in Section 11-24), but we wish to establish the following point: Given a situation in which there is uncertainty, in which we have some knowledge that is relevant and in which we have certain expectations, there are many possible assignments of prior probabilities. However, some of these probability distributions are less plausible than others. Indeed, some of them are downright implausible. If we wish to be true to the desiderata for plausible reasoning, then we shall look for that assignment of priors which is consistent with all we know and expect but beyond that is maximally noncommittal (or minimally prejudiced).

And to conclude this section, we characterize the general situation of uncertainty as follows:

1. We are considering a variable whose range of values is known. (This range can be finite and discrete, or it can be continuous.)

2. We have information concerning the expected value of this variable (or some function of it).

3. We want to assign a prior probability distribution which is consistent with all we know and expect but beyond that is maximally noncommittal.

## 11-24   The Maximum Entropy Priors

It will have to be understood that the mathematical details underlying this section are somewhat beyond the expected preparation of the reader of this text. Details aside, however, the general reader should go through the section with a view to following the procedures and to understanding that the assignment of maximum entropy priors is a significant step forward in the Bayesian approach. It was mentioned earlier that one of the bones of contention concerning the Bayesian approach was the question of how to assign priors, and in this section we shall indicate that the assignment of maximum entropy priors goes a long way toward settling this contention.

What we plan to demonstrate is straightforward. Consider a general situation of uncertainty as characterized in the previous section:

1. We are dealing with a variable $Y$ that can take on $k$ distinct values, $Y_1$ through $Y_k$.

2. We know the expected value of $Y$ to be $E(Y) = C$, where $C$ is some constant.

3. We want to know how to assign the maximally noncommittal prior.

How do we do it? We maximize the entropy of the prior probability distribution subject to the constraints that ($i$) the sum of the probabilities must be unity and ($ii$) $E(Y) = C$. Remember that entropy is defined as

$$H = - \sum_{i=1}^{k} p_i \log_2 p_i \qquad (11\text{-}1)$$

so that the problem can be stated concisely as follows:

*Maximize H subject to the constraints*

(i)
$$\sum_{i=1}^{k} p_i = 1$$

(ii)
$$E(Y) = \sum_{i=1}^{k} (p_i Y_i) = C$$

*The set of priors, $p_1$ through $p_k$, which result constitute the maximum entropy priors.*

The problem examined in Section 11-23 would be stated as follows:

*Maximize $H = -\sum_{i=1}^{5} p_i \log_2 p_i$ subject to the constraints*

(i)
$$\sum_{i=1}^{5} p_i = 1$$

(ii)
$$E(Y) = \sum_{i=1}^{5} (p_i Y_i) = 2$$

*The set of priors, $p_1$ through $p_5$, which result constitute the maximum entropy priors.*

Without going into the details of the solution, we can obtain the following maximum entropy distribution:

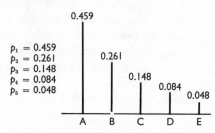

$p_1 = 0.459$
$p_2 = 0.261$
$p_3 = 0.148$
$p_4 = 0.084$
$p_5 = 0.048$

To make sure that the assignment above satisfies constraints (i) and (ii), we sum the five probabilities and find that

$$\sum_{i=1}^{5} p_i = 1.000$$

and we check the expected value by computing

$$E(Y) = \sum_{i=1}^{5} p_i Y_i$$

$$= (0.459)1 + (0.261)2 + (0.148)3 + (0.084)4 + (0.048)5$$

$$= 2.001$$

For this distribution the entropy is found to be

$$H = - \sum p_i \log_2 p_i = 1.940 \text{ bits}$$

and it is interesting to compare this amount of uncertainty with that obtained by assuming no relevant information (that is, the uniform prior where all $p_i = \frac{1}{5}$). If we encode our prior knowledge in the form of a uniform probability distribution, then we are saying that the uncertainty of the situation is

$$H = \log_2 5 = 2.32 \text{ bits}$$

COMMENT. This particular problem of grade expectation serves to demonstrate what can be done with the maximum-entropy approach. Note the following points:

1. If we are true to the desiderata for plausible reasoning, we must encode all we know. If the student had assigned a uniform prior distribution against his better judgment, then the measure of uncertainty would be 2.32 bits. This is the maximum entropy distribution with no constraints other than Rule 2 (that the probabilities must sum to unity). If he has other knowledge that can be encoded in the form of expectations, then he should do so, and under these circumstances the measure of uncertainty will be less than 2.32 bits. In the problem above, the maximum-entropy priors, subject to an expected grade of B, defined a situation with 1.94 bits of uncertainty. As you encode more of what you know, you reduce the uncertainty. The maximum entropy solution can be thought of as a recipe for being maximally noncommittal after you have encoded all that you know.

2. It might occur to you that the maximum-entropy solution as obtained above is still unsatisfactory—meaning that you have some more information to encode. The fact that the largest probability is assigned to grade A seems contrary to common sense. Let us consider this objection carefully. Part of the trouble may be that the word "expectation" has both a colloquial and a statistical meaning. Colloquially we might say, "I expect a B," meaning, "The largest probability should be assigned to grade B." If this is what we mean, then we must be careful to encode our knowledge accordingly. This encoding will be different from the encoding performed above. In the example above we interpreted "The grade expectation is a B" to mean "$E(Y) = Y_2$, where $Y_2$ was the numerical equivalent of a B." For comparative purposes let us consider what kind of priors we should have assigned if we had argued as follows: We say, "I expect a B," and we mean, "Given all I know, the chances of my getting a B are 0.5":

$$p(\text{my grade will be B} \mid X) = 0.5 = p_2$$

In addition to this, let us also say that the expectation $E(Y)$ is still going to be $Y_2$, which is the equivalent of a B. So now the problem will be phrased as follows:

> *Maximize H subject to the following constraints:*
> (i)         $p_2 = 0.5$
> (ii)        $p_1 + p_2 + p_3 + p_4 + p_5 = 1$
> (iii)       $p_1 Y_1 + p_2 Y_2 + p_3 Y_3 + p_4 Y_4 + p_5 Y_5 = 2$
>
> *The set of priors, $p_1$ through $p_5$, which result constitute the maximum entropy priors.*

The solution for this rephrased problem is as follows:

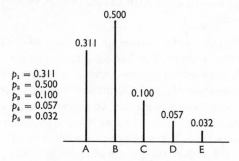

$$p_1 = 0.311$$
$$p_2 = 0.500$$
$$p_3 = 0.100$$
$$p_4 = 0.057$$
$$p_5 = 0.032$$

Check that the various constraints are satisfied:

$$p_2 = 0.5$$

$$\sum_{i=1}^{5} p_i = 1.000$$

$$E(Y) = 1.999$$

This maximum-entropy prior has an uncertainty measure of

$$H = 1.751 \text{ bits}$$

Returning now to the objection stated earlier (concerning the interpretation of the word "expectation"), we see now that it is quite possible to produce a maximum-entropy prior that is consistent with the colloquial meaning of the phrase "I expect a B." The probability distribution assigned above seems to be acceptable, and we shall not pursue this example any further.

## 11-25   Case 1: Uniform Priors

Under what circumstances will the maximum-entropy prior be the uniform prior? The situation is indicated below:

*Maximize $H = - \sum_{i=1}^{k} p_i \log_2 p_i$ subject to the one constraint that*

$$\sum_{i=1}^{k} p_i = 1 \qquad (Rule\ 2)$$

*The priors, $p_1$ through $p_k$, which result will all be equal to $1/k$—that is, the uniform prior.*

If all you know about the problem is that the sum of the probabilities must be unity, then there is no alternative but to assign uniform priors. When this is done, the entropy measure will be a maximum (see Section 11-13). In other words, you will be facing a situation of maximum uncertainty.

Thus we see that the case of the uniform prior is a special case of the maximum-entropy prior.

You are asked to bet on the outcome of throwing a loaded dice, but nobody tells you how it is loaded. If you are to be true to the desiderata for plausible reasoning and wish to assign maximally noncommittal priors consistent with all you know, then the maximum-entropy priors will be the uniform priors:

$$p(1 \mid X) = \tfrac{1}{6} \qquad p(2 \mid X) = \tfrac{1}{6} \qquad p(3 \mid X) = \tfrac{1}{6}$$
$$p(4 \mid X) = \tfrac{1}{6} \qquad p(5 \mid X) = \tfrac{1}{6} \qquad p(6 \mid X) = \tfrac{1}{6}$$

## 11-26   Case 2: The Normal Distribution

In traditional statistics we do not often talk about prior probabilities, but they are always present. Consider a typical statistical model involving the two basic assumptions that (*i*) the population is normally distributed, $ND(\mu,\sigma)$, and (*ii*) the sampling plan is SIRS. Assumption (*ii*) involves one kind of prior probability distribution—the rectangular distribution (uniform distribution). The SIRS plan is based upon the notion of equal probability of occurrence for any member of the population, and this is one way to talk about the uniform prior. Assumption (*i*) involves another kind of prior probability distribution—the normal distribution with mean $\mu$ and standard deviation $\sigma$. Whether they are called prior distributions or not makes no difference; they *are* prior probability distributions.

Now what we need to ask is: Are these two prior distributions consistent with what we know about the experimental situation? Consider the uniform distribution assumption (*ii*). With all we know about the sampling plan actually used and with all we know about the experimental situation in general, is it plausible to assign uniform priors over the set of population members? In some cases it will no doubt be quite plausible. In other cases it will not be plausible. Whenever we knowingly assign uniform priors in the face of contrary knowledge, we are operating against the desiderata for plausible reasoning. We have seen in Section 11-25 just what kind of situation leads to a maximum-entropy distribution that is uniform.

What about the assumption of normality? Under what circumstances will the maximum-entropy prior be a normally distributed prior?

The situation of uncertainty that results in a normally distributed maximum-entropy prior may be characterized as follows:

1. Consider a variable $Y$ whose range of values is infinite and continuous:

$$-\infty \leq Y \leq \infty$$

2. We have information concerning the average value (expected value) of this variable:

$$E(Y) = \mu$$

3. We have information concerning the variance (since this is also an average or mean, we define it as an expected value, too) of this variable:

$$E([Y - E(Y)]^2) = \sigma^2$$

4. We want to assign the prior probability distribution over the range of values of $Y$ in such a way as to be maximally noncommittal yet consistent with all we know. (Parenthetically, you should note that the expression in 3 for variance is similar to the more familiar form:

$$V = \text{mean value of squared deviations from mean}$$
$$= \text{mean value of } (Y - \mu)^2$$

The expected-value form is very common in theoretical work.)

If we rephrase the problem in the form of a maximum-entropy problem, we have

*Maximize H subject to the following constraints:*

(i) $$\int_{-\infty}^{\infty} p(Y \mid X) \, dY = 1$$

*Since we are dealing with a continuous distribution, we want the area under the curve to be unity—this is Rule 2 for continuous distributions.*

(ii) $$E(Y) = \mu$$

(iii) $$E([Y - E(Y)]^2) = \sigma^2$$

*The solution to this maximization problem is a normally distributed maximum entropy prior:* $\text{ND}(\mu, \sigma)$.

Now, this is a satisfying result. What has been shown may be described more informally as follows. An experimenter is interested in some measure, such as the height of college men, and he knows only two items of information: (*i*) the expected height (average height) across the nation is 69.5 in., and (*ii*) the variance of the heights across the nation is 4.1 sq. in. Given this information, he wants to define a population distribution of heights. The easy thing to do is to say that the population distribution is normal with mean 69.5 and variance 4.1. It is more satisfying, however, to be sure that such a prior probability distribution is maximally noncommittal with respect to all the experimenter knows. Let us allow one approximation—that the heights range from minus infinity to plus infinity (we shall relax this approximation in a moment). Then, according to the results indicated above, we shall find that the maximum-entropy prior (the minimally prejudiced probability assignment) is indeed a normal distribution with mean 69.5 and variance 4.1.

WHAT HAPPENS WHEN THE RANGE OF *Y* IS NOT INFINITE? Clearly, in practice, the range of the dependent measure is not infinite. In the example above it would be plausible to argue that the range of heights would be between the limits 48 and 86 in., for example. Now, what happens to the maximum entropy prior under this restricted range? The answer is simple: We get a *truncated* normal distribution, that is, part of a normal distribution.

## 11-27   Other Cases

We leave the subject of maximum-entropy priors after the following general comments. The notion of maximum-entropy priors is very recent and has rarely been used in social science research. In view of the importance of assigning prior probabilities in the Bayesian approach and in view of the criticism leveled at just this aspect of the approach, it is useful to know that there is a way of assigning priors—a way that is consistent with all you know and yet maximally noncommittal (minimally prejudiced) beyond this. The maximum-entropy priors satisfy the desiderata for plausible reasoning, and it is expected that the procedure for obtaining such priors will become commonplace in the next few years.

It is appropriate to ask about the more traditional probability distributions and the assumptions underlying commonly used tests (such as those discussed in Part One of this text). We have just seen in Section 11-25 that the normal distribution (and truncated normal distributions) is a maximum-entropy prior under the following circumstances:

1. The measure is continuous within a stated range.
2. The expected value of the measure is known.
3. The variance of the measures is known.

There are other kinds of probability distributions (the sampling distributions of $t$, $F$, and $\chi^2$, the binomial distribution, the multinomial distribution, and others not mentioned in this text) that are used in practical research, and some engineers have taken pleasure in describing the constraints that give rise to maximum-entropy priors that match a given probability distribution. The interested reader should consult Tribus[2] for further details.

## EXERCISES

1. Check the entropy measures for the probability assignments in Sections 11-23 and 11-24.
2. For the grade problem in Section 11-23, what would the prior assignment be in the following cases?
   (a) "I know I shall never get an A, but beyond that I wish to be maximally noncommittal." What would the entropy be?
   (b) "I expect a C, but beyond that I wish to be minimally prejudiced." Is this different from knowing nothing at all? What is the entropy for this situation?
   (c) "Whatever my chances are of obtaining an A, my chances for B are half as good, my chances for C are half as good as my chances for B, my chances for D are half as good as my chances for C, and my chances for E are half as good as my chances for D." What is the entropy of this unusual situation?
   (d) "My chances of getting C are twice as good as my chances for getting B or D, but I shall surely not get an A or an E."
3. Consider the following binomial experiments and define (i) the range of permissible outcomes, (ii) the probability assignment on these outcomes, and (iii) the entropy of the situation:

   (a) $n = 2, p = 0.5$
   (b) $n = 3, p = 0.5$
   (c) $n = 4, p = 0.5$
   (d) $n = 4, p = 0.2$
   (e) $n = 4, p = 0.8$

4. Consider a fourfold contingency table. There are two row-probability parameters ($p_1$ and $q_1$) and two column-probability parameters ($p_2$ and $q_2$). For each of the following cases compute the entropy on the row marginals, the entropy on the column marginals, and the entropy within the table under the hypothesis of independence:
   (a) No relevant prior information for $p_1$ and $q_1$ or $p_2$ and $q_2$.
   (b) $p_1 = 0.3$ but no relevant information on $p_2$ and $q_2$.
   (c) $p_1 = 0.3$ and $p_2 = 0.7$.
   (d) The experimenter examines $N$ cases and lets them fall as they will within the fourfold table, but he has no prior information on the marginal probabilities.
   (e) The experimenter examines 20 controls and 20 experimentals, and finds out how the controls distribute themselves in two categories, high and low, and

    [2] Myron Tribus. *Rational descriptions, decisions, and designs.* New York: Pergamon Press, 1969.

how the experimentals distribute themselves in these two categories. If the table is of the following form:

|              | High | Low |     |
|--------------|------|-----|-----|
| Controls     |      |     | 20  |
| Experimentals |     |     | 20  |

what are the required entropies?

(f) An experimenter fixes both the row totals and the column totals at 6. How many different contingency tables are possible under these constraints? If each of these possibilities is equally likely, what is the entropy within the table? What are entropies on the marginals? What is the entropy within the table under the hypothesis of independence?

## 11-3   HOW TO COMPREHEND NEW INFORMATION

### 11-31   Introduction

In any given problem the experimenter must describe the experimental setup and the hypotheses of interest in the form of unambiguous proposition-like statements. He must define a mutually exclusive and exhaustive set of hypotheses, and he must consider each of these hypotheses in turn in terms of what kinds of measure he is likely to encounter under that particular hypothesis. Briefly we shall refer to this as (i) providing a rational description of the problem and (ii) assigning prior probabilities. The latter activity is of two kinds: assigning priors (a) over the set of hypotheses—$p(H_i \mid X)$—and (b) over the data ($D$, the dependent measures) for each hypothesis—$p(D \mid H_i X)$.

Having proceeded this far, we want to know how the experimenter is going to comprehend new information. By this we shall mean two things: (i) how to *extend the conversation* to comprehend a new set of mutually exclusive and exhaustive statements and (ii) how to *change an assignment* of probabilities when new data are available.

### 11-32   The Extension Rule

We are considering a probability assignment $p(A \mid X)$, and we wish to extend the conversation to comprehend a new set of mutually exclusive and exhaustive statements, $B_1$ through $B_n$. First we note that, since $B_1$ to $B_n$ constitute a mutually exclusive and exhaustive set,

$$\sum_{i=1}^{n} p(B_i \mid X) = 1$$

Now, regardless of the meaning of $A$, the following relationship is also true:

$$\sum_{i=1}^{n} p(B_i \mid AX) = 1 \qquad (11\text{-}2)$$

Given the information $X$, we know that one of the events $B_1$ through $B_n$ must occur (that is, one of the statements $B_1$ through $B_n$ must be true). Given the information $X$ and the information $A$, this is still true, unless $A$ happens to be the denial of $X$. But we do not allow this special case, since it is contrary to the model of plausible reasoning. We do not define a probability that is conditional upon contradictory information.

Multiply both sides of Equation (11-2) by $p(A \mid X)$, and switch sides:

$$p(A \mid X) = \sum_{i=1}^{n} p(A \mid X) p(B_i \mid AX)$$

and using the product rule (Rule 1), we have

$$p(A \mid X) = \sum_{i=1}^{n} p(AB_i \mid X)$$

$$= \sum_{i=1}^{n} p(A \mid B_iX) p(B_i \mid X) \qquad (11\text{-}3)$$

These equations are independent of the meanings of $A$ and $B_i$, and we shall refer to Equation (11-3) as the *extension rule*.

ILLUSTRATION.   You are signed up for a math course that is to be taught in two sections by two different professors, but you do not know in which section you will be placed. Of interest to you is the statement

$$A \equiv \text{``I will get an A in the course.''}$$

and you are trying to encode your knowledge about $p(A \mid X)$, where

$X \equiv$ "Everything you know about the course and the professors and your ability, etc."

Having talked to other students, you wish to extend the conversation to include the following information:

$$P_1 \equiv \text{``My instructor will be Professor } P_1 \text{.''}$$
$$P_2 \equiv \text{``My instructor will be Professor } P_2 \text{.''}$$
$$p(A \mid P_1X) = 0.75$$
$$p(A \mid P_2X) = 0.35$$

These last two conditional priors indicate that you have given yourself a much better chance of getting an A if you have Professor $P_1$ than if you have Professor $P_2$. The size of these probabilities indicates that you have some confidence that you can attain an A, but you happen to know that Professor $P_2$ is more reluctant to grant A's than Professor $P_1$.

Making use of the extension rule, we write

$$p(A \mid X) = \sum_{i=1}^{2} p(AP_i \mid X)$$

$$= \sum_{i=1}^{2} p(A \mid P_i X)p(P_i \mid X)$$

$$= p(A \mid P_1 X)p(P_1 \mid X) + p(A \mid P_2 X)p(P_2 \mid X)$$

$$= (0.75)p(P_1 \mid X) + (0.35)p(P_2 \mid X)$$

If you have no relevant information to indicate which section you will be assigned to, then the priors $p(P_1 \mid X)$ and $p(P_2 \mid X)$ would both be established as $\frac{1}{2}$, and the problem would be completed as follows:

$$p(A \mid X) = (0.75)(0.5) + (0.35)(0.5) = 0.55$$

At any stage in an investigation, it is possible to introduce new information by means of the extension rule. As you become aware of new matters that bear on the original problem, you establish a new set of mutually exclusive and exhaustive statements (or hypotheses) and apply the extension rule.

*The extension rule for:*
  1. *One new set of mutually exclusive and exhaustive statements,* $B_1$ *through* $B_n$:

$$p(A \mid X) = \sum_{i=1}^{n} p(AB_i \mid X)$$

  2. *Several new sets of mutually exclusive and exhaustive statements:*

$$B_i \quad for \ \ i = 1, \dots, n$$
$$C_j \quad for \ \ j = 1, \dots, m$$
$$D_k \quad for \ \ k = 1, \dots, r$$

*etc.*

$$p(A \mid X) = \sum_{i=1}^{n} \sum_{j=1}^{m} \sum_{k=1}^{r} \cdots p(AB_i C_j D_k \cdots \mid X)$$

## 11-33   How to Change an Assignment

This section can be brief. In order to change an assignment of prior probabilities when new data become available, we simply make use of Bayes' theorem, which tells us how to convert priors into posteriors. Consider a set of mutually exclusive and exhaustive hypotheses, $H_1$ through $H_k$, for which priors have been established:

$$p(H_i \mid X) \qquad \text{for} \quad i = 1, \ldots, k$$

Next consider new data, $D$, for which the following priors have also been established:

$$p(D \mid H_i X) \qquad \text{for} \quad i = 1, \ldots, k$$

Under these circumstances Bayes' equation tells us how to change the prior assignment into a posterior assignment:

$$p(H_i \mid DX) = p(H_i \mid X) \frac{p(D \mid H_i X)}{p(D \mid X)}$$

In order to evaluate the denominator $p(D \mid X)$, we make use of the extension rule as follows:

$$p(D \mid X) = \sum_{i=1}^{k} p(DH_i \mid X) = \sum_{i=1}^{k} p(D \mid H_i X) p(H_i \mid X)$$

Alternatively we might make use of the odds form of Bayes' theorem:

$$O(H_i \mid DX) = O(H_i \mid X) \frac{p(D \mid H_i X)}{p(D \mid \bar{H}_i X)}$$

$$\text{where } \bar{H}_i = (H_1 + H_2 + \cdots + H_{i-1} + H_{i+1} + \cdots + H_k)$$
$$= \text{(any hypothesis other than } H_i)$$

or the evidence form:

$$\text{ev}(H_i \mid DX) = \text{ev}(H_i \mid X) + 10 \log_{10} \frac{p(D \mid H_i X)}{p(D \mid \bar{H}_i X)}$$

where $\bar{H}_i = $ (denial of $H_i$).

HOW TO HANDLE $p(D \mid \bar{H}_i X)$. In the odds form and the evidence form, we have to evaluate the probability of obtaining the data under the denial of $H_i$. How do we do this? To keep the problem simple, consider just three hypotheses—$H_1$, $H_2$, and $H_3$—these being mutually exclusive and exhaustive. Consider $p(D \mid \bar{H}_1 X)$:

$$p(D \mid \bar{H}_1 X) = p(D \mid [H_2 + H_3] X)$$

since the denial of $H_1$ is the occurrence of either $H_2$ or $H_3$. Now the multiplication rule (Rule 1) would give us

$$p(D[H_2 + H_3] \mid X) = p(D \mid [H_2 + H_3] X) p([H_2 + H_3] \mid X)$$

so that

$$p(D \mid [H_2 + H_3] X) = \frac{p(D[H_2 + H_3] \mid X)}{p([H_2 + H_3] \mid X)}$$

We need to evaluate the numerator and denominator in this equation. Consider the numerator:

$$p(D[H_2 + H_3] \mid X) = p([DH_2 + DH_3] \mid X)$$
$$= p(DH_2 \mid X) + p(DH_3 \mid X) \qquad \text{(addition rule)}$$
$$= p(D \mid H_2X)p(H_2 \mid X) + p(D \mid H_3X)p(H_3 \mid X)$$

Consider the denominator:

$$p([H_2 + H_3] \mid X) = p(H_2 \mid X) + p(H_3 \mid X) \qquad \text{(addition rule)}$$

Putting all these findings together, we have

$$p(D \mid \bar{H}_1X) = p(D \mid [H_2 + H_3]X)$$
$$= \frac{p(D \mid H_2X)p(H_2 \mid X) + p(D \mid H_3X)p(H_3 \mid X)}{p(H_2 \mid X) + p(H_3 \mid X)} \qquad (11\text{-}4)$$

This formula can easily be extended to the case where there are more than three hypotheses and to the case where there are only two hypotheses.

ILLUSTRATION. You are a reporter at a closed-door ecumenical conference and are waiting in a corridor for the session to end. You review your knowledge about the following statements:

$$D \equiv \text{``This churchman is a smoker.''}$$
$$H_1 \equiv \text{``This churchman is a Roman Catholic.''}$$
$$H_2 \equiv \text{``This churchman is a Baptist.''}$$
$$H_3 \equiv \text{``This churchman is a Methodist.''}$$
$$H_4 \equiv \text{``This churchman is a Buddhist.''}$$

and come up with the following priors:

$$p(H_1 \mid X) = 0.60 \quad \text{and} \quad p(D \mid H_1X) = 0.70$$
$$p(H_2 \mid X) = 0.10 \quad \text{and} \quad p(D \mid H_2X) = 0.30$$
$$p(H_3 \mid X) = 0.25 \quad \text{and} \quad p(D \mid H_3X) = 0.50$$
$$p(H_4 \mid X) = 0.05 \quad \text{and} \quad p(D \mid H_4X) = 0.10$$

The door of the conference room opens, and out walks a man who is smoking. Before getting down to the task of reporting, you decide to evaluate the odds on this churchman being a Baptist, that is,

$$O(H_2 \mid DX) = O(H_2 \mid X)\frac{p(D \mid H_2X)}{p(D \mid \bar{H}_2X)}$$

$$= \left(\frac{0.10}{0.90}\right)\frac{0.3}{p(D \mid \bar{H}_2X)}$$

Consider $p(D \mid \bar{H}_2 X)$ and Equation (11-4):

$$p(D \mid \bar{H}_2 X)$$
$$= p(D \mid [H_1 + H_3 + H_4]X)$$
$$= \frac{p(D \mid H_1 X)p(H_1 \mid X) + p(D \mid H_3 X)p(H_3 \mid X) + p(D \mid H_4 X)p(H_4 \mid X)}{p(H_1 \mid X) + p(H_3 \mid X) + p(H_4 \mid X)}$$
$$= \frac{(0.7)(0.60) + (0.5)(0.25) + (0.1)(0.05)}{(0.60) + (0.25) + (0.05)} = 0.611$$

Therefore,

$$O(H_2 \mid DX) = \frac{1}{9}\left(\frac{0.3}{0.611}\right) = \frac{1}{18}$$

In other words, the posterior odds are about half the prior odds. If a man walked out of the conference room and you did not know anything about the smoking habits of the participants, the odds on his being a Baptist would be 1 in 9. If you consider new information in the form of smoking habits, then the odds on a man who is smoking being a Baptist are about 1 in 18.

## EXERCISES

1. Consider the illustration in Section 11-32 (the probability of getting an A in a course taught by either professor $P_1$ or professor $P_2$).
   (a) What is the probability of getting an A if $p(P_1 \mid X) = 0.40$?
   (b) What value should be assigned to $p(P_1 \mid X)$ if your chances of getting an A are to be 50:50?
   (c) Expand $p(AB \mid C)$ and $p(ABC \mid D)$.
   (d) Consider the introduction of new information as follows. You hear that you are definitely going to be in Section 1. (There is no uncertainty here.) You learn that Section 2 will definitely be given at 9:30 A.M., but section 1 will be given at either 8:00 A.M. or 11:00 A.M. Let this information be designated:

$$Q_1 \equiv \text{``Section 1 will be given at 8 A.M.''}$$
$$Q_2 \equiv \text{``Section 1 will be given at 11 A.M.''}$$

   Consider the probabilities $p(P_1 \mid X)$ and $p(P_2 \mid X)$ in the light of this new information. Using the extension rule, write the expression for $p(A \mid X)$ when new information concerning $P_1$ and $P_2$ and new information concerning $Q_1$ and $Q_2$ are brought into the conservation.
   (e) If it is known that $p(P_1 \mid Q_1 X) = 0.1$ (this professor hates to teach that early), and $p(P_1 \mid Q_2 X) = 0.6$ (this professor prefers the later hour), compute the value $p(A \mid X)$. (Assume for the moment that you don't know anything relevant about the prior probabilities on $Q_1$ and $Q_2$.)
   (f) If $p(Q_1 \mid X) = 0.2$, what is $p(A \mid X)$?
2. Consider the illustration in Section 11-33 (the ecumenical conference and smoking habits of the participants).
   (a) What is the posterior probability that a man who is smoking is (i) Roman Catholic? (ii) Methodist? (iii) Buddhist?

(*b*) Convert these posterior probabilities to odds ratios and decibels of evidence.

(*c*) What are the prior probabilities, odds ratios, and evidences for smokers among Roman Catholics, Baptists, Methodists, and Buddhists?

(*d*) What is the posterior evidence that a nonsmoker is (*i*) Roman Catholic? (*ii*) Baptist? (*iii*) Methodist? (*iv*) Buddhist?

(*e*) A churchman comes out of the conference. How much uncertainty is there concerning his church membership? (Answer in entropy measure.)

(*f*) If a churchman comes out of the conference smoking, how much uncertainty is there concerning his church membership? (*Hint;* First find out what $p(DH_i \mid X)$ is for each *i*.)

(*g*) If a nonsmoking churchman comes out of the conference, how much uncertainty is there concerning his church membership?

3. You are feeling unwell and take your temperature. The thermometer reads 110°F. What new information do you introduce into the conservation?

4. You are employing a statistical model and are informed by a statistician that under the assumptions of the null hypothesis the chances of getting a chi-square value larger than 20 for 10 df are less than 0.05. If you reject the null hypothesis (when you know it is true, though with probability less than 0.05), what new information have you introduced into the situation?

5. If you perform a statistical test of significance and find that the null hypothesis (which you hoped to reject) could not be rejected at the 0.05 level but was close, what new information are you introducing if you say, "There tends to be a significant difference"?

6. (*a*) If you compute a statistic, such as the variance for example, is there any uncertainty in the situation? (We are referring here to the actual computation of the statistic.)

(*b*) If you use a sample statistic to estimate a population parameter, wherein lies the uncertainty of the situation?

(*c*) If you are interested in estimating the population mean and you take an SIRS sample of size $N$ to obtain an estimate, what happens to the uncertainty of the estimate as $N$ increases? Can you figure out why the uncertainty changes as $N$ increases? If your sample was, in fact, the whole population, how much uncertainty would there be in using the sample mean as the population mean?

## 11-4  SOME WORKED EXAMPLES

### 11-41  Example 1: A Problem in Self-evaluation

The following example is based on an actual study by a student at Dartmouth College. At this institution a student takes three courses in each of three terms per academic year. The maximum grade is 5.0, corresponding to an A, and the minimum is zero. Thus in any one term a student receives three grades that sum to a value between 15 and 0 inclusive. The purpose of this exercise was to let each student evaluate his own career in a Bayesian manner in order to produce evidence of "potential success"— something other than a mere grade-point average. Three hypotheses were to be examined:

$$H_1 \equiv \text{"I am an excellent student."}$$

$$H_2 \equiv \text{"I am an average student."}$$

$$H_3 \equiv \text{"I am a poor student."}$$

PRIOR TO THE FIRST TERM

$X \equiv$ "I am accustomed to getting mostly A's in high school; I know the
competition is tough at Dartmouth; my College Board scores were
mediocre by Dartmouth standards; but I plan to set my standards
high."

$p(H_1 \mid X) = 0.50$

$p(H_2 \mid X) = 0.25$ } since "If I do not look like an excellent
$p(H_3 \mid X) = 0.25$ } student, I don't know what to expect."

Now, under each hypothesis this student must decide the prior assignments. Without going through the details of a maximum-entropy prior
assignment but keeping the principle in mind, he establishes the priors shown
in Table 11-1. He excludes the possibility that he would ever obtain less than

Table 11-1   The Priors $p(D \mid H_i X)$

| Grade sum | $H_1$ | $H_2$ | $H_3$ |
|-----------|-------|-------|-------|
| 15 | 0.20 | 0.005 | $\cdots$ |
| 14 | 0.25 | 0.005 | $\cdots$ |
| 13 | 0.25 | 0.015 | $\cdots$ |
| 12 | 0.15 | 0.100 | $\cdots$ |
| 11 | 0.10 | 0.125 | $\cdots$ |
| 10 | 0.01 | 0.250 | $\cdots$ |
| 9 | 0.01 | 0.250 | 0.005 |
| 8 | 0.01 | 0.125 | 0.015 |
| 7 | 0.01 | 0.100 | 0.05 |
| 6 | 0.01 | 0.015 | 0.10 |
| 5 | $\cdots$ | 0.005 | 0.30 |
| 4 | $\cdots$ | 0.005 | 0.33 |
| 3 | $\cdots$ | $\cdots$ | 0.20 |

3 as a grade sum per term. The rather widely spread distributions for $H_1$ and
$H_2$ indicate his unwillingness to relinquish these hypotheses too readily. If
he has a bad time in his first term, he will not necessarily give up on the $H_1$
hypothesis, and he feels that it will take a couple of terms before he will be
able to make a more meaningful assignment of priors over the various grade
sums.

AFTER THE FIRST TERM.   We shall indicate the grade sum in term 1 as
follows:

$D_1 \equiv$ "Grade sum in term 1 is 8."

The prior evidence for each hypothesis gives

$$\text{ev}(H_1 \mid X) = 10 \log_{10} \frac{0.5}{0.5} = 0$$

$$\text{ev}(H_2 \mid X) = 10 \log_{10} \frac{0.25}{0.75} = -4.771 \text{ db}$$

$$\text{ev}(H_3 \mid X) = 10 \log_{10} \frac{0.25}{0.75} = -4.771 \text{ db}$$

The posterior evidence for each hypothesis yields

$$\text{ev}(H_1 \mid D_1 X) = \text{ev}(H_1 \mid X) + 10 \log_{10} \frac{p(D_1 \mid H_1 X)}{p(D_1 \mid \bar{H}_1 X)}$$

$$= 0 - 8.451 = -8.451 \text{ db}$$

$$\text{ev}(H_2 \mid D_1 X) = -4.771 + 10.299 = 5.528 \text{ db}$$

$$\text{ev}(H_3 \mid D_1 X) = -4.771 - 5.082 = -9.853 \text{ db}$$

Using Appendix I, we may convert these posterior evidences into posterior probabilities, as follows:

$$p(H_1 \mid D_1 X) = 0.125$$
$$p(H_2 \mid D_1 X) = 0.781$$
$$p(H_3 \mid D_1 X) = 0.094$$

Now these posterior probabilities will serve as the priors for the second term.

### AFTER THE SECOND TERM

$$D_2 \equiv \text{"Grade sum in term 2 is 11."}$$

At this stage the prior evidence for each hypothesis is the posterior evidence after the first term, that is, $-8.451$ db, $5.528$ db, and $-9.853$ db for $H_1$, $H_2$, and $H_3$, respectively. The posterior evidence after term 2 is calculated as follows:

$$\text{ev}(H_1 \mid D_2 D_1 X) = \text{ev}(H_1 \mid D_1 X) + 10 \log_{10} \frac{p(D_2 \mid H_1 D_1 X)}{p(D_2 \mid \bar{H}_1 D_1 X)}$$

$$= -8.451 - 0.476 = -8.927 \text{ db}$$

$$\text{ev}(H_2 \mid D_2 D_1 X) = 5.528 + 3.404 = 8.932 \text{ db}$$

$$\text{ev}(H_3 \mid D_2 D_1 X) = -9.853 + (\text{indeterminate})$$

Using Appendix I, we convert these posterior evidences into posterior probabilities, as follows:

$$p(H_1 \mid D_2 D_1 X) = 0.11$$
$$p(H_2 \mid D_2 D_1 X) = 0.89$$
$$p(H_3 \mid D_2 D_1 X) = \text{indeterminate}$$

The Bayesian analysis shows that hypothesis $H_3$ is no longer in contention; or, in the student's own words, "At this point I rejected the hypothesis that I would disappoint myself by being a poor student."

RECONSIDERATION. At this stage the student reconsidered the conditional priors, $p(D \mid H_iX)$. On the basis of the experience gained during the past two terms, he began to believe that brilliance and grade sum were not quite so intimately connected. In other words, he allowed that a brilliant student might well *not* get a grade sum of 15 all the time, or even 14 or 13. His conception of hypothesis $H_1$ underwent a change on the basis of new knowledge (in the form of experience at Dartmouth in general). To symbolize this reconsideration, we introduce a new $X$, calling it $X'$:

$X' \equiv$ "All that I know about the Dartmouth system and my own ability at this time."

New priors were established as follows:

$$p(H_1 \mid X') = \tfrac{1}{3} \quad \text{and} \quad p(H_2 \mid X') = \tfrac{2}{3}$$

Notice that $H_3$ no longer features in this self-evaluation (Table 11-2). Note that values below 6 are now ruled out.

Table 11-2   The Priors $p(D \mid H_iX')$

| Grade sum | $H_1$ | $H_2$ |
|:---:|:---:|:---:|
| 15 | 0.15 | $\cdots$ |
| 14 | 0.20 | $\cdots$ |
| 13 | 0.25 | 0.01 |
| 12 | 0.20 | 0.03 |
| 11 | 0.15 | 0.06 |
| 10 | 0.03 | 0.10 |
| 9 | 0.01 | 0.20 |
| 8 | 0.01 | 0.30 |
| 7 | $\cdots$ | 0.20 |
| 6 | $\cdots$ | 0.10 |

AFTER THE THIRD TERM

$$D_3 \equiv \text{"Grade sum in term 3 is 11."}$$

The prior evidence was

$$\text{ev}(H_1 \mid X') = -3.01 \text{ db} \quad \text{and} \quad \text{ev}(H_2 \mid X') = +3.01 \text{ db}$$

The posterior evidence is

$$\text{ev}(H_1 \mid D_3 X') = \text{ev}(H_1 \mid X') + 10 \log_{10} \frac{p(D_3 \mid H_1 X')}{p(D_3 \mid H_2 X')}$$

$$= -3.01 + 3.979 = +0.969 \text{ db}$$

$$\text{ev}(H_2 \mid D_3 X') = +3.01 - 3.979 = -0.969 \text{ db}$$

Converting these evidences to probabilities gives

$$p(H_1 \mid D_3 X') = 0.56 \quad \text{and} \quad p(H_2 \mid D_3 X') = 0.44$$

These become the new priors for the next term.

Note that the evidence seems to favor the $H_1$ hypothesis now. From the student's point of view, this inference agrees with common sense because in term 3 he obtained his first A in a course. This boosted his morale and kept him optimistic over the summer vacation. In his own words, "I returned in September a little overconfident."

### AFTER THE FOURTH TERM

$$D_4 \equiv \text{"Grade sum in fourth term was 9."}$$

"This forced me to give up (temporarily) the idea that I was brilliant." The posterior evidence after this term was

$$\text{ev}(H_1 \mid D_4 D_3 X') = \quad 0.969 - 13.010 = -12.041 \text{ db}$$
$$\text{ev}(H_2 \mid D_4 D_3 X') = -0.969 + 13.010 = \quad 12.041 \text{ db}$$

Converting to probabilities, we have

$$p(H_1 \mid D_4 D_3 X') = 0.06 \quad \text{and} \quad p(H_2 \mid D_4 D_3 X') = 0.94$$

There is no need to pursue this problem any further except in the interests of closure. This student obtained a grade sum of 8 in the fifth term and decided to leave school. He traveled widely for 14 months and then returned with radically different priors on the hypotheses $H_1$, $H_2$, and $H_3$. In Exercise 1 at the end of this section, the further history of this student is presented.

The purpose of giving this illustration is to show the flexibility of the Bayesian approach in handling a very personal matter—that of self-evaluation. There is no obvious way of dealing with such a problem by traditional methods. By successively encoding our knowledge at various stages in the problem and making use of Bayes' theorem to reason plausibly from priors to posteriors, we can maintain very close identification with the problem of interest.

### 11-42   Example 2: Reaction Time to Light and Sound

By way of comparison let us consider the problem given in Section 5-31. An experimenter has a hunch that human beings respond more quickly to sound than to light, and he performs an experiment in whole-body jumping. How could we handle this problem from the Bayesian point of view?

First we must state the set of mutually exclusive and exhaustive hypotheses of interest to the experimenter. Reaction time to light and sound will be designated $RT_L$ and $RT_S$, respectively:

$$H_1 \equiv \text{"}RT_L > RT_S \text{ for subject } i\text{"}$$
$$H_2 \equiv \text{"}RT_L \leq RT_S \text{ for subject } i\text{"}$$

Next the experimenter must encode his knowledge concerning these two hypotheses. We designate "all that he knows about the subject matter and the experimental apparatus and its limitations, etc." by the symbol $X$. Thus

$$X \equiv \text{"experimenter's prior knowledge"}$$

On the basis of $X$ the experimenter must assign priors to $H_1$ and $H_2$, and he does so as follows:

$$p(H_1 \mid X) = 0.75$$
$$p(H_2 \mid X) = 0.25$$

Note that there is no reason to make these two hypotheses equally likely. In view of what is known about the neurophysiology of the auditory and visual systems, it is irrational to assign equal probabilities, except, of course, if we have never learned about these two systems. The reason the experimenter does not assign probabilities 1 and 0 to $H_1$ and $H_2$, respectively, is a practical one. He knows that apparatus has limitations, and cooperation from human subjects invariably falls short of perfection. In other words, experimental data are unlikely to verify one or the other hypothesis infallibly.

Given the fallibility of experimental data, the following conditional priors are established:

$$p(D_1 \mid H_1 X) = 0.85 \qquad p(D_2 \mid H_1 X) = 0.15$$
$$p(D_1 \mid H_2 X) = 0.20 \qquad p(D_2 \mid H_2 X) = 0.80$$

where $D_1 \equiv$ "The data for subject $i$ show $RT_L > RT_S$."
$D_2 \equiv$ "The data for subject $i$ show $RT_L \leq RT_S$."

Treating the experiment as a sequential experiment, consider the data for the first subject (see Section 5-31):

$$RT_L = 0.75 \text{ sec} \qquad \text{and} \qquad RT_S = 0.72 \text{ sec}$$

Therefore, this is an instance of $D_1$.

We now evaluate the evidence for $H_1$, given $D_1$:

$$\text{ev}(H_1 \mid D_1 X) = \text{ev}(H_1 \mid X) + 10 \log_{10} \frac{p(D_1 \mid H_1 X)}{p(D_1 \mid H_2 X)}$$

$$= 10 \log_{10} \frac{0.75}{0.25} + 10 \log_{10} \frac{0.85}{0.20}$$

$$= 4.771 + 6.284 = 11.055 \text{ db}$$

$$\text{ev}(H_2 \mid D_1 X) = -11.055 \text{ db}$$

The next subject yields the following data:

$$RT_L = 0.66 \text{ sec} \qquad \text{and} \qquad RT_S = 0.67 \text{ sec}$$

and this is an instance of $D_2$. The new posterior evidence is thus

$$\text{ev}(H_1 \mid D_2 D_1 X) = \text{ev}(H_1 \mid D_1 X) + 10 \log_{10} \frac{p(D_2 \mid H_1 D_1 X)}{p(D_2 \mid H_2 D_1 X)}$$

$$= 11.055 - 7.269 = 3.786 \text{ db}$$

$$\text{ev}(H_2 \mid D_2 D_1 X) = -3.786 \text{ db}$$

Note that $p(D_2 \mid H_1 D_1 X) = p(D_2 \mid H_1 X)$, since the experimenter believes one subject's data to be independent of every other subject's data. Note also that every time the data are $D_1$, 6.284 db of evidence accrue to $H_1$, and every time the data are $D_2$, 7.269 db of evidence is subtracted from the evidence for $H_1$. We can therefore write the following formula for evidence for $H_1$:

$$\text{ev}(H_1 \mid DX) = 4.771 + 6.284(n_1) - 7.269(n_2) \text{ db}$$

where $n_1 = $ number of instances of $D_1$

$n_2 = $ number of instances of $D_2$

The 10 subjects described in Section 5-31 included 7 instances of $D_1$ and 3 instances of $D_2$, so that the final evidence in favor of $H_1$ after running these 10 subjects would be

$$\text{ev}(H_1 \mid D_1 D_1 D_2 D_2 D_1 D_1 D_1 D_1 D_2 D_1 X) = 4.771 + 6.284(7) - 7.269(3)$$

$$= 25.952 \text{ db}$$

Looking up Appendix I, we find that this evidence corresponds to odds of about 500 to 1 in favor of $H_1$.

COMMENT. This very simple analysis of the experimental data gives a satisfyingly direct evaluation of hypothesis $H_1$. It is possible to elaborate the analysis by elaborating the assignment of conditional priors. For example, the assignment could have been made as in Table 11-3.

Table 11-3   Conditional   Priors
$p(D_i \mid H_j X)$

|       | $H_1$ | $H_2$ |
|-------|-------|-------|
| $D_1$ | 0.20  | 0.01  |
| $D_2$ | 0.30  | 0.04  |
| $D_3$ | 0.30  | 0.10  |
| $D_4$ | 0.15  | 0.40  |
| $D_5$ | 0.05  | 0.45  |

where   $D_1 \equiv$ "$RT_L - RT_S$ lies above $+0.08$ sec."

$D_2 \equiv$ "$RT_L - RT_S$ lies in the interval 0.05 through 0.07 sec."

$D_3 \equiv$ "$RT_L - RT_S$ lies in the interval 0.02 through 0.04 sec."

$D_4 \equiv$ "$RT_L - RT_S$ lies in the interval $-0.01$ through 0.01 sec."

$D_5 \equiv$ "$RT_L - RT_S$ lies in the interval $-0.04$ through $-0.02$ sec."

It is left as an exercise to evaluate the final evidence in favor of $H_1$, given the conditional priors in Table 11-3.

### 11-43   Example 3: A Contingency Table Problem

In Chapter 8 contingency tables were examined, and the $\chi^2$ goodness-of-fit test was used to decide whether there was significant dependence between two attributes. In this section we examine a Bayesian approach to the analysis of contingency table data.[3] To keep the discussion as simple as possible, consider a $2 \times 2$ (fourfold) contingency table.

Before gathering data, the experimenter must define a mutually exclusive and exhaustive set of hypotheses:

$H_d \equiv$ "The variables $A$ and $B$ are dependent."

$H_i \equiv$ "The variables $A$ and $B$ are independent."

The probabilities of interest are as follows:

|       | $B_1$ | $B_2$ | |
|-------|-------|-------|-------|
|       | $B_1$ | $B_2$ |       |
| $A_1$ | $p(A_1B_1 \mid X)$ | $p(A_1B_2 \mid X)$ | $p(A_1 \mid X)$ |
| $A_2$ | $p(A_2B_1 \mid X)$ | $p(A_2B_2 \mid X)$ | $p(A_2 \mid X)$ |
|       | $p(B_1 \mid X)$ | $p(B_2 \mid X)$ | 1 |

[3] The details of this kind of analysis are given in Tribus, chapter 6.

The four joint probabilities within the table must sum to unity, the row marginal probabilities must sum to unity, the column marginal probabilities must sum to unity, and the joint probabilities must sum rowwise and columnwise to the marginal probability values.

The experimenter must say something about these probabilities before obtaining data.

UNDER HYPOTHESIS $H_d$. If $A$ and $B$ are believed to be dependent on each other, then the following priors must be established:

|       | $B_1$      | $B_2$      |
|-------|------------|------------|
| $A_1$ | $\omega_1$ | $\omega_2$ |
| $A_2$ | $\omega_3$ | $\omega_4$ |

where $\qquad \omega_1 + \omega_2 + \omega_3 + \omega_4 = 1$

Using whatever information he may have, the experimenter will establish a maximum entropy prior over these joint probabilities. The marginal probabilities will be obtained by adding across rows and adding down columns.

UNDER HYPOTHESIS $H_i$. If attributes $A$ and $B$ are believed to be independent of each other, then the following priors must be established:

|       | $B_1$     | $B_2$     |            |
|-------|-----------|-----------|------------|
| $A_1$ |           |           | $\alpha_1$ |
| $A_2$ |           |           | $\alpha_2$ |
|       | $\beta_1$ | $\beta_2$ | $1$        |

where $\qquad \alpha_1 + \alpha_2 = 1 = \beta_1 + \beta_2$

Using whatever information he may have, the experimenter will establish a maximum entropy prior over these two sets of marginal probabilities. According to the independence hypothesis $H_i$, the joint probabilities within the table are simply products of the marginal probabilities, as follows:

$$p(A_1B_1 \mid X) = p(A_1 \mid X)p(B_1 \mid X) = \alpha_1\beta_1$$
$$p(A_1B_2 \mid X) = \alpha_1\beta_2$$
$$p(A_2B_1 \mid X) = \alpha_2\beta_1$$
$$p(A_2B_2 \mid X) = \alpha_2\beta_2$$

SPECIAL CASES OF PRIOR INFORMATION.   The following special cases of prior information may arise in a particular experimental problem:

1. No relevant prior information
2. Exact information on either the row or column marginals
3. Exact information on both row and column marginals
4. Some relevant information on one marginal
5. Some relevant information on both marginals

At this time solutions have not been found for all these cases, but we shall illustrate the first two cases below.

SPECIAL CASES OF DESIGN INFORMATION.   The experimenter has a certain amount of freedom when it comes to running the actual experiment. For instance, he can decide how many subjects will be classified in the table or how many subjects of type $A_1$ will be classified. In general, we designate the design information in terms of the following quantities:

$$\begin{array}{ccc} & B_1 \quad B_2 & \\ A_1 & \boxed{\phantom{XXXXXX}} & N_{A_1} \\ A_2 & & N_{A_2} \\ & N_{B_1} \quad N_{B_2} & N \end{array}$$

Thus we can distinguish the following cases:

$A$. Only the total number of cases $N$ is fixed ahead of time.
$B$. The marginal totals for either the $A$ attribute or the $B$ attribute are fixed—either $N_{A_1}$ and $N_{A_2}$ or $N_{B_1}$ and $N_{B_2}$.
$C$. The marginal totals for both attributes are fixed ahead of time.

Perhaps the most common case is $B$, because it has become conventional to perform experiments on so many controls and so many experimentals. The experimenter studying the aggressive behavior of schizophrenics might design the following classification scheme:

| | Aggression | No aggression | |
|---|---|---|---|
| Schizophrenics | | | 40 |
| Normals | | | 40 |

In other words, he plans to use 40 schizophrenics and 40 normals (as controls), making a total of 80 subjects. This is an instance of special case $B$.

CASE 1$A$: MINIMUM PRIOR INFORMATION AND MINIMUM DESIGN INFORMATION. Suppose that the data for an experiment are designated $D$, where

$$D = \begin{array}{|c|c|} \hline n_1 & n_2 \\ \hline n_3 & n_4 \\ \hline \end{array} \begin{array}{c} N_{A_1} \\ \\ N_{A_2} \end{array}$$
$$\quad\quad N_{B_1} \quad N_{B_2} \quad N$$

Our interest is focused on the following two equations:

$$\mathrm{ev}(H_d \mid DX) = \mathrm{ev}(H_d \mid X) + 10 \log_{10} \frac{p(D \mid H_d X)}{p(D \mid H_i X)} \tag{11-5}$$

$$\mathrm{ev}(H_i \mid DX) = \mathrm{ev}(H_i \mid X) + 10 \log_{10} \frac{p(D \mid H_i X)}{p(D \mid H_d X)} \tag{11-6}$$

In view of the fact that there are only two hypotheses, we need consider only one of the above, and the basic task is to evaluate the two probabilities $p(D \mid H_d X)$ and $p(D \mid H_i X)$. In other words, we have to assign values to these two conditional priors. What is the probability of obtaining the data $D$ under hypothesis $H_d$, and what is the probability under hypothesis $H_i$?

The details involved in finding these two probabilities are spelled out in the reference given at the beginning of this section. For now we simply report that

$$p(D \mid H_d X) = \frac{N!(4-1)!}{(N+4-1)!}$$

$$p(D \mid H_i X) = \frac{(2-1)!(2-1)!N!}{n_1!n_2!n_3!n_4!} \frac{N_{A_1}!N_{A_2}!N_{B_1}!N_{B_2}!}{(N+2-1)!(N+2-1)!}$$

Note that cell frequencies, the marginal frequencies, and the total frequency appear as factorials in these expressions.

Substituting these values in Equation (11-5), we obtain

$$\mathrm{ev}(H_d \mid DX) - \mathrm{ev}(H_d \mid X) = 10 \log_{10} \underbrace{\frac{(4-1)!}{(2-1)!(2-1)!}}_{\text{Term 1}}$$

$$+ 10 \log_{10} \underbrace{\frac{(N+2-1)!(N+2-1)!}{(N+4-1)!}}_{\text{Term 2}}$$

$$+ \underbrace{\sum_{i=1}^{4} 10 \log_{10} n_i!}_{\text{Term 3}} - \underbrace{\sum_{i=1}^{2} 10 \log_{10} N_{A_i}!}_{\text{Term 4}}$$

$$- \underbrace{\sum_{i=1}^{2} 10 \log_{10} N_{B_i}!}_{\text{Term 5}} \tag{11-7}$$

Now this equation may look formidable, but this change in evidence for hypothesis $H_d$ is written in the form of five terms for a good reason. Each of these terms can be interpreted directly:

Term 1 depends only upon the size of the contingency table.

Term 2 depends upon the number of cases, $N$, relative to the size of the table.

Term 3 depends upon the cell frequencies only and can be rephrased in the form of an entropy measure—the *entropy within the table*, or the uncertainty of the experimenter with respect to what values $n_1$, $n_2$, $n_3$, and $n_4$ will take on.

Term 4 depends on the row marginals only and can be rephrased in the form of an entropy measure—the *row-marginal entropy*, or the uncertainty of the experimenter with respect to what values $N_{A_1}$ and $N_{A_2}$ will take on.

Term 5 depends upon the column marginals only and can be rephrased as *column-marginal entropy*, or the uncertainty of the experimenter with respect to what values $N_{B_1}$ and $N_{B_2}$ will take on.

The advantage of the above breakdown into five terms is that when we consider design $B$, in which the experimenter controls the row-marginal totals, then we know that he has no uncertainty with respect to the values $N_{A_1}$ and $N_{A_2}$. Thus the row-marginal-entropy term is zero, and that term drops out. Similarly, for other cases of prior information and design information, the breakdown into five terms should give a clue as to what to expect. To illustrate this feature, we present next the change in evidence for $H_d$ for the special case $1B$.

CASE $1B$: MINIMUM PRIOR INFORMATION BUT ROW TOTALS CONTROLLED. The change in evidence for $H_d$ is as follows:

$$\text{ev}(H_d \mid DX) - \text{ev}(H_d \mid X) = \underbrace{10 \log_{10} [(2 - 1)!]^2}_{\text{Term 1}}$$

$$+ \underbrace{10 \log_{10} \frac{(N + 2 - 1)!}{(N_{A_1} + 2 - 1)!(N_{A_2} + 2 - 1)!}}_{\text{Term 2}}$$

$$+ \underbrace{\sum_{i=1}^{4} 10 \log_{10} n_i!}_{\text{Term 3}} - \underbrace{(0)}_{\text{Term 4}} - \underbrace{\sum_{i=1}^{2} 10 \log_{10} N_{B_i}!}_{\text{Term 5}}$$

$$(11\text{-}8)$$

ILLUSTRATION 1.    Consider the data discussed in Section 8-41:

|  | Cognitive system | | |
|---|---|---|---|
|  | Complex | Simple |  |
| High conflict | 18 | 6 | 24 |
| Low conflict | 17 | 19 | 36 |
|  | 35 | 25 | 60 |

The experimenter is interested in deciding whether or not complexity of the cognitive system and degree of conflict are dependent on each other. In the more conventional chi-square analysis, the value $\chi^2 = 4.57$ was obtained, and for a $\chi^2$ distribution with 1 df this value was significant beyond the 0.05 level. In other words, the hypothesis of independence $H_i$ was rejected in favor of $H_d$.

This is an instance of case 1A in the Bayesian analysis of contingency tables, and so we use Equation (11-7) to evaluate the change in evidence in favor of $H_d$, that is, the change from prior to posterior evidence after examining the data. Note that when we actually perform the computation involved in Equation (11-7), we do so in the following form:

Change in evidence for $H_d$

$$= 10 \log_{10} \frac{(rc - 1)!(N + r - 1)!(N + c - 1)!n_1!n_2!n_3! \cdots}{(r - 1)!(c - 1)!(N + rc - 1)!N_{A_1}!N_{A_2}! \cdots N_{B_1}!N_{B_2}! \cdots} \quad (11\text{-}7')$$

where $r$ = number of rows
$c$ = number of columns.

The breakdown into five terms is essentially for exposition. For the data above we obtain

$$\text{ev}(H_d \mid DX) - \text{ev}(H_d \mid X) = 10 \log_{10} \frac{3!61!61!18!6!17!19!}{1!1!63!24!36!35!25!}$$

$$= 6.237 \text{ db}$$

In other words, the data in the contingency table add support to the dependent hypothesis. If we assume that the experimenter was quite undecided about $H_i$ and $H_d$ to start with—that is, the prior evidence for $H_d$ was zero—then the examination of these 60 subjects increases the evidence for $H_d$ by 6.237 db. Looking up Appendix I, we note that this amount of evidence corresponds to a probability of

$$p(H_d \mid DX) = 0.81$$

and an odds ratio of

$$O(H_d \mid DX) = 4.26$$

Neither of these measures of plausibility of $H_d$ is overwhelming, and the experimenter might well defer judgment until further studies have been completed.

ILLUSTRATION 2. In the following experimental problem, an experimenter set out to examine the relationship between opinion change and introversion–extroversion. He chose 40 introverts and 40 extroverts and classified them according to whether they could be induced to change their opinions or not. The data were as follows:

|  | Opinion change | |  |
|  | Yes | No |  |
| Introvert | 16 | 24 | 40 |
| Extrovert | 30 | 10 | 40 |
|  | 46 | 34 | 80 |

This particular experimental design is an instance of case $1B$ of the Bayesian approach. Thus we use Equation (11-8) to evaluate the posterior evidence for $H_d$ (or $H_i$). Instead of splitting the computation into five terms, as in Equation (11-8), we use the form

Change in evidence in favor of $H_d$

$$= 10 \log_{10} \frac{[(c-1)!]^r (N+c-1)! n_1! n_2! n_3! \cdots}{(N_{A_1}+c-1)!(N_{A_2}+c-1)! \cdots (c-1)! N_{B_1}! N_{B_2}! \cdots} \quad (11\text{-}8')$$

where $r$ = number of rows
$c$ = number of columns

Using the data above, we obtain

$$\text{ev}(H_d \mid DX) - \text{ev}(H_d \mid X) = 10 \log_{10} \frac{[1!]^2 81! 16! 24! 30! 10!}{41! 41! 1! 1! 46! 34!}$$

$$= 16.004 \text{ db}$$

This is considerable *change in evidence* in favor of $H_d$, and we note that 16.004 db corresponds to a probability of

$$p(H_d \mid DX) = 0.975$$

(assuming prior evidence to be zero) and an odds ratio of

$$O(H_d \mid DX) = 39/1$$

The data strongly support the argument that extroverts are more susceptible to induced opinion change than introverts. The odds are 39 to 1 in favor of the dependent hypothesis.

## EXERCISES

1. Consider the example in Section 11-41. When this student returned to school after 14 months' absence, he established the following priors:

$$p(H_1 \mid X'') = 0.6 \qquad p(H_2 \mid X'') = 0.4 \qquad p(H_3 \mid X'') = 0.0$$

where $X'' \equiv$ "All he knew at that time." Using the priors in Table 11-2, follow the evidence in favor of $H_1$ over the next five terms, in which he obtained grade sums of 12, 11, 13, 14, and 13.

2. The moral of the story about the student in Section 11-41 and Exercise 1 above is not that you should leave school for 14 months. What is important is the comparison between grade-point average over 10 terms and the evidence for $H_1$ at the end of this time. Since the grade-point average is anchored to the first term of the freshman year and since means have smaller standard errors as time progresses (in the case of grades), because they are based on more and more grades, it is not easy to demonstrate that new information (like a change of priors) has been added during a four-year career. Consider your own grades over the past few years, and make a sincere and uncompromisingly honest Bayesian analysis of $H_1$, $H_2$, and $H_3$ (or some other more meaningful hypotheses) for yourself.

3. Consider the reaction-time experiment discussed in Section 11-42. In Table 11-3, you will find a set of priors that could be used with the data for this experiment (see Section 5-31 for the original data). Using the evidence form of Bayes' theorem, perform a sequential analysis of the hypotheses $H_1$ and $H_2$ for these data. How does the analysis with the more refined priors compare with the simpler analysis in Section 11-42?

4. Consider the priors given in Table 11-3. If the range of $D$ had been extended above $+0.08$ sec, would you expect the $p(D \mid H_1 X)$ to decrease or increase? Why?

5. Check Exercise 5 in Section 4-4 to find out about Stirling's approximation for $k$!
   (a) For illustration 1 in Section 11-43, check the value obtained for the increment in evidence for $H_d$.
   (b) For illustration 2 in Section 11-43, check the value obtained for the increment in evidence for $H_d$.

6. Consider a fourfold contingency table whose marginal totals are all 5. Give each of the possible outcomes within the table. For each of these possible outcomes compute the change in evidence for $H_d$ using (i) Equation (11-7) and (ii) Equation (11-8).

7. For each of the following compute the change in evidence for $H_d$, using the specified equation:
   (a) Exercise 3 in Section 8-4, using Equation (11-8),
   (b) Exercise 4 in Section 8-4, using Equation (11-7),
   (c) Exercise 5 in Section 8-4, using Equation (11-8) but with rows and columns switched,
   (d) Exercise 7a in Section 8-4, using Equations (11-7) and (11-8).

# APPENDICES

Note: All tables with the exception of Appendix F (the $F$-tables) were produced on a GE-635 time-shared computer using the computer language BASIC. The $\chi^2$, $t$, and ND(0,1) tables involved the use of a fourth-order Runga-Kutta rule for approximating definite intergals.

# Values Sampled by SIRS from a Rectangular Distribution on the Interval (0,1)

Note: These tables may be used in several ways. If we are simulating SIRS sampling from a continuous rectangular distribution, then the five-digit entries in the table may be read as decimal numbers; for example, the first sampled value is 0.22156. If we are simulating SIRS sampling from a discrete distribution having only 10 possible values—0, 1, 2, 3, 4, 5, 6, 7, 8, 9—then, reading columnwise or rowwise, we may think of each digit in the table as a sampled value. If we are simulating binomial experiments, this table may be used with any value for $p$, the probability of success.

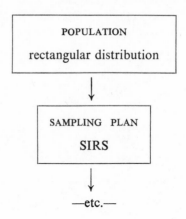

| | | | | | | | | | |
|---|---|---|---|---|---|---|---|---|---|
| 22156 | 88594 | 43097 | 21643 | 57110 | 33324 | 12168 | 87109 | 79615 | 05626 |
| 95179 | 89340 | 44305 | 12395 | 95111 | 48755 | 31329 | 46863 | 50723 | 54325 |
| 27096 | 05695 | 17794 | 97756 | 93031 | 58527 | 98330 | 47332 | 31175 | 22416 |
| 76147 | 16856 | 01808 | 38062 | 75137 | 16089 | 36447 | 44508 | 35750 | 20013 |
| 79434 | 79499 | 83176 | 08626 | 12831 | 84898 | 35222 | 34530 | 05931 | 57928 |
| | | | | | | | | | |
| 45081 | 52134 | 88297 | 15370 | 44600 | 80093 | 18509 | 36275 | 42602 | 70597 |
| 04829 | 20853 | 27656 | 32591 | 69380 | 75455 | 34463 | 36455 | 65163 | 61216 |
| 26318 | 76672 | 13459 | 69301 | 15660 | 39864 | 13104 | 92968 | 08289 | 29245 |
| 14777 | 19579 | 29152 | 95055 | 78303 | 50434 | 77176 | 47468 | 47552 | 94895 |
| 72930 | 84883 | 02903 | 82074 | 20732 | 62558 | 20429 | 37815 | 85527 | 56192 |
| | | | | | | | | | |
| 12282 | 03733 | 09850 | 02287 | 76454 | 02227 | 50858 | 47015 | 62137 | 52097 |
| 91875 | 56791 | 33491 | 35035 | 40543 | 77287 | 69740 | 27189 | 46434 | 55181 |
| 73004 | 57811 | 53861 | 52116 | 20840 | 97380 | 21749 | 65148 | 05616 | 53856 |
| 78559 | 98128 | 90551 | 30380 | 29645 | 00920 | 52459 | 39519 | 09514 | 58978 |
| 43223 | 85823 | 58763 | 04773 | 84670 | 84254 | 50774 | 52760 | 51752 | 92541 |
| | | | | | | | | | |
| 66219 | 64260 | 07786 | 82064 | 65997 | 56832 | 78271 | 97220 | 99382 | 61574 |
| 03350 | 81011 | 92130 | 96126 | 17411 | 17191 | 23628 | 09724 | 39570 | 35851 |
| 38788 | 16035 | 87397 | 28451 | 91958 | 31991 | 20367 | 47504 | 85263 | 68011 |
| 03663 | 05530 | 32298 | 01939 | 06024 | 60500 | 46472 | 03141 | 52005 | 79310 |
| 14836 | 72069 | 18847 | 05107 | 65109 | 38033 | 15335 | 53913 | 60328 | 18133 |
| | | | | | | | | | |
| 57330 | 49811 | 54480 | 97333 | 82324 | 90834 | 01499 | 74883 | 48347 | 27498 |
| 05380 | 24564 | 99842 | 49366 | 58972 | 40338 | 83717 | 31385 | 64235 | 43786 |
| 87237 | 37008 | 71596 | 39118 | 19451 | 49267 | 07499 | 21435 | 03096 | 72767 |
| 24195 | 62506 | 10465 | 45279 | 27657 | 11779 | 39615 | 33116 | 84029 | 73011 |
| 32118 | 92721 | 04076 | 53623 | 93542 | 88449 | 98699 | 06201 | 50789 | 34154 |
| | | | | | | | | | |
| 87114 | 71061 | 10910 | 04708 | 33694 | 96897 | 05481 | 55227 | 84132 | 05165 |
| 59459 | 97843 | 26878 | 59455 | 46856 | 09909 | 63140 | 16684 | 01242 | 68966 |
| 13520 | 83723 | 54637 | 71690 | 50499 | 51106 | 44451 | 06068 | 90914 | 39814 |
| 29070 | 66553 | 26784 | 26341 | 92023 | 14324 | 00167 | 83770 | 41757 | 05104 |
| 37504 | 18552 | 23847 | 21356 | 54431 | 00648 | 76582 | 51130 | 44865 | 49344 |
| | | | | | | | | | |
| 12725 | 56228 | 25793 | 06080 | 61346 | 83511 | 11988 | 14559 | 59615 | 33723 |
| 45110 | 16591 | 01708 | 59535 | 70041 | 48653 | 82462 | 83302 | 49416 | 96876 |
| 54433 | 68578 | 61414 | 26679 | 40181 | 02322 | 51930 | 79357 | 27526 | 84893 |
| 25487 | 30494 | 86541 | 32836 | 22571 | 60310 | 70829 | 70984 | 50025 | 35777 |
| 50638 | 16243 | 69349 | 47972 | 94935 | 49628 | 37062 | 92209 | 58261 | 04196 |
| | | | | | | | | | |
| 37845 | 90821 | 21387 | 10761 | 68043 | 35518 | 96073 | 95275 | 45503 | 54468 |
| 67871 | 06393 | 33428 | 98354 | 68577 | 91495 | 12769 | 89494 | 99352 | 00687 |
| 06852 | 79812 | 91538 | 14797 | 42323 | 51287 | 13824 | 94012 | 50842 | 12430 |
| 92796 | 59549 | 93499 | 16351 | 51987 | 70531 | 88471 | 81673 | 23214 | 86802 |
| 22147 | 68651 | 19088 | 88905 | 92676 | 05305 | 75412 | 19206 | 57710 | 09543 |

# APPENDIX B
## Values Sampled by SIRS
## from the Standard Normal
## Distribution ND(0,1)

Note: These tables are sometimes known as random normal deviates.

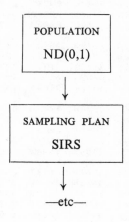

```
 0.116   1.441   0.603   0.393   2.296  -0.575  -0.878  -0.487   0.781  -0.995
 0.188   1.372  -0.094  -0.586   1.491   0.311  -0.207  -0.377  -1.684  -0.207
-1.157   0.221  -1.401   0.549   0.818  -0.417   0.072  -1.115  -0.236  -0.665
 0.739  -0.389   0.414  -0.977  -1.457   0.467  -0.477  -0.695   0.767   0.276
-0.189   0.926   0.498   0.693  -1.250  -0.281  -0.700  -2.204   0.848  -0.200

 0.385  -0.293   0.591   0.911   1.564   0.447   0.488   1.534   0.915  -1.844
-2.161   2.624  -0.149   0.132   0.502   0.169  -0.799  -1.201   0.417   1.094
 0.065  -0.499   1.519  -0.541  -0.011   1.115  -0.280   0.264  -1.808  -2.185
-0.879  -2.307   0.906  -0.629   0.056  -0.073  -0.514   1.129   1.720  -0.145
 0.951  -0.414   1.022   0.569   0.449  -1.220  -0.131   0.028  -2.173  -0.011

-0.305  -0.497  -0.714  -1.589   1.065   0.569  -1.676   0.260   0.312  -0.778
 0.911  -0.714  -1.057   0.469  -0.121  -2.316   0.216  -0.549   0.317  -0.695
 1.159   1.104   1.096  -0.216  -1.987  -1.185   0.821  -0.217   1.063   2.160
-1.316  -0.345  -1.910   0.360  -2.378  -0.391  -0.645   0.695  -0.727  -0.471
-0.131   0.756   0.928  -0.038   0.738   0.968   1.335  -1.305   1.323   0.557

 0.231  -0.135  -0.205   1.067   2.141  -1.484  -0.910   1.990   0.117  -0.027
 1.160   0.074  -0.085  -0.737  -1.014   0.473   1.117   0.182   0.413  -0.039
 0.867  -0.207  -1.443  -0.965  -0.042   0.770  -0.695  -0.094   0.062  -0.238
 0.713  -1.480  -2.798   0.323   0.777   1.337  -0.689  -0.050   0.150   1.470
-0.364  -0.711   0.850   1.219  -0.441   1.047   0.088  -0.398   0.216   0.376

-2.909  -0.517   0.499   0.612   0.709   0.250  -1.410   0.708  -0.702   0.707
-0.605   1.597   0.448   0.169  -0.842  -1.459   1.064   0.261  -0.499   0.092
 1.101  -0.849   0.148  -0.879  -0.751  -1.940  -0.077   1.613   0.007   0.059
 0.700  -1.618  -0.417   0.880   0.285   0.058   0.830   0.044  -0.247  -1.901
 0.348   0.560   1.745  -0.249  -0.802  -0.931  -0.718  -0.787   2.336  -0.593

 0.474  -0.631   0.791   1.669   0.226   0.318   2.004  -1.599  -1.010   1.075
 0.734  -0.424   1.392  -1.276   1.219  -1.398   0.322   0.158  -0.578   0.953
-0.309   1.117   0.745   1.410   0.667  -0.089  -1.115  -0.264  -1.664   0.011
-0.109  -1.322   0.058   0.563  -0.348   0.146   0.609  -0.529  -0.908  -0.703
-2.679  -0.016   0.418  -1.828  -0.301  -1.100   0.516   0.602   0.100  -0.829

 1.140  -0.333   1.482   0.262  -0.394   0.473  -0.163  -0.896  -0.558  -0.310
-1.106  -1.647   0.702   0.594   0.686  -1.029  -0.106  -1.142   0.237   1.257
 0.419  -0.174  -0.199   1.284  -1.551  -0.263   0.525   0.016  -0.228  -0.388
-0.054   0.482   0.919   1.233  -2.608   0.297   1.049   0.387   0.950   0.331
-1.235   1.723  -1.566   0.049   0.492  -0.280  -0.618   0.133   0.346   1.314

 1.020   1.466  -1.308  -0.641  -1.118  -0.839  -0.390  -0.042  -0.973  -0.720
 1.378  -1.382   0.933   1.748  -0.002   1.959   0.087   0.721   1.208  -1.642
-1.487  -0.591   0.808   0.507  -0.732   0.962  -0.659  -0.005  -1.970  -1.161
-0.297  -0.183   0.858  -0.603   0.306  -0.417  -1.330   1.729   1.050   1.770
-1.075  -0.620  -0.276   0.837   0.035  -0.133   1.923  -0.644   0.069   0.211
```

# APPENDIX C
## The Standard Normal
## Distribution ND(0,1)

*Example:* Suppose $z = 1.25$. Then part $a$ shows that the area beyond 1.25 is 0.1056, and part $b$ shows that the ordinate at $z = 1.25$ is $Y = 0.1826$.

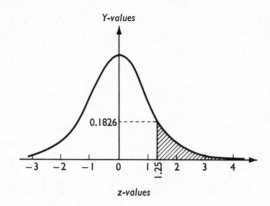

## (*a*) Areas beyond a Given *z*-Value

| z | Area | z | Area | z | Area | z | Area |
|------|--------|------|--------|------|--------|------|--------|
| 0.00 | 0.5000 | 0.50 | 0.3085 | 1.00 | 0.1586 | 1.50 | 0.0668 |
| 0.01 | 0.4960 | 0.51 | 0.3050 | 1.01 | 0.1562 | 1.51 | 0.0655 |
| 0.02 | 0.4920 | 0.52 | 0.3015 | 1.02 | 0.1538 | 1.52 | 0.0642 |
| 0.03 | 0.4880 | 0.53 | 0.2980 | 1.03 | 0.1515 | 1.53 | 0.0630 |
| 0.04 | 0.4840 | 0.54 | 0.2945 | 1.04 | 0.1491 | 1.54 | 0.0617 |
| 0.05 | 0.4800 | 0.55 | 0.2911 | 1.05 | 0.1468 | 1.55 | 0.0605 |
| 0.06 | 0.4760 | 0.56 | 0.2877 | 1.06 | 0.1445 | 1.56 | 0.0593 |
| 0.07 | 0.4720 | 0.57 | 0.2843 | 1.07 | 0.1423 | 1.57 | 0.0582 |
| 0.08 | 0.4681 | 0.58 | 0.2809 | 1.08 | 0.1400 | 1.58 | 0.0570 |
| 0.09 | 0.4641 | 0.59 | 0.2775 | 1.09 | 0.1378 | 1.59 | 0.0559 |
| 0.10 | 0.4601 | 0.60 | 0.2742 | 1.10 | 0.1356 | 1.60 | 0.0548 |
| 0.11 | 0.4562 | 0.61 | 0.2709 | 1.11 | 0.1334 | 1.61 | 0.0536 |
| 0.12 | 0.4522 | 0.62 | 0.2676 | 1.12 | 0.1313 | 1.62 | 0.0526 |
| 0.13 | 0.4482 | 0.63 | 0.2643 | 1.13 | 0.1292 | 1.63 | 0.0515 |
| 0.14 | 0.4443 | 0.64 | 0.2610 | 1.14 | 0.1271 | 1.64 | 0.0505 |
| 0.15 | 0.4403 | 0.65 | 0.2578 | 1.15 | 0.1250 | 1.65 | 0.0494 |
| 0.16 | 0.4364 | 0.66 | 0.2546 | 1.16 | 0.1230 | 1.66 | 0.0484 |
| 0.17 | 0.4325 | 0.67 | 0.2514 | 1.17 | 0.1210 | 1.67 | 0.0474 |
| 0.18 | 0.4285 | 0.68 | 0.2482 | 1.18 | 0.1190 | 1.68 | 0.0464 |
| 0.19 | 0.4246 | 0.69 | 0.2450 | 1.19 | 0.1170 | 1.69 | 0.0455 |
| 0.20 | 0.4207 | 0.70 | 0.2419 | 1.20 | 0.1150 | 1.70 | 0.0445 |
| 0.21 | 0.4168 | 0.71 | 0.2388 | 1.21 | 0.1131 | 1.71 | 0.0436 |
| 0.22 | 0.4129 | 0.72 | 0.2357 | 1.22 | 0.1112 | 1.72 | 0.0427 |
| 0.23 | 0.4090 | 0.73 | 0.2326 | 1.23 | 0.1093 | 1.73 | 0.0418 |
| 0.24 | 0.4051 | 0.74 | 0.2296 | 1.24 | 0.1074 | 1.74 | 0.0409 |
| 0.25 | 0.4012 | 0.75 | 0.2266 | 1.25 | 0.1056 | 1.75 | 0.0400 |
| 0.26 | 0.3974 | 0.76 | 0.2236 | 1.26 | 0.1038 | 1.76 | 0.0392 |
| 0.27 | 0.3935 | 0.77 | 0.2206 | 1.27 | 0.1020 | 1.77 | 0.0383 |
| 0.28 | 0.3897 | 0.78 | 0.2176 | 1.28 | 0.1002 | 1.78 | 0.0375 |
| 0.29 | 0.3859 | 0.79 | 0.2147 | 1.29 | 0.0985 | 1.79 | 0.0367 |
| 0.30 | 0.3820 | 0.80 | 0.2118 | 1.30 | 0.0968 | 1.80 | 0.0359 |
| 0.31 | 0.3782 | 0.81 | 0.2089 | 1.31 | 0.0950 | 1.81 | 0.0351 |
| 0.32 | 0.3744 | 0.82 | 0.2061 | 1.32 | 0.0934 | 1.82 | 0.0343 |
| 0.33 | 0.3706 | 0.83 | 0.2032 | 1.33 | 0.0917 | 1.83 | 0.0336 |
| 0.34 | 0.3669 | 0.84 | 0.2004 | 1.34 | 0.0901 | 1.84 | 0.0328 |
| 0.35 | 0.3631 | 0.85 | 0.1976 | 1.35 | 0.0885 | 1.85 | 0.0321 |
| 0.36 | 0.3594 | 0.86 | 0.1948 | 1.36 | 0.0869 | 1.86 | 0.0314 |
| 0.37 | 0.3556 | 0.87 | 0.1921 | 1.37 | 0.0853 | 1.87 | 0.0307 |
| 0.38 | 0.3519 | 0.88 | 0.1894 | 1.38 | 0.0837 | 1.88 | 0.0300 |
| 0.39 | 0.3482 | 0.89 | 0.1867 | 1.39 | 0.0822 | 1.89 | 0.0293 |
| 0.40 | 0.3445 | 0.90 | 0.1840 | 1.40 | 0.0807 | 1.90 | 0.0287 |
| 0.41 | 0.3409 | 0.91 | 0.1814 | 1.41 | 0.0792 | 1.91 | 0.0280 |
| 0.42 | 0.3372 | 0.92 | 0.1787 | 1.42 | 0.0778 | 1.92 | 0.0274 |
| 0.43 | 0.3335 | 0.93 | 0.1761 | 1.43 | 0.0763 | 1.93 | 0.0268 |
| 0.44 | 0.3299 | 0.94 | 0.1736 | 1.44 | 0.0749 | 1.94 | 0.0261 |
| 0.45 | 0.3263 | 0.95 | 0.1710 | 1.45 | 0.0735 | 1.95 | 0.0255 |
| 0.46 | 0.3227 | 0.96 | 0.1685 | 1.46 | 0.0721 | 1.96 | 0.0249 |
| 0.47 | 0.3191 | 0.97 | 0.1660 | 1.47 | 0.0707 | 1.97 | 0.0244 |
| 0.48 | 0.3156 | 0.98 | 0.1635 | 1.48 | 0.0694 | 1.98 | 0.0238 |
| 0.49 | 0.3120 | 0.99 | 0.1610 | 1.49 | 0.0681 | 1.99 | 0.0232 |

| z | Area | z | Area | z | Area | z | Area |
|---|------|---|------|---|------|---|------|
| 2.00 | 0.0227 | 2.50 | 0.0062 | 3.00 | 0.0013 | 3.50 | 0.0002 |
| 2.01 | 0.0222 | 2.51 | 0.0060 | 3.01 | 0.0013 | 3.51 | 0.0002 |
| 2.02 | 0.0216 | 2.52 | 0.0058 | 3.02 | 0.0012 | 3.52 | 0.0002 |
| 2.03 | 0.0211 | 2.53 | 0.0057 | 3.03 | 0.0012 | 3.53 | 0.0002 |
| 2.04 | 0.0206 | 2.54 | 0.0055 | 3.04 | 0.0011 | 3.54 | 0.0002 |
| 2.05 | 0.0201 | 2.55 | 0.0053 | 3.05 | 0.0011 | 3.55 | 0.0001 |
| 2.06 | 0.0197 | 2.56 | 0.0052 | 3.06 | 0.0011 | 3.56 | 0.0001 |
| 2.07 | 0.0192 | 2.57 | 0.0050 | 3.07 | 0.0010 | 3.57 | 0.0001 |
| 2.08 | 0.0187 | 2.58 | 0.0049 | 3.08 | 0.0010 | 3.58 | 0.0001 |
| 2.09 | 0.0183 | 2.59 | 0.0048 | 3.09 | 0.0010 | 3.59 | 0.0001 |
| 2.10 | 0.0178 | 2.60 | 0.0046 | 3.10 | 0.0009 | 3.60 | 0.0001 |
| 2.11 | 0.0174 | 2.61 | 0.0045 | 3.11 | 0.0009 | 3.61 | 0.0001 |
| 2.12 | 0.0170 | 2.62 | 0.0043 | 3.12 | 0.0009 | 3.62 | 0.0001 |
| 2.13 | 0.0165 | 2.63 | 0.0042 | 3.13 | 0.0008 | 3.63 | 0.0001 |
| 2.14 | 0.0161 | 2.64 | 0.0041 | 3.14 | 0.0008 | 3.64 | 0.0001 |
| 2.15 | 0.0157 | 2.65 | 0.0040 | 3.15 | 0.0008 | 3.65 | 0.0001 |
| 2.16 | 0.0153 | 2.66 | 0.0039 | 3.16 | 0.0007 | 3.66 | 0.0001 |
| 2.17 | 0.0150 | 2.67 | 0.0037 | 3.17 | 0.0007 | 3.67 | 0.0001 |
| 2.18 | 0.0146 | 2.68 | 0.0036 | 3.18 | 0.0007 | 3.68 | 0.0001 |
| 2.19 | 0.0142 | 2.69 | 0.0035 | 3.19 | 0.0007 | 3.69 | 0.0001 |
| 2.20 | 0.0139 | 2.70 | 0.0034 | 3.20 | 0.0006 | 3.70 | 0.0001 |
| 2.21 | 0.0135 | 2.71 | 0.0033 | 3.21 | 0.0006 | 3.71 | 0.0001 |
| 2.22 | 0.0132 | 2.72 | 0.0032 | 3.22 | 0.0006 | 3.72 | 0.0001 |
| 2.23 | 0.0128 | 2.73 | 0.0031 | 3.23 | 0.0006 | 3.73 | 0.0000 |
| 2.24 | 0.0125 | 2.74 | 0.0030 | 3.24 | 0.0005 | 3.74 | 0.0000 |
| 2.25 | 0.0122 | 2.75 | 0.0029 | 3.25 | 0.0005 | 3.75 | 0.0000 |
| 2.26 | 0.0119 | 2.76 | 0.0028 | 3.26 | 0.0005 | 3.76 | 0.0000 |
| 2.27 | 0.0116 | 2.77 | 0.0028 | 3.27 | 0.0005 | 3.77 | 0.0000 |
| 2.28 | 0.0113 | 2.78 | 0.0027 | 3.28 | 0.0005 | 3.78 | 0.0000 |
| 2.29 | 0.0110 | 2.79 | 0.0026 | 3.29 | 0.0005 | 3.79 | 0.0000 |
| 2.30 | 0.0107 | 2.80 | 0.0025 | 3.30 | 0.0004 | 3.80 | 0.0000 |
| 2.31 | 0.0104 | 2.81 | 0.0024 | 3.31 | 0.0004 | 3.81 | 0.0000 |
| 2.32 | 0.0101 | 2.82 | 0.0024 | 3.32 | 0.0004 | 3.82 | 0.0000 |
| 2.33 | 0.0099 | 2.83 | 0.0023 | 3.33 | 0.0004 | 3.83 | 0.0000 |
| 2.34 | 0.0096 | 2.84 | 0.0022 | 3.34 | 0.0004 | 3.84 | 0.0000 |
| 2.35 | 0.0093 | 2.85 | 0.0021 | 3.35 | 0.0004 | 3.85 | 0.0000 |
| 2.36 | 0.0091 | 2.86 | 0.0021 | 3.36 | 0.0003 | 3.86 | 0.0000 |
| 2.37 | 0.0088 | 2.87 | 0.0020 | 3.37 | 0.0003 | 3.87 | 0.0000 |
| 2.38 | 0.0086 | 2.88 | 0.0019 | 3.38 | 0.0003 | 3.88 | 0.0000 |
| 2.39 | 0.0084 | 2.89 | 0.0019 | 3.39 | 0.0003 | 3.89 | 0.0000 |
| 2.40 | 0.0081 | 2.90 | 0.0018 | 3.40 | 0.0003 | 3.90 | 0.0000 |
| 2.41 | 0.0079 | 2.91 | 0.0018 | 3.41 | 0.0003 | 3.91 | 0.0000 |
| 2.42 | 0.0077 | 2.92 | 0.0017 | 3.42 | 0.0003 | 3.92 | 0.0000 |
| 2.43 | 0.0075 | 2.93 | 0.0016 | 3.43 | 0.0003 | 3.93 | 0.0000 |
| 2.44 | 0.0073 | 2.94 | 0.0016 | 3.44 | 0.0002 | 3.94 | 0.0000 |
| 2.45 | 0.0071 | 2.95 | 0.0015 | 3.45 | 0.0002 | 3.95 | 0.0000 |
| 2.46 | 0.0069 | 2.96 | 0.0015 | 3.46 | 0.0002 | 3.96 | 0.0000 |
| 2.47 | 0.0067 | 2.97 | 0.0014 | 3.47 | 0.0002 | 3.97 | 0.0000 |
| 2.48 | 0.0065 | 2.98 | 0.0014 | 3.48 | 0.0002 | 3.98 | 0.0000 |
| 2.49 | 0.0063 | 2.99 | 0.0013 | 3.49 | 0.0002 | 3.99 | 0.0000 |

## (b) Ordinates (y-Values) for Given z-Values

| z | y | z | y | z | y | z | y |
|---|---|---|---|---|---|---|---|
| 0.00 | 0.3989 | 0.50 | 0.3520 | 1.00 | 0.2419 | 1.50 | 0.1295 |
| 0.01 | 0.3989 | 0.51 | 0.3502 | 1.01 | 0.2395 | 1.51 | 0.1275 |
| 0.02 | 0.3988 | 0.52 | 0.3484 | 1.02 | 0.2371 | 1.52 | 0.1256 |
| 0.03 | 0.3987 | 0.53 | 0.3466 | 1.03 | 0.2347 | 1.53 | 0.1237 |
| 0.04 | 0.3986 | 0.54 | 0.3448 | 1.04 | 0.2322 | 1.54 | 0.1218 |
| 0.05 | 0.3984 | 0.55 | 0.3429 | 1.05 | 0.2298 | 1.55 | 0.1200 |
| 0.06 | 0.3982 | 0.56 | 0.3410 | 1.06 | 0.2274 | 1.56 | 0.1181 |
| 0.07 | 0.3979 | 0.57 | 0.3391 | 1.07 | 0.2250 | 1.57 | 0.1163 |
| 0.08 | 0.3976 | 0.58 | 0.3371 | 1.08 | 0.2226 | 1.58 | 0.1145 |
| 0.09 | 0.3973 | 0.59 | 0.3352 | 1.09 | 0.2202 | 1.59 | 0.1127 |
| 0.10 | 0.3969 | 0.60 | 0.3332 | 1.10 | 0.2178 | 1.60 | 0.1109 |
| 0.11 | 0.3965 | 0.61 | 0.3312 | 1.11 | 0.2154 | 1.61 | 0.1091 |
| 0.12 | 0.3960 | 0.62 | 0.3291 | 1.12 | 0.2130 | 1.62 | 0.1074 |
| 0.13 | 0.3955 | 0.63 | 0.3271 | 1.13 | 0.2106 | 1.63 | 0.1056 |
| 0.14 | 0.3950 | 0.64 | 0.3250 | 1.14 | 0.2083 | 1.64 | 0.1039 |
| 0.15 | 0.3944 | 0.65 | 0.3229 | 1.15 | 0.2059 | 1.65 | 0.1022 |
| 0.16 | 0.3938 | 0.66 | 0.3208 | 1.16 | 0.2035 | 1.66 | 0.1005 |
| 0.17 | 0.3932 | 0.67 | 0.3187 | 1.17 | 0.2012 | 1.67 | 0.0989 |
| 0.18 | 0.3925 | 0.68 | 0.3165 | 1.18 | 0.1988 | 1.68 | 0.0972 |
| 0.19 | 0.3918 | 0.69 | 0.3144 | 1.19 | 0.1965 | 1.69 | 0.0956 |
| 0.20 | 0.3910 | 0.70 | 0.3122 | 1.20 | 0.1941 | 1.70 | 0.0940 |
| 0.21 | 0.3902 | 0.71 | 0.3100 | 1.21 | 0.1918 | 1.71 | 0.0924 |
| 0.22 | 0.3894 | 0.72 | 0.3078 | 1.22 | 0.1895 | 1.72 | 0.0908 |
| 0.23 | 0.3885 | 0.73 | 0.3056 | 1.23 | 0.1872 | 1.73 | 0.0893 |
| 0.24 | 0.3876 | 0.74 | 0.3033 | 1.24 | 0.1849 | 1.74 | 0.0877 |
| 0.25 | 0.3866 | 0.75 | 0.3011 | 1.25 | 0.1826 | 1.75 | 0.0862 |
| 0.26 | 0.3856 | 0.76 | 0.2988 | 1.26 | 0.1803 | 1.76 | 0.0847 |
| 0.27 | 0.3846 | 0.77 | 0.2965 | 1.27 | 0.1781 | 1.77 | 0.0832 |
| 0.28 | 0.3836 | 0.78 | 0.2943 | 1.28 | 0.1758 | 1.78 | 0.0818 |
| 0.29 | 0.3825 | 0.79 | 0.2920 | 1.29 | 0.1736 | 1.79 | 0.0803 |
| 0.30 | 0.3813 | 0.80 | 0.2896 | 1.30 | 0.1713 | 1.80 | 0.0789 |
| 0.31 | 0.3802 | 0.81 | 0.2873 | 1.31 | 0.1691 | 1.81 | 0.0775 |
| 0.32 | 0.3790 | 0.82 | 0.2850 | 1.32 | 0.1669 | 1.82 | 0.0761 |
| 0.33 | 0.3778 | 0.83 | 0.2826 | 1.33 | 0.1647 | 1.83 | 0.0747 |
| 0.34 | 0.3765 | 0.84 | 0.2803 | 1.34 | 0.1625 | 1.84 | 0.0734 |
| 0.35 | 0.3752 | 0.85 | 0.2779 | 1.35 | 0.1603 | 1.85 | 0.0720 |
| 0.36 | 0.3739 | 0.86 | 0.2756 | 1.36 | 0.1582 | 1.86 | 0.0707 |
| 0.37 | 0.3725 | 0.87 | 0.2732 | 1.37 | 0.1560 | 1.87 | 0.0694 |
| 0.38 | 0.3711 | 0.88 | 0.2708 | 1.38 | 0.1539 | 1.88 | 0.0681 |
| 0.39 | 0.3697 | 0.89 | 0.2684 | 1.39 | 0.1518 | 1.89 | 0.0668 |
| 0.40 | 0.3682 | 0.90 | 0.2660 | 1.40 | 0.1497 | 1.90 | 0.0656 |
| 0.41 | 0.3667 | 0.91 | 0.2636 | 1.41 | 0.1476 | 1.91 | 0.0643 |
| 0.42 | 0.3652 | 0.92 | 0.2612 | 1.42 | 0.1455 | 1.92 | 0.0631 |
| 0.43 | 0.3637 | 0.93 | 0.2588 | 1.43 | 0.1435 | 1.93 | 0.0619 |
| 0.44 | 0.3621 | 0.94 | 0.2564 | 1.44 | 0.1414 | 1.94 | 0.0607 |
| 0.45 | 0.3605 | 0.95 | 0.2540 | 1.45 | 0.1394 | 1.95 | 0.0595 |
| 0.46 | 0.3588 | 0.96 | 0.2516 | 1.46 | 0.1374 | 1.96 | 0.0584 |
| 0.47 | 0.3572 | 0.97 | 0.2492 | 1.47 | 0.1354 | 1.97 | 0.0573 |
| 0.48 | 0.3555 | 0.98 | 0.2468 | 1.48 | 0.1334 | 1.98 | 0.0561 |
| 0.49 | 0.3538 | 0.99 | 0.2443 | 1.49 | 0.1314 | 1.99 | 0.0550 |

| z | y | z | y | z | y | z | y |
|------|--------|------|--------|------|--------|------|--------|
| 2.00 | 0.0539 | 2.50 | 0.0175 | 3.00 | 0.0044 | 3.50 | 0.0008 |
| 2.01 | 0.0529 | 2.51 | 0.0170 | 3.01 | 0.0043 | 3.51 | 0.0008 |
| 2.02 | 0.0518 | 2.52 | 0.0166 | 3.02 | 0.0041 | 3.52 | 0.0008 |
| 2.03 | 0.0508 | 2.53 | 0.0162 | 3.03 | 0.0040 | 3.53 | 0.0007 |
| 2.04 | 0.0498 | 2.54 | 0.0158 | 3.04 | 0.0039 | 3.54 | 0.0007 |
| 2.05 | 0.0487 | 2.55 | 0.0154 | 3.05 | 0.0038 | 3.55 | 0.0007 |
| 2.06 | 0.0477 | 2.56 | 0.0150 | 3.06 | 0.0036 | 3.56 | 0.0007 |
| 2.07 | 0.0468 | 2.57 | 0.0146 | 3.07 | 0.0035 | 3.57 | 0.0006 |
| 2.08 | 0.0458 | 2.58 | 0.0143 | 3.08 | 0.0034 | 3.58 | 0.0006 |
| 2.09 | 0.0449 | 2.59 | 0.0139 | 3.09 | 0.0033 | 3.59 | 0.0006 |
| 2.10 | 0.0439 | 2.60 | 0.0135 | 3.10 | 0.0032 | 3.60 | 0.0006 |
| 2.11 | 0.0430 | 2.61 | 0.0132 | 3.11 | 0.0031 | 3.61 | 0.0005 |
| 2.12 | 0.0421 | 2.62 | 0.0128 | 3.12 | 0.0030 | 3.62 | 0.0005 |
| 2.13 | 0.0412 | 2.63 | 0.0125 | 3.13 | 0.0029 | 3.63 | 0.0005 |
| 2.14 | 0.0404 | 2.64 | 0.0122 | 3.14 | 0.0028 | 3.64 | 0.0005 |
| 2.15 | 0.0395 | 2.65 | 0.0119 | 3.15 | 0.0027 | 3.65 | 0.0005 |
| 2.16 | 0.0387 | 2.66 | 0.0116 | 3.16 | 0.0027 | 3.66 | 0.0004 |
| 2.17 | 0.0378 | 2.67 | 0.0112 | 3.17 | 0.0026 | 3.67 | 0.0004 |
| 2.18 | 0.0370 | 2.68 | 0.0109 | 3.18 | 0.0025 | 3.68 | 0.0004 |
| 2.19 | 0.0362 | 2.69 | 0.0107 | 3.19 | 0.0024 | 3.69 | 0.0004 |
| 2.20 | 0.0354 | 2.70 | 0.0104 | 3.20 | 0.0023 | 3.70 | 0.0004 |
| 2.21 | 0.0347 | 2.71 | 0.0101 | 3.21 | 0.0023 | 3.71 | 0.0004 |
| 2.22 | 0.0339 | 2.72 | 0.0098 | 3.22 | 0.0022 | 3.72 | 0.0003 |
| 2.23 | 0.0331 | 2.73 | 0.0096 | 3.23 | 0.0021 | 3.73 | 0.0003 |
| 2.24 | 0.0324 | 2.74 | 0.0093 | 3.24 | 0.0020 | 3.74 | 0.0003 |
| 2.25 | 0.0317 | 2.75 | 0.0090 | 3.25 | 0.0020 | 3.75 | 0.0003 |
| 2.26 | 0.0310 | 2.76 | 0.0088 | 3.26 | 0.0019 | 3.76 | 0.0003 |
| 2.27 | 0.0303 | 2.77 | 0.0086 | 3.27 | 0.0019 | 3.77 | 0.0003 |
| 2.28 | 0.0296 | 2.78 | 0.0083 | 3.28 | 0.0018 | 3.78 | 0.0003 |
| 2.29 | 0.0289 | 2.79 | 0.0081 | 3.29 | 0.0017 | 3.79 | 0.0003 |
| 2.30 | 0.0283 | 2.80 | 0.0079 | 3.30 | 0.0017 | 3.80 | 0.0002 |
| 2.31 | 0.0276 | 2.81 | 0.0076 | 3.31 | 0.0016 | 3.81 | 0.0002 |
| 2.32 | 0.0270 | 2.82 | 0.0074 | 3.32 | 0.0016 | 3.82 | 0.0002 |
| 2.33 | 0.0264 | 2.83 | 0.0072 | 3.33 | 0.0015 | 3.83 | 0.0002 |
| 2.34 | 0.0258 | 2.84 | 0.0070 | 3.34 | 0.0015 | 3.84 | 0.0002 |
| 2.35 | 0.0252 | 2.85 | 0.0068 | 3.35 | 0.0014 | 3.85 | 0.0002 |
| 2.36 | 0.0246 | 2.86 | 0.0066 | 3.36 | 0.0014 | 3.86 | 0.0002 |
| 2.37 | 0.0240 | 2.87 | 0.0064 | 3.37 | 0.0013 | 3.87 | 0.0002 |
| 2.38 | 0.0234 | 2.88 | 0.0063 | 3.38 | 0.0013 | 3.88 | 0.0002 |
| 2.39 | 0.0229 | 2.89 | 0.0061 | 3.39 | 0.0012 | 3.89 | 0.0002 |
| 2.40 | 0.0223 | 2.90 | 0.0059 | 3.40 | 0.0012 | 3.90 | 0.0001 |
| 2.41 | 0.0218 | 2.91 | 0.0057 | 3.41 | 0.0011 | 3.91 | 0.0001 |
| 2.42 | 0.0213 | 2.92 | 0.0056 | 3.42 | 0.0011 | 3.92 | 0.0001 |
| 2.43 | 0.0208 | 2.93 | 0.0054 | 3.43 | 0.0011 | 3.93 | 0.0001 |
| 2.44 | 0.0203 | 2.94 | 0.0052 | 3.44 | 0.0010 | 3.94 | 0.0001 |
| 2.45 | 0.0198 | 2.95 | 0.0051 | 3.45 | 0.0010 | 3.95 | 0.0001 |
| 2.46 | 0.0193 | 2.96 | 0.0049 | 3.46 | 0.0010 | 3.96 | 0.0001 |
| 2.47 | 0.0188 | 2.97 | 0.0048 | 3.47 | 0.0009 | 3.97 | 0.0001 |
| 2.48 | 0.0184 | 2.98 | 0.0047 | 3.48 | 0.0009 | 3.98 | 0.0001 |
| 2.49 | 0.0179 | 2.99 | 0.0045 | 3.49 | 0.0009 | 3.99 | 0.0001 |

# APPENDIX D
## Chi-square Values Corresponding to Specific Probability Levels

*Example:* Consider a chi-square distribution with 4 df. According to Section 4-4, the equation for this distribution is

$$Y_{(4)} = \tfrac{1}{4}(\chi^2)e^{-(\chi^2)/2}$$

The column headings in this appendix are specific probability levels, and for 4 df the corresponding $\chi^2$ values are shown below:

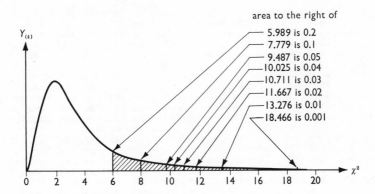

area to the right of
5.989 is 0.2
7.779 is 0.1
9.487 is 0.05
10.025 is 0.04
10.711 is 0.03
11.667 is 0.02
13.276 is 0.01
18.466 is 0.001

*Note:* For df larger than 30, compute the quantity $(\sqrt{2\chi^2} - \sqrt{2n - 1})$ and look up ND $(0,1)$.

| df | 0.2 | 0.1 | 0.05 | 0.04 | 0.03 | 0.02 | 0.01 | 0.001 |
|---|---|---|---|---|---|---|---|---|
| 1 | 1.642 | 2.705 | 3.841 | 4.217 | 4.709 | 5.411 | 6.634 | 10.827 |
| 2 | 3.219 | 4.605 | 5.991 | 6.437 | 7.013 | 7.824 | 9.210 | 13.815 |
| 3 | 4.642 | 6.251 | 7.814 | 8.311 | 8.947 | 9.837 | 11.344 | 16.266 |
| 4 | 5.989 | 7.779 | 9.487 | 10.025 | 10.711 | 11.667 | 13.276 | 18.466 |
| 5 | 7.289 | 9.236 | 11.070 | 11.644 | 12.374 | 13.388 | 15.086 | 20.514 |
| 6 | 8.558 | 10.644 | 12.591 | 13.197 | 13.967 | 15.033 | 16.811 | 22.457 |
| 7 | 9.803 | 12.016 | 14.067 | 14.702 | 15.508 | 16.622 | 18.475 | 24.321 |
| 8 | 11.030 | 13.361 | 15.507 | 16.170 | 17.010 | 18.168 | 20.090 | 26.124 |
| 9 | 12.242 | 14.683 | 16.918 | 17.608 | 18.479 | 19.678 | 21.665 | 27.877 |
| 10 | 13.442 | 15.987 | 18.306 | 19.020 | 19.921 | 21.160 | 23.209 | 29.588 |
| 11 | 14.631 | 17.274 | 19.674 | 20.411 | 21.341 | 22.617 | 24.724 | 31.263 |
| 12 | 15.812 | 18.549 | 21.025 | 21.784 | 22.741 | 24.053 | 26.216 | 32.909 |
| 13 | 16.985 | 19.811 | 22.361 | 23.142 | 24.124 | 25.471 | 27.688 | 34.527 |
| 14 | 18.151 | 21.063 | 23.684 | 24.485 | 25.492 | 26.872 | 29.141 | 36.123 |
| 15 | 19.310 | 22.306 | 24.995 | 25.815 | 26.847 | 28.259 | 30.577 | 37.697 |
| 16 | 20.465 | 23.541 | 26.295 | 27.135 | 28.190 | 29.632 | 31.999 | 39.252 |
| 17 | 21.614 | 24.768 | 27.586 | 28.444 | 29.522 | 30.994 | 33.408 | 40.789 |
| 18 | 22.759 | 25.989 | 28.868 | 29.744 | 30.844 | 32.345 | 34.804 | 42.312 |
| 19 | 23.900 | 27.203 | 30.143 | 31.036 | 32.157 | 33.687 | 36.190 | 43.819 |
| 20 | 25.037 | 28.411 | 31.410 | 32.320 | 33.461 | 35.019 | 37.565 | 45.314 |
| 21 | 26.171 | 29.614 | 32.670 | 33.596 | 34.758 | 36.343 | 38.931 | 46.796 |
| 22 | 27.301 | 30.812 | 33.923 | 34.866 | 36.048 | 37.659 | 40.289 | 48.267 |
| 23 | 28.428 | 32.006 | 35.171 | 36.130 | 37.331 | 38.967 | 41.638 | 49.727 |
| 24 | 29.553 | 33.195 | 36.414 | 37.388 | 38.608 | 40.269 | 42.979 | 51.178 |
| 25 | 30.675 | 34.381 | 37.652 | 38.641 | 39.879 | 41.565 | 44.313 | 52.619 |
| 26 | 31.794 | 35.562 | 38.884 | 39.888 | 41.145 | 42.855 | 45.641 | 54.051 |
| 27 | 32.911 | 36.740 | 40.112 | 41.131 | 42.406 | 44.139 | 46.962 | 55.475 |
| 28 | 34.026 | 37.915 | 41.336 | 42.369 | 43.661 | 45.418 | 48.277 | 56.891 |
| 29 | 35.139 | 39.086 | 42.556 | 43.603 | 44.912 | 46.692 | 49.587 | 58.300 |
| 30 | 36.250 | 40.255 | 43.772 | 44.833 | 46.159 | 47.961 | 50.891 | 59.702 |

# t-Values Corresponding to Specific Probability Levels

*Example:* Consider a $t$ distribution with 10 df. According to Section 4-5, the equation for this distribution is

$$Y_{(10)} = \frac{315}{\sqrt{10\ 256}} \left(1 + \frac{t^2}{10}\right)^{-5.5}$$

The column headings in this Appendix are specific probability levels, and for 10 df the corresponding $t$ values are shown below:

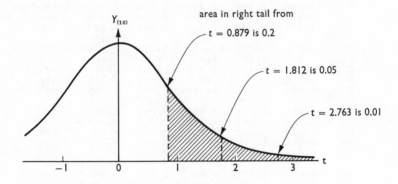

Note: For df larger than 40, $t$ is approximately ND(0,1).

| df | 0.2 | 0.1 | 0.05 | 0.025 | 0.01 | 0.005 |
|---|---|---|---|---|---|---|
| 1 | 1.376 | 3.077 | 6.313 | 12.707 | 31.827 | 63.694 |
| 2 | 1.060 | 1.885 | 2.919 | 4.302 | 6.964 | 9.926 |
| 3 | 0.978 | 1.637 | 2.353 | 3.182 | 4.540 | 5.841 |
| 4 | 0.940 | 1.533 | 2.131 | 2.776 | 3.747 | 4.604 |
| 5 | 0.919 | 1.475 | 2.015 | 2.570 | 3.364 | 4.032 |
| 6 | 0.905 | 1.439 | 1.943 | 2.446 | 3.142 | 3.707 |
| 7 | 0.896 | 1.414 | 1.894 | 2.364 | 2.997 | 3.499 |
| 8 | 0.888 | 1.396 | 1.859 | 2.305 | 2.896 | 3.355 |
| 9 | 0.883 | 1.383 | 1.833 | 2.262 | 2.821 | 3.249 |
| 10 | 0.879 | 1.372 | 1.812 | 2.228 | 2.763 | 3.169 |
| 11 | 0.875 | 1.363 | 1.795 | 2.200 | 2.718 | 3.105 |
| 12 | 0.872 | 1.356 | 1.782 | 2.178 | 2.681 | 3.054 |
| 13 | 0.870 | 1.350 | 1.770 | 2.160 | 2.650 | 3.012 |
| 14 | 0.868 | 1.345 | 1.761 | 2.144 | 2.624 | 2.976 |
| 15 | 0.866 | 1.340 | 1.753 | 2.131 | 2.602 | 2.946 |
| 16 | 0.864 | 1.336 | 1.745 | 2.119 | 2.583 | 2.920 |
| 17 | 0.863 | 1.333 | 1.739 | 2.109 | 2.566 | 2.898 |
| 18 | 0.862 | 1.330 | 1.734 | 2.100 | 2.552 | 2.878 |
| 19 | 0.860 | 1.327 | 1.729 | 2.092 | 2.539 | 2.860 |
| 20 | 0.859 | 1.325 | 1.724 | 2.085 | 2.527 | 2.845 |
| 21 | 0.859 | 1.323 | 1.720 | 2.079 | 2.517 | 2.831 |
| 22 | 0.858 | 1.321 | 1.717 | 2.073 | 2.508 | 2.818 |
| 23 | 0.857 | 1.319 | 1.713 | 2.068 | 2.499 | 2.807 |
| 24 | 0.856 | 1.317 | 1.710 | 2.063 | 2.492 | 2.796 |
| 25 | 0.856 | 1.316 | 1.708 | 2.059 | 2.485 | 2.737 |
| 26 | 0.855 | 1.314 | 1.705 | 2.055 | 2.478 | 2.773 |
| 27 | 0.855 | 1.313 | 1.703 | 2.051 | 2.472 | 2.770 |
| 28 | 0.854 | 1.312 | 1.701 | 2.048 | 2.467 | 2.763 |
| 29 | 0.854 | 1.311 | 1.699 | 2.045 | 2.461 | 2.756 |
| 30 | 0.853 | 1.310 | 1.697 | 2.042 | 2.457 | 2.749 |
| 31 | 0.853 | 1.309 | 1.695 | 2.039 | 2.452 | 2.744 |
| 32 | 0.852 | 1.308 | 1.693 | 2.036 | 2.448 | 2.733 |
| 33 | 0.852 | 1.307 | 1.692 | 2.034 | 2.444 | 2.733 |
| 34 | 0.852 | 1.306 | 1.690 | 2.032 | 2.441 | 2.728 |
| 35 | 0.851 | 1.306 | 1.689 | 2.030 | 2.437 | 2.723 |
| 36 | 0.851 | 1.305 | 1.688 | 2.028 | 2.434 | 2.719 |
| 37 | 0.851 | 1.304 | 1.687 | 2.026 | 2.431 | 2.715 |
| 38 | 0.851 | 1.304 | 1.685 | 2.024 | 2.428 | 2.711 |
| 39 | 0.850 | 1.303 | 1.684 | 2.022 | 2.425 | 2.707 |
| 40 | 0.850 | 1.303 | 1.683 | 2.021 | 2.423 | 2.704 |

# APPENDIX F

## F-Values Corresponding to the 0.05 and the 0.01 Probability Levels

*Example:* Consider an $F$ distribution with (2,2) df. According to Section 4-6 the equation for this distribution is

$$Y_{(2,2)} = \frac{1}{(1 + F)^2}$$

Looking up the $m = 2$, $n = 2$ entry in part (*a*), the 0.05 level is represented by an $F$-value of 19; and looking up the appropriate cell in part (*b*), the 0.01 level is found to be $F = 99$.

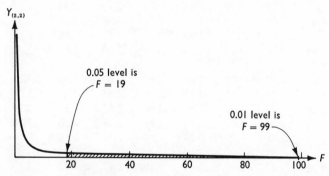

*Acknowledgment:* Reproduced from R. Fisher and F. Yates, *Statistical Tables for Biological, Medical and Agricultural Research*, Oliver and Boyd Ltd., Edinburgh, by kind permission of the publishers.

PART (*a*): Values of *F* with (*m*,*n*) df at the 0.05 Level

| $n$ \ $m$ | 1 | 2 | 3 | 4 | 5 | 6 | 8 | 12 | 24 |
|---|---|---|---|---|---|---|---|---|---|
| 1 | 161.40 | 199.50 | 215.70 | 224.60 | 230.20 | 234.00 | 238.90 | 243.90 | 249.00 |
| 2 | 18.51 | 19.00 | 19.16 | 19.25 | 19.30 | 19.33 | 19.37 | 19.41 | 19.45 |
| 3 | 10.13 | 9.55 | 9.28 | 9.12 | 9.01 | 8.94 | 8.84 | 8.74 | 8.64 |
| 4 | 7.71 | 6.94 | 6.59 | 6.39 | 6.26 | 6.16 | 6.04 | 5.91 | 5.77 |
| 5 | 6.61 | 5.79 | 5.41 | 5.19 | 5.05 | 4.95 | 4.82 | 4.68 | 4.53 |
| 6 | 5.99 | 5.14 | 4.76 | 4.53 | 4.39 | 4.28 | 4.15 | 4.00 | 3.84 |
| 7 | 5.59 | 4.74 | 4.35 | 4.12 | 3.97 | 3.87 | 3.73 | 3.57 | 3.41 |
| 8 | 5.32 | 4.46 | 4.07 | 3.84 | 3.69 | 3.58 | 3.44 | 3.28 | 3.12 |
| 9 | 5.12 | 4.26 | 3.86 | 3.63 | 3.48 | 3.37 | 3.23 | 3.07 | 2.90 |
| 10 | 4.96 | 4.10 | 3.71 | 3.48 | 3.33 | 3.22 | 3.07 | 2.91 | 2.74 |
| 11 | 4.84 | 3.98 | 3.59 | 3.36 | 3.20 | 3.09 | 2.95 | 2.79 | 2.61 |
| 12 | 4.75 | 3.88 | 3.49 | 3.26 | 3.11 | 3.00 | 2.85 | 2.69 | 2.50 |
| 13 | 4.67 | 3.80 | 3.41 | 3.18 | 3.02 | 2.92 | 2.77 | 2.60 | 2.42 |
| 14 | 4.60 | 3.74 | 3.34 | 3.11 | 2.96 | 2.85 | 2.70 | 2.53 | 2.35 |
| 15 | 4.54 | 3.68 | 3.29 | 3.06 | 2.90 | 2.79 | 2.64 | 2.48 | 2.29 |
| 16 | 4.49 | 3.63 | 3.24 | 3.01 | 2.85 | 2.74 | 2.59 | 2.42 | 2.24 |
| 17 | 4.45 | 3.59 | 3.20 | 2.96 | 2.81 | 2.70 | 2.55 | 2.38 | 2.19 |
| 18 | 4.41 | 3.55 | 3.16 | 2.93 | 2.77 | 2.66 | 2.51 | 2.34 | 2.15 |
| 19 | 4.38 | 3.52 | 3.13 | 2.90 | 2.74 | 2.63 | 2.48 | 2.31 | 2.11 |
| 20 | 4.35 | 3.49 | 3.10 | 2.87 | 2.71 | 2.60 | 2.45 | 2.28 | 2.08 |
| 21 | 4.32 | 3.47 | 3.07 | 2.84 | 2.68 | 2.57 | 2.42 | 2.25 | 2.05 |
| 22 | 4.30 | 3.44 | 3.05 | 2.82 | 2.66 | 2.55 | 2.40 | 2.23 | 2.03 |
| 23 | 4.28 | 3.42 | 3.03 | 2.80 | 2.64 | 2.53 | 2.38 | 2.20 | 2.00 |
| 24 | 4.26 | 3.40 | 3.01 | 2.78 | 2.62 | 2.51 | 2.36 | 2.18 | 1.98 |
| 25 | 4.24 | 3.38 | 2.99 | 2.76 | 2.60 | 2.49 | 2.34 | 2.16 | 1.96 |
| 26 | 4.22 | 3.37 | 2.98 | 2.74 | 2.59 | 2.47 | 2.32 | 2.15 | 1.95 |
| 27 | 4.21 | 3.35 | 2.96 | 2.73 | 2.57 | 2.46 | 2.30 | 2.13 | 1.93 |
| 28 | 4.20 | 3.34 | 2.95 | 2.71 | 2.56 | 2.44 | 2.29 | 2.12 | 1.91 |
| 29 | 4.18 | 3.33 | 2.93 | 2.70 | 2.54 | 2.43 | 2.28 | 2.10 | 1.90 |
| 30 | 4.17 | 3.32 | 2.92 | 2.69 | 2.53 | 2.42 | 2.27 | 2.09 | 1.89 |
| 40 | 4.08 | 3.23 | 2.84 | 2.61 | 2.45 | 2.34 | 2.18 | 2.00 | 1.79 |
| 60 | 4.00 | 3.15 | 2.76 | 2.52 | 2.37 | 2.25 | 2.10 | 1.92 | 1.70 |
| 120 | 3.92 | 3.07 | 2.68 | 2.45 | 2.29 | 2.17 | 2.02 | 1.83 | 1.61 |
| $\infty$ | 3.84 | 2.99 | 2.60 | 2.37 | 2.21 | 2.09 | 1.94 | 1.75 | 1.52 |

PART (b): Values of F with (m,n) df at the 0.01 Level

| n \ m | 1 | 2 | 3 | 4 | 5 | 6 | 8 | 12 | 24 |
|---|---|---|---|---|---|---|---|---|---|
| 1 | 4,052 | 4,999 | 5,403 | 5,625 | 5,764 | 5,859 | 5,981 | 6,106 | 6,234 |
| 2 | 98.49 | 99.00 | 99.17 | 99.25 | 99.30 | 99.33 | 99.36 | 99.42 | 99.46 |
| 3 | 34.12 | 30.81 | 29.46 | 28.71 | 28.24 | 27.91 | 27.49 | 27.05 | 26.60 |
| 4 | 21.20 | 18.00 | 16.69 | 15.98 | 15.52 | 15.21 | 14.80 | 14.37 | 13.93 |
| 5 | 16.26 | 13.27 | 12.06 | 11.39 | 10.97 | 10.67 | 10.27 | 9.89 | 9.47 |
| 6 | 13.74 | 10.92 | 9.78 | 9.15 | 8.75 | 8.47 | 8.10 | 7.72 | 7.31 |
| 7 | 12.25 | 9.55 | 8.45 | 7.85 | 7.46 | 7.19 | 6.84 | 6.47 | 6.07 |
| 8 | 11.26 | 8.65 | 7.59 | 7.01 | 6.63 | 6.37 | 6.03 | 5.67 | 5.28 |
| 9 | 10.56 | 8.02 | 6.99 | 6.42 | 6.06 | 5.80 | 5.47 | 5.11 | 4.73 |
| 10 | 10.04 | 7.56 | 6.55 | 5.99 | 5.64 | 5.39 | 5.06 | 4.71 | 4.33 |
| 11 | 9.65 | 7.20 | 6.22 | 5.67 | 5.32 | 5.07 | 4.74 | 4.40 | 4.02 |
| 12 | 9.33 | 6.93 | 5.95 | 5.41 | 5.06 | 4.82 | 4.50 | 4.16 | 3.78 |
| 13 | 9.07 | 6.70 | 5.74 | 5.20 | 4.86 | 4.62 | 4.30 | 3.96 | 3.59 |
| 14 | 8.86 | 6.51 | 5.56 | 5.03 | 4.69 | 4.46 | 4.14 | 3.80 | 3.43 |
| 15 | 8.68 | 6.36 | 5.42 | 4.89 | 4.56 | 4.32 | 4.00 | 3.67 | 3.29 |
| 16 | 8.53 | 6.23 | 5.29 | 4.77 | 4.44 | 4.20 | 3.89 | 3.55 | 3.18 |
| 17 | 8.40 | 6.11 | 5.18 | 4.67 | 4.34 | 4.10 | 3.79 | 3.45 | 3.08 |
| 18 | 8.28 | 6.01 | 5.09 | 4.58 | 4.25 | 4.01 | 3.71 | 3.37 | 3.00 |
| 19 | 8.18 | 5.93 | 5.01 | 4.50 | 4.17 | 3.94 | 3.63 | 3.30 | 2.92 |
| 20 | 8.10 | 5.85 | 4.94 | 4.43 | 4.10 | 3.87 | 3.56 | 3.23 | 2.86 |
| 21 | 8.02 | 5.78 | 4.87 | 4.37 | 4.04 | 3.81 | 3.51 | 3.17 | 2.80 |
| 22 | 7.94 | 5.72 | 4.82 | 4.31 | 3.99 | 3.76 | 3.45 | 3.12 | 2.75 |
| 23 | 7.88 | 5.66 | 4.76 | 4.26 | 3.94 | 3.71 | 3.41 | 3.07 | 2.70 |
| 24 | 7.82 | 5.61 | 4.72 | 4.22 | 3.90 | 3.67 | 3.36 | 3.03 | 2.66 |
| 25 | 7.77 | 5.57 | 4.68 | 4.18 | 3.86 | 3.63 | 3.32 | 2.99 | 2.62 |
| 26 | 7.72 | 5.53 | 4.64 | 4.14 | 3.82 | 3.59 | 3.29 | 2.96 | 2.58 |
| 27 | 7.68 | 5.49 | 4.60 | 4.11 | 3.78 | 3.56 | 3.26 | 2.93 | 2.55 |
| 28 | 7.64 | 5.45 | 4.57 | 4.07 | 3.75 | 3.53 | 3.23 | 2.90 | 2.52 |
| 29 | 7.60 | 5.42 | 4.54 | 4.04 | 3.73 | 3.50 | 3.20 | 2.87 | 2.49 |
| 30 | 7.56 | 5.39 | 4.51 | 4.02 | 3.70 | 3.47 | 3.17 | 2.84 | 2.47 |
| 40 | 7.31 | 5.18 | 4.31 | 3.83 | 3.51 | 3.27 | 2.99 | 2.66 | 2.29 |
| 60 | 7.08 | 4.98 | 4.13 | 3.65 | 3.34 | 3.12 | 2.82 | 2.50 | 2.12 |
| 120 | 6.85 | 4.79 | 3.95 | 3.48 | 3.17 | 2.96 | 2.66 | 2.34 | 1.95 |
| ∞ | 6.64 | 4.60 | 3.78 | 3.32 | 3.02 | 2.80 | 2.51 | 2.18 | 1.79 |

# APPENDIX G
## The r-to-z Transformation

*Example:* According to Section 9-15, the r-to-z transformation for $r = 0.68$ would be as follows:

$$z = \frac{1}{2} \log \frac{(1 + r)}{(1 - r)} = \frac{1}{2} \log \frac{(1.68)}{(0.32)} = 0.829$$

These logarithms are to base $e$ ($=2.7182818284$).

| r | z | r | z | r | z | r | z |
|---|---|---|---|---|---|---|---|
| 0.00 | 0.000 | 0.25 | 0.255 | 0.50 | 0.549 | 0.75 | 0.972 |
| 0.01 | 0.010 | 0.26 | 0.266 | 0.51 | 0.562 | 0.76 | 0.996 |
| 0.02 | 0.020 | 0.27 | 0.276 | 0.52 | 0.576 | 0.77 | 1.020 |
| 0.03 | 0.030 | 0.28 | 0.287 | 0.53 | 0.590 | 0.78 | 1.045 |
| 0.04 | 0.040 | 0.29 | 0.298 | 0.54 | 0.604 | 0.79 | 1.071 |
| 0.05 | 0.050 | 0.30 | 0.309 | 0.55 | 0.618 | 0.80 | 1.098 |
| 0.06 | 0.060 | 0.31 | 0.320 | 0.56 | 0.632 | 0.81 | 1.127 |
| 0.07 | 0.070 | 0.32 | 0.331 | 0.57 | 0.647 | 0.82 | 1.156 |
| 0.08 | 0.080 | 0.33 | 0.342 | 0.58 | 0.662 | 0.83 | 1.188 |
| 0.09 | 0.090 | 0.34 | 0.354 | 0.59 | 0.677 | 0.84 | 1.221 |
| 0.10 | 0.100 | 0.35 | 0.365 | 0.60 | 0.693 | 0.85 | 1.256 |
| 0.11 | 0.110 | 0.36 | 0.376 | 0.61 | 0.708 | 0.86 | 1.293 |
| 0.12 | 0.120 | 0.37 | 0.388 | 0.62 | 0.725 | 0.87 | 1.333 |
| 0.13 | 0.130 | 0.38 | 0.400 | 0.63 | 0.741 | 0.88 | 1.375 |
| 0.14 | 0.140 | 0.39 | 0.411 | 0.64 | 0.758 | 0.89 | 1.421 |
| 0.15 | 0.151 | 0.40 | 0.423 | 0.65 | 0.775 | 0.90 | 1.472 |
| 0.16 | 0.161 | 0.41 | 0.435 | 0.66 | 0.792 | 0.91 | 1.527 |
| 0.17 | 0.171 | 0.42 | 0.447 | 0.67 | 0.810 | 0.92 | 1.589 |
| 0.18 | 0.181 | 0.43 | 0.459 | 0.68 | 0.829 | 0.93 | 1.658 |
| 0.19 | 0.192 | 0.44 | 0.472 | 0.69 | 0.847 | 0.94 | 1.738 |
| 0.20 | 0.202 | 0.45 | 0.484 | 0.70 | 0.867 | 0.95 | 1.831 |
| 0.21 | 0.213 | 0.46 | 0.497 | 0.71 | 0.887 | 0.96 | 1.945 |
| 0.22 | 0.223 | 0.47 | 0.510 | 0.72 | 0.907 | 0.97 | 2.092 |
| 0.23 | 0.234 | 0.48 | 0.522 | 0.73 | 0.928 | 0.98 | 2.297 |
| 0.24 | 0.244 | 0.49 | 0.536 | 0.74 | 0.950 | 0.99 | 2.646 |

# The z-to-r Transformation

According to Section 9-15, the *r*-to-*z* transformation is

$$z = \frac{1}{2} \log \frac{(1 + r)}{(1 - r)}$$

Turning this around, we find that the equation for *z*-to-*r* transformations is

$$r = \frac{(e^{2z} - 1)}{(e^{2z} + 1)}$$

*Example:* Given a *z*-value of 1.81, note that the table gives $r = 0.946$ for $z = 1.80$ and $r = 0.948$ for $z = 1.82$. Interpolating, we would argue that the *r* value corresponding to $z = 1.81$ is 0.947.

| z | r | z | r | z | r | z | r |
|------|-------|------|-------|------|-------|------|-------|
| 0.00 | 0.000 | 0.25 | 0.244 | 0.50 | 0.462 | 0.75 | 0.635 |
| 0.01 | 0.009 | 0.26 | 0.254 | 0.51 | 0.469 | 0.76 | 0.641 |
| 0.02 | 0.019 | 0.27 | 0.263 | 0.52 | 0.477 | 0.77 | 0.646 |
| 0.03 | 0.029 | 0.28 | 0.272 | 0.53 | 0.485 | 0.78 | 0.652 |
| 0.04 | 0.039 | 0.29 | 0.282 | 0.54 | 0.492 | 0.79 | 0.658 |
| 0.05 | 0.049 | 0.30 | 0.291 | 0.55 | 0.500 | 0.80 | 0.664 |
| 0.06 | 0.059 | 0.31 | 0.300 | 0.56 | 0.507 | 0.81 | 0.669 |
| 0.07 | 0.069 | 0.32 | 0.309 | 0.57 | 0.515 | 0.82 | 0.675 |
| 0.08 | 0.079 | 0.33 | 0.318 | 0.58 | 0.522 | 0.83 | 0.680 |
| 0.09 | 0.089 | 0.34 | 0.327 | 0.59 | 0.529 | 0.84 | 0.685 |
| 0.10 | 0.099 | 0.35 | 0.336 | 0.60 | 0.537 | 0.85 | 0.691 |
| 0.11 | 0.109 | 0.36 | 0.345 | 0.61 | 0.544 | 0.86 | 0.696 |
| 0.12 | 0.119 | 0.37 | 0.353 | 0.62 | 0.551 | 0.87 | 0.701 |
| 0.13 | 0.129 | 0.38 | 0.362 | 0.63 | 0.558 | 0.88 | 0.706 |
| 0.14 | 0.139 | 0.39 | 0.371 | 0.64 | 0.564 | 0.89 | 0.711 |
| 0.15 | 0.148 | 0.40 | 0.379 | 0.65 | 0.571 | 0.90 | 0.716 |
| 0.16 | 0.158 | 0.41 | 0.388 | 0.66 | 0.578 | 0.91 | 0.721 |
| 0.17 | 0.168 | 0.42 | 0.396 | 0.67 | 0.584 | 0.92 | 0.725 |
| 0.18 | 0.178 | 0.43 | 0.405 | 0.68 | 0.591 | 0.93 | 0.730 |
| 0.19 | 0.187 | 0.44 | 0.413 | 0.69 | 0.597 | 0.94 | 0.735 |
| 0.20 | 0.197 | 0.45 | 0.421 | 0.70 | 0.604 | 0.95 | 0.739 |
| 0.21 | 0.206 | 0.46 | 0.430 | 0.71 | 0.610 | 0.96 | 0.744 |
| 0.22 | 0.216 | 0.47 | 0.438 | 0.72 | 0.616 | 0.97 | 0.748 |
| 0.23 | 0.226 | 0.48 | 0.446 | 0.73 | 0.623 | 0.98 | 0.753 |
| 0.24 | 0.235 | 0.49 | 0.454 | 0.74 | 0.629 | 0.99 | 0.757 |

| z | r | z | r | z | r | z | r |
|------|-------|------|-------|------|-------|------|-------|
| 1.00 | 0.761 | 1.50 | 0.905 | 2.00 | 0.964 | 2.50 | 0.986 |
| 1.02 | 0.769 | 1.52 | 0.908 | 2.02 | 0.965 | 2.52 | 0.987 |
| 1.04 | 0.777 | 1.54 | 0.912 | 2.04 | 0.966 | 2.54 | 0.987 |
| 1.06 | 0.785 | 1.56 | 0.915 | 2.06 | 0.968 | 2.56 | 0.988 |
| 1.08 | 0.793 | 1.58 | 0.918 | 2.08 | 0.969 | 2.58 | 0.988 |
| 1.10 | 0.800 | 1.60 | 0.921 | 2.10 | 0.970 | 2.60 | 0.989 |
| 1.12 | 0.807 | 1.62 | 0.924 | 2.12 | 0.971 | 2.62 | 0.989 |
| 1.14 | 0.814 | 1.64 | 0.927 | 2.14 | 0.972 | 2.64 | 0.989 |
| 1.16 | 0.821 | 1.66 | 0.930 | 2.16 | 0.973 | 2.66 | 0.990 |
| 1.18 | 0.827 | 1.68 | 0.932 | 2.18 | 0.974 | 2.68 | 0.990 |
| 1.20 | 0.833 | 1.70 | 0.935 | 2.20 | 0.975 | 2.70 | 0.991 |
| 1.22 | 0.839 | 1.72 | 0.937 | 2.22 | 0.976 | 2.72 | 0.991 |
| 1.24 | 0.845 | 1.74 | 0.940 | 2.24 | 0.977 | 2.74 | 0.991 |
| 1.26 | 0.851 | 1.76 | 0.942 | 2.26 | 0.978 | 2.76 | 0.992 |
| 1.28 | 0.856 | 1.78 | 0.944 | 2.28 | 0.979 | 2.78 | 0.992 |
| 1.30 | 0.861 | 1.80 | 0.946 | 2.30 | 0.980 | 2.80 | 0.992 |
| 1.32 | 0.866 | 1.82 | 0.948 | 2.32 | 0.980 | 2.82 | 0.992 |
| 1.34 | 0.871 | 1.84 | 0.950 | 2.34 | 0.981 | 2.84 | 0.993 |
| 1.36 | 0.876 | 1.86 | 0.952 | 2.36 | 0.982 | 2.86 | 0.993 |
| 1.38 | 0.880 | 1.88 | 0.954 | 2.38 | 0.983 | 2.88 | 0.993 |
| 1.40 | 0.885 | 1.90 | 0.956 | 2.40 | 0.983 | 2.90 | 0.993 |
| 1.42 | 0.889 | 1.92 | 0.957 | 2.42 | 0.984 | 2.92 | 0.994 |
| 1.44 | 0.893 | 1.94 | 0.959 | 2.44 | 0.984 | 2.94 | 0.994 |
| 1.46 | 0.897 | 1.96 | 0.961 | 2.46 | 0.985 | 2.96 | 0.994 |
| 1.48 | 0.901 | 1.98 | 0.962 | 2.48 | 0.986 | 2.98 | 0.994 |

# APPENDIX I

## Table for Converting Probability, Odds, and Evidence into One Another

*Example:* (*a*) Given $p = 0.61$, find $O$ and ev.

    *Answer:* $O$ = odds = 1.564

                ev = evidence = 1.942 db

      (*b*) Given $O = 1.5$, find $p$ and ev.

    *Answer:* $p = 0.60$

                ev = 1.76 db

      (*c*) Given ev = $-3.00$ db, find $p$ and $O$.

    *Answer:* $p = 0.333$ (by interpolation)

              $O = 0.500$ (by interpolation)

| $p$ | Odds | Evid | $p$ | Odds | Evid | $p$ | Odds | Evid |
|---|---|---|---|---|---|---|---|---|
| 0.01 | 0.010 | -19.957 | 0.34 | 0.515 | -2.881 | 0.67 | 2.030 | 3.075 |
| 0.02 | 0.020 | -16.902 | 0.35 | 0.538 | -2.689 | 0.68 | 2.124 | 3.273 |
| 0.03 | 0.030 | -15.097 | 0.36 | 0.562 | -2.499 | 0.69 | 2.225 | 3.474 |
| 0.04 | 0.041 | -13.803 | 0.37 | 0.587 | -2.312 | 0.70 | 2.333 | 3.679 |
| 0.05 | 0.052 | -12.788 | 0.38 | 0.612 | -2.127 | 0.71 | 2.448 | 3.888 |
| 0.06 | 0.063 | -11.950 | 0.39 | 0.639 | -1.943 | 0.72 | 2.571 | 4.101 |
| 0.07 | 0.075 | -11.234 | 0.40 | 0.666 | -1.761 | 0.73 | 2.703 | 4.319 |
| 0.08 | 0.086 | -10.607 | 0.41 | 0.694 | -1.581 | 0.74 | 2.846 | 4.542 |
| 0.09 | 0.098 | -10.048 | 0.42 | 0.724 | -1.402 | 0.75 | 3.000 | 4.771 |
| 0.10 | 0.111 | -9.543 | 0.43 | 0.754 | -1.225 | 0.76 | 3.166 | 5.006 |
| 0.11 | 0.123 | -9.080 | 0.44 | 0.785 | -1.048 | 0.77 | 3.347 | 5.247 |
| 0.12 | 0.136 | -8.654 | 0.45 | 0.813 | -0.872 | 0.78 | 3.545 | 5.496 |
| 0.13 | 0.149 | -8.256 | 0.46 | 0.851 | -0.697 | 0.79 | 3.761 | 5.754 |
| 0.14 | 0.162 | -7.884 | 0.47 | 0.886 | -0.522 | 0.80 | 3.999 | 6.020 |
| 0.15 | 0.176 | -7.534 | 0.48 | 0.923 | -0.348 | 0.81 | 4.263 | 6.297 |
| 0.16 | 0.190 | -7.202 | 0.49 | 0.960 | -0.174 | 0.82 | 4.555 | 6.585 |
| 0.17 | 0.204 | -6.887 | 0.50 | 1.000 | 0.000 | 0.83 | 4.882 | 6.886 |
| 0.18 | 0.219 | -6.586 | 0.51 | 1.040 | 0.173 | 0.84 | 5.249 | 7.201 |
| 0.19 | 0.234 | -6.298 | 0.52 | 1.083 | 0.347 | 0.85 | 5.666 | 7.533 |
| 0.20 | 0.249 | -6.021 | 0.53 | 1.127 | 0.521 | 0.86 | 6.142 | 7.883 |
| 0.21 | 0.265 | -5.755 | 0.54 | 1.173 | 0.696 | 0.87 | 6.692 | 8.255 |
| 0.22 | 0.282 | -5.497 | 0.55 | 1.222 | 0.871 | 0.88 | 7.333 | 8.653 |
| 0.23 | 0.298 | -5.248 | 0.56 | 1.272 | 1.047 | 0.89 | 8.090 | 9.079 |
| 0.24 | 0.315 | -5.007 | 0.57 | 1.325 | 1.224 | 0.90 | 8.999 | 9.542 |
| 0.25 | 0.333 | -4.772 | 0.58 | 1.380 | 1.401 | 0.91 | 10.111 | 10.047 |
| 0.26 | 0.351 | -4.543 | 0.59 | 1.439 | 1.580 | 0.92 | 11.499 | 10.606 |
| 0.27 | 0.369 | -4.320 | 0.60 | 1.499 | 1.760 | 0.93 | 13.285 | 11.233 |
| 0.28 | 0.388 | -4.102 | 0.61 | 1.564 | 1.942 | 0.94 | 15.666 | 11.949 |
| 0.29 | 0.408 | -3.889 | 0.62 | 1.631 | 2.126 | 0.95 | 18.999 | 12.787 |
| 0.30 | 0.428 | -3.680 | 0.63 | 1.702 | 2.311 | 0.96 | 23.999 | 13.802 |
| 0.31 | 0.449 | -3.475 | 0.64 | 1.777 | 2.498 | 0.97 | 32.333 | 15.096 |
| 0.32 | 0.470 | -3.274 | 0.65 | 1.857 | 2.688 | 0.98 | 48.999 | 16.901 |
| 0.33 | 0.492 | -3.076 | 0.66 | 1.941 | 2.880 | 0.99 | 98.999 | 19.956 |

# APPENDIX J

## Table for Converting Probability Values into Uncertainty Measures $-p \log_2 p$

The rational measure of uncertainty introduced in Section 11-13 was defined as:

$$H = -\sum_{i=1}^{k} p_i \log_2 p_i$$

where $k$ is the number of alternatives. This table gives value of $(-p \log_2 p)$, and these are positive values.

*Example:* Given $p = 0.34$, how much does this contribute to the uncertainty of a situation?

*Answer:* $-p \log_2 p = -0.34 \log_2 0.34 = 0.5291$ bit

| 0.01 | 0.0664 | 0.34 | 0.5291 | 0.67 | 0.3871 |
| 0.02 | 0.1128 | 0.35 | 0.5301 | 0.68 | 0.3783 |
| 0.03 | 0.1517 | 0.36 | 0.5306 | 0.69 | 0.3693 |
| 0.04 | 0.1857 | 0.37 | 0.5307 | 0.70 | 0.3602 |
| 0.05 | 0.2160 | 0.38 | 0.5304 | 0.71 | 0.3508 |
| 0.06 | 0.2435 | 0.39 | 0.5297 | 0.72 | 0.3412 |
| 0.07 | 0.2685 | 0.40 | 0.5287 | 0.73 | 0.3314 |
| 0.08 | 0.2915 | 0.41 | 0.5273 | 0.74 | 0.3214 |
| 0.09 | 0.3126 | 0.42 | 0.5256 | 0.75 | 0.3112 |
| 0.10 | 0.3321 | 0.43 | 0.5235 | 0.76 | 0.3009 |
| 0.11 | 0.3502 | 0.44 | 0.5211 | 0.77 | 0.2903 |
| 0.12 | 0.3670 | 0.45 | 0.5184 | 0.78 | 0.2795 |
| 0.13 | 0.3826 | 0.46 | 0.5153 | 0.79 | 0.2686 |
| 0.14 | 0.3971 | 0.47 | 0.5119 | 0.80 | 0.2575 |
| 0.15 | 0.4105 | 0.48 | 0.5082 | 0.81 | 0.2462 |
| 0.16 | 0.4230 | 0.49 | 0.5042 | 0.82 | 0.2347 |
| 0.17 | 0.4345 | 0.50 | 0.5000 | 0.83 | 0.2231 |
| 0.18 | 0.4453 | 0.51 | 0.4954 | 0.84 | 0.2112 |
| 0.19 | 0.4552 | 0.52 | 0.4905 | 0.85 | 0.1992 |
| 0.20 | 0.4643 | 0.53 | 0.4854 | 0.86 | 0.1871 |
| 0.21 | 0.4728 | 0.54 | 0.4800 | 0.87 | 0.1747 |
| 0.22 | 0.4805 | 0.55 | 0.4743 | 0.88 | 0.1622 |
| 0.23 | 0.4876 | 0.56 | 0.4684 | 0.89 | 0.1496 |
| 0.24 | 0.4941 | 0.57 | 0.4622 | 0.90 | 0.1368 |
| 0.25 | 0.5000 | 0.58 | 0.4558 | 0.91 | 0.1238 |
| 0.26 | 0.5052 | 0.59 | 0.4491 | 0.92 | 0.1106 |
| 0.27 | 0.5100 | 0.60 | 0.4421 | 0.93 | 0.0973 |
| 0.28 | 0.5142 | 0.61 | 0.4350 | 0.94 | 0.0839 |
| 0.29 | 0.5179 | 0.62 | 0.4275 | 0.95 | 0.0703 |
| 0.30 | 0.5210 | 0.63 | 0.4199 | 0.96 | 0.0565 |
| 0.31 | 0.5237 | 0.64 | 0.4120 | 0.97 | 0.0426 |
| 0.32 | 0.5260 | 0.65 | 0.4039 | 0.98 | 0.0285 |
| 0.33 | 0.5278 | 0.66 | 0.3956 | 0.99 | 0.0143 |

# INDEX